PERCEPTIONS OF THE OTHER

Eurocentrism in the Historiography of Islam from the Medieval Period to the Modern Era: Clash of Civilisations or Dialogue of Cultures?

REVISED EDITION

METIN MUSTAFA

Centre for Ottoman Renaissance and Civilisation
Sydney, Australia
©2025

Copyright ©2025 by Centre for Ottoman Renaissance and Civilisation

21 19 18 17 1 2 3 4

All rights reserved. No part of this book may be reproduced or transmitted in any form or by any means, electronic or mechanical, including photocopying, recording or by any information storage and retrieval system without permission in writing from the Publisher and Author.

Published by Centre for Ottoman Renaissance and Civilisation

Website: ottomanrenaissance.org

Email: info@ottomanrenaissance.org

ISBN: 978-0-646-71277-2

Cover Design: Centre for Ottoman Renaissance and Civilisation

To control a people, you must first control what they think about themselves and how they regard their history and culture. And when your conqueror makes you ashamed of your culture and your history, he needs no prison walls and no chains to hold you.

John Henrik Clarke (1915-1998)

OTHER BOOKS BY THE AUTHOR

I am Süleyman, Sultan of the Sultans of East and West ~ The Making of an Image: Majestic Caesar, Sultan, Evliyâ'ya Pâd-şâh-i and Poet ~ A Cultural Perspective

Oriental Imaginings, Occidental Refashioning:
Turquerie, the Tulip Age and Ottoman Modernity, 1683-1867

Legacy of Ottoman Renaissance Material and Visual Culture in Early Modern Europe, 1400-1699

The Ottoman Renaissance and the Early Modern World, 1400-1699 (Essays Series Complete Edition)

'The Divine Comedy' of Süleyman Çelebi and Mir Heidar: A Sufi Mystical Reading of Early Modern Turkic Representations of Prophet Muhammad's 'Isra' and Mi'raj'

The Mediterranean Zeitgeist: Re-Orienting the Renaissance

Renaissance Women:
Nuns, Sultanas and Queens Legitimising Female Sovereignty

Michelangelo meets Sinan:
Representations of the Divine, Salvation and Paradise in Renaissance Art

History of Ottoman Renaissance Art:
From Mehmed I to Selim II. Revised Edition.

The Ottoman Renaissance:
A Reconsideration of Early Modern Ottoman Art, 1413-1575

Tragedy of Sultan Süleyman (a play)

CONTENTS

Preface	ix
Introduction	1
Part I	29
1. The Rise and Expansion of Islam	31
2. Islamic Contribution to Western Civilisation	37
3. Impact of Islam on Medieval European Consciousness	65
4. The Renaissance Mindset	77
The idealisation of a dead world	
5. The Ottoman Threat	81
Division in the Mediterranean	
6. Observing the Other and Shifting Identities in the Sixteenth Century	91
7. European Perceptions of Islam and the Ottoman Turks in the Seventeenth Century	101
8. Birth of Man's Hubris	109
The Age of Enlightenment	
9. The Age of Enlightenment and the Orient in the Eighteenth Century	115
10. A Critique of Orientalism	131
11. The Era of Imperialism and the Subservience of the Other	141
Europe's supremacy over the Muslim Other	
12. From the Imagined Orient to the Orient Express	163
"Awful, disappointing and dirty Orient"	
ADDENDUM	171
Part II	173
13. Where did the Muslims go Wrong?	175
Eclipse of Reason: A Religious Perspective	
14. Challenging Imperialism, Eurocentrism & Muslim Radicalism	203
Atatürk's Vision of Modernisation and the Future of the Muslim World	
15. Re-awakening of Islam	241
Double Standards of Western Representations of Resurgent Islam: 1970-1995	

16. The Clash of Civilisations or Dialogue of Cultures? 251
    The Muslim Response
17. The New Millennium and the Muslim Other 269
    9/11 and the Clash of Civilisations Debate Revisited

    Part III 285

18. Decolonising Orientalism 287
    Critiquing Euro-American Intellectual Hegemony in Academia
19. Religion, Politics and the Emerging World Order 309
20. The Global South in the 21st century 317
    The Voice of the Other in the Multipolar World
21. America: The Last Bastion of Western Imperialism 337
    The Illusion of Greatness
22. From Europe to America 381
    Evangelical White Christianity and Islamophobia
23. Challenging Western Cultural Imperialism and Soft Power Politics 395
    Television as a Medium in Representing the Muslim Other in the 21st Century

    Conclusion 415
    Epilogue 433

    Notes 441
    Bibliography 477

PREFACE

Upon the publication of the first edition of this book in 1999, I believed I would not return to it once its completion. However, with the benefit of hindsight, history continually offers us new events and evidence to analyse, enhancing our comprehension of the world we inhabit. Given the significant developments that have occurred since the initial release of this book, I, as a historian, deemed it essential to contribute further to the ongoing discourse surrounding the themes of 'them versus us' and the 'clash of civilisations'. Consequently, the addendum for the second edition began to evolve into a distinct entity, guiding me toward topics I had not originally intended to explore.

To comprehend the concept of Muslim "backwardness", it is essential to delve into the fundamental aspects of the topic from a modern perspective. This entails investigating the role of higher education in Muslim nations, the allocation of governmental resources for research and innovation, the pursuit of academic validation within Western paradigms, and the representation of Muslims by Muslims through the use of soft power techniques. Furthermore, the evolving negative perceptions of Islam in Europe, which have transformed into what is now termed Islamophobia, require examination within the framework of the 21st century. The events of September 11, 2001, reignited the enduring discourse between Islam and the West, echoing the Christian Crusades worldview of the eleventh century. This revival highlights the clash of civilisations thesis articulated by Samuel P. Huntington in 1993, necessitating a reassessment of the original edition of my book through a contemporary lens. However, this analysis would be incomplete for today's audience without a comprehensive investigation of the book's initial focus—Muslim contributions to the advancement of Western civilisation and the evolving perceptions of Islam that have emerged in Europe since the Middle Ages, which continue to have relevance in the present day.

The exploration of civilisations has been a significant endeavour for many historians. To what degree can one civilisation affect the evolution of another? Are cultural influences capable of being so strong that they alter the viewpoints of adjacent civilisations? In what ways has the study of the "Other," particularly Islam, facilitated the progress of Europe and Western civilisation? In the tenth century, Western Christendom was geographically constrained. Nevertheless, to its south lay a dynamic civilisation that would greatly influence its historical trajectory, both in terms of geography and intellect. This civilisation was Islam.

Initially, Western Christendom regarded its theological, intellectual, and military counterpart with scrutiny, a perspective that persisted into the Renaissance with the rise of early modern Europe. Over the years, European perceptions of the Mediterranean Orient (encompassing the contemporary Middle East, including Turkey and Iran) have evolved, leading to the emergence of Orientalism. This framework fostered ideas such as the dichotomy of Islam versus the West and the notion of Islam as a looming threat, thereby planting the seeds of prejudice and skewed perceptions towards Islam.

In the 21st century, Islam and nations of the Global South are reaffirming their presence by contesting Western hegemony and influence. They are actively decolonising the Eurocentric concepts of Orientalism that emerged in the 19th century, fostering an epistemological unity that values diverse forms of knowledge and thereby undermining the Euro-American supremacy in academic discourse. Furthermore, the sanctions levied against Russia following its invasion of Ukraine in 2022 have instilled fear among numerous nations in the Global South, who are concerned that the West may utilise global financial mechanisms as instruments of coercion against them. In the wake of the conflict in Gaza, both Russia and China have adeptly tapped into this anti-Western sentiment, leveraging discontent regarding perceived double standards from the West, as well as the imposition of sanctions and economic pressure. This does not imply that middle powers including Turkey and other Islamic nations are eager to exchange American hegemony for Chinese influence; rather, it indicates their willingness to collaborate with Russia and China in pursuit of a more fragmented, multi-polar and independent global order.

The revised version of this book seeks to enhance understanding of the historical forces that have shaped our past and continue to impact the present, examined through the perspective of historical determinism. By recognising and addressing these elements within our society, we can become better informed and make decisions that safeguard marginalised voices and those considered different from the majority, thereby averting their demonisation and dehumanisation. As our understanding of the human experience evolves, we are confronted with critical choices and responsibilities concerning cultural interconnectedness and exchanges. It is through the respect and recognition of the 'Other' that our differences can be perceived not as barriers to social cohesion and advancement, but as essential contributions to the rich tapestry of the intercultural mosaic that defines our world.

INTRODUCTION

The study of civilisations has been a pursuit undertaken by numerous historians. To what extent can one civilisation influence the development of another? Can cultural influences be so potent that they can reshape the perceptions of neighbouring civilisations? How has the examination of the 'Other', specifically Islam, contributed to the advancement of Europe and Western civilisation? In the tenth century, Western Christendom was geographically confined. However, to its south existed a vibrant civilisation that would profoundly shape its historical trajectory, both geographically and intellectually. This civilisation was Islam. Initially, Western Christendom regarded its theological, intellectual, and military counterpart with scrutiny, a perspective that persisted into the Renaissance and the rise of early modern Europe. Over the centuries, European perceptions of the Mediterranean Orient (which includes the former Ottoman territories and Iran) have evolved, leading to the emergence of Orientalism. This concept fostered ideas such as the dichotomy of Islam versus the West and the notion of Islam as a looming threat following the disintegration of communism in the former Soviet Union, thereby planting the seeds of prejudice and skewed perceptions against Islam.

It has been argued that these observations have resulted in an ideological and geographical division between Christendom and Islam, which persisted throughout their interactions and eventually culminated in the conflict between the Western world and Islam. This division, also referred to as the "immutable barrier" by Braudel, initially shifted from the Iberian Peninsula in the west after 1492 and later moved eastward to southeastern Europe in the Balkans due to the rising influence of the Ottomans. It continued to exist until the decline of the Ottoman Empire in the early decades of the twentieth century. The conceptual divide between Islam and the West emerged as a significant subject of scholarly debate in the Western world during the latter half of the twentieth century. This discourse was largely prompted by the crises associated with the Bosnian War (1992-1995) and the Nagorno-Karabakh conflict involving Armenia and Azerbaijan in the Caucasus (1988-1994).

Following the conclusion of the Second World War, there arose significant challenges to both orientalism and European dominance on a global scale. Following the end of the Cold War, Islam re-emerged as a central theme in Western historiography, particularly through the perspectives of postmodern thinkers like Francis Fukuyama and Samuel P. Huntington. Huntington, in particular, posits that the emerging world order in the post-Soviet era will be characterised by a bipolar division between the West and Islam. However, Turkish historians and other Muslim writers hold differing viewpoints. The questions then arise: is Islam poised to become the next threat to Western hegemony? Will it pose a challenge to Western civilisation, or can it peacefully coexist alongside other major civilisations in the world?

Modern historiography has undeniably been shaped by its roots in the Western world, a fact that is evident in the methodologies, narratives, and frameworks that dominate historical scholarship today. The extensive spread of Western influence, particularly since the Age of Enlightenment, has led to the predominance of Western historiographical perspectives within the global historical community. This dominance is not merely a reflection of geographical or political power; it is also a manifestation of cultural hegemony, where Western narratives often overshadow or marginalise alternative viewpoints and interpretations.

Nevertheless, these Western influences present considerable obstacles when striving to comprehend non-Western cultures in their own contexts. The challenge lies in the tendency of Western historians to project their own cultural values, assumptions, and historical experiences onto societies that may operate under entirely different paradigms. This projection can lead to a skewed understanding of non-Western histories, where the complexities and nuances of these cultures are oversimplified or misrepresented. As a result, the rich tapestry of non-Western historical experiences risks being reduced to mere footnotes in a predominantly Western narrative.

Is it feasible for contemporary Western historiography to completely evade this predicament? This question is fraught with complexity. While some historians strive to adopt more inclusive and pluralistic approaches, the ingrained biases and frameworks of Western thought can be difficult to dismantle entirely. The challenge is not only intellectual but also methodological; historians must grapple with the tools and concepts that have been developed within a Western context, which may not be fully applicable or relevant to non-Western societies.

When historians examine topics such as Islam and the Ottoman Empire, can they truly avoid the pitfalls of Orientalism? Edward Said's seminal work, *Orientalism* (1978), highlights how Western scholarship has often portrayed Eastern societies as exotic, backward, and fundamentally different from the rational, progressive West. This framework can lead to a distorted understanding of Islamic cultures and the Ottoman Empire, reducing them to stereotypes that fail to capture their historical realities. While some historians are aware of these pitfalls and actively seek to counteract them by incorporating local perspectives and voices, the risk of falling into Orientalist tropes remains ever-present.

These inquiries are intricate and do not lend themselves to straightforward answers, making it increasingly challenging for historians to extricate themselves from this dilemma. The very act of interpreting history is influenced by the historian's own cultural background, biases, and the prevailing historiographical trends of their time. As a result, these reflections have contributed to the ongoing dichotomy between the Occident and the Orient, perpetuating a divide that complicates cross-cultural interactions.

The relationship between Europe and Islam, as well as the perceptions and attitudes of Europeans towards Islam, had distinct differences. Unlike the other Old World civilisations of China and India, Europeans and Muslims had a deeper understanding of each other. While China and India were geographically defined places, Islam was a religion. The civilisations of China, East Asia, India, South-east Asia, and pre-Columbian America may have been highly advanced and sophisticated, but they were primarily regional in nature. Apart from expanding and influencing neighbouring areas, these civilisations were confined to specific locations, cultures, and even races to a significant extent.

In contrast to the ethnically defined and geographically limited civilisations, Islam was fundamentally universal in its beliefs, self-perception, and aspirations. Muslims considered themselves fortunate possessors of God's final revelation and believed it was their duty to disseminate God's truth to all of humanity. Despite its universalist goals and assertions, Christianity remained predominantly European, and even its holy wars, crusades, and conquests were undertaken to spread God's message to the rest of humanity. Consequently, it was inevitable for these two civilisations to clash. However, the question remains: will the conflict between the West and Islam persist into the twenty-first century? This matter will be explored in greater detail in the final section of the book.

Europeans often express a deep-seated apprehension when discussing Islam and the Muslim communities they have come across, including the Moors, Saracens, Tatars, and Turks. Through various forms of expression such as poetry, polemics, historical accounts, and literature, they convey a strong awareness of a Christian Europe that feels besieged and endangered by a powerful Islamic world. This Europe, to some extent, was shaped and confined by the boundaries of Muslim influence in the eastern, southeastern, and southern regions.[1]

Communication between Islam and Christianity, as well as between Islam and post-Christian culture, has faced significant challenges. The writing produced in the West about Islam, commonly referred to as the work of orientalists, has often been influenced by the contentious debates of the Middle Ages.[2] During the period when Christianity gained control of the Roman Empire until the seventh century, it seemed inevitable that the Christian message would universally spread without hindrance. However, Islam emerged in the seventh century and halted this expansion. Consequently, Christians were confronted with the unsettling notion that God had made a grave error, unless they possessed a profound piety capable of enduring severe shocks. The sudden appearance of Islam, originating from the Arabian sands, quickly established its presence in the territories of the Byzantine Empire (Eastern Roman Empire) including Palestine, Syria, Iraq, Persia and Christian Egypt, causing the foundations of the world to tremble and casting a dark shadow over the heart of Christendom, the Holy Land.

Western Christendom was compelled to rediscover its identity, reassess its dogma, and delineate its boundaries, ultimately shaping Europe as a representation of Western civilisation. This endeavour fostered cultural and doctrinal differentiation and separation from its ideological adversary, Islam. The process of introspection involved observing, analysing, and engaging in military confrontations with Islam, which was perceived as the principal 'Other' within the orientalist framework.

Before the seventh century, various civilisations, including Persia, Africa, and the so-called 'barbarian' world, were regarded as 'the Other'. However, this study concentrates solely on European views of the 'Islamic Other.' Over the centuries, these views have fostered misunderstandings and a strained relationship between the two civilisations, a dynamic that persists to this day. Such misconceptions significantly shape Western historiography, complicating the ability of scholars and students to engage with Islam in an objective manner. The study of Islam in Europe reached its peak in the nineteenth century, coinciding with the era of European imperialism when almost all Muslim lands, with the notable exception of Turkey, came under European dominion.

Due to the military strength of Islam and the perceived weakness of Christendom, verbal attacks became the primary means of combating what was initially viewed as 'heresy' and later as a false religion of satanic origin. Pope Innocent III labelled Muhammad as the Anti-Christ, while Doughty referred to him as "a dirty and treacherous Arab" nearly 700 years later. Throughout medieval and modern literature, a clear bias against Muhammad and Islam is evident. The presence of the Turks in Islamic history further contributed to both European admiration and prejudice against the Ottoman Empire and Islam. However, by the nineteenth century, when the tide had turned against Islam, the term 'Turk' had become synonymous with 'Muslim', 'tyrant', and 'barbarian'. These biased depictions have been deeply ingrained in the Western psyche and continue to persist today.

Regrettably, the prevailing perception that Europeans hold of Islam is that of 'the religion of the sword'. This perception originated during the Middle Ages and was perpetuated by both the church and the state for centuries. This bias, held by ordinary individuals, along with vague notions of harems and veiled women, stems from a widespread and profound lack of knowledge about Islam. The accounts of European travellers who ventured into the Ottoman lands and other Muslim regions such as Persia from the 16th to the 18th century served as the foundation for a new wave of oriental exoticism in art and literature. Eventually, this tradition evolved into the well-known academic orientalism of the 19th and 20th centuries, which was closely intertwined with European imperialist aspirations. The extent to which these perceptions have influenced European and Western perspectives on Islam will be further examined in the subsequent chapters.

The rapid spread of Islam is a remarkable phenomenon that occurred within a century after the death of the Prophet in 632 AD. The Muslim

Empire expanded extensively, stretching from China to the Adriatic, France to India, and the Caspian Sea to the Sahara. This extraordinary growth was achieved by a people who were often disregarded as ignorant nomads by the wider world beyond the Arabian peninsula. They conquered and governed over four-and-a-half million square miles of land, reshaping the course of history. Christianity was subdued by Islam in its original territories in the Near East, North Africa, and Spain. Additionally, the Muslim Empire posed a significant threat to the Byzantine Roman Empire and transformed the Persian Empire into a stronghold of Islam.

No other accomplishment in human history can be compared to this. While Alexander the Great's conquests were impressive, they only left behind legends and a few inscriptions. On the other hand, wherever the Arabs went, they established a civilisation and a complete way of life that has endured and continues to endure. Their influence decisively shaped the future of Europe by blocking access to the prosperous lands of the east. This, in turn, prompted the voyages of exploration to the west and south centuries later, which ultimately fuelled European power. Therefore, the Arabs were poised to alter the trajectory of European history.

In the year 720, the Muslims successfully traversed the challenging Pyrenees and gained access to all of western Europe. However, their advancement was halted by the Franks in a battle near the present-day cities of Tours and Poitiers. Nevertheless, the significance of this battle remains uncertain, especially considering that the eastern wing of the Muslim army was already making progress into the Swiss Valais region. Regardless of the reasons behind it, there is undeniable evidence that the immense wave of expansion had temporarily ceased and reached its inherent boundary.

Following the failed expedition into France, western Europe constantly faced the looming threat of Islam, which had become the dominant civilisation. Christendom, on the other hand, was confined to a small region within the Euro-Asian land mass, always vulnerable and only finding respite during periods of Muslim disunity. The Crusaders arrived in Palestine but were eventually expelled, and in the 13th century, the Arab world suffered devastation at the hands of the Mongol armies. However, the Mongols and later the Turks converted to Islam, becoming its champions. The fall of Constantinople in 1453 marked a turning point, as the Ottomans emerged as a formidable force against the European enclave. They captured Belgrade in 1521 and Rhodes the following year. Süleyman the Magnificent ventured into Hungary and achieved a significant victory at Mohacs. In the 1530s, the French King, Francis I, sought Ottoman support against the Hapsburgs and even encouraged their plans to invade Italy. Subsequently, Protestant princes also sought Muslim assistance against the Pope and the Emperor, leading the Sultan to prepare for an invasion of Germany. Consequently, the boundary between the Orient and Europe was gradually pushed further into the heartland of the continent. The Turkish onslaught left a lasting impact on European perceptions, shaping not only their views of the Turks but also of the entire Muslim world.

The possibility of the Islamic threat being empty cannot be disregarded, as Europe had already surpassed the Muslim world in terms of effective power due to advancements in firearms and shipbuilding. However, this threat resonated with the long-standing perception of the world held by Europeans, which had been shaped over nearly nine centuries. The "menace of Islam" had consistently remained a significant factor amidst the ever-changing landscape, leaving a lasting imprint on the European consciousness. This branding is still evident to this day.

By the conclusion of the seventeenth century, the dynamics in Europe were undergoing significant transformation. In 1683, the Ottomans besieged Vienna for the second and final time, following their initial attempt in 1529 under Sultan Süleyman (d. 1566). Their power had already diminished, a reality acknowledged in the Treaty of Karlowitz, which was ratified in 1699. The Islamic realm, if it can still be characterised as such, had been on the defensive for several years, and its defences were starting to crumble. The British had solidified their foothold in India, the Dutch in Indonesia, and the Russian conquest of Azov brought their most persistent adversary into the Balkans. The

European powers were consolidating their strength. A new crusade had begun, aimed at eradicating the Islamic threat from Europe once and for all.

Treaty of Karlowitz (1699) and the Muslim advance into southern France (720) were separated by nearly a millennium, while our present time is distanced by just over three centuries from Karlowitz. Throughout this interval, Europe and the West managed to momentarily set aside their deep preoccupation with Islam. Nevertheless, this focus was not easily removed from their collective awareness. Hichem Djait, a Tunisian author, contends that the prejudices of the medieval period have become firmly embedded in the Western mindset, raising concerns about the possibility of ever completely eliminating these biases.[3]

Undoubtedly, the years of European imperial dominance were marked by a collective amnesia. In the late 18th century, Edward Gibbon (d. 1794) recognised the importance of dedicating nine out of the seventy-one chapters of his renowned work, *The Decline and Fall of the Roman Empire*, to Islam. However, European historians in the subsequent century chose to overlook this significant aspect. Nevertheless, it is evident that there has been a revival of concern regarding Islam. Samuel P. Huntington's seminal work, *The Clash of Civilizations* (1996), along with other scholarly writings, embodies the views of postmodern historians who regard Islam as the primary ideology capable of contesting Western hegemony in the so-called New World Order that emerged after the collapse of communism.

The events that unfolded were not merely about physical conquest. In the past, those who had exerted their influence on the Muslim world were either militarily powerful but lacking in cultural strength, such as the Mongols, or vice versa. However, when confronted with Western power, the Muslims encountered a combination of physical force and cultural dominance. If colonialism had been characterised by brutal oppression, the impact would have been relatively shallow, leaving only surface-level scars. The dead are quickly buried, and massacres are forgotten. Yet, for Islam and the rest of the non-European world, this was an experience of being under the guidance of well-intentioned masters who believed it was their moral duty to educate and improve the natives. According to Amy Allen:

> Imperialism as a political project cannot sustain itself without the ideas of empire, and the idea of empire, in turn, is noursihed by a philosophical and cultural imaginary that justifies the political subjugation of distant territories and their native populations through claims that such peoples are less advanced, cognitively inferior, and therefore naturally subordinate.[4]

These European masters displayed a polite contempt for the fundamental values that tradition holds, which is far more destructive than persecution. They did not destroy bodies, but rather souls - or at the very least, the nourishment upon which human souls thrive. Western colonialism dismantled the barriers and any other divisions that had been established between itself and Islam since the Middle Ages. As long as the West was supreme in terms of ideology, culture, economy, military power, and technology, there was no barrier.

During the middle of the twentieth century, the Europeans initiated the process of withdrawing from their colonies. However, they left behind a lasting impact that the 'developing' world is still grappling with. With the exception of Algeria and Indonesia, it cannot be claimed that the Europeans were forcefully expelled from their colonies. Instead, the collapse of European empires can be attributed to a lack of determination, self-doubt, exhaustion from two major wars, and economic factors. Nevertheless, in their abdication, they attempted to fulfil their responsibilities by imposing unsuitable systems of government and administration on the newly independent nations. Perhaps there was no alternative, as the traditional structures of governance and social life had been significantly disrupted.

The independence movements in the colonies and protectorates emerged not as a result of a return to indigenous values, but rather through the adoption of Western ideas and ideologies, whether liberal or revolutionary. Contrary to expectations, this process of modernisation, which can be seen as synonymous with Westernisation, was actually accelerated rather than halted. Turkey, under the leadership of Mustafa Kemal Atatürk (1881-1938), underwent a profound cultural and political transformation. Atatürk viewed modernisation as synonymous with Westernisation, even if it meant disregarding six centuries of Ottoman and Islamic heritage. Consequently, Turkey became the sole Islamic country in the Middle East to embrace secularism and separate religion from politics. The new rulers' enthusiasm for all things "modern" was not tempered by any self-doubt, unlike their former masters. The tragic irony of this situation became evident during the Vietnam War (1955-1975), when the Vietnamese people fought not to preserve their own traditions or assert their true identity, but rather under the banner of Western ideology, striving to emulate their former colonisers in terms of nationalism and socialism. The West found itself at odds with its own reflection. Hence, it could be argued that the Cold War was a conflict of ideologies that the West both fostered and fought against, giving rise to the very "isms" it sought to combat.

Western values continue to serve as the benchmark against which all others are evaluated, and the majority willingly accept this standard. The Europeans' self-assurance, which once allowed them to maintain control over native populations during the era of imperialism, still persists. It is widely assumed that the rest of the world must adhere to the rules established by Western civilisation, rules that have evolved from European history. Although the European powers constitute a small minority within the United Nations, a cursory examination of the organisation's Charter reveals that it exclusively incorporates principles originating from Western sources. This same pattern holds true for the current understanding of international law. Consequently, the influence of Eurocentrism and the pressure to adopt Western practices remain highly pronounced in developing nations today.

In recent years, the importance of religion has undeniably increased not only in Islamic societies but also in other cultures. However, what are the specific factors contributing to this phenomenon? The endeavour to integrate the economies of Islamic nations into the global economy has impacted both societies and individuals in this region.

Elements of "Westernisation" can be observed in every country and city: local products often struggle to compete against Western goods, educators have received their training abroad, and television broadcasts Western culture and standards of living even in the most remote areas. As a result, many individuals have developed a desire to safeguard and preserve their own cultural identity against the overpowering influence of the West. They perceive Islam and Islamic values as a means to achieve this goal, as it represents their own culture and stands apart from Western influences.

Islam and Western historiography

In the last century, historians have made efforts to analyse history from a global perspective, devoid of personal biases. However, it is important to acknowledge that this approach has not been flawless. The concept of objectivity in historical accounts is unattainable as writers inevitably convey their viewpoints influenced by their specific time and geographical context. Various scholars, such as Spengler, Toynbee, Hodgson, Fukuyama, and Huntington, have endeavoured to present an impartial understanding of human history. Nevertheless, their challenges in achieving this equilibrium become evident, especially when addressing the topic of Islam.

Oswald Spengler's work, *The Decline of the West* (1918), brought to the forefront of European consciousness the realisation of its failure caused by the Great War, despite its belief in progress. As Paul Valery succinctly put it, "We later civilizations ... we now know that we are mortal".[5] Spengler observed that "world history is our world picture and not all mankind's".[6] Unlike other cultures and civilisations such as the Indian, Greek, and Roman, who did not conceive of a progressing world, Spengler speculated that the civilisation of the West may also meet its demise in due course.[7] However, he does not desire to confirm the ultimate downfall of the West, but rather sees it as the only civilisation capable of achieving universality for all of humanity. On the other hand, Hegel argues that universal history does not exist.

Spengler distanced himself from a narrow linear perspective on the past, rejecting the idea of any continuity between classical antiquity and the present. He criticised the division of history into ancient, medieval, and modern periods as a simplistic and meaningless framework that has unfortunately dominated our historical thinking. As a result, we have failed to grasp the true significance of the overall history of humanity.[8] By freeing himself from these constraints, Spengler was able to objectively examine the cycles of history and analyse each culture on its own terms. Unlike Hegel and other thinkers, Spengler did not assign a predetermined destiny to Islam or any other culture. According to Spengler, all cultures are destined to decline, but the manner in which they decline differs. Arab culture, for instance, has already experienced irreversible decline, while the decline of the West remains a possibility. Despite potential threats or weakening due to war, the West still maintains a tangible superiority, albeit one based primarily on material and power.[9]

Is the Islamic civilisation on the verge of decline, or will it successfully confront the challenges posed by the modern era? This notion of cultural demise has been contested by Arnold Toynbee in his book *A Study of History*. Toynbee meticulously examined twenty-one civilisations in an attempt to unravel the essence of history and its revelations. Among these civilisations, Toynbee identifies five cultures that continue to thrive in the twentieth century: the Western and Orthodox (both rooted in Hellenic civilisation), the Islamic, the Indian, and the Far Eastern. Remarkably, this cultural classification has remained unchanged since the eighth century of the commom era. According to Toynbee, the four non-Western cultures that persist today have yet to have their final say.[10]

According to Toynbee, the Anglo-Saxons have implemented white racism through colonialism in its most extreme manifestation. This is due to the conscious association and identification of Western Christians with Israel, positioning themselves as the chosen people.[11] As a result, white racism has reached its peak in the form of Western imperialism during the 19th and early 20th centuries. However, Toynbee encounters a dilemma when it comes to Islam. Despite rejecting the notion of a clear divide between Europe and the Orient, he cannot help but attribute the fracture caused by the emergence of Islam. This massive Islamic road-block was a challenge which evoked proportionally energetic responses from pioneer communities in the two blockaded Christian societies.[12]

Simultaneously, he highlights that the division between the East and West may have existed even before the rise of Islam, implying that this dichotomy was present during the Roman era. Toynbee views civilisations as "intelligible historical entities" and endeavours to comprehend their decline.[13] He argues that the process of 'Westernisation' or 'modernisation' does not necessarily result in the complete disintegration of other cultures. Instead, Western modernity compels these cultures to come into contact with it. A prime example of this is the complete political and military downfall of the Ottoman Empire, while Turkey still maintains its Islamic identity in the form of the Republic of Turkey.

Toynbee proposes that cultures have the ability to adopt elements from one another as needed. In this particular scenario, the East adopted Western techniques without adopting its institutions, suggesting that a culture is not a unified entity that must be fully embraced or rejected. Similarly, Western Christendom during the Middle Ages borrowed intellectual ideas from Islam while disregarding its faith and beliefs. However, the question arises as to how adopting technical aspects from the West can contribute to the preservation of the Other's cultural identity. Toynbee does not address this matter. Despite the West's temporary technical and material superiority, Toynbee unintentionally assigns a certain historical significance to the West.[14]

The interaction between the global community and the Western world could potentially be regarded as the most significant event in contemporary history when looking back. The Other is perceived as someone who imitates while still valuing their own distinctiveness. Is there any fault in that? Throughout the Middle Ages, Christian Europe borrowed concepts from the Muslims - were they merely imitating? Nevertheless, they successfully maintained and safeguarded their unique identity! It can be contended that cultures that merely replicate without ultimately creating anything original and distinctive in place of the imitated elements are destined to fall behind and remain perpetually reliant on those who innovate and develop new technologies or methods to progress their societies.

In Francis Fukuyama's work, *The End of History and the Last Man* (1992), Eurocentrism and Eurocentric ideology are prominently featured. Fukuyama asserts that Western ideology, specifically liberalism, has achieved ultimate triumph with the collapse of communism during the Cold War. However, he also predicts that Muslim fundamentalism, particularly from Islam, poses a significant threat to Western dominance, potentially leading to conflict. Numerous critics, including Turkish and Muslim scholars and writers, argue that Fukuyama's thesis merely reflects the spiritual turmoil experienced in the West. The book explores this perspective further in the subsequent chapters.[15]

Samuel P. Huntington, a renowned scholar, has categorised the post-Cold War world into six distinct civilisations: Sinic, Japanese, Hindu, Islamic, Western, and Latin American. In his analysis, he emphasises the potential clash of civilisations in the post-Cold War era and the upcoming millennium. Huntington delves into the complexities of modernisation in non-Western countries, particularly in the Islamic, Asian, and Third World nations. He raises a significant question regarding whether these civilisations can achieve modernisation without adopting Western values. Samuel Huntington perceives a civilisation-based world order where societies which share cultural kinship co-operate with each other and countries grouping themselves around "the lead or core states of their civilization".[16] He describes the West's ambitions for ideological, cultural, and military expansion as "universalist aspirations", which inevitably lead to clashes with other prominent civilisations in the world, namely Islam and China. In this struggle for political supremacy, both Muslim and non-Muslim nations unite with their kin-countries for support.[17] The fall of the Berlin Wall and the end of the Cold War brought about a sense of euphoria, creating an "illusion of harmony". However, the post-Cold War era in the 1990s did not necessarily become more peaceful. Contrary to expectations, democracy did not prevail at the end of World War I. This exposed the weakness of the West, which had dominated the world through colonialism for centuries, in its attempt to establish its ideological supremacy. Instead, the aftermath of World War I gave rise to extreme forms of antithesis to democracy: fascism and communism. These ideologies eventually led to another global conflict and resulted in the Cold War, a clash of ideologies between the so-called free world (Western Europe and the United States) and the Soviet Union, which ultimately collapsed in 1990. The West then claimed victory over communism, but this triumph was merely an illusion. It unleashed a Pandora's box of ethnic conflicts and "ethnic cleansing" in the Balkans, particularly between the Serbian Christian Orthodox and the Muslims of Bosnia and Kosovo, fuelling a clash between Christianity and Islam. However, the Berlin Wall, according to Kaplan has been replaced by a "cultural curtain ... in Bosnia, ... a curtain separating the Christian and Islamic worlds".[18] This raises the question: Is the world currently experiencing a clash of civilisations as envisioned by Huntington? The book focusses on examining the perspectives of Turkish historians and other Muslim writers challenging Huntington's thesis in subsesquent chapters.

Samuel P. Huntington perceives the West as a distinct entity, while the remaining five non-Western civilisations differ significantly in terms of cultural values, religion, and social structure. Consequently, whenever the West engages with these civilisations, be it through cultural, military, or political means, clashes are inevitable. This is because the non-Western civilisations perceive the West's intervention as an attempt to assert its global dominance over them.[19] Throughout history, it has become apparent that the concept of Europe began to permeate the minds of its inhabitants during the Renaissance period. This notion gained even more significance during the 17th and 18th centuries, known as the era of Enlightenment and the Scientific Revolution.

The people of Europe cultivated a sense of superiority over the Islamic Other, largely attributed to their economic and technological progress. The Enlightenment period and the subsequent division of religion from state affairs are regarded as pivotal factors in establishing Western superiority. From a Western standpoint, states or nations that fail to embrace this separation are perceived as immature and limited by their religious convictions. Motivated by this self-perception,

Europe actively pursued secularism, capitalism, liberalism, nationalism, colonialism, and imperialism to reinforce its identity and ideological preeminence. Interestingly, this identity and hegemony were shaped by the contributions of the peoples and cultures of the Near East, specifically the Mesopotamian, Hellenic, and Islamic civilisations, often categorised as the history of the 'Other.' In its assertion of superiority over the 'Other,' Europe ideologically progressed, leading to the emergence of various 'isms' associated with European-Western civilisation, including secularism, fascism, Nazism, and communism. The effects of these ideologies continue to resonate today among numerous nations and peoples worldwide.

At what point in history did a distinct awareness of Europe begin to take shape? How has the West's perspective on its nearest Other, the Mediterranean Orient, evolved? In what ways did Islam play a role in shaping the 'idea of Europe'? To what degree did the perceptions of the Islamic Other influence the development of a European identity? Have these European views of Islam created a definitive or imagined divide between the West and the East? Europe's substantial engagement with Islamic culture during the Middle Ages raises the question of why Islam is perceived as a potential threat in the aftermath of communism's decline and the shifting global landscape that followed the post-9/11 era, which has posed challenges to Western ideologies. Since the eighth century, when the worlds of Christendom and Islam first intersected, Europeans have persistently endeavoured to assert their cultural and technological dominance over the peoples of the eastern Mediterranean. This pursuit reached its peak during the age of imperialism and colonialism in the nineteenth century, which solidified European dominance across the globe.

In addition to the aforementioned sources, the book utilises secondary sources from Western historiography on Islam. Noteworthy individuals such as Henri Pirenne, Ernest Renan, Arnold Toynbee, Oswald Spengler, Edward Gibbon, Hegel, Hodgson, Kinross, Braudel, Runciman, Wheatcroft, Shaw, and Norman Daniel will be consulted. Moreover, non-Western writers including Asrar, Djait, Esposito, Hourani, İnalcık, Zakaria, Schioun, and Bammate will also be incorporated. The study also encompasses the viewpoints of contemporary orientalists including Bernard Lewis, Maxime Rodinson, Thierry Hentsch, and Edward Said. Primary sources, particularly translations of works by orientalists, ambassadors, and envoys who journeyed to the Orient and played a role in shaping Orientalism. Notable figures in this context include Émeric Crucé (d. 1648), Pierre Belon (d. 1564), Guillaume Postel (d. 1581), Jean de Thevenot (d. 1667), Jean Siméon Chardin (d. 1779), Lady Mary Wortley Montagu (d. 1762), Montesquie (d. 1755), as well as others who wrote about Islam and the Turks, including Machiavelli (d. 1527), the French playwright Jean Racine (d. 1699) and his play *Bajazed*, Voltaire, Antoine Galland (d. 1715), Mozart (d. 1791) and his compositions inspired by Turkish themes, as well as nineteenth-century artists like Ingres, known for his significant portrayals of the Ottoman harem and the Turkish bath.

Maxime Rodinson presents a compelling argument against the validity of the concepts of East and West. According to him, these terms oversimplify the rich diversity of people, countries, regions, societies, and cultures that exist in reality.[20] By categorising societies and cultures as either western or eastern, we unintentionally perpetuate biases and prejudices that contribute to racist tendencies. Regrettably, this labelling has become deeply ingrained in history, particularly in western historiography, making it challenging to overcome. As a historian myself, I also struggle to avoid using the terms "East" and "West". However, in specific historical contexts, I may resort to terms like Occident, Europe, Franks, Orient, Middle East, and the Mediterranean Orient to represent the concepts of East and West. This conscious choice aims to distance myself from any orientalist agenda.

Structure

The book extensively examines the origins and substance of these debates, providing a comprehensive analysis of the historical and political dynamics between Islam and Europe throughout different epochs. It covers the Rise of Islam, the Middle Ages, the Renaissance, the Enlightenment, the Orientalism of the nineteenth century, European imperialism and colonialism, and the contemporary era characterised by the so-called New World Order.

The structure of the book is organised into three sections:

a) the initial encounters between Western Christendom and Islam, highlighting how Christendom assimilated Islamic knowledge into its own intellectual tradition;

b) European perceptions of Islam, which include medieval, Renaissance, and 17th and 18th-century historiography that contributed to the development of Orientalism;

c) the impact of European imperialism on Orientalism and the evolving relationship between Islam and the New World Order in the modern context.

In first two chapters of Part I of the book, I examine the rise of Islam, and how Europeans viewed the Islamic Other in the Middle Ages. These chapters explore the emergence of Islam and its profound impact on the consciousness of Latin Christendom. The first century after the Prophet Muhammad's passing witnessed the rapid expansion of Islam, stretching from Spain in the west to the borders of China in the east. This expansion is widely recognised as a global phenomenon in human history. The achievements and contributions of Muslim Spain (Al-Andalus) to the development of Western civilisation should not be overlooked. In fact, it was in this region that Christendom encountered a fully developed and thriving civilisation. Western historiography often neglects the intellectual and philosophical inspiration that Islam sparked in Latin Christendom during the Middle Ages. The main objective of this chapter is to demonstrate the extent to which this intellectual exchange contributed to the formation of Western civilisation.

Chapters three, four, five, and six examine the rise of the Turks during the eleventh century and the ensuing clash between the civilisations of Christendom and Islam. Chapter three looks at the first millennium in Europe commenced with the confrontation between Christianity and Islam during the Crusades. The struggle undertaken by Latin Christendom against the Seljuk Turks in both Anatolia and the Holy Land, referred to as the Crusades, significantly shaped the view of Islam as the "Other." This period marked the emergence of the Muslim world as the principal adversary to Christendom in the quest for universal dominance. Following the collapse of the Seljuk Empire of Rum in Anatolia in the late thirteenth century, the rise of the Ottoman Turks posed a subsequent threat for Latin Christendom. This chapter explores the gradual resurgence of Europeans from a prolonged period of stagnation, taking into account the political, military, and economic challenges presented by the Ottomans. It emphasizes their attempts to rejuvenate a former era of the Greco-Roman civilisation, commonly referred to by historians as the Renaissance. In the context of nineteenth-century European nationalism, the narrative of the Renaissance was reinterpreted and distorted, as it became a historical phase during which Europeans endeavoured to reclaim a sense of belonging to a collective European identity, seeking to differentiate themselves from the more dominant and often perceived as 'backward' Muslim adversaries of that time.

Chapter five focusses on the reigns of the two prominent Ottoman Sultans, Mehmed the Conqueror (d.1481) and Süleyman the Magnificent (r. 1520-1566), shedding light on the division in the Mediterranean world caused by the Ottoman presence. After establishing themselves in Constantinople (Istanbul) in 1453 and the Janissaries' siege of Vienna in 1529, the negative connotations of perception of the Turk began to spread throughout the Western world. This perception gained even more prominence in the nineteenth century, dominating European newspapers with the label, the "Terrible Turk". The Christian world faced the Turkish onslaught and it is worth exploring how they responded to this existential challenge. The following chapter 'Observing the Other and Shifting Identities in the Sixteenth Century' examines how European observations shaped the image of the Ottoman Turks during the sixteenth century, the zenith of Turkish power in the Mediterranean Orient, the Balkans, and North Africa.

In the seventeenth century, travellers like Jean de Thévenot (1633-1667) set out on voyages to the Orient. This time period also witnessed an increasing European consciousness, as scholars and writers endeavoured to portray the 'Other' in a more impartial way. Racine's play, *Bajazet*, for example, sought to accurately depict Turkish characters without modifying their traditions or behaviours. The seventeenth century was marked by a confident self-assurance and a sincere interest in the histories of diverse cultures. Chapter seven explores the exploration of European consciousness in this era.

During the Enlightenment of the eighteenth century, notable figures such as Henri de Boulainvilliers (1658-1722), Voltaire (1694-1778), Montesquieu (1689-1755), and Edward Gibbon (1737-1794) sought to present an impartial representation of the Orient. This discussion also explores the emergence of the term 'despot' and the connection between exoticism and the Orient during this period. The 1704 translation of Antoine Galland's *The Tales of the Arabian Nights* played a pivotal role in shaping the view of the Orient as a land of exotic allure. Furthermore, Lady Mary Wortley Montagu's journey to Turkey in 1717 sparked a wave of curiosity and intrigue regarding the Ottoman Empire. European interest in various elements of Turkish culture flourished, evident in Mozart's compositions inspired by Turkish themes and French artist Jean-Auguste-Dominique Ingres' depictions of Turkish baths (1862) and harem scenes. However, as the Ottoman Empire's influence waned in southeastern Europe and the West experienced a series of military setbacks, leading to unfavorable peace agreements with the Turkish sultans, the perception of the Ottomans as despotic intensified. It became the perceived frailty of the Turks, rather than their might, that presented a challenge for Europe. Chapters eight and nine provide a deeper examination of this historical context.

Chapter ten centres on the critique of Orientalism and the changing European views of Islam, examining it through the lens of nineteenth-century European imperialism. On the other hand, Chapter eleven delves into the portrayal of the Other from the standpoint of Islam's subordination and submissive position in the face of European imperialism and colonialism. Following Turkey's unsuccessful second attempt to seize Vienna in 1683 and the subsequent Treaty of Karlowitz in 1699, the once mighty Ottoman Empire was compelled to accept peace terms imposed by the victorious powers. With Napoleon's expedition to Egypt, European control over Ottoman territories gained momentum. Over time, the French and British gradually took hold of the Sultan's possessions in North Africa, while Russian and Austrian ambitions in the Balkans weakened the Empire's influence in that region. The Greek war of Independence and the Balkan conflicts of the 1870s marked the pinnacle of anti-Turk propaganda in Europe. The Turks were portrayed as 'barbaric' and 'savage', while Europe turned a blind eye to the Christian atrocities committed against Muslim populations in the Balkans, Morea, and Crete.

In the 19th century, Europe aimed to reconnect with its classical roots to shape its identity, yet the notion of the imagined Orient continued to captivate the Western mindset. The concept of the imagined Orient materialised for the aristocracy and the curious intellectual circles before the dawn of the 20th century. Opulent train journeys to the Orient allured the wealthy to exotic places like Istanbul, the heart of the Ottoman Empire. However, the adverse views of the Muslim Orient gradually influenced the literary works of writers, such as Agatha Christie's crime novels, particularly her famous series featuring the murder on the Orient Express and others. Chapter twelve delves deeper into this subject.

Part II of the book consists of five chapters, specifically chapters thirteen to seventeen. This section opens with a thorough analysis of the shortcomings and vulnerabilities of Muslims during the period from the 18th century to the early 20th century, prior to the disintegration of the Ottoman Empire. This analysis requires an objective and persistent approach to develop a comprehensive evaluation. Chapter thirteen, entitled 'Where Did the Muslims Go Wrong?', investigates the key elements that led to the decline of Muslim civilisation and aims to offer alternative suggestions for future progress. Subsequent chapters address the challenges that the West encounters in the twentieth century due to the increased self-assurance and resurgent Islam.

Chapter fourteen centres on the deterioration of Europe and the obstacles it encountered in maintaining its global supremacy. European ethnocentrism was profoundly shaken by the events of the early twentieth century. The outbreak of World War I in 1914, followed by World War II in 1939, utterly shattered European self-assurance in its own advancement. Europe commenced a process of reevaluating its shortcomings and attempting to reconcile with its political and economic downfall. This marked the inception of Europe's decline. Despite the profound shock to eurocentrism, by the conclusion of the First World War, Europe still exerted control over eighty five percent of the world's territories.[21] The British and French dismantled the Ottoman Empire, dividing its territories among themselves. Syria and Lebanon became French mandates, while Transjordan, Iraq, and Palestine fell under British control. The victorious powers also divided Asiatic Turkey, gaining control over the Straits and Constantinople. This consolidation of power in Europe led to a determination to suppress any resistance to their dominance. However, Mustafa Kemal emerged as a formidable obstacle to complete European domination of the Mediterranean Orient. Kemal's call for Turkish nationalism inspired his people to overthrow Western imperialism, making Turkey the first post-war country to do so. This movement sparked nationalist movements throughout the Middle East, India, and Indonesia. Failing to subjugate Turkey, Britain and France turned their attention to Russian bolshevism, which ultimately contributed to the tensions of the Cold War. The Cold War persisted until the 1990s, when it was replaced by the re-emergence of Islam as the only ideology capable of challenging Western hegemony. Unfortunately, due to the instantaneous reporting of conflicts by the Western media, the portrayal of Islam in the news and media has been largely negative.

Furthermore, Chapter fifteen titled "Re-awakening of Islam: Double Standards of Western Representations of Resurgent Islam ~ 1970-1995", examines the representation of Islam in the media and its role in the resurgance of the perceived 'Islamic threat' during this era, which became an increasing concern for the Western world. To substantiate my analysis, I will draw upon articles from magazines and newspapers, along with Edward Said's work, *Covering Islam - How the Media and the Experts Determine How We See The Rest of the World.*

In Chapter sixteen, an evaluation is conducted concerning the Muslim viewpoint on Samuel Huntington's contentious theory, widely recognised as the 'clash of civilisations'. The Islamic perspective predominantly underscores the significance of promoting intercultural dialogue instead of endorsing conflict in the present context. In the final section of this chapter, I explore the reactions of Turkish historians and various Muslim authors to eurocentrism and the New World Order articulated by Huntington and Fukuyama in the early 1990s following the collapse of communism in the Soviet Union, while also offering a critique of orientalism. Additionally, Muslim scholars draw attention to historical instances of intolerance within Christian Europe to demonstrate the shortcomings of the Western world.

In contemporary era, it is essential to examine the perceptions of the Muslim 'Other' in the 21st century in the aftermath of the 9/11 attacks on New York and Washington in Chapter seventeen 'The New Millennium and the Muslim Other'. This allows historians to obtain a more profound insight into the changing dynamics or the consistent psyche of the Western mindset.

Part III examines the acknowledgment of the Other in the 21st century, highlighting the assertiveness of Muslims as it challenges Orientalism and the prevailing global narrative shaped by Western perspectives. The section commences with Chapter eighteen, titled 'Decolonising Orientalism: Critiquing Euro-American Intellectual Hegemony in Academia'. This chapter sets the stage for a thorough critique of the ways in which Euro-American scholarship has historically marginalised non-Western perspectives. It highlights the need for a decolonised approach to knowledge production that recognises and values the contributions of Muslim scholars and thinkers, thereby challenging the intellectual dominance that has long characterised academic discourse. Following this foundational critique, Chapter nineteen, 'Religion, Politics and the Emerging World Order', shifts the focus to the intersection of religion and politics in shaping global power dynamics. The chapter examines how religion is used as a justification to propagate political aspirations and objectives in the context of the quest for a new world order.

The discussion then transitions to 'The Global South in the 21st Century' in Chapter twenty, which contextualises the aspirations of the United States within a framework of neo-colonialism and imperialism that has persisted since the conclusion of the Second World War. This chapter critically assesses the resurgence of these imperialistic tendencies during Donald Trump's presidency, exploring how they have impacted global perceptions of the Other, particularly in relation to Muslim identities.

In Chapter twenty-one, titled 'America: The Last Bastion of Western Imperialism', the concept of American exceptionalism is scrutinized. This chapter interrogates the narratives that position the United States as a unique force for good in the world or the myth of American exceptionalism revealing how such claims often obscure the realities of imperialism and its consequences for marginalised communities, including Muslims.

Chapter twenty-two, 'From Europe to America: Evangelical White Christianity and Islamophobia', shifts the lens to contemporary expressions of Islamophobia in the United States, linking these sentiments to the broader Christian Evangelical movement. This chapter explores how religious ideologies can fuel xenophobia and discrimination, contributing to a climate of fear and misunderstanding surrounding Muslim communities.

Finally, Part III of the book concludes with Chapter twenty-three, 'Challenging Western Cultural Imperialism and Soft Power Politics'. The chapter delves into the complex dynamics of representation and identity, focusing specifically on how Muslims portray the Muslim Other within the context of 21st-century television media. The chapter begins by contextualising the concept of cultural imperialism, particularly as it pertains to Western narratives that often dominate global media landscapes. It explores the historical roots of these narratives and how they have shaped perceptions of Muslims and Islamic culture in the West. I argue that such representations frequently perpetuate stereotypes and reinforce a monolithic view of Islam, which fails to capture the diversity and richness of Muslim identities. As the chapter progresses, it shifts to an analysis of contemporary television shows, documentaries, and films that feature Muslim characters and themes. I highlight both positive and negative portrayals, examining how these representations can either challenge or reinforce existing stereotypes. By analysing specific case studies, the chapter illustrates the ways in which Muslim creators and storytellers are actively working to reclaim narratives and present more nuanced, authentic depictions of their culture. Furthermore, the chapter addresses the concept of soft power politics, discussing how media can serve as a tool for cultural diplomacy and influence. It examines the role of television in shaping public opinion and fostering understanding between cultures, while also critiquing the ways in which it can perpetuate division and misunderstanding. The chapter emphasises the importance of representation in media, arguing that it has the potential to challenge dominant narratives and promote a more inclusive and accurate understanding of the Muslim experience. In conclusion, Chapter twenty-three serves as a critical examination of the intersection between media representation, cultural imperialism, and identity politics. It calls for a more conscious and responsible approach to storytelling in television, advocating for the inclusion of diverse voices and perspectives that reflect the complexities of the Muslim experience in the modern world. Through this exploration, the chapter not only highlights the challenges faced by Muslim communities in the media landscape but also celebrates the resilience and creativity of those who strive to redefine their narratives in the face of cultural hegemony.

The Arab conquests of the seventh century represented a significant expansion that spanned across North Africa, crossing the Straits of Gibraltar into the Iberian Peninsula, which includes modern-day Spain and southern France to the west. Simultaneously, these conquests progressed eastward, reaching as far as Iran, Central Asia, China, India, and South Asia. This period of expansion was pivotal in the formation of a vast, unified empire that, for the first time since antiquity, brought together a diverse array of cultures under the umbrella of the Islamic faith.

Contrary to the common Western narrative that suggests Islam was propagated through force and violence, the reality is that the principles of Islam, which prioritize intellectual engagement, religious tolerance, and social justice, played a crucial role in the ability of Muslim leaders to sustain their influence in the territories they had conquered for centuries. This approach not only facilitated the integration of various cultures but also established a rich legacy that continues to resonate in contemporary society. The first part of the book delves into this extraordinary historical development, exploring its implications and the dynamics that shaped this era.

PART I

FROM MECCA TO AL-ANDALUS

ENCOUNTERS IN THE WEST

[T]he Arab conquests of the seventh century have continued to play an important role in human history, down to the present day. It is this unparalleled combination of secular and religious influence which I feel entitles Muhammad to be considered the most influential single figure in human history.

Michael H. Hart

The world is held up by four pillars: the wisdom of the learned, the justice of the great, the prayers of the righteous, and the valour of the brave.

An inscription on one of the main buildings of the Madrasa of Granada (1340).

CHAPTER 1

THE RISE AND EXPANSION OF ISLAM

During the seventh century, the primary focus of Roman Christendom was on Byzantium rather than the Arab expansion. It wasn't until the tenth century that Christendom became aware of Baghdad, Damascus, and Cordoba. The West had no interest in delving deeper into their knowledge of Islam and the Arabs. However, this doesn't mean that Christian Europe was completely ignorant of the Arabs. They had been acquainted with the Saracens, or Arabs, long before the rise of Islam, and initially, the Saracens' conversion to Islam went unnoticed. It is worth noting that the division between the West and the Orient in the form of Christianity versus Islam had not yet emerged. What did emerge was a powerful new force in the eastern Mediterranean that challenged the Byzantine and Persian empires. A vibrant civilisation quickly emerged from the convergence of Greek, Persian, and Arab cultures, one that Europe would later borrow from more than it would like to acknowledge. However, these two cultures would also clash both ideologically and militarily. Islam from its inception distanced itself from Christianity by asserting that "There is no God but God" and that "He begetteth not neither is He begotten and He hath no peer".[1] After embracing both the Torah and the New Testament, Islam embarked on a path towards unity. By proclaiming its mission and universality, it expressed its opposition to the Christian universal message. Despite Muslims considering Christians as infidels and idolaters, Muslim literature has never defamed the name of Jesus Christ, unlike the Christian slanders directed towards the Prophet of Islam.

Hence, when we reflect on history, we cannot trace the division between the Orient and Occident back to ancient times because that division did not emerge until many centuries later. After the Prophet's death in 632 C.E., the spread of Islam from the Atlantic Ocean and the Iberian peninsula (711) in the West, to China (c.616) and the borders of India (c. 1200) in the East, has been recognised as a significant global event - a truly transformative occurrence. In the century following the Prophet's passing, Islam had incorporated Kabul, Bokhara, and Samarkand in the East, as well as Carthage and Tangier in the West. In 711, after crossing the Straits of Gibraltar (named after Jabel al-Tariq, the leader of the expedition), they conquered Visigothic Spain and named it Al-Andalus, the Land of the Vandals. By 732, they had advanced as far as Tours on the Loire River in southern France. This marked the arrival of al-Tariq and the establishment of the emirate of Cordova, which would become the most enduring Muslim presence on the European continent, lasting for nearly eight centuries. Al-Andalus came to symbolise the Orient within the Occident. From that point onward, Islam maintained a permanent presence in Europe, initially in the southwest (Iberia) and later in the southeast (Balkans and Black Sea regions). The interaction between Christians and Muslims has been a defining aspect of Europe's political and cultural landscape. After their defeat at the Battle of Poitiers in 732, Muslims reached their furthest point of expansion in the West and were thereafter contained at the Pyrenees, which became the boundary of Western Christendom. In the East, the Byzantine forces temporarily held the boundary.

By the mid-eighth century, a universal message was being firmly established across the known world, extending from Spain to China. The worldview of the medieval Muslim was markedly different from that of their Chinese or Hindu counterparts. Ultimately, God appointed Muhammad to deliver the final law, which refined all prior truths and gradually asserted its dominance globally, replacing all previous legal

THE RISE AND EXPANSION OF ISLAM   33

frameworks. As Muhammad was born in Mecca, Muslims began to view themselves as the central point of the Earth. In a similar vein, the first Europeans, who were among the initial explorers of new territories, later contributed to a transformed understanding of the world. Ethnocentrism is not a recent phenomenon; medieval Europeans regarded Jerusalem as the center of the world. They held a strong belief that, just as Paradise was situated in the east where the sun rises, the centre of divine representation on Earth was in the west where the sun sets, leading to Rome, rather than Jerusalem, becoming the epicentre of both spiritual and temporal authority for western Christendom. By the mid-eighth century, a universal message was being firmly established across the known world, extending from Spain to China. The worldview of the Medieval Muslim diverged significantly from that of their Chinese or Hindu counterparts. Ultimately, God appointed Muhammad to deliver the final law, which refined all prior truths and gradually asserted its dominance globally, replacing all previous legal frameworks. As Muhammad was born in Mecca, Muslims began to view themselves as the central point of the Earth. In a similar vein, the first Europeans, who were among the initial explorers of new territories, later contributed to a transformed understanding of the world. Ethnocentrism is not a recent phenomenon; medieval Europeans regarded Jerusalem as the center of the world. They held the conviction that, just as Paradise was situated in the east where the sun rises, the center of divine representation on Earth was in the west where the sun sets, with Rome emerging as the epicenter of both spiritual and temporal authority for Western Christendom. As a result, all that originated from the Orient became integrated into the heritage of the Occident. Following the conquest of Jerusalem by Islam in 638 and the swift expansion of Islamic influence in both eastern and western directions, the focal point of Christianity shifted considerably westward and inward. The Islamic conquests ultimately transformed Europe into the principal bastion of Christianity.

The expansion of Islam posed a challenge to the dominant position of Christianity in the Mediterranean region, leading to a fracture in Christian dominance. This raised concerns about unity within the Christian territories of the Orient and resulted in Western Christendom being cut off from direct contact with other religions and civilisations. The division between Islam and Western Christendom at the Pyrenees caused the continent to turn inward, disrupting previous lines of commerce, intellectual exchange, and political interaction. However, this isolation ultimately benefited Western Christendom. Intellectually, it allowed for the absorption of Islamic knowledge from Al-Andalus and paved the way for the Renaissance. In terms of religious conflict and ideology, the dichotomy left Christendom with two main tasks: combating Islam and converting the remaining pagans in Europe. This isolationism, if one may label it as such, gave rise to feudalism and the emergence of northern kingdoms, such as 'Francia'.

Was the Arab expansion the true catalyst for a lasting division between the Occident and Orient during the era of the Crusades? This question must be answered within the timeframe of the eleventh to thirteenth centuries. Can the military conflicts between the Muslim Arabs and the Christian Europeans (specifically the Latin Holy Roman Empire, which was predominantly Germanic, as well as Spain, Sicily, and the Franks) be attributed to a clash of religious ideologies or rather a clash between two distinct cultures? The perception of Islam was not solely shaped by the Crusades, as some argue, but rather by the gradual ideological unity that developed within the Latin Christian world. This unity created a clearer image of the enemy and directed the focus of the European powers towards the Crusades. Simultaneously, the Muslim world remained the primary adversary, as Christendom successfully converted the Normans, Hungarians, and some Slavs to Christianity. Undoubtedly, the rapid rise of Islam between the seventh and eighth centuries brought about significant political, religious, and geographical transformations in the Mediterranean region. It toppled existing regimes and dynasties, thereby shaping the future of the societies and cultures it encountered. Christianity and Islam were now forced to interact as communities and individuals in the lands conquered by the Arabs, as well as on a state and empire level. However, each encounter between the two was unique in its own right.

The relationship between Christendom and Islam fostered a perception that the Muslim world was predominantly a hostile political and ideological entity, while simultaneously being recognised as a distinct and unique civilisation. Nevertheless, Christians occupied significant roles within the bureaucratic framework of the Islamic Caliphate, which enabled them to cultivate a relatively harmonious perspective of the Islamic faith. The Byzantine Empire and the Arab states were well-acquainted, engaging in both military confrontations and commercial exchanges. Despite their hostilities, a degree of mutual respect was preserved. Consequently, the dynamics between the Caliph and the Byzantine Emperor oscillated between warfare and peace, as well as between hostility and courtesy.

Prior to the ninth century, the Christian realms of inner Eurasia and the Mediterranean basin possessed limited knowledge or understanding of the Muslim world, despite the prolonged conflict that had existed between the Arabs and the Italian city-states for almost four centuries. The Franks, who had experienced centuries of invasions causing political, social, and economic turmoil in Christendom from the fourth to the tenth centuries, suddenly found themselves confronted with a vibrant and thriving civilisation. Some historians argue that Islamic societies entered a period of decline around 945 C.E. and only resurfaced in the nineteenth century. However, it should be noted that many of the most renowned cultural, scientific, and artistic figures of Islamic civilisation, including Ibn Sina (d. 1037), al-Ghazali (d. 1111), al-Buruni (d. 1048), and al-Firdawsi (d. 1020), lived after this period. This perspective warrants a re-evaluation of historical narratives. Following this period, both Arabic and Persian, as well as Turkish, began to significantly influence the development of a sophisticated Islamic culture. This era is undoubtedly distinguished in Islamic history as a time of extraordinary advancement. Marshall Hodgson posits that during this time, "Islamic civilisation had already achieved a degree of refinement and flowering totally beyond the ability of the Carolingian empire ... Islam had produced a scientific outpouring which Europe would only truly begin to grasp and to equal from the thirteenth century onward".[2]

Medieval Europe was not the only conduit linking the ancient and modern eras. During its height, Islamic civilisation arguably served as a more effective bridge from antiquity to contemporary society. A comparative analysis of medieval Christendom and medieval Islam indicates that the Islamic world provided a more advantageous pathway toward modern civilisation. The Islamic realm was extensive and properous, spanning a vast territory with diverse peoples and abundant resources. Like Western Christendom, it inherited the traditions of Hellenistic civilisation but excelled with a far greater mastery of science and philosophy. Furthermore, it enriched this heritage through interactions with other civilisations and its own creative endeavours. Islamic civilisation paved the way for a remarkable renaissance in science and literature centuries before the European movement typically associated with that term. In contrast, Christian Europe was relatively resource-scarce, limited in its reach, and primarily preoccupied with local issues. In many respects, though not universally, it lagged behind the achievements of Islamic civilisation.[3]

The Islamic civilisation was the pioneer in being truly universal, as it encompassed individuals from diverse races and cultures across three continents. It thrived in various regions, including Spain, southern Italy, the Russian steppes, and the Balkan Peninsula, thereby establishing its presence in Europe. Additionally, it was undeniably Asian and African, incorporating individuals of different ethnicities, including white, black, brown, and yellow. Geographically, it stretched from southeastern Europe to the core of Africa, surpassing the borders of India and China, and even reaching Indonesia.[4]

CHAPTER 2

ISLAMIC CONTRIBUTION TO WESTERN CIVILISATION

To fully comprehend the impact of Islam on European consciousness, it is imperative to possess a historical understanding of the contributions made by Islam to the realm of knowledge. Unfortunately, this aspect of history has been largely overlooked by Western historians and Orientalist writers. In what manner can we perceive medieval Islam as being responsible for the formation of Western civilisation? What exactly constituted Islamic learning? Where did it originate and how did it disseminate to Europe? Did Muslims merely adopt ideas from the Ancient Greeks without any original contributions of their own, as believed by most orientalists? How did Islamic learning shape the development of the European Renaissance? To what extent did Europe incorporate and integrate these borrowed ideas into its own heritage?

In this concise overview, it is impossible to enumerate the numerous ways in which Islamic culture contributed to the advancement of Western civilisation. Therefore, we must confine ourselves to briefly mentioning a few of the most significant discoveries attributed to Muslim research, as well as acknowledging the scholars, philosophers, and writers who brought prestige to the fields of science and literature, and exerted a noteworthy influence on Western thought.

Abu al-Hajjaj Yusuf ibn Ismail (1318-1354), the Sultan of the Emirate of Granada (r. 1333-1354), established the Madrasah of Granada or Madrasa Yusufiyya in 1340, with the entrance embellished by majestic stone lions.[1] The educational program encompassed a wide range of subjects such as medicine, chemistry, astronomy, philosophy, and theology.[2] Among the notable figures associated with the university was Lisanu din ibn al-Khatib (1313-1374), a poet historian who penned approximately sixty books. A profound inscription graced the facade of one of the prominent buildings, conveying:

> The world is held up by four pillars: the wisdom of the learned, the justice of the great, the prayers of the righteous, and the valour of the brave.[3]

Notably, wisdom takes precedence in this list, which is unsurprising considering that Islam extols the virtues of knowledge in various verses of the Qur'an. The Prophet Muhammad himself proclaimed that "the ink of a scholar is more precious than the blood of a martyr", and encouraged believers to "seek after learning, even if they should have to go as far as China to find it".[4] For centuries, the Muslims steadfastly adhered to this fundamental principle of their faith, harmonising divine revelation with the pursuit of knowledge, which consequently fostered progress in the realm of learning.

During the early part of the Middle Ages, no other people contributed as significantly to human progress as the Arabs did. This includes not only those living in the Arabian Peninsula but also all those whose mother tongue was Arabic. Arabic served as the language of learning, culture, and intellectual advancement for the civilised world, except for the Far East. From the ninth to the twelfth century, more works in various fields such as philosophy, medicine, history, religion, astronomy, and geography were written in Arabic than in any other language.[5]

When Islam emerged in the world during the mid-seventh century, the Greco-Roman civilisation was already declining. The Byzantium Empire, tasked with carrying on the legacy of Athens and Rome, had failed in its duty. Not only did Byzantium fail to preserve the cultural treasures entrusted to it, but this "second Rome" was also responsible for the destruction of numerous scientific and artistic works from antiquity.

The uninformed emperors of Byzantium, motivated by the zealotry of orthodox adherents, vigorously endeavoured to eliminate the vestiges of what they regarded as a pagan civilisation. Emperor Theodorius II (r. 402-450), in particular, gained a notorious reputation for his extensive destruction in North Africa. Contrary to a false legend, it was under his orders, not those of Caliph Omar, that the renowned library in Alexandria was destroyed.[6] In 489, Emperor Zeno closed the prestigious school in Edessa, which had been a hub for the dissemination of the Syriac language and Greek knowledge throughout the Orient since the second century. Emperor Justinian (r. 527-565) further tarnished his reputation by closing the equally renowned Platonic school in Athens and the schools in Alexandria.

The Nestorian monks from Edessa and Nisibia, along with philosophers from Athens and Alexandria, encountered persecution from the Orthodox Church and the Byzantine authorities. Consequently, they sought refuge in Persia. In Persia, they found freedom and protection under the tolerant rule of the Sassanids. This allowed them to continue their important work of translating the Holy Scriptures of the Church Fathers, as well as the philosophical and scientific works of Greece. It is because of the diligent efforts of these scholars in exile that the Arabs, upon conquering Syria and Persia, discovered a significant portion of Greece's intellectual heritage.

The Arabs, known for their innate curiosity, were profoundly captivated by the wealth of new ideas and knowledge presented by this ancient scholarship. As the victors, they eagerly began to study the arts and sciences of their newly-conquered subjects. At first, they commissioned Arabic translations of the Eastern adaptations of Greek authors, and subsequently, they undertook the translation of the original texts that had not been previously converted into Syriac or Chaldean.

The Syrian Umayyads' reign (r. 661-750), however, served as a period of growth and maturation for the Muslim civilisation. Undoubtedly, the most remarkable era of Muslim civilisation was that of the Abbasid Caliphs of Baghdad (750 - 1258) and the Spanish Umayyads (755-1492). Gustave Le Bon asserts:

> While the rest of Europe was engulfed in darkness and barbarism, Baghdad and Cordova, the two prominent cities under Islamic rule, shone as beacons of civilisation, illuminating the entire world with their brilliance.[7]

For five hundred years, Islam exerted its dominance over the world through its power, knowledge, and advanced civilisation. Inheriting the scientific and philosophical wealth of the Greeks, Islam not only preserved it but also enhanced it before transmitting it to Western Europe. Consequently, it broadened the intellectual horizons of the Middle Ages and left a profound impact on European life and thinking.[8]

The establishment of the Bayt al Hikmat (House of Learning) in Baghdad by Caliph Al Mamun (r. 813-833) in 830 was a significant event during the Middle Ages. The role played by this institution, which can be described as a combination of an academy, library, and translation centre, cannot be overstated. It played a crucial role in transmitting the knowledge of ancient civilisation to the Western world. This esteemed establishment, consisting of scholars from Christian, Jewish, and Muslim Arab backgrounds, primarily focused on the study of Greek science and philosophy, as well as the works of Galen, Hippocrates, Plato, Aristotle, and various commentators such as Alexander of Aphrodis, Themistenes, and others. This intellectual exchange can be seen as an invasion of sorts, leading to a state of intellectual intoxication among the learned individuals involved.[9]

The Bayt al Hikmat was the foundation-stone of the Baghdad School, which was to exert its influence right up to the second half of the fifteenth century. To this illustrious school falls the signal merit of having ensured the continuity of civilisation by repairing the chain of human knowledge so brutally broken in the sixth century by the decline and fall of Rome. If Muslim civilisation had restricted itself merely to saving ancient learning, guarding it carefully and then passing it on intact to future generations, the service rendered humanity would in itself have been inestimable. But such was not the case. The scholars and philosophers of the Baghdad School, heirs of the spirit and tradition of the School of Alexandria, enlarged and enriched the learning of antiquity by new and original additions in all branches of science, by countless discoveries in the applied arts, and also, and above all, by new methods of research and investigation. The Arabs of the ninth century were already in possession of the rich scientific method of observation, deducing causes and effects, to accept as fact only what has been proved by experiment, which long afterwards in the hands of European scientists was to be instrumental in making their greatest discoveries.[10] By concentrating their thought on individual events Muslim scholars were able to develop scientific method much further than their Greek or Alexandrian predecessors. They were responsible for the introduction or the restoration of scientific method to medieval Europe.[11]

The Baghdad School played a crucial role in the resurgence of medieval Europe while simultaneously spreading enlightenment across multiple regions in Asia. Notably, it impacted India during the Ghaznavid period circa 1016, influenced the Seljuk Turks through the works of Omar Khayyam around 1076, and reached the Mongols via Nasr ed Dine Tusi in 1260. Additionally, it affected the Ottomans around 1337. Furthermore, Islamic philosophy and intellectual traditions permeated into China during Kublai Khan's rule in 1280.

Trade Routes in the Middle Ages

The interaction between these two civilisations, Christian and Muslim, was established through established and well-established routes. Commerce and pilgrimage played a crucial role in facilitating this contact. Even before the eleventh century, there was already thriving land and sea trade between the East and the West. Islamic civilisation entered Europe through regions such as Spain, Sicily, and the South of France, which were under direct Saracen rule.[12]

During the ninth century, Muslim civilisation had already established its dominance in Spain. At that time, the Spaniards recognised Arabic as the sole language for scientific and literary pursuits. Its significance was so profound that the Ecclesiastical Authorities were compelled to translate the collection of canons used in Spanish churches into the Romanic language, which eventually evolved into modern Spanish. Both Arabic and Romanic languages were widely used throughout Muslim Spain. Christian Spain acknowledged the superiority of the Muslims, as demonstrated by King Alphonse the Great of the Asturias, who in 830 invited two Saracen scholars to serve as tutors for his son and heir. Subsequently, Alphonse VI (d. 1109), the conqueror of Toledo, who had married the daughter of the Muslim king of Seville, and Alphonse the Wise, played significant roles in fostering intellectual collaboration between Christians and Muslims. The establishment of the renowned translator's school in Toledo in 1130, under the reign of Alphonse VII, further solidified this intellectual rapprochement. This school, often referred to as the Spanish equivalent of Baghdad's House of Learning, owed its success to the diligent efforts of translators in Toledo, as well as their counterparts in Burgos, Sicily, and Naples. These translators provided European scholars with Latin translations of the works of Arab astronomers, mathematicians, philosophers, doctors, chemists, and botanists. It was not until the late thirteenth century that translations began to be made directly from the original Greek texts.

The scientific achievements of the Muslims had gained widespread recognition and attracted the intellectual elite of the Western world to regions such as Andalusia, Sicily, and the South of Italy. For instance, Gerbert d'Aurillac, who later became the first French Pope under the title Sylvester II (r. 999-1003), spent three years in Toledo studying mathematics, astronomy, chemistry, and other subjects under the guidance of Muslim scholars. Numerous prelates and scholars from France, England, Germany, and Italy pursued their studies at the universities of Muslim Spain. Among them were Gerard of Cremona (1114-1187), who translated Aristotle's physics from Arabic texts, Campanus of Navarra (1220-1296), Abelard of Bath (1080-1152), Albert and Daniel of Morley (d. 1210), Michel Scot, Hermann the Dalmatian (1100-1160), and numerous others. These individuals owe their fundamental education to the Saracens.

Regarding France, the influence of Muslim civilisation on the southern part of the country was undoubtedly shaped by its proximity to Spain. However, the direct Saracen occupation of Septimania, a vast region encompassing the Mediterranean, the Cevennes, the Pyrennes, and the Rhone, played an even more significant role. This occupation, which lasted for over fifty years, introduced various industries and universal machines of Arab origin to the south of France.[13] Even after the expulsion of the Arabs, their influence persisted through trade and friendship with France.[14]

It is important to acknowledge the intermediary role played by Spanish and Aquitanian Jewry in bridging the gap between Islamic civilisation and Christian culture. The profound theological influence of the Arabs on scholastic theology in the Middle Ages primarily came through Hebrew translations. Furthermore, it is essential to recognise the debt of gratitude that Judaism owes to Muslim civilisation. The literary culture of Jews in the Middle Ages was merely a reflection of Muslim culture, which resonated more with their native genius than Christian civilisation.[15] In fact, the first Hebrew grammar was compiled by Yehuda ben Qoraish in the ninth century based on Arabic grammars.[16] The Middle Ages witnessed the emergence of a rich literature in theology and philosophy written in Arabic by Jewish scholars such as Maimonides (d. 1204), Sa'adia Fayyumi (d. 942), Yehuda Halevy (d. 1141), Bahya ibn Paquda (d. 1120), Ibn Gabirol (d. 1070), and many others.

Astronomy

Muslim scholars were initially drawn to the fields of astronomy and mathematics, which piqued their curiosity. The Arabs, known for their practical mindset, were particularly interested in the exact sciences. Astronomy, in particular, captivated not only scientists but also various Caliphs, Seljuk Sultans, and Khans who descended from Genghis Khan (d. 1227) and Timur (d. 1405). As a result, observatories were established in key centres throughout the Islamic Empire, including Baghdad, Cairo, Cordova, Toledo, and Samarkand, which gained well-deserved recognition.

The Baghdad School of Astronomy originated during the reign of Al Mansur, the second Abbassid Caliph (754-755), who himself was an astronomer. Under the leadership of his successors, Harun al Rasheed (r. 786-809) and Al Mamun (r. 813-33), the School of Baghdad produced significant works. They revised ancient theories, rectified errors in Ptolemy's work, and corrected Greek tables. The Baghdad School is credited with discovering the movement of the sun's apogee, evaluating the obliquity of the elliptical and its gradual decrease, and conducting detailed studies on the duration of the year. Scholars from Baghdad also observed the irregularity of the moon's highest latitude and identified a third lunar inequality known as variation. They made predictions about sunspots, studied eclipses and the appearance of comets and other celestial phenomena, questioned the immobility of the earth, and laid the groundwork for future astronomers like Copernicus (D. 1543) and Kepler (d. 1630).

The School of Baghdad meticulously documented their observations in the Verified Table, with Yahya ben Abu Mansur (d. 830) being recognised as the primary author of this significant work. Among the esteemed scholars affiliated with this institution, Al Batani (d. 929) stands out as one of the twenty most influential astronomers worldwide, according to Lanade. Additionally, Abul Wefa's (d. 998) name is associated with a fundamental aspect of astronomy, specifically the third lunar inequality. Remarkably, this Muslim astronomer made this discovery a whole ten centuries before the Danish scholar Tycho Brahe (d. 1601), who has been mistakenly credited with this finding.

Ali Ibn Younis (d. 1009), a renowned figure, is credited with inventing the pendulum and the sun-dial. The Fatimid Caliph Al Hakem (r. 990-1021) recognised his brilliance and commissioned the construction of an observatory on Mount Mocattam, establishing the esteemed School of Cairo. Ali Ibn Younis also curated the remarkable Hakemite Table, which surpassed the accuracy of all its predecessors. This table gained widespread recognition, replacing Ptolemy's Almagest and the Baghdad treatises not only in the Orient but also as far as China.

Simultaneously, Hassan Ibn Al Haitan (d. 1040), another esteemed astronomer and mathematician from the School of Cairo, authored a celebrated treatise on optics. This work served as a foundation for the subsequent works of Roger Bacon (d. 1292) and Kepler. It is worth mentioning that Ibn Haitan was the first to propose the construction of a dam at Aswan to regulate the water level of the Nile, a concept of great significance.

Astronomical studies held great importance in Muslim Spain, with the Emir of Cordova, Abd ar Rahman II (r. 822-52), displaying a particular interest in this field. Unfortunately, very few astronomical works from Muslim Spain have survived. Most of their works were destroyed during the reconquest and the period of religious persecution. However, we do know that the observatories in Toledo and Cordova were highly renowned during their time. History has preserved the names of several Andalusian scholars and those born elsewhere, who worked in Al Andalus, such as Maslamah Al Mahrebi, Ibn Khaldun (d. 1406), Ibn Rushd (Averroes, d. 1198), and others. The high quality of the lost works of these Muslim scholars can be inferred from the numerous contemporary Christian authors who borrowed from them. It is evident that the astronomic tables of Alphonse X (r. 1252-84), known as the Alphonsine Tables, were greatly influenced by Arab works, if not entirely based on them.

The wars and internal conflicts that ravaged Asia from the eleventh century onwards had a significant impact on the intellectual life of Muslim society. While they certainly hindered the progress of civilisation, they did not completely halt it. The School of Baghdad managed to survive the political decline of the Oriental Caliphate and the fragmentation of the Arab-Islamic Empire, now under the rule of the Seljuk Turks. The Baghdad school continued its activities until the mid-fifteenth century, and its influence spread to Central Asia, India, and China. One of the most distinguished scholars of Islam, Abdur Rahman Mohammad Ben Ahmad Al Biruni (d. 1048), served as a bridge between the traditions of the School of Baghdad and those of Indian scholars. He lived at the court of Mahmud of Ghazna (r. 997-1030) and authored numerous works on various subjects, including lists of the latitude and longitude of the world's major cities.

During his reign, the Seljuk Sultan Melik Shah (r. 1072-1092) had a deep interest in astronomy and surrounded himself with scholars and literary figures. His support led to significant advancements in the field, including a calendar reform that was ten centuries ahead of the Gregorian reform and more accurate. The credit for this reform goes to Abdur Rahman Haseni and Omar Khayyam (d. 1131), the renowned poet whose verses have immortalised his name.

Similarly, the Mongol rulers also played a crucial role in promoting science. Despite his notorious reputation for the destruction of Baghdad, Hulagu Khan (d. 1265), the grandson of Genghis Khan, established a model observatory at Meragah. Nasr Ed Dine Thusi (1201-1274), the author of the Ilkhanian Tables and the director of this observatory, perfected numerous observation instruments. As a result, the works of astronomers from Baghdad and Cairo reached China during the reign of Kublai Khan (d. 1294).

However, it was during the reign of Ulugh Beg (d. 1449), the grandson of Timur, that Muslim astronomy reached its pinnacle. Ulugh Beg, closely associated with the Timurid Renaissance, was a passionate devotee of astronomy. He is considered the last representative of the School of Baghdad and his comprehensive work, published in 1437, provided a comprehensive overview of contemporary astronomical knowledge. Remarkably, he bridged the astronomy of the Ancients with that of the modern era, a century before Kepler.

Mathematics

The science that the Arabs favoured the most, alongside astronomy, was mathematics. Muslim scholars made significant discoveries in arithmetic, geometry, and algebra, establishing many fundamental principles. The numerals and counting method invented by the Arabs are still widely used in arithmetic today. The Arabs are also credited with the invention of algebra, a claim that is highly likely to be true. Caliph Al Mamun appointed Muhammad Ben Musa Khwarizmi (c. 780-850) as the head of the House of Learning, where he wrote a treatise on algebra titled *Al Gebr Wa'l Maakalala* (Calculation by Symbols). The word "algebra" is derived from the first part of the title of this work, and the word "algorism" comes from a variant of the author's name, "Alkarizmi". Gerard of Cremona's translation of this work played a crucial role in introducing Western colleagues to the beauty of algebraic calculus and decimal arithmetic.[17] Al Khwarizmi is regarded as one of the most influential figures in mathematical thought during the Middle Ages.[18] Thabit Ben Garrah (d. 910), the translator of Ptolemy's Almagest, further developed algebra and recognised its application to geometry, carrying on the work initiated by Al Khwarizmi.

Trigonometry, a branch of mathematics, was diligently cultivated by the Arabs due to its application in astronomy. The origins of this scientific field can be traced back to Al Batani, who had the brilliant idea of replacing the subtenses of arcs used by the Greeks in their trigonometric calculations with the half subtense of the double arc, known as the sine of the arc. Al Batani was the first to introduce the terms 'sine' and 'cosine' in his works, referring to them as extended shadow in gnomic calculus. In modern trigonometry, we now refer to this concept as the tangent.[19] The introduction of tangents in trigonometry proved to be of great significance, although it took another five hundred years for modern mathematicians to make this discovery. The mathematician Regiomontanus (d. 1476) is credited with this discovery, but even Copernicus was unaware of it almost a century later.[20]

The invention of the numeral 'zero' by Mohammad Ben Ahmad in 976 revolutionised mathematics, although it wasn't adopted in the Western world until the early twelfth century. Lastly, Nasr Ed Dine Thusi was the first to question the inviolability of Euclidean geometry. He can be considered as the distant precursor to Lobatchevsky (d. 1856) and Riemann (d. 1866) in the field of non-Euclidean geometry.

Physiscs

Regrettably, the principal Arab treatises on physics have been lost, leaving us with only their titles as a glimpse into their content. However, the limited number of surviving works serves as a testament to the significance of their studies. One particularly noteworthy treatise is the work on optics by Hasan Ibn al-Haytham, also known as Alhasen in the Western world, who lived from 965 to 1039. This treatise marked a pivotal moment in the field of science and is considered to be the beginning of modern science of optics.[21] It delves into various topics such as the apparent position of images in mirrors, refraction, the apparent size of objects, and the utilisation of the dark room, which later proved crucial in the development of photography and other disciplines. Furthermore, Ibn al-Haytham's research on magnifying lenses served as inspiration for Western scientists like Roger Bacon and Kepler, who conducted experiments with microscopes and telescopes. Notably, he also criticised the theories of Euclid and Ptolemy and became the first to provide an accurate description of the eye itself, as well as lenses and binocular vision.

Arab scholars of that era also possessed advanced knowledge in mechanics. This can be inferred from the various ingenious instruments they used in their research, many of which eventually made their way to the Western world. Edward Bernard (1638-1697) of Oxford has even suggested that it was the Arabs who first discovered the use of the pendulum in clocks. Regardless, it is undeniable that they had weight-driven clocks that differed significantly from the clepsydra. Benjamin of Tudela (d. 1173), a traveller who visited Jewish communities in the Levant during the twelfth century, provided a description of the renowned clock in the Mosque at Damascus.

It is undeniable that the Chinese were the inventors of the compass; however, it was the Muslims who refined and effectively utilised it by incorporating the magnetic needle into navigation techniques.

Chemistry

It can hardly be overstated that chemistry as a scientific discipline did not exist prior to the contributions of the Arabs. While the Greeks had some understanding of certain elements, they were completely unaware of crucial substances like alcohol, sulphuric acid, acqua regia, and nitric acid. These discoveries, along with potassium, sal ammoniac, silver nitrate, corrosive sublimate, and the preparation of mercury, were made by the Arabs. Additionally, many terms used in chemistry, such as alcohol, alembic, alkali, elixir, and more, have their origins in Arabic. Furthermore, the Arabs were the first to employ techniques such as distillation, sublimation, crystallisation, coagulation, and cupellation for the extraction and combination of substances, making their contribution to the field of chemistry truly significant.

Undoubtedly, the most prominent Arab chemist was Abu Musa Djafar Al Kufi, also known as Djeber, who lived in the latter half of the eighth century. His works served as a comprehensive scientific encyclopaedia and provided a summary of contemporary chemistry. Several of his works were translated into Latin, with the most notable being the Sum of Perfection, which was translated into French in 1672. Another influential figure was Abu Bakr Zakaria Al Razi (d. 925), known as Razes in the West, who described the process of producing sulphuric acid and alcohol in his book, *Al Hawi*. Alcohol was obtained through the distillation of fermented starches or sugars.

The Arabs not only conducted theoretical research but also applied their knowledge practically. The application of chemistry to pharmacy is one of the significant contributions made by Muslim scholars to the Western world. Many everyday products, such as camphor, distilled water, plasters, syrups, and various ointments, can be traced back to Arab origins. The advancements they made in industrial chemistry are evident in the exceptional skills of their artisans in dyeing, leather curing, and steel tempering.

Gunpowder and the manufacture of paper from cotton, linen, or rags were among the inventions that greatly benefited the industry. The names of Roger Bacon, Albertus Magnus (d. 1280), and Berthold Schwarz (d. 1384) were long associated with the invention of gunpowder, although it is also often credited to the Chinese. However, research conducted by Reinaud and Fave has clearly demonstrated that while the Chinese discovered saltpetre and its use in fireworks, it was solely the Arabs who invented gunpowder as an explosive substance capable of propelling projectiles. They notably utilised it in 1342 to defend Algeciras against the attack of Alphonse XI.[22]

The invention of paper holds immense significance and ushered in a new era for civilisation. It enabled the widespread availability of affordable books and the democratisation of knowledge, which became possible only after the Arabs replaced the parchment used in the ancient world and the silk paper used by the Chinese with the ordinary paper we are familiar with today.

Natural Sciences

In the field of natural sciences, the Arabs embarked on a journey of studying nature itself and conducting their own observations, following their initial commentaries on Greek authors. As a result, they significantly expanded Dioscorides's (d. 90CE) *Herbal* by introducing two thousand new species. The Arab pharmacopoeia included numerous plants and medical substances that were completely unfamiliar to the Greeks. They were responsible for the introduction of rhubarb, tamarind pulp, cassia, manna, senna leaves, and camphor. Moreover, their preference for sugar over honey led to the development of a wide range of delightful and health-promoting preparations. By utilising sugar, they crafted syrups, juleps, and preserved herbs and fruits.

The Arabs played a pivotal role in introducing the Western world to perfumes and spices. They brought forth incense and other fragrant resins from Arabia, attar of roses, nutmegs, cloves, and pepper. From the Muslim regions of the East, they introduced vegetables like tomatoes, asparagus, artichokes, as well as an array of delectable sweets and an abundance of exquisite flowers such as lilac, jasmine, tulips, camellias, Japanese roses, and many more. Coffee, which originated in Yemen, made its way to Europe through the Ottoman Empire during the sixteenth century. Prior to that, coffee was condemned by the Pope as the devil's drink.

In terms of domestic animals, Arabia was renowned for producing the finest horses, Asia Minor for breeding superior goats, and Morocco for its renowned sheep. Additionally, the Arabs had achieved remarkable advancements in agriculture and displayed a strong interest in geology.

Medicine

After mathematics and chemistry, medicine was the field of study that most captivated the Muslims. In the early centuries of the Hegira, it was an essential component of a comprehensive education. As a result, there was a significant number of doctors and medical treatises. Muslim physicians played a crucial role in advancing medical science in the Western world. For many centuries, the writings of Rhazes, Ibn Sina (Avicenna, d. 1037), Abul Cassis (d. 1013), and Ibn Zohr (d. 1162) formed the foundation of medical education in European universities. The Schools of Medicine at Salerno and particularly Montpellier gained worldwide renown. The medical knowledge compiled by Rhazes (d. 925), known as Abu Bakr Ibn Zakaria Al Razi, in his book *Havi* (The Chaste Life), as well as his other work "Mansuri," dedicated to the Caliph Al Mansur, remained highly esteemed and widely used for several hundred years as a medical manual. In fact, *Havi* was one of the nine volumes that comprised the entire library of the Paris Faculty of Medicine in 1395. It contained the initial descriptions of certain eruptive fevers such as smallpox and measles. Al Razi introduced the use of mild purgatives in pharmacy, employed cupping for cases of apoplexy, and advocated the use of cold water for persistent fevers. He is also credited with inventing the sexton, which he frequently utilised. Al Razi's works were translated into Latin and printed multiple times, notably in 1509 in Venice and in 1528 and 1578 in Paris. His treatise on smallpox was last republished in 1745.

Abu Ali Al Hussein Ibn Abdallah, known in the East as Ibn Sina (d. 1037) and in the West as Avicenna, undoubtedly stood as the greatest Muslim physician. His work *Canun Fi'l Tib* or *Precepts of Medicine* was published in Arabic in Rome in 1593. It consisted of five volumes that covered physiology, hygiene, pathology, therapeutics, and materia medica. For six hundred years, from the twelfth to the seventeenth century, this remarkable work served as the cornerstone of medical education in French and Italian universities.

Muslim doctors made significant advancements in the field of surgery, with their knowledge dating back to the eleventh century. They were skilled in treating various conditions such as cataracts, utilising techniques like prolapse or extraction of the crystalline lens. They were also proficient in lithotrity, managing haemorrhages, employing caustics, setons, and cauterisation. Additionally, they possessed knowledge of anaesthetics, which was considered a modern discovery at the time. Prior to a painful operation, they would administer a drug derived from the plant darnel to induce complete unconsciousness in the patient. Arab science played a crucial role in the development of ophthalmology, as evidenced by Ali Ibn Issa's *Memorandum for Oculists*, which remained relevant until the nineteenth century. Ibn Al-Mahasin performed the first cataract suction operation in 1256 and is credited with inventing the hollow needle.

One of the most prominent Muslim surgeons was Abul Qasim Khalaf Ben Abbas (Abulcassis) of Cordova (d. 1013). Renowned physiologist Haller asserts that "his works were the primary source of inspiration for all surgeons from that time until the fourteenth century".[23] Abulcassis's surgical works were eventually printed in Latin in 1497.

Muslim Spain was a hub of medical advancements, producing renowned doctors such as Ibn Zohr and Averroes. Ibn Zohr's notable contribution was the incorporation of scientific observation into medicine. He emphasised the body's natural ability to heal itself in certain illnesses, making him the first to integrate medicine, surgery, and pharmacy. His writings on surgery introduced the concept of bronchotomy and provided detailed instructions for treating dislocations and fractures. Averroes, known more for his commentary on Aristotle, also made significant contributions as a doctor. He wrote commentaries on Avicenna's *Canun* and Galen's works. Averroes' treatise on theriac and his book on poisons and fevers were highly valued in the West. His principal medical work, *The Kulliyet*, was first printed in Venice in 1490 and later reprinted in various countries. Additionally, Ibn Al Nafis (d. 1289), a Syrian physician, accurately demonstrated the circulatory system of blood three hundred years before the Portuguese Michael Servetus (1511-53), who is commonly credited with this discovery.

Muslim doctors in general emphasised the importance of hygiene in their medical practices. This emphasis on hygiene, including frequent bathing or ablutions before prayer, and the avoidance of alcohol and pork, has been observed in Islam for centuries. Arab hospitals were built with superior hygiene conditions compared to contemporary establishments. These hospitals were spacious, allowing for free circulation of air and water. The Aphorisms of the School of Salerno, a renowned European medical institution, contained valuable instructions on hygiene, which were influenced by Arab medical knowledge.[24]

Philosophy

If one were to attempt to chronicle the progress of Muslim thought in the realm of philosophy, it would be an overwhelming task due to the sheer magnitude of information. However, we can provide a general overview of the contributions made by Muslim thinkers and their impact on the development of philosophical ideas in the West. The origins of philosophical speculation in the Islamic world can be traced back to an early period. At one point, certain biased writers joined forces to outright deny the existence of Muslim philosophy. They claimed that any doctrines contradicting the teachings of the Qur'an or raising doubts about religious dogmas would not have been able to flourish in the intolerant atmosphere of Islam. However, these assertions have long been discredited in the face of abundant and compelling evidence to the contrary.

It is also unjust and inaccurate to relegate Muslim thought to a subordinate role as a mere follower of Greek philosophy. Arabian philosophical speculation emerged as early as the first century of the Muslim era, primarily in relation to the theodicy of Islam. The nature of God, His unity, power, justice, clemency, and other divine attributes became the subjects of intricate and profound dissertations. These discussions gave rise to various schools of thought, often engaging in passionate debates. Topics such as predestination, moral freedom, salvation through deeds or faith, the succession to the Prophet as the spiritual and temporal leader of the Muslim community, and numerous other matters became focal points of intellectual exploration.

Muslim thought became more complex and subtle with the dissemination and assimilation of the works of Antiquity. In the third century of the Muslim era, the Muslim school of scholasticism was founded under Al Kindi (d. 873). This school was closely connected to the Hellenistic tradition and had a dominant influence of Neoplatonic tendencies. Many writers from this school took on the task of reconciling Plato and Aristotle, aligning their teachings with revealed religion. Among the most renowned philosophers of this school were Al Farabi (d. 950), who hailed from Turkestan and wrote the treatise *The Perfect City* which foreshadowed Thomas Moore's (d. 1852) *Utopia*, Ibn Badja (Avempace, d. 1138), Ibn Tofayl (d. 1185), and Ibn Rushd (Averroes). It is widely acknowledged today that Christian scholasticism drew heavily from their writings.

In both philosophy and science, Muslim thought played a crucial role as a bridge between the ideas of Antiquity and modern speculation. It is an established fact that Islam successfully reconciled monotheism, the primary contribution of the ancient Semitic world, with Greek philosophy, which was the main contribution of the ancient Indo-European world.[25] It is crucial to acknowledge that within the realm of philosophical contemplation, scholasticism represents only a fraction of Muslim thought. This section is deemed less significant and certainly less innovative compared to the intellectual movement instigated by theological sects. Muslim thinkers, both in philosophy and science, exhibited a comprehensive intellectual curiosity. They explored various issues concerning primary causes, engaging in diverse forms of philosophical contemplation that ranged from empirical approaches to elevated mysticism, passing through stages of scepticism and rationalism. These ideas found expression in numerous philosophical sects and schools. We delve deeper into Muslim scholasticism because its prominent proponents had a particularly significant influence on religious and secular philosophy in medieval Europe. Avicenna and Averroes gained immense renown in the Christian West, surpassing their fame in the Islamic East, where they were primarily recognised as doctors.

Avicenna holds great significance in the intellectual history of the Middle Ages, being regarded by some as the pinnacle of this era. What sets him apart is the comprehensive nature of his work, which encompasses various fields of knowledge. While his contributions to medicine have been previously mentioned, his impact on science and philosophy should not be overlooked. Avicenna's greatest achievement lies in establishing a scientific system that endured for centuries. As a prominent figure in scholasticism, he not only fully developed this philosophy but also provided it with a broad and visionary perspective. Despite being influenced by Aristotle and Plato, Avicenna's originality of thought remains intact. He engages with Aristotle on an equal intellectual footing, often offering corrections or taking his arguments to their logical conclusions. Avicenna's notable works include *The Art of Healing* (Kitab Al Shifa), *Guide to Wisdom* (Al Hidayat Fi'l Hikmat), *The Story of Hayy Ibn Yagzan,* and *Manual of Instruction and Warning* (Kitab Al Icharat Wa'l Tanbihat). The initial translations of Avicenna's works can be traced back to the early twelfth century.

Avicenna's influence on Western philosophical thought cannot be overstated. Every thesis on medieval philosophers examines their relationship with Avicennian philosophy. The more in-depth these examinations go, the clearer it becomes that Avicenna was not merely a source of inspiration for these philosophers, but one of the primary forces shaping their thinking.[26] Albertus Magnus regarded him as a role model, despite his opposition to Arab philosophy. In his work on *Averroes and Averroism*, Renan boldly asserted that the esteemed mentor of St. Thomas Aquinas "owed everything to Averroes".[27] St. Thomas Aquinas himself, greatly influenced by Averroes, was also familiar with Avicennian thinking. Prior to ascending to the papal throne, Pope John XXI (r. 1276-77) taught a theory of knowledge in which Avicenna replaced Aristotle. Similarly, William of Auvergne (d. 1249), Alexander of Hales (d. 1245), and many others also drew inspiration from these respected Muslim scholars.

Averroes, whose name is a distortion of Abul Walid Mohammad Ibn Rushd, achieved even greater success in the West than Avicenna. His commentaries on Aristotle earned him unparalleled fame among Muslim authors and the title The Great Commentator. It is believed that Michel Scott deserves credit for introducing Averroes to the Latin world. By the mid-thirteenth century, all significant works of this

Andalusian philosopher had been translated into Latin. Averroes, despite himself, played a dual role in the history of medieval scholasticism. While some worshipped him as the eminent commentator on Aristotle, an authority universally admired, others attacked him as the embodiment of perversity and ungodliness. Despite the infrequent references made by Albertus Magnus, the influence of the Muslim philosopher on the case of St. Thomas Aquinas (d. 1274) is undeniable. St. Thomas emerges as both the strongest opponent of Averroist doctrine and, paradoxically, the first disciple of The Great Commentator. While Albertus owes his entire intellectual foundation to Avicenna, St. Thomas owes a significant portion of his philosophical development to Averroes.[28] The striking resemblance in their ideas is evident through the employment of remarkably similar expressions, leaving no doubt about the profound impact the Muslim philosopher had on the preeminent Catholic theologian.

During the fourteenth and fifteenth centuries, Averroes' influence in Europe reached its peak. In universities of Europe, his commentaries were preferred over Aristotle's treatises as required readings. John of Baconthorp (d. 1347), an English Carmelite Provincial and doctor of the Order, established Averroism as the traditional teaching in his school. Paul of Venice, an esteemed member of the Augustinian Order, openly expressed his support for the most radical Averroist theories. In 1473, when Lois XI organised the teaching of philosophy, the study of Aristotle's doctrine and his commentator Averroes became a mandatory subject. Vicomercato, appointed by Francois I, taught this subject at the College de France from 1543 to 1567.

However, during that time, the University of Padua emerged as the primary stronghold of Arab peripateticism. Averroes, without a doubt, was its most prominent advocate. This tradition persisted well into the seventeenth century, with Bologna, Ferrara, and Venice following Rome's intellectual lead. While these cities received enthusiastic support, there was also a vehement backlash against Arabian Aristotelianism and its main proponent. This opposition primarily originated from orthodox theology and eventually extended to the Humanists of the Renaissance.

In 1240, William of Auvergne, the Bishop of Paris, issued a condemnation of various writings influenced by Arabism. In 1269, Bishop Etienne Tempier of Paris reaffirmed this verdict. However, these measures were not enough to eradicate the movement entirely. Arab philosophy continued to flourish, with Siger de Brabant (d. 1280), considered the founder of Latin Averroism or Christian Averroism, teaching at the University of Paris between 1266 and 1277. In 1277, the Pope initiated a new investigation, resulting in the banning of 219 subversive writings. Despite these efforts, Averroism continued to gain traction.

The European Humanists were equally vehement in their opposition to Avicenna. They viewed the Commentator as the embodiment of Arab philosophy and the Arab spirit. With direct access to ancient sources, the Arabs became the target of vicious attacks. Disregarding the significant contributions they made to European civilisation by preserving Greek knowledge, they were accused of intellectual depravity and corrupting ancient civilisation.

The impact of Averroes' ideas was so extensive that understanding the true essence of the philosopher requires a significant effort, given the contradictory criticism surrounding his work. It is important to differentiate between the philosophy of Averroes and Averroism itself. Nevertheless, it is evident from the aforementioned that Averroes' influence endured in Western philosophy for many centuries. Despite distortions and misrepresentations by both fervent supporters and staunch opponents, his doctrine brought about a revolution in the thinking of Europe's intellectual elite and played a role in liberating Western thought from certain restrictive barriers.

Literature

Undoubtedly, one of the most notable accomplishments of the Muslim intellect was its significant contribution to philosophical thought. However, in comparison, its impact on literature was not as remarkable. Nevertheless, in a specific domain, it played a decisive role. To dispel any doubts regarding this matter, one must consider the emergence of modern lyric poetry in Europe.

Emerging almost simultaneously in Spain and France during the early twelfth century, it subsequently spread to Italy and the rest of Europe. The Spanish romances and the Provencal *trobas* served as its expressive forms. The literary renaissance in the *langue d'Oc* countries transcends the boundaries of literary history, signifying a pivotal moment in Western civilisation.

The creative and inspirational value of Provencal poetry, both in the realm of emotions and in the realm of art, cannot be overstated. It is indeed the progenitor of modern poetry, perhaps even more so than Latin poetry. Without it, Italian poetry, Spanish poetry, the German Minnesingers, and certainly the courtly poetry of Northern France would be inexplicable.[29] However, what exactly constitutes the "song" of the troubadours? The essential characteristic of this poetry, setting it apart from all other forms of love poetry known prior to that time, is the idealisation of woman, her veneration as a divine entity, and the exaltation of love in its purest and most spiritual form. This serves as the recurring theme in the poetry of William IX, Duke of Aquitaine (d. 1127), Marcabru (d. 1150), Jauffre Rudel (d. 1147?), and other troubadours who followed in their footsteps, as well as in the works of Dante and Petrarch.

The research conducted by Julien, Ramon Menendez Pidal, and R. Nycle leaves no room for doubt that the troubadours' poetry, which reflects significant changes in Western thought and emotion, directly originates from popular Arabo-Andalusian poetry. The recent studies by the new Spanish school of history have revealed such striking similarities and clear analogies between Andalusian lyric poetry, which first emerged in the ninth century, and that of Provence, that it is impossible to explain them without acknowledging the decisive influence of one on the other.[30] The themes of Platonic love, complete devotion to one's lady, service offered in the name of love, and the melancholic pleasure derived from love-induced suffering, have all been prevalent in Arab poetry since the eighth century. In Andalusia, this form of poetry appeared in the ninth century in the popular 'zajal'. It represents one of the most captivating outcomes of the encounter between the Arab and Romance civilisations.

The tragic error of the Crusades dealt a fatal blow to the emerging synthesis between the two Mediterranean civilisations - a synthesis that, if allowed to develop naturally, would have brought immeasurable artistic and cultural riches to humanity. However, even during the Crusades, economic, scientific, and artistic exchanges did not come to a complete halt. The interactions between Muslim states, Spanish principalities, and Provencal courts continued. Poetry and music undoubtedly held a significant position in these exchanges. The Moorish principalities served as a breeding ground for poets, musicians, and dancers who would captivate the courts of Southern Europe. Through their songs and dances, which provided a bridge between people that was both accessible and enjoyable, the path was paved for lyric poetry, which at that time was inseparable from music.

Asin Palacios's remarkable research on the Muslim origins of *The Divine Comedy* has revealed the profound influence of two great figures, Muhy Ad Dine Ibn Arabi (d. 1240) and Abul Ala Al Maari (d. 1057), on Dante (d. 1321). The poetry of Al Maari, with its unparalleled splendour, embodies a philosophy that is deeply pessimistic and sceptical. Furthermore, the philosophical novel *Hay Ibn Yakzan* by Ibn Tofayl (d. 1185), which was translated into Latin by Edward Pococke the Younger in 1671 and then into numerous European languages, served as a source of inspiration for Daniel Defoe (d. 1731) and became a model for his famous work Robinson Crusoe.

Ibn Hazm (d. 1064), a brilliant intellect from Muslim Spain, left a lasting impact on Western literature. With his prolific writing, he composed a multitude of fables, tales, and apologues that spread throughout Europe from the thirteenth century onwards. These fables were translated into Spanish by Alphonse the Wise, King of Castile (r. 1252-84), and later into Latin, Hebrew, Persian, and French. Lafontaine acknowledged Ibn Hazm's fables as one of his sources, while Boccaccio, Chaucer, and various German storytellers were influenced to varying degrees. Additionally, *The Thousand and One Nights* captivated a large number of European readers.

Geography and History

The Arab character is distinguished by their strong passion for travel, which has played a significant role in shaping the course of civilisation. Prior to the Spanish and Portuguese advancements in navigation during the 15th and 16th centuries, no other people had contributed as much as the Arabs in expanding mankind's understanding of the universe and providing an accurate depiction of our planet, a prerequisite for any real progress.[31] As early as the ninth century, Arab merchants were the first to venture into distant regions, including China, Africa, and the far North of what is now Central Asia. The account of Süleyman's journey, written by Abu Zeyd in 851 and completed in 880, was the first published work on China. Al Masudi (d. 956), whose remarkable achievements were acknowledged by the scientific community in the late 18th century, extensively travelled the vast empire of the Caliphs during the mid-10th century. He also visited Ceylon, Madagascar, and Zanzibar, documenting the nature of the countries he encountered in his renowned work, *Golden Pastures*.

Ibn Haykal Al Biruni (d. 1048), Muhammad Idrissi (d. 1066?), and Ibn Batuta (d. 1369) are renowned travellers and scholars who have made significant contributions to the field of geography. Their invaluable works have played a crucial role in expanding the Western understanding of the world. Idrissi, born in Ceuta in 1099 and having resided at the Court of Palermo, wrote a treatise on geography for Roger II of Sicily (d. 1154). This treatise became a cornerstone for European cartographers for over three hundred and fifty years, with minimal alterations.[32] Additionally, the West relied on works such as Ulug Beg's general map of the world and the famous astrological tables attributed to him. Ulug Beg drew inspiration from the writings of Nasr Ed Dine Thusi and the observations of Ali Kuşçu (Ali Qushji, d. 1474), who had undertaken a voyage to China to verify measurements of the meridian and the size of the world. Arab sea charts also played a significant role, with Vasco da Gama (d. 1524) utilising one belonging to Malem Can, a Moor from Gujerat, as a guide to Melinda in 1497. Another chart, created by the Arab Omar, aided Albuquerque in navigating the Sea of Oman and the Persian Gulf.[33] It is plausible that the works of Muslim scholars may have influenced the discovery of America. In fact, Christopher Columbus himself mentioned Aventuez (Averroes) as one of the authors who inspired him to speculate about the existence of the New World in a letter written from Haiti in October 1498.[34]

The number of Muslim writers who have contributed to historical works is extensive. In the historical dictionary of the Ottoman historian Katib Çelebi (d. 1657), known as Hadja Khalfa, one can find numerous names of renowned historians. The earliest historical writings date back to the Umayyad era. One of the initial writers was likely Abu Minaf, mentioned by Al Masudi (d. 956) in his *Golden Pastures*.

Western scholars criticise Muslim historians for their excessive focus on factual reporting, neglecting broader concepts and the interconnection of historical events. While this criticism may hold some validity, it is only partially true. Indeed, the majority of Muslim historians did not engage in constructing elaborate theories that increasingly captivated the Western mind and characterised contemporary historical science. Instead, they saw themselves as collectors of information and preservers of records for future generations. They refrained from assuming the role of interpreters and judges of past events.

Undoubtedly, this perspective on history differs from that of the West. However, whether it is advantageous or detrimental is a matter of debate. Nonetheless, it is reasonable to argue that an author who faithfully transmits the tradition entrusted to them, without commentary or criticism, demonstrates greater sincerity and impartiality than those who present us with documents that have been censored, altered, or falsified to align with their own beliefs. Nevertheless, it would be unfair to accuse Muslim historians of narrow-mindedness and a lack of critical judgment. On the contrary, they gained renown for their broad-mindedness and approached questions with an enlightened interest that Western history considered beyond its scope. Consequently, literary history holds a significant place in their works.

Al Makkari (d. 1632), the most prominent historian of Muslim Spain, was born towards the end of the sixteenth century and passed away in

1631. His significant work, *Analects on the History and Literature of the Arabs in Spain*, was published in Leyden between 1855 and 1859. This treatise serves as a valuable source of information regarding the various regions of Spain, shedding light on the daily life, customs, and personalities of its inhabitants. With a style that is both lively and precise, the author vividly portrays the vibrant intellectual atmosphere not only in major cities like Cordova, Granada, and Seville, but also throughout the entire country. The insights provided about the lives of lawyers, doctors, musicians, singers, and educated women, including lawyers and poetesses, are of immeasurable worth in reconstructing the illustrious society of Muslim Spain.

Political Science and Sociology

The literary works dedicated to political philosophy and sociology are considered to be valuable treasures in Muslim literature. These works, written in Arabic, Persian, and Turkish, present profound and diverse perspectives on the art of governance and the various challenges of community life. Al Farabi, a prominent Muslim philosopher who preceded Avicenna, authored a treatise entitled *The Model City*, which delves into the realm of spirituality and noble sentiments. Drawing inspiration from Plato's belief that humans are meant to live in society, Al Farabi concludes that the perfectly organised State should encompass the entire inhabited world and include all of humanity. The notion of a universal state is frequently associated with the Roman Empire, the power struggles between the Papacy and the Empire in the Middle Ages, or the ideologies of some contemporary Utopians in Europe, but it is not a novel concept in Islamic philosophical thinking. In fact, it is implicitly present in the theocratic conception of Islam, and *The Model City* serves as an expression of this concept. Al Farabi, influenced by the mystical tendencies of his philosophy, ascribes lofty moral objectives to the universal state and its rulers. He believes that the duty of this state is to ensure perfect governance on earth for its citizens and bring them happiness in the afterlife. According to Al Farabi, the ideal city should be governed by a supreme ruler who possesses qualities such as great intelligence, infallible memory, eloquence, studiousness, temperance, magnanimity, a love for justice, unwavering determination, and a firm commitment to doing good. If it is not possible to find all these qualities in a single individual, then the government of the state should be entrusted to two, three, or more individuals who collectively possess all the necessary qualities. In this way, Al Farabi arrives at a similar idea as Plato, advocating for government by the wise or an aristocratic republic.

The open-minded perspectives of Al Farabi stand in stark contrast to the teachings of Ibn Zahir (d. 1293), a Sicilian Arab from the thirteenth century. His work, *Salan Al Mota*, was compared to Machiavelli's book *The Prince* and contains certain principles that are conceived in a similar vein as those of the Florentine secretary, but even more cunning and deceitful.

Al Mawerdi (972-1058), a renowned jurist who served as the Grand Judge in Ostawa, near Nishapur, is the author of the famous *Kitab Al Ahkam Es Sultaniah* (The Book of the Rules of Power). This work delves into a highly intriguing theory of the Caliphate and explores the key political, social, and legal institutions of the Islamic state. *Al Ahkam Es Sultaniah*, along with another of Al Mawerdi's works titled *Governmental Statutes*, has been translated into French.

Those who criticise Islamic civilisation, viewing it merely as a pale reflection of Hellenic culture and denying its originality, are compelled to acknowledge that the world owes its first-ever philosophy of history to the genius of Ibn Khaldun (d. 1406). No writer, be it Arab or European, had ever before presented such a comprehensive and philosophical perspective on history as Ibn Khaldun did. The consensus among critics of Ibn Khaldun is that he was the most exceptional historian to emerge from Islam and one of the greatest in history.[35] Long before modern sociologists like Comte, Vico, Marx, and Spengler, Ibn Khaldun dedicated himself to studying the evolution of human society and sought to provide a rational explanation for the progress of history.

Ibn Khaldun authored a comprehensive history of the world, consisting of three books, an introduction, and an autobiography. The first book, along with the introduction, forms a distinct section known as the Prolegomena.[36] This section stands as a timeless monument on its own, and it is through this work that the author gained worldwide recognition. Within it, one can find the earliest general reflections on history, the various forms of civilisation influenced by climate and nomadic lifestyles, and the unique customs of each civilisation. Additionally, Ibn Khaldun delves into the social institutions, sciences, and arts that these civilisations fostered. The author also discusses topics such as Qur'anic sciences, mathematics, singing and instrumental music, agriculture, and crafts. This work can be considered a true encyclopaedia, infused with a deeply philosophical spirit, where history is viewed as an integral part of philosophy. Ibn Khaldun explored the fundamental nature of the discipline of history. For Kahldun, history encompasses the careful examination and verification of facts, the thorough exploration of their underlying causes, and a deep comprehension of the unfolding and origins of events. Hence, history assumes great significance as a field of study within philosophy and deserves recognition as a scientific endeavour.[37] This perspective already reflects a modern understanding of history, emphasising its primary role in analysing facts and searching for causes. It presupposes a comprehensive knowledge of human civilisation and psychology.

It is nearly impossible to analyse the vast body of work produced by Ibn Khaldun. His brilliant and knowledgeable observations on the vulnerability of civilisations, the cyclical nature of evolution, and the crucial role played by the elite in the establishment of states, which he employs to support his theory, are truly captivating. Ibn Khaldun's starting point is the assertion that there exists a complete parallel between the life of a state and that of a human being or any other living being. Just like man, states are born, develop, and eventually perish. They too are subject to certain laws of natural progression. Ibn Khaldun dedicated himself to uncovering and elucidating this process of evolution.

CHAPTER 3
IMPACT OF ISLAM ON MEDIEVAL EUROPEAN CONSCIOUSNESS

The acknowledgment of Islam's influence on Europe is now widely accepted among serious Orientalists. However, despite recognising Islam's crucial role in transmitting ancient civilisation to the West, some Orientalists still hesitate to acknowledge the creative brilliance of the Arabs. Recent studies have made it impossible to deny that the Arabs completely reevaluated Greek knowledge, and without their transformative efforts, the Renaissance would not have been possible. The French School of Oriental Studies, led by the late Provencal Levi, and the notable Spanish historians Sanchez-Albornoz, Asin Palacios, Gomez Moreno, and Emile Gomez, have conducted scientific research on Muslim Spain, which fully supports this theory. As Sanchez-Albornoz in his book *Spain and Islam* wrote:

> Without question, it is no longer possible to discuss the dark Middle Ages in today's world. Instead, it is important to acknowledge the existence of the magnificent civilisation of Muslim Spain alongside a Europe suffering from misery and decline. Present-day leaders in Arab studies in Spain are expanding our understanding of the far-reaching impact and brilliance of this Hispano-Moorish culture. They have reaffirmed that it played a crucial role in the advancement of philosophy,

science, poetry, and all aspects of culture in Christian Europe. They have demonstrated that its influence extended even to the intellectual heights of medieval thinkers such as St. Thomas and Dante. Undoubtedly, there are still individuals on both sides of the Pyrenees or the Mediterranean who refuse to recognise its superiority and formative role. However, there is already an abundance of evidence supporting this, and new discoveries continue to emerge every day. Centuries before the Renaissance revitalised dormant springs, the stream of civilisation that flowed from Cordova preserved and transmitted the essence of ancient thought to the modern world.[1]

It is not surprising that Islam showed little interest in learning about the Franks during this period. In the early 11th century, these two civilisations had minimal interaction and remained unfamiliar with each other. This limited contact occurred primarily in southern Italy, particularly in Sicily, and Spain. However, it is important to note that the encounter between the Islamic and Christian worlds at this time cannot be considered a hostile one between the East and the West. Nevertheless, there were indications of its beginnings during this era.

Medieval Europe's response to Islamic Learning

Between 1100 and 1140, Latin writers focused on the life of Muhammad, disregarding accurate details, due to popular demand. These authors portrayed Muhammad as a "sorcerer" and magician who deceitfully destroyed Christianity in Africa and the East. Muslims were viewed as idolaters, and according to the German author Der Stricker, Muhammad was worshipped as part of a trinity alongside Tervagant and Apollo, as an attempt to align Islam with the despised Jewish faith. However, the Franks began to show interest in acquiring knowledge from their rival civilisation. Gerbert of Aurillac, who later became Pope Sylvester II (999-1003), conducted studies in Spain and brought back a wealth of technical and scientific information. Consequently, the dissemination of Islamic scientific knowledge to England, France, and Spain began gradually through Latin translations of Arabic works.[2] According to Maxime Rodinson:

The translation effort was developed and well organised in Spain after the fall in 1085 of Toledo, which was not only a great city, but one of the intellectual centers of the time... No one sought in these Arab manuscripts an image if Islam or the Muslim experience, but rather an objective knowledge of the natural world.[3]

Peter the Venerable, while in Spain, employed translators such as Robert of Kelton. In 1143, they completed a translation of the Qur'an along with other Arabic texts. However, despite these scholarly efforts, there was still no significant study of Islam. During this period, Latin Christendom also sought philosophical knowledge, primarily from the Arabic texts of Ibn Sina, also known as Avicenna in Christendom, and Arabic translations of Aristotle's works in Greek, which were previously thought to be lost. Consequently, a few scholars now had access to Aristotle's works through Arabic translations. The translated works of Avicenna's philosophical encyclopaedia, the *Kitab al-shifa* (Book of the Cure), garnered particular interest. This book gained widespread recognition throughout Christendom and provided the Latin West with a model of original synthesis, known as the "Aristotelian synthesis". Avicenna's comprehensive analysis of humanity and the world further enhanced this scientific perception of the world. As Roger Bacon proclaimed in the thirteenth century, "Thus philosophy was revived chiefly by Aristotle in Greek and then chiefly by Avicenna in Arabic".[4] This perception led Christian thinkers to create an image of the Muslim world as the birthplace of the greatest and most diverse philosophers and thinkers of the period. For the first time, this thinking contradicted the prevailing negative perception of Muslims. In addition to the literary and philosophical knowledge gained by the Franks from Muslims, another significant element that stimulated the advancement of Islamic learning was the economic interests of Frankish merchants and traders. The merchants from the Frankish region recognised the Muslim East as a crucial economic and trading hub. The Crusades played a role in further boosting this economic activity.

The Crusades and the Islamic Other

The Crusades unveiled the biases and hostilities of Christendom towards the Orient, specifically targeting the Islamic faith. The Crusaders were convinced that the Holy Land needed to be liberated from the non-believers, leading to the inclusion of the Seljuk Turks as the 'Other' in this narrative. Jerusalem for the Crusaders was a symbolic place, "an adventure within Western Christendom, not only in the religious, but in the social and political sense".[5] The migration of Turkish tribes into Asia Minor had made the land route for Christian pilgrims on their way to the Holy Land impossible. This migration became possible after the Byzantine defeat by the Seljuks at Manzikert in 1071. As a result, the Byzantine emperor Alexis Comnenos (r. 1081-1118) saw an opportunity to regain the lost lands in Anatolia and sought help from Pope Urban II. For the Pope, this was a chance not only to unite the warring knights of western Europe but also to bring an end to Christian disunity. By enlisting Frankish knights to combat the Turks, the Pope not only enhanced his prestige and authority but also strengthened the Papacy as a unifying force in western Europe. As Maxime Rodinson concurs, the "Council of Clermont's decision to embark on the First Crusade to the Holy Land in 1095 was tied to the movement toward papal supremacy".[6] If the Pope had not initiated the Crusades against the Turks, it would have been politically catastrophic for Christendom due to the ongoing conflicts waged by feudal lords. These conflicts included the Normans' battles in Italy, Sicily, and England, the French engagements in Spain, and the Germans' campaigns in northeast Europe.[7] Thus, he created an enemy, an anti-Christian enemy for the peoples of northern Europe of whom they knew very little about.

The initial impact of the unofficial or People's Crusade was borne by the Byzantine Empire. These individuals, lacking discipline, training, and wealth, were a disruptive force as they traversed the lands they encountered. When they reached Constantinople, as Runciman mentions, they were nothing but a "horde of undisciplined marauders whom the Byzantines promptly transported across the Bosphorus - and to slaughter at the hands of the Turks".[8] It is undeniable that the

Byzantine emperor Alexis would have been filled with anger. The precise terms of the agreement between the emperor and the Pope remain unknown, yet there are indications that the emperor might have desired to enlist Western mercenaries who would be under his authority.[9] The emperor harboured suspicion towards the Franks, whose knights were subject to the authority of feudal lords. This distrust stemmed from the belief that these lords were driven by a desire to establish their own realms by seizing territories that the Byzantines regarded as their own, despite being presently held by the Seljuk Turks.

The effects of the Crusades were more than economic activity. They introduced political contacts and interest. However, according to Maxime Rodinson what the Crusades and their mythology were to create was "a huge market for comprehensive, integral, entertaining and satisfying image of the enemy's ideology".[10] Saladin's (d. 1193) achievements continued to be revered in Christian Europe even a century after his time. Despite being a Muslim, Western Christendom struggled to acknowledge his true identity, leading to his inclusion in the Christian narrative. To integrate him into their own history, it was claimed that Saladin had a Christian mother who was stranded in Egypt due to a storm, and he himself converted to Christianity on his deathbed. This narrative of the Christian failure to conquer Jerusalem now appropriates one of Islam's most renowned heroes, making him a part of their own legacy.

During the eleventh and twelfth centuries, Western Christendom developed strong biases against Islam. These biases took root in the collective unconscious and subconscious, ensuring that the image would remain alive and easily revived in Western public opinion.[11] The portrayal of Muslims in the media and the global perceptions of them can be observed by examining the Gulf War of 1990-91, the wars in Iraq (2003-2011) and Afghanistan (2001-2021). The 'Mohammedan' heresy, which originated in the eleventh century, has continued to manifest in various forms up to the present day.

The Crusades facilitated contact between the Occident and Orient, but the condemnation of Islam during this time coincided with the emergence of the Crusades' spirit. This condemnation served to justify the Catholic Church's authority in uniting western Christendom against a shared adversary, whose beliefs Europe was just beginning to comprehend. The Catholic Church gradually recognised the religious influence of Islam and its advancements in North Africa and Spain. Europe eventually realised that both religions originated in the eastern Mediterranean and shared a common heritage, encompassing Jewish monotheism, Greek philosophy and science, Roman law and governance, and the traditions of ancient civilisations in the region.[12] However, the Western Church could not tolerate the corrections brought by Islam against Christianity. Islam asserted that Jesus Christ was not divine, but merely a human being, and that Muhammad was the greatest of all prophets and the final messenger of God to humanity. The Western Church, unable to accept these beliefs, deemed them heretical. Consequently, the Christian doctrine was called into question, leading to the conclusion that Muhammad was a fraudulent figure and a servant of Satan. Thus, the Church had to grasp an understanding of the Qur'an: "the Other must be studied the better to be refuted".[13]

The admiration of Arab philosophy by Christendom was evident, with the term 'philosopher' being commonly associated with 'Muslim'.[14] However, it raises the question of how they reconciled this admiration with the harsh criticism of Islam and its founder. Maxime Rodinson explains:

> One could escape these apparent contradictions about the Muslim world by assuming that their philosophers opposed the official religion of their own countries. Although both simplistic and too general, this opinion can be substantiated from accurate accounts. From the Western perspective, the Muslim philosophers seemed to accept certain religious dogmas and doctrines that could benefit the ignorant and barbaric among their people. By exaggerating the gap between reason and faith in Islam, some in the West went even further, claiming that the philosophers secretly ridiculed the Quran and were persecuted by the authorities.[15]

In the high Middle Ages, the understanding of Islam was profoundly embedded in the minds of Western Christendom, largely influenced by the effects of popular literature on the less educated populace. However, amidst this prevailing mindset, there were a few notable exceptions. Two prominent figures from the thirteenth century, Frederick II of Hohenstaufen and Thomas Aquinas, stood out as individuals who not only reflected the prevailing attitudes of their time but also played a significant role in shaping them. Frederick II, who ascended to the throne of Sicily in 1197 and later became the Emperor of the Holy Roman Empire from 1212 to 1250, along with Thomas Aquinas, who lived between 1225 and 1274, exerted a powerful influence on the perception of Islam during this era. Frederick II possessed a deep appreciation for Arab culture and had a profound interest in Islam. He engaged in intellectual discussions with Muslims, conversing fluently in Arabic about various subjects such as philosophy, science, logic, and mathematics. His admiration for Muslims was evident in his actions, as he even established a Saracen colony in Lucera, Italy, complete with a mosque. Frederick II treated Muslims with tolerance and respect. Consequently, when the Normans arrived in Sicily, they embraced and assimilated the political, scientific, and cultural advancements of the Muslim society as their own. The coexistence of Islam and Christianity in Sicily was, therefore, partially a result of the Arab heritage. Sicily experienced a renaissance and prosperity, distinguishing it from other European countries of that era, except for Spain and Italy, thanks to the contributions of Muslim civilisation. Thus, Hodgson claims that, "the greatest impact on the Occidental cultural and political life was made by the Latin rulers of the island [Sicily], notably by Frederick II".[16] It was here that the Europeans began to study works in Arabic. Hodgson states, "Even the Greeks were translating works from Arabic and Persian, for they were the most vital languages of the age this side of Chinese".[17]

In the year 1229, Frederick II, the sovereign of Sicily, forged a treaty with Sultan Al-Kamil of Egypt (r. 1218-1238) to discuss affairs pertaining to the Holy Land. This notable accord symbolised the bond between the Orient and the West, highlighting their shared involvement. Furthermore, it recognised the significance and value of the

Mediterranean region. As a result of his favourable stance towards Islam, Pope Gregory IX excommunicated Frederick II in 1239. However, Arab culture permeated not only Sicily but also the southern regions of Italy and the reconquered Spain. The Islamic influence was inescapable. This entire region of Europe absorbed from the Islamic civilisation, "whose ideas pervaded the learned guild structures of the day and extended their influence as far afield as England and Germany".[18] Learned men from Christendom, like Michael Scot, Robert Grossetete, Roger Bacon, Siger de Brabant, Albert the Great and Thomas Acquinas all encountered Aristotle via Averroes and Avicenna. Thus, according to Hodgson, "the most important consequence of the translations from Arabic was to raise the occidental thinking to a higher level of sophistication".[19]

Thomas Acquinas caused apprehension when he endeavoured to harmonise reason and faith. In terms of intellectual alignment, he found himself more closely aligned with Muslim philosophers like al-Kindi, al-Farabi, Avicenna, and Averroes, rather than the prominent figures within his own Church. Averroes, a Muslim philosopher, greatly influenced Acquinas by asserting that faith and reason exist solely within distinct and isolated realms. Acquinas's work centred on the bible, the Greek and the Islamic - or the *Orients*. As Henri Corbin remarked:

> [...] The names of Avicenna and of Averroes could well be taken as symbols of the respective spiritual destinies which awaited the Orient and the West.[20]

Hence, Christendom was destined to assimilate the philosophy that resided in its immediate vicinity. On certain occasions, Thomas Aquinas criticises Christendom as being uncivilised. This claim represents a recurring inconsistency in the Western viewpoint of Mediterranean history, as well as history in its entirety, as Aquinas himself foreshadowed the development of the West which he subsequently influenced. At the same time, for the thirteenth century Occident, its culture was "confined to its own little peninsulas. Thomas Acquinas was read from Spain to Hungary and from Sicily to Norway. Ibn al-

Arabi was read from Spain to Sumatra and from the Swahili coast to Kazan on the Volga".[21] Therefore, the cultural boundaries of Europe were significantly narrower in comparison to those of Islam.

Despite the lack of knowledge gained by Muslims from Europeans, the Europeans, on the other hand, actively embraced various cultural practices and ideas from the Islamic world. This assimilation played a significant role in the development of European culture. The advancement of Western culture can largely be attributed to the exceptional cultural proficiency of the Islamic civilisation.[22] To what extent did Islam shape Europe's cultural landscape? This phenomenon of one culture adopting elements from another prompts us to ponder the impact of Islamic intellectual culture on the modern West. It is often argued that Islamic intellectual culture primarily built upon Greek ideas, albeit with some additional advancements.[23] What must be addressed here is that Islam stirred "the imagination and the challenge to the ingenuity of the Occidentals".[24]

Ultimately, a full cycle has been completed: the Occident assimilates the ancient legacies of Egypt and Babylon, incorporating them into its own culture, embraces the influences of Hellenism, and subsequently focuses on the burgeoning civilisation of Rome. However, at the time of the Crusades, Hodgson notes that Europe:

> [...] never returning east of the Adriatic again, but rather turning as far as possible to the forests of Britain, Gaul, and Germany ... [and then they were] amazed at the time of the Crusades to find that the *east* is better developed then they.[25]

To their astonishment, Europe discovered that the East was more advanced than they had anticipated. Hence, the Crusades can be interpreted as an endeavour by uninformed Europe to establish a stronger connection with the global hub. Although Christendom held great admiration for the scientific and philosophical advancements of the Arabs during that era, it unfortunately left a profound and enduring mark of anti-Muslim prejudice on the Western mindset. While only a small fraction of the Franks were influenced by Arab knowledge, the

Church's teachings against the alleged imposter, Muhammad, "constituted the illiterate common people's sole source of information about Islam".[26] The dissemination of false information and the ignorance surrounding the Muslim faith permeated across Europe. While Dante demonstrated his ability to rescue Avicenna, Averroes, Saladin, Hector, Aeneas, Abraham, Socrates, Plato, and Aristotle from hell and transfer them to purgatory, he did not extend the same mercy to Muhammad. Muhammad, being condemned to the eighth circle of Hell, was excluded from Dante's act of redemption.[27] Nevertheless, Western Christendom swiftly embraced the Muslim philosophers and scientists, assimilating them into their own culture by distorting their names, making it challenging to discern their true identities today. For instance, Ibn Bajah was transformed into Avempace, Ibn Rushd became Averroes, Ibn Sina was renamed Avicenna, Abul Hasan became Alboacen, and Ibn al-Haytham was altered to Alhazen. However, it is undeniable that Europe during the Middle Ages, or more specifically, Western Christendom, started to learn from the advancements of Islamic civilisation. Albert Champdor in his book appropriately sums up this point:

> Our ancestors acquired the knowledge of weaving luxurious fabrics from the Orient, which later brought fortune to Venice and parts of France. The Orient introduced the art of creating satin, velvet, brocades made of gold and silver, as well as lightweight fabrics like muslin, gauze, and taffeta. Throughout history, the Orient excelled in producing deep-pile carpets, inspiring European craftsmen to master this craft. Venice, in turn, learned the techniques of glassblowing and mirror cutting from the markets of the Near East. The West borrowed the art of paper-making and the skill of creating syrups from Syrian craftsmen. This peaceful invasion had a profound impact on commerce and the early stages of industry in Europe. Drapery underwent transformation, Europe acquired the ability to manufacture textiles, luxury trades flourished and expanded, production increased, and techniques advanced. In essence, an economic revolution swept through society and the entire continent.[28]

Thus, the Orient was transforming the Occident. The arrival of a new set of ideas, primarily philosophical in nature, had a profound impact on scientific and philosophical thinking as well as on theology in later periods. Influenced by Arab thought and inspired by rediscovering ancient Greek knowledge, Europeans became increasingly interested in scholarship and philosophy. This curiosity propelled them towards an autonomous and swiftly evolving intellectual journey, the benefits of which we continue to experience today.[29]

There is no denying that Islam played a significant role in the emergence of early modern European civilisation. According to Henri Pirenne, "The Frankish Empire would probably never have existed without Islam, and Charlemagne without Mahomet would be inconceivable".[30] To discuss Muhammad and Charlemagne alone would be insufficient. The emergence of Islam established the parameters of a fresh, cohesive entity known as 'Christendom'. Above all, Islam provided the intellectual and philosophical impetus that allowed European identity to take shape. The existence of Europe, not to mention Charlemagne, would be unimaginable without the influence of Muhammad.

Parallel campaigns to reconquer Europe had commenced. In the western region, the Normans seized Messina by 1001 and proceeded to reclaim Sicily for the Christian faith. Alfonso VI captured Toledo in 1085, marking significant progress in the Christian reconquest of the Iberian Peninsula. The battle of Las Navas de Tolosa in 1212 served as a pivotal moment for the Christians, turning the tide in their favour during the reconquest. Granada remained as the last remaining Muslim state. In Eastern Europe, Prince Dimitri Donskoi of Moscow achieved a decisive victory over the Tatars at the Battle of Kulikovo in 1380. Similar to Spain, a prolonged and arduous struggle ensued, but in 1480, Ivan III, also known as Ivan the Great, successfully repelled the final Tatar advance on Moscow, liberating themselves from the "Tatar yoke". While the Reconquista triumphed in Iberia and Russia, it faltered in the Levant, succumbing to the overwhelming power of the emerging Ottoman Empire. These conflicts initially arose between Western Christendom and the Seljuk Turks, and later, from the fourteenth century onwards, between Europe and the Ottoman Empire, persisting animosities between Christendom and Islam well into the twentieth century.[31]

The rise of the Ottoman Turks in Asia Minor after the fall of the Seljuk Sultanate of Rum in 1299, and their ongoing territorial expansion into the Balkans and Central Europe over the following centuries, nevertheless led to a notable alteration in the frontier matter between Christendom and Islam, drawing it nearer to the core of Europe. This coincided with the simultaneous Renaissances in Italy and Ottoman Istanbul.[32] However, the Renaissance in Europe had a long-lasting influence on the perception of Islam in the subsequent centuries. As a result, the term 'Turk' became synonymous with 'Muslim' and vice versa. The European outlook on the Turk went through a significant change, shifting from admiration for their political and military systems during the fifteenth and sixteenth centuries, to a sense of intrigue and captivation with life in the Sultan's palace, and eventually to a perception of tyranny and savagery in the nineteenth century. This unfavourable depiction of Islam has endured until the present time.

CHAPTER 4

THE RENAISSANCE MINDSET
THE IDEALISATION OF A DEAD WORLD

At the start of the 5th century, the Western Roman Empire crumbled and was divided among various Germanic tribes. Meanwhile, in the East, Byzantium emerged with Christianity reshaping the once thriving Roman Empire. In the West, Christianity encountered a tribal society, introducing new beliefs and ways of living. The Crusades, commencing with the capture of Jerusalem in 1099, marked the beginning of Western Christendom's interactions with Islam and Byzantium. Urbanisation surged, markets flourished, and cities emerged. However, the monastic Christianity of the West struggled to adapt from a predominantly rural society to a fully developed urban civilisation. This led to an unexpected turn of events: the Renaissance. A civilisation that had been dormant for a millennium was revived and repurposed to meet the changing times.

The Greco-Roman 'Classical World', now known as such, was considered to have achieved the pinnacle of civilisation and became the standard to be followed. The separation of religion and culture occurred: the warrior took the place of the saint at the top of society; the Greek and Latin classics supplanted the Bible in education; museums were constructed to preserve and study the remnants of the Classical World; classical architecture replaced the organic forms that had developed naturally within Christendom, resulting in an orderly yet artificial environment; artists brought the gods from heaven to the human realm, and the exaltation of God and the saints was replaced by the exaltation of Man. Man was now deemed 'the measure of all things'.

However, a new separate entity gazed upon the world. No longer a part of an organic culture, this entity was captivated by a lifeless world, which had been revived and idealised through the power of imagination. Culture was no longer internally developed, but rather obtained from an external, deceased source. We transition from an era where individuals were shaped by a holistic process, to one where civilisation was acquired by learning about another world from a different time. This gave rise to a new type of 'civilised' individual who, residing in an idealised imaginary world, felt more connected to dead cultures and civilisations than those that were alive.

The Renaissance had a significant social impact by creating a divide between the elite and the rest of society. Classical education and culture were inaccessible to the majority, leading to the emergence of a warrior class. The values of courage, self-sacrifice, and discipline were glorified, overshadowing Christian virtues like love, forgiveness, and humility. Literary works shifted from focusing on saints to celebrating heroes. Monuments of great warriors and statesmen adorned public spaces, while their grand palaces dominated urban and rural landscapes. Even in death, the Church paid tribute to them by housing their tombs and memorials in churches and cathedrals.

The Roman Empire served as a blueprint and source of motivation for the recently established independent nations to establish their own empires. Failing to subdue their neighbouring territories, they ventured abroad and enforced their own interpretation of civilisation on the global stage, resulting in the destruction of the indigenous cultures they encountered and the preservation of their remnants in newly established museums for scholarly examination. According to Ahmed Paul Keeler in *Islam & The West: A New Narrative for the Age of Crises*:

Western Christendom's inability to make the transition from a rural to an urban civilisation ushered in the Renaissance, and the idealisation of a dead world. With 'Man becoming the measure of all things' humanism was born. In that which now regarded itself as the civilised world, humanism aspired to the virtues of the classical age. With the descent into our modern world, humanism has been transformed into the rights demanded by, and granted to, the sovereign individual.[1]

This mindset initiated centuries of unfavourable attitudes towards Muslims. As the following chapters will explain, the judgements made by Europeans towards Muslims, particularly the Turks, based on this mentality, would greatly impact the relationship between Islam and the West for centuries.

During the Renaissance, there was significant turmoil within the Christian Church and it made its way into the Papacy. Over the course of a century, from the mid-15th to the mid-16th century, a succession of popes, influenced by the new humanism, acted in a manner reminiscent of the most decadent Roman emperors, much to the dismay of the devout. They embarked on a project to restore the splendour of Rome and reconstruct St Peter's in the classical style. To finance this ambitious endeavour, the popes issued indulgences, allowing the faithful to pay for the reduction of time spent in Purgatory for themselves and their loved ones. This was the catalyst for the events that led to the Reformation and the division of Christendom.[2] As a result of this division, the Ottoman Turks would take advantage and keep Europe divided.

CHAPTER 5

THE OTTOMAN THREAT
DIVISION IN THE MEDITERRANEAN

Following the conquest of Constantinople by Sultan Mehmed the Conqueror in 1453, the Ottoman Turks acquired a new imperial capital, which they renamed Istanbul. This marked the beginning of a new era of expansion for the empire. Under the rule of Selim I and his son Süleyman the Magnificent, the Ottoman Empire experienced significant growth. Politically, it extended its influence from the Atlantic Ocean in the west, with Süleyman's commander Salih Pasha briefly occupying Morocco in 1554, to the gates of Vienna in southeastern Europe. It also gained control over the Gulf of Aden in the south and the Persian Gulf in the east, effectively bringing the house of Islam under its dominion. Socially, the empire transformed into a diverse and tolerant society, accommodating people of different races and religions. Economically, it gained control over the traditional trading routes of the East and the Silk Road.[1] According to Hentsch, "The expansion of the Ottoman Empire re-opened - in Western eyes - the rift which the Arab invasions of the seventh century had allegedly inflicted on the Mediterranean, and made it irreversible".[2]

During the mid-fourteenth century, the Byzantine Empire had reached a state of extreme weakness and vulnerability. Emperor Manuel II was willing to relinquish control of Constantinople to anyone who would pledge to protect it. However, the fervour and enthusiasm for the Crusades that had characterised the eleventh century no longer resonated with the Christian world, especially as the Turks rapidly conquered the Balkans. Surprisingly, the Ottomans were often viewed as liberators by the people of the Balkans. Paul Coles' research has revealed that throughout the fifteenth and sixteenth centuries, the peasant populations in the Balkans and central Hungary frequently welcomed and even aided the Ottoman advancement. As Paul Coles states, "The explanation lies in the more primitive and less exacting character of the Turkish feudalism in comparison with its European counterpart".[3] The Ottoman feudal system revolved around the *timar*, a non-hereditary land grant given to the *sipahi*, a cavalry soldier, in exchange for their military services. According to Bernard Lewis, even in the nineteenth century, European travellers in southeastern Europe noted the prosperity and satisfaction of the Balkan peasants, which they found to be superior to certain regions in Christian Europe. Nevertheless, the distinction was significantly more pronounced during the fifteenth and sixteenth centuries, a time when Europe experienced the profound peasant uprisings. It is worth mentioning that despite the widespread criticism, the *devsirme* levy had its merits, allowing the most destitute villagers to ascend to influential positions within the Ottoman Empire. Many individuals seized this opportunity and relocated their families to the empire's capitals, thereby establishing a unique "form of social mobility that was unattainable in the aristocratic societies of contemporary Christendom".[4] The Slavs, in contrast to the Catholic west, preferred living under Ottoman rule due to the Turks' greater tolerance towards other religions. It is worth noting that the Ottomans displayed a remarkably high level of religious toleration towards their non-Muslim subjects, especially when compared to the missionary zeal and sectarian intolerance prevalent in contemporary Europe. The conversion of Balkan peoples to Islam was a gradual process and appeared to be more closely tied to personal, social, or economic factors rather than any aggressive proselytising pursued by Ottoman administrators. These factors included the expectation of reduced taxation or exemption from mandatory government service for converts.[5] During the 14th century, Slavic people sought refuge from the Catholic crusade that targeted the Orthodox East. This crusade, sanctioned by the Pope, led to the coerced conversion of approximately two hundred thousand Bulgarians from Orthodox Christianity to Catholicism through the efforts of Franciscan missionaries. Lord Kinross highlights the severity of their persecution, stating that the Muslim conquest was seen by many as a means to regain their religious freedom.[6] The lands conquered by the Turks were not subjected to denationalisation. Over a span of nearly five centuries, the inhabitants of the Balkans successfully maintained their language and culture. It is undeniable that this policy, which was already implemented during the reign of Mehmed II, played a significant role in the gradual weakening and eventual downfall of Turkish dominance in the region.[7] Refugees from Europe, specifically the Iberian Jews who sought refuge from the Inquisition's forced conversion torment in Christian Spain, migrated to Ottoman society. Alongside the Greeks, Slavs, and Armenians within the empire, these Jewish refugees not only preserved their religious beliefs, language, and culture, but also exerted significant influence in Ottoman politics, administration, and economy. According to Paul Coles:

> Ottomans created the modern civilisation of religious tolerance and multi-ethnic, multi-religious societies and saved Europe from the narrow-minded intolerant barbarity of the Middle Ages.[8]

The Ottoman Empire's policy of religious and cultural tolerance towards its people proved to be detrimental to their ambitions of establishing a lasting power in southeastern Europe. The decline of the empire was already apparent in the fifteenth century, but the disunity within Christendom during that time further prolonged the Turkish threat for an additional two centuries.

During the fourteenth century, Christendom experienced a period of fragmentation and disintegration. Feuding feudal lords posed a threat to the stability of the region, leading to the emergence of small monarchical kingdoms that were often at odds with one another. This process was accompanied by the growth of independent cities and republics, particularly in Italy. The Frankish rulers were too preoccupied with their own conflicts to pay much attention to the struggles faced by Constantinople.

The lack of unity among the Christian monarchies in Europe was evident. They failed to take advantage of the interregnum that occurred in the Ottoman Empire in 1402, when it was weakened by the invasion of Timur. It was not until Mehmed II ascended the throne for the second time in 1451 and consolidated the power of the Osman dynasty that the era of Ottoman expansionism truly began. By 1453 any help that arrived from Christendom was slow and even too late. But the lamentation of the West and the image of the Turk were evident in Cardinal Bessarion's letter *The Turkish Menace* to Francesco Foscari, Doge of Venice, dated 13 July, 1453: "[…] while in hope of victory fresh forces were being brought against the enemy, the barbarians conquered the city [29 May, 1453]".[9] However, there were others like John of Segovia (c.1400-1458) who in 1454 suggested a series of conferences with the Muslim jurists even if they did not result in the conversion of the parties involved.[10]

Sultan Mehmed II's death in 1480 was pronounced in Italy as "La grande aquila e morta!" (The great eagle is dead).[11] The demise of Mehmed brought great joy to the Europeans. Guillaume Coursin, the vice-chancellor of the Order of St. John, convened the Knights of Rhodes and delivered the news that Mehmed's resting place remained empty. Furthermore, he revealed that the powerful earthquake that coincided with his death was a result of his entrails descending from one abyss to another, ultimately reaching the depths of hell. Coursin proceeded to enumerate the multitude of atrocities and offenses committed by the Sultan against humanity. In the eyes of Christendom, Mehmed was not only a harbinger of death but also the embodiment of evil as the Antichrist.[12] As Babinger has shown, Mehmed was not alone in his tyrannical behaviour. Among his Italian contemporaries, Ferranto of Aragon fits perfectly in Aristotle's analysis of a tyrant's character - "dissolute vice, hideous cruelty, bloodthirstiness, unrestrained sexual lust and bestial intemperance …"[13] Similarly, Jacob Burckhardt called Ferrante "the most terrible of all the princes of his day, a demonic nature […]"[14]

The end of the fifteenth century marked a significant period of expansion for Europe. This expansion occurred simultaneously in both the eastern and western regions, with the primary goal of overthrowing Muslim dominance that had persisted for centuries. In the east, the Russians engaged in a prolonged battle and eventually emerged victorious over the Tatars. Similarly, in the west, the Christians brought an end to the Moorish rule that had been established eight centuries earlier, gradually eradicating their presence. In both parts of Europe, the resurgent Christians took the fight to the enemy's territory. In the east, the Russians pursued the Tatars into Tartary, establishing their dominance over central and northern Asia. In the west, the Spaniards and Portuguese, followed by other maritime nations, pursued the Moors into Africa and Asia, and incidentally stumbled upon and colonised America.[15]

The conquest of Granada by Ferdinand of Aragon and Isabella of Castille on 2 January 1492 marked the ultimate triumph of Christianity over Islam in the prolonged eight-century battle for control over the Iberian Peninsula. Consequently, the power struggle between Christendom and Islam shifted significantly towards southeastern Europe, particularly in the Balkans under Ottoman rule. This ongoing conflict between the two religious factions would subsequently engulf the entire Mediterranean region throughout the sixteenth century.[16]

By the conclusion of the 15th century, the Ottoman Empire emerged as not just a force in the Mediterranean, but also as a significant player in Europe. This transformation commenced with the capture of Constantinople by Mehmed II in 1453. Subsequently, Selim I expanded the empire's territories by acquiring Syria, Egypt, and the revered Islamic sites of Mecca and Medina through successful campaigns in 1516-1517. These territorial gains were further consolidated under the reign of Süleyman the Magnificent:

> [...] Sultan of the Sultans of East and West, Lord born under a fortunate conjunction, of the kingdoms of the Roman and Persians and Arabs, hero of all that is, pride of the arena of earth time; of the Mediterranean and the Black Sea, and the glorified Ka'ba and the illumined Medina,

> the noble Jerusalem and the throne of Egypt, the rarity of the age, and the province of Yemen, and Aden and Sana, and Baghdad the abode of rectitude, and Basra and al-Hasa and the Cities of Nushiravan, and the lands of Algiers and Azerbaijan, the steppes of the Kipchak and the land of the Tatars, and Kurdistan and Luristan, and of the countries of Rumelia and Anatolia and Karaman and Wallachia and Moldavia and Hungary all together, and many more kingdoms and lands mighty of esteem: Sultan and Padishah [...][17]

Consequently, the Ottoman Empire transformed the eastern Mediterranean into a vast expanse under its control. Süleyman successfully elevated the empire to a prominent position as both a formidable force on land and a dominant naval power. The military prowess of the Ottomans garnered widespread acclaim. Paolo Giovio in his *Turcicarum Rerum Commentarius* of 1539 wrote: "Their military discipline has such justice and severity as easily to surpass the ancient Greeks and Romans".[18] Süleyman's retreat only occurred at the gates of Vienna in 1529. This particular setback has been a subject of debate among historians. However, it is highly probable that due to the persistent rainfall in September, Süleyman made the decision to orderly retreat (in contrast to the chaotic second siege of Vienna in 1683) and embark on a three-month journey back to Istanbul before the onset of winter. Approximately at the same time a bronze medal was struck depicting Emperor Charles V supported by an angel on his right and "haunted by the turbaned profile of Süleyman" on his left.[19] Therefore, according to the perspective of the Franks, the Grand Turk emerged as a haunting figure in the European mindset and "summed up what was to remain the status quo" throughout the sixteenth century.[20]

During a period of religious upheaval, there existed individuals who perceived the Turkish menace as an imminent danger to Christendom. This perception was so deeply ingrained that some even held the belief that a Turkish invasion would serve as a divine retribution for Europe's transgressions. In certain regions, the sound of the "Turkbells" resonated daily, summoning the faithful to engage in acts of penitence and prayer.[21] During this era, the Turkish people emerged as a significant concern for the Western world, primarily in political rather than religious terms. As Rodinson claims, the Turks were "seen more as a secular or cultural menace than an ideological threat".[22] The West no longer regarded the Sultans as "leaders of rabbles".[23] Veronese, the Renaissance painter, depicted the renowned figures of his time in his artwork, *the Marriage at Cana*. Notably, he included Süleyman the Magnificent, "the Shadow of God on earth ... and Padishah", within the painting.

Süleyman comprehended the lack of unity among Christians, which led him to manipulate their divisions by forming an alliance with Francis I of France in 1536. This strategic move further deepened the divide between the conflicting factions in Europe. The French King, in an attempt to justify his alliance with the Turk, expressed his apology and emphasised his reliance on Christian doctrine and ideology. According to Heath:

> I cannot deny that I very much want to see the Turk powerful and ready for war, not for his own sake, for he is an infidel and the rest of us are Christians, but to erode the power of the Emperor (Charles V) and involve him in crippling expense.[24]

However, when the French granted the Turks rights to a port in southern France, they were perceived as betrayers of Europe.

Nevertheless, it should be acknowledged that the Europeans also employed the Safavids as a means to counter the Sultan. Although Christian unity may not have been prevalent, it became evident during the Battle of Lepanto in 1571. At this decisive encounter, the combined forces of Venice, Genoa, and Charles V inflicted a significant naval defeat upon the Turks. But this triumph did not last as the Grand Vizier, Sokollu tells the Venetian minister in Istanbul regarding the Venetian loss of Cyprus:

> There is wide difference between your loss and ours. In capturing Cyprus from you we have cut off one of your arms; in defeating our fleet you have merely shaved off our beard; the lopped arm will not grow again, but the shorn beard will grow stronger than before.[25]

Shortly afterwards Venice made peace with Turkey and the euphoria of Lepanto was short-lived.

In the late sixteenth century, the Ottomans found themselves entangled in conflicts with Iran (1578-1590), diverting their attention from the Mediterranean. Concurrently, the Spanish shifted their focus towards the Atlantic and the New World. According to Braudel:

> [...] the Hispanic bloc and the Ottoman bloc, so locked together in a struggle for the Mediterranean, at last disengaged their forces and at a stroke, the inland sea was freed from the international war which had from 1550-1580 been its major feature.[26]

Both the Spanish and Turkish monarchs came to realise the importance of achieving peace in the Mediterranean. This was crucial for them to shift their focus towards other significant matters. Philip II of Spain needed peace in order to consolidate his power over the Aztecs, Incas, and the Mayas in the New World. He aimed to extract valuable resources such as gold and other precious goods from these indigenous peoples. On the other hand, Murad III of Turkey sought peace to effectively combat the Safavids in the name of Sunni Islam, extending his influence across the Tigris.

Religious debates were entirely overshadowed by political circumstances. This led to the establishment of partially diplomatic connections between the Western world and the East, although the nature of this relationship remained uncertain. In 1581, Queen Elizabeth I initiated trade with the Ottoman Empire by engaging with the Turkey Company. In 1588 she informed Sultan Murad III that "as far as she was concerned, Spain was nothing but a nation of idolaters with Philip II as their leader".[27] As Norman Daniel claims this was an alliance based "solely on ideology ... strict monotheists against untrustworthy Catholics". Elizabeth also sent an unofficial ambassador to Istanbul to accompany Sultan Mehmed III on his war against the Austrians in 1593, "for he had borne the English armes upon his tent ... in the Turkes campe against Christians".[28] When James I assumed the English throne, he rejected the notion of a formal embassy from Istanbul as it would not be fitting for a Christian ruler. The Italian city-states made it clear to their oppressive governments that they would gladly welcome a potential Turkish invasion, just like some Balkan Christians had done before. Hale describes this period of Frankish diplomacy and perception of the Other as an:

> [...] atmosphere of double-think about Europe's alien, infidel but permanent lodger, two strands of opinion ... One focused upon monstrous inhumanity; the other on high standards of material well-being. The Turks were still judged as much in terms of behaviour as of belief.[29]

From an external perspective, the Ottoman Empire appeared to be uncivilised, savage, and merciless. The act of a monarch eliminating all his brothers upon ascending to the throne, which was established as a palace law by Mehmed II, seemed particularly brutal (this measure was implemented to prevent any challenges to the throne). It is important to acknowledge that during this period, Europe also had its share of cruel practices such as torture, witch burnings, the Spanish Inquisition, and mutilation. However, it was the Turks who were predominantly associated with impalement, as depicted by German artists like Erhard Schoen in his portrayal of the siege of Vienna in 1529. This anti-Turkish propaganda became increasingly evident during the conflicts between the Turks and the Venetians, as well as the Turks and the Habsburgs in the sixteenth century. As the Turkish threat increased "both the Ottoman Empire and Islam itself came under closer scrutiny".[30] For Albert Lybyer, a twentieth century historian, the Ottoman Turks remained 'Mohammedan' and this "has constituted the real tragedy of the Turk".[31]

CHAPTER 6

OBSERVING THE OTHER AND SHIFTING IDENTITIES IN THE SIXTEENTH CENTURY

Those who embarked on a journey to the Orient had unique experiences that shaped their perceptions. Ogier Ghiselin de Busbecq (d. 1592), the Austrian imperial ambassador who resided in Istanbul between 1555 and 1562, was among those individuals. Busbecq developed a profound admiration for the Ottoman system of governance during his time there. He observed that in the Ottoman Empire, people from all walks of life, including slaves and shepherds, had the opportunity to rise through the social ranks and attain influential positions. This starkly contrasted with the Frankish lands, where one's social status was predetermined by birth, either into nobility or slavery. According to Busbecq:

> It is by merit that men rise in the service, a system which ensures that posts should be assigned only to the competent...those who receive the highest offices from the Sultan are for the most part the sons of shepherds or herdsmen, and so far from being ashamed of their parentage, they actually glory in it...they do not believe that high qualities are either natural or hereditary, nor do they think that they can be handed down from father to son [...][1]

Busbecq identified these factors as the underlying causes for the triumph of the Turks. Furthermore, he asserts that these attributes were not commonly found in Europe, where social status was determined solely by one's lineage rather than individual merit.[2] In his correspondence, Busbecq expresses profound pessimism regarding the peril Europe faces as a result of Ottoman conquests. He fails to comprehend why Europe is fixated on exploring the Indies and the Antipodes in pursuit of wealth, while it is confronted by a formidable and potent adversary. Simultaneously, Busbecq mourns over the lack of unity among Christians. Busbecq in his letters state:

> On their side are the resources of a mighty empire, strength unimpaired, experience and practice in fighting, a veteran soldiery, habituation to victory, endurance of toil, unity, order, discipline, frugality, and watchfulness. On our side is public poverty, private luxury, impaired strength, broken spirit, lack of endurance and training; the soldiers are insubordinate, the officers avaricious; there is contempt for discipline; licence, recklessness, drunkenness, and debauchery are rife; and, worst of all, the enemy is accustomed to victory and we to defeat.[3]

It was clear to Busbecq and his peers that Europe was destined for failure while the Turks would emerge victorious. Even Thomas Moore (d. 1535), in his work *Utopia* (1516) written four decades prior to Busbecq's letters, acknowledged that the Ottoman Turks would probably retain control over Greece and the Balkans, a significant portion of Albania, and the entirety of Bosnia.[4] Thankfully, Europe proved them wrong. Although Turkish dominance persisted for a while, signs of decline were gradually emerging.

In 1554, Pierre Belon, a fellow traveller to the Orient, published his observations on Greece, Asia Minor, Palestine, Egypt, and Arabia. He dedicated two out of his three books to ancient and contemporary Greece, the ruins of ancient Troy, and the prominent cities of the region, namely Istanbul and Jerusalem. The third book focused on the social customs of the Turks. What made Belon's work noteworthy was his consistent tone and detached manner when describing both the customs of the region and the essential aspects of Asia Minor. Unlike

Busbecq, Belon drew a comparison between the slaves in Turkey and those in Europe, noting that they experienced happiness based on the master they served.[5] Ottoman slavery differed significantly from the practices of Anglo-Saxons. It did not involve a colour-based hierarchy, as old Islamic customs disregarded differences in skin colour. Moreover, being a slave did not leave an indelible mark on one's identity. Once freed, a slave immediately gained full rights and privileges.

The concept of slavery in the Ottoman Empire did not possess any inherent characteristic. It was always conceivable for an Ottoman slave to attain freedom. As stated by Lybyer, "The idea of Aristotle, that some men are born to be slaves, was wholly absent".[6] Nonetheless, Belon does express admiration for the Sultan's religious and cultural acceptance towards his subjects:

> For the Turk oblige no man to live in the Turkish manner and thus is it permitted to for each to live according to his law.[7]

Guillaume Postel (d. 1581) took his visionary observations of the Other to the next level by envisioning a utopia or a universal republic where Catholics, Orthodox, and Muslims would unite under a single faith. He firmly believed that Christian Europe could coexist harmoniously with the Muslim East, and if the West failed to rejuvenate itself, it would be up to the Turks to fill the void and establish the universal republic.[8] These early travellers to the Orient provide historians with the initial glimpses of true oriental exoticism. According to Rodinson, these observers "began to dress like the Turks".[9] However, that marked the extent of its reach. In the realm of literature, although the pieces were entirely fictional and derived from Eastern history, such as Marlowe's *Tambourlaine*, they captivated the literary community. Nevertheless, they were not regarded as credible sources for understanding the history or essence of the Muslim East or the Ottoman Empire.

The political analysis of the Ottoman Empire persisted. In *The Prince* by Machiavelli, there are limited references to the Turk. Although this may not provide sufficient grounds to evaluate the Turkish political system, it holds significance as it draws a comparison between the governing systems of the Franks and the Muslim Orient. Machiavelli declares that "all princedoms of which we have record are governed in two ways: in one there is a prince, and all the others are as servants ... In the other, there is a prince, with barons ..."[10] Machiavelli's comparison of the governing methods of the Turks and the King of France reveals that the concept of the Other is no longer based on religious differences, but rather on purely political disparities. This highlights Europe's growing political awareness of both itself and the Other. Machiavelli's perspective on the Other is significant as it signifies the political emergence of the West and its distinct identity, separate from the vision of the Other. During the sixteenth century, the Ottoman Empire's religious tolerance and equality towards its citizens, regardless of their ethnicity or nationality, were highly regarded by the Franks and Western intellectuals. Influential thinkers like Machiavelli, Voltaire, and Rousseau criticised the inequalities within their own societies, influenced by the Turkish-Islamic perspectives they encountered. Additionally, travellers to the Levant during this period, such as Busbecq, Thevenot and Lady Mary Wortley Montagu, also expressed admiration for the Turkish system. However, the Turkish threat began to decline particularly from seventeenth century onwards - a surprising achievement for an Empire which most European historians today consider to have begun its decline at the end of the previous century: an easy judgement in hindsight. For others the decline became more obvious in the eighteenth century. If this era can be marked as the beginning of the end of Turkish military threat to Christendom what about the economic threat? According to Pirenne and other Western historians one of the main reasons for Europe's venture into the seas during the fifteenth and sixteenth centuries was the result of Turkish expansionism and the closing off the Orient to European trade, which eventually caused the economic decline of the Mediterranean and thus the decline of the image of the eastern Mediterranean.[11] This is true to an extent. As Halil İnalcık has shown, Mehmed the Conqueror, due to political tensions in the Morea and Albania which led to a long war with Venice from 1463 to 1479 took economic reprisals against the Italian kingdom. But at the same time he maintained trading relations with the West by encouraging Florence and Dubrovnik to take the place of Venice.[12]

Italian traders had access to Egyptian goods both before and after the Ottoman expansion. When Vasco de Gama rounded the Cape of Good Hope in 1497 he did not do it as a result of Ottomans closing off the Orient to European trade, but to compete with Venice. When the old spice route Syria, Egypt, and the Red Sea came under the control of the Topkapı Palace in Istanbul in 1517, and later the Persian Gulf in 1534, Venice continued to have trading access through these areas. Thus, the Ottomans did not restrict the Mediterranean trade. As İnalcık and Braudel agree - the trade thrived:

> What is quite clear is that the Mediterranean had captured large portion of the pepper trade...trade with the Levant was flourishing...from the Persian Gulf ... to Red Sea [...][13]

Similarly, as Braudel clearly points out, after 1550 "the difficult gateway to the Red Sea stood wide open, and a huge volume of trade flowed through".[14] When the Ottomans and Venetians were not involved in military conflict:

> [...] the Ottomans unhesitatingly restored to the Venetians their commercial privileges. Venice always dominated the spice trade in the ports of Egypt and Syria, and in 1546 the Ottomans granted Venice the monopoly of alum mining in return for a payment of twenty-five thousand ducats.[15]

Venetian economy continued to grow despite military conflicts with the Ottomans. Venice obtained its silk brocades and satins, paper, glassware and mirrors from the ports of the eastern Mediterranean, and its spices, drugs, silk, dyes and cotton from Egypt and Syria. During the sixteenth century the Ottoman ports became "richer and more attractive than before, and second half of the century, France, England and Holland were actively participating in the trade, eventually confining Ragusan and Venetian commerce to the Adriatic".[16] Under Süleyman the Magnificent's rule (1520-1566) the Ottomans granted the West certain economic rights in the Empire which came to be known as capitulations. After Venice, these rights were granted to France in 1569 and later to England, Holland and other European monarchies except the Habsburgs. Süleyman and the later sultans "always tried to use these commercial privileges as a political weapon".[17]

The Calvinists in France received support from the Ottomans in their conflict against the Spanish Catholics. However, the rise of the mercantilist states in Europe had a transformative effect on the capitulations, gradually turning the Ottoman economy into a dependency of Europe. This had detrimental consequences for the Ottoman Empire, not only in terms of its economy but also in terms of its perception as an oriental despot, especially after the Industrial Revolution and up until the end of the Ottoman dynasty in the twentieth century. The influx of cheap European silver into the Ottoman economy starting from the 1580s led to a price revolution that severely impacted the Ottoman economy and disrupted the established traditions of the state and society.[18] As Lewis points out, together with the capitulations and "the extraterritorial immunities bestowed on them [Europeans] - as an act of condescension - by Muslim rulers made it easier for them to exploit and, in time, to dominate the open markets of the Islamic world".[19]

Hentsch argues that the era spanning from the late fifteenth century to the sixteenth century marked a significant shift in European history, one that the Turks and other civilisations failed to achieve.[20] However, in contrast to this notion, Hodgson asserts that the Ottomans and the Timurid Mughals not only upheld their political dominance but also exhibited remarkable cultural ingenuity throughout this era.[21] According to Hodgson, the Ottomans and the Muslims of the Indian Ocean "had themselves matched the Portuguese technical advantages and had succeeded in containing them, reducing them to one element among others in the multinational trading world of the Southern Seas".[22] Both Hentsch and Hodgson concur that "something happened in sixteenth century Europe which was to leave its imprint on society as a whole, something which happened nowhere else".[23] What were the influences that shaped the course of history? Was it the European

Renaissance, the great discoveries, the rise of mercantilism leading to the Industrial Revolution, or the pursuit of individualism, humanism, and a return to the original Greek sources? Despite lingering fears of the Ottoman Empire's expansion, significant transformations were taking place in the economic and scientific realms of the Western world by the end of the sixteenth century. These transformations ultimately propelled Christian European powers to global dominance within a span of two centuries.[24] The key factor behind Europe's success was its commercial dynamism, which paradoxically stemmed from its lack of unity and fostered intense competition in both trade and military endeavours. The economic growth of the Franks, driven by the exploration of new markets and resources in the New World, pitted them against the Ottomans in an economic conflict that ultimately resulted in the Ottoman Empire's decline. It is worth noting that while both Eastern Europe and the Islamic world experienced growth, European growth rates accelerated at a faster pace. According to Braudel, the demise of the Ottoman Empire was evident:

> The 16th century saw her final defeat in the course of an unprecedented economic upheaval when the opening up of the Atlantic destroyed the age-old privilege of the Levant which for a time had been the sole repository of the riches of the 'Indies'.[25]

Europe's shift in economic and political ambitions towards the Atlantic had a significant impact on how Europeans perceived the Orient. The European mindset gradually accepted the presence of the Turks in southeastern Europe, justifying it based on their presence in America. The expansionist endeavours of Europe in the sixteenth century resulted in a society divided into wealthy and influential dynasties, such as England, France, Italy, and Spain, and a burgeoning population of impoverished individuals in Islamic lands. The true extent of this disparity was unveiled in the seventeenth century.[26]

By the conclusion of the sixteenth century, the notions of European culture and heritage underwent a transformation as they traversed the Atlantic, incorporating North America into the expanding concept of the "West". Consequently, the term "Western" gradually gained a more widespread significance in the subsequent centuries, culminating in its zenith during the latter half of the 20th century.

The frontier of the Muslim Other in the 16th century

If we are able to establish the European border of the Ottoman Empire, we can effectively distinguish between the Orient and the Occident. Braudel has difficulty determining that division, as he calls it the "immutable barrier which runs between Zagreb and Belgrade [...]"[27] Similarly, for Hentsch, this is also very troubling because "the Ottomans, heirs of Byzantium, stabilised their European dominions at the same longitude," as the Romans.[28] Can we conclude that the western frontier of the Hellenic world, which was established by Rome, Byzantium, and eventually Istanbul, serves as the dividing line between the Occident and the Orient? It is important to acknowledge the confusion surrounding this "immutable barrier". The Eastern Mediterranean has traditionally been associated with the Orient, but the meaning has evolved over time. For instance, many Western historians consider ancient Greece as part of inner Eurasia, despite its location on this perplexing longitude. However, as European focus shifted towards the Atlantic during the fifteenth and sixteenth centuries, and the Turks expanded their territories from the Balkans to Algiers, various concepts of Europe and the Other emerged: "the Mediterranean and Atlantic, Catholic and Protestant, Western and Eastern".[29] By the conclusion of the sixteenth century, the term "Turk" had become interchangeable with "Muslim". Although the Ottoman Turks may have been acknowledged as a form of Europeans during this period, they were far from being fully assimilated into every aspect of the European way of life. The Europeans were greatly influenced by the grandeur of the Sublime Porte, leaving a lasting impact on them due to its overpowering presence.[30] However, during the late sixteenth century, a significant shift occurred in the ecological and historical underpinnings of Islamic culture. This marked a turning point where the Orient ceased to fulfil the intellectual aspirations of a world that was becoming more cosmopolitan and driven by commerce. Instead, it encountered a completely transformed world, characterised by a cosmopolitanism rooted in entirely new foundations.[31]

As the sixteenth century came to a close, "from myth and map, chorography, history and survey, Europe passed into the mind".[32] Europe began to witness the emergence of a collective European identity among the educated and privileged individuals within Christian societies. As early as 1516, Thomas Moore highlighted the political dynamics within Europe in his work, *Utopia*. This marked a significant turning point as Europe sought to explore and understand itself through interactions with the 'Other'. According to Hale, "By 1600 a concern for 'them' had become marginalised by a clamant interest in 'us'".[33] The Europeans started to contemplate their own identity more deeply, particularly when their curiosity about the people and customs of other continents led to comparisons. The emergence of the Reformation, the rise of humanism, the spread of secular ideology, the growth of mercantilism, and the era of exploration and expansionism all contributed to instilling a sense of Europeanness and unity within Christendom. However, the shift from 'Christendom' to 'Europe' as a secular term of identification did not entail the eradication of the Christian element. The profession of Christianity remained necessary and, in the eyes of most individuals, even more significant than being European. This newfound strength of Europe marked the beginning of viewing the 'Other' through a lens of superiority.

CHAPTER 7

EUROPEAN PERCEPTIONS OF ISLAM AND THE OTTOMAN TURKS IN THE SEVENTEENTH CENTURY

The differences between the Turks and the Europeans were significant: Europeans engaged in extensive global exploration, conquered America, and initiated the slave trade, while the Turks remained confined within the borders of their land empire and accepted peace terms imposed by Europe for the first time. Europe not only established the foundation for its economic supremacy but also started perceiving the world from a distinct perspective. Islam and the Ottoman Empire were now viewed as subjects to be conquered, subjugated, traded, exploited, or simply studied by Europe. This chapter explores the European viewpoints on Islam and the Ottoman Turks in the seventeenth century, analysing them from a standpoint of superiority that emerged following the decline of the Ottoman threat.

During the seventeenth century, as more and more people travelled to the East, the Orient started to be seen as a fascinating and intriguing place. It marked the beginning of a period where the Orient became a subject of comparison and contemplation, serving as both a window and a mirror. Although Europe had not yet fully dominated the Orient, there was still a certain level of control: Europe had trading rights in the Levant, its merchants and traders journeyed to the ports of the Ottoman Empire and the Porte in search of new economic opportunities, ambassadors and consuls had permanent residences in Pera, Istanbul, and the number of travellers to this exotic land continued to rise. While orientalism emerged in the nineteenth century, it actually predates Europe's initial incursion into the Levant since the time of the Crusades.

Orient of the Seventeenth Century Observers

Paul Hazard defined the seventeenth and eighteenth centuries as the "crisis of European consciousness".[1] This was the era, according to Foucault, where the thoughts of the seventeenth and eighteenth centuries had "no real chasm anywhere separating the two periods".[2] In the eyes of seventeenth century Europe, the Turks were perceived as no longer posing a threat. It was believed that they had no intentions of expanding their empire beyond its borders, rendering them insignificant. Over the course of two centuries, Europe experienced a significant transformation in its perception of itself and its curiosity about the history of other civilisations. The European monarchs maintained peaceful relations with one another, which greatly influenced their exploration of foreign lands and contributed to the development of their own identity. The 17th century witnessed a surge in global exploration, with Europe envisioning a comprehensive plan for the world. Travellers documented their voyages and provided detailed descriptions of the lands they encountered. During this period, the focus of exploration shifted towards the Turkish Empire, which became the epitome of the Orient for European scholars. Religious differences and notions of heresy were no longer the primary concerns. Instead, the Turks assumed a mythical political role in the European mindset, serving as a catalyst for the idea of a united Europe. The Europeans began to believe that the disintegration of the Ottoman Empire was necessary for the realisation of European unity. However, this dream would only materialise two centuries later, when the victorious Allied powers entered Istanbul in 1919 following the Ottoman Empire's defeat in World War 1.

One of the least known intellectuals of the seventeenth century is the French political writer, Émeric Crucé (1590-1648). His pioneer work on international relations, *Nouveau Cynée* (1623), is the first major treatise advocating for universal peace and global free trade among nations. Published anonymously, it proposed a pacifist international utopia, the Senate of Nations, to replace warfare with diplomacy. Crucé argued that rejecting aggressive expansionism would lead to peaceful coexistence and significant material wealth, regardless of geographical or religious differences.[3] Crucé and his supporters advocated for the participation of the Ottomans in the peace negotiations, even going so far as to include the Sultan in his Senate of Nations, ranking him below the Pope.[4] For Crucé, the inclusion of the Sultan was significant because the Turkish monarch occupied the seat of the Eastern Roman Empire.[5] Conversely, many others argued that achieving peace required sacrificing the interests of the Turks. Although Crucé's work received considerable immediate recognition at the time, inspiring many writers to explore the theme of peace, it later fell into obscurity.[6] Moreover, the European imperial powers displayed blatant hypocrisy as each monarch sought to outshine the others in securing more advantageous trade and economic benefits from the Porte.

During their journeys to the Orient, European explorers not only encountered the Turkish Empire, its diverse population and meritocratic structure, but also discovered the characteristics of Persia and its people. However, this diversity was an integral part of the broader concept of the Orient or Levant. For European travellers, their curiosity about the Orient held greater significance than their economic interests. Initially, these travellers returned home with detailed accounts of their observations of the Other. Later on, they even managed to bring back physical artefacts such as sculptures, bas-reliefs, and obelisks. The combination of these travellers' observations and the historical knowledge of the Arab and Turkish peoples eventually led to the creation of the earliest comprehensive work on the Orient - the Bibliotheque Orientale in 1697. In terms of historical records, there were over two hundred voyages to the Orient throughout the seventeenth century.

During the years 1655 to 1659, Jean de Thevenot (1633-1667) embarked on a journey to Turkey. He held great admiration for the Turks due to their unwavering commitment to Islam and their remarkable religious tolerance towards various communities, including Christians and

Jews. Recognising the prevailing biases in Europe during that era, Thevenot felt compelled to rectify these misconceptions. According to Thevenot:

> Many in Christendom believe that the Turks are great devils, barbarians and faithless people, but those who have known them and conversed with them have a different sentiment; for it is certain that the Turks are good ... honest people [...][7]

At the same time Thevenot saw things he did not like about the Turks. In his travels account, Thevenot writes, "And in regard to their vices, they are supremely arrogant ... show scorn ... toward all other nations ... little involved toward the sciences ... strongly inclined to love ... brutal nature ... and ... great sodomites".[8] He does, however, say that although the Turks are little inclined toward the sciences, they have their doctors of law.[9] But putting these last words aside, to Thevenot the Turks "are a proud people, conscious of their strength and valour". When Thevenot travelled to Egypt he described these people as "dogs" and "slaves" of the Turks and later in his trip to Persia he mentioned the decadence and depravity of the shah's court and the ill-built and dreary capital, Isphahan.[10] Jean Simeon Chardin (1699-1779), however, is more conciliatory towards Persia and went as far as declaring that "after the Christians of Europe, they are the most learned people in the world, without excepting the Chinese".[11] But he concluded that the Persians like the Turks "would be much greater had they the excellent methods of ... Europe [...]"[12] A century ago, it would have been inconceivable to comment on the perceived absence of method among the peoples of the Orient. In the European mindset, a comparison with the Orient led to the belief that Europe was more "modern" and "civilised" than its counterpart. This laid the foundation for the debate surrounding the notion of "oriental despotism". However, a more thorough analysis of the Ottoman administration reveals a notable constraint on the authority of the Ottoman sultan—namely, the Sharia, or Sacred Law of Islam. This legal framework asserted its supremacy over the sultan and was beyond his capacity to amend. Even if he violated its provisions through force, he could not damage it; it remained unchanged. The sultan knew that he must not transgress too often or touch certain matters, otherwise, he would be deemed unfit for the throne. The Sacred Law shared the loyalty of his Muslim subjects; it required consultation before executing a criminal or engaging in war with an enemy. It also claimed a significant portion of his lands' revenues, controlling the imposition of general taxation and causing financial difficulties. Furthermore, it protected his Christian subjects from his attempts to forcefully subjugate them. The Sharia influenced his mindset, leading him to give up harmless pleasures while supporting him in executing capable and worthy brothers and sons. The Sharia acted as a rigid constitution that could not be amended. It aimed to regulate matters indefinitely. Although it could be slightly modified through legal interpretation, it was likely one of the most unchanging systems in human history. The sovereign had no authority to modify it in any way. Therefore, constrained by an unalterable constitution, deep-rooted laws and institutions, and the conservative customs of the people, the power of the Ottoman sultan could only be exerted in specific directions. Like the Ruling Institution, the Muslim Institution contained and embodied an educational system which was of its essential structure. Through it, great majority of the members of the institution, including all who expected promotion, were required to pass; accordingly, they bore as a body the name Ulema, or learned men. The *mektebs* or schools taught Arabic, reading and writing and the Qur'an; the *madrasah* have a course of ten studies resembling the Seven Arts of the West; the law schools taught the group of sciences connected with the Qur'an and Sharia and including both law and theology. A number of the Ulema who had finished the law course, and who at some previous time had chosen to become counsellors and jurists rather than take up the more severe and active judicial career, constituted a distinct body, the muftis. The mufti of Istanbul had the title of Sheik-ul-Islam assigned to him by Mehmed II. The Mufti was definitely constituted by Süleyman the Magnificent the head of the Ulema; and as such outranked all officials of government. Sixteenth century Westerners compared the Mufti with a cardinal but more often with the pope. The Mufti could give responses only when his opinion was asked. He was frequently consulted by the sultan as to the conformity of proposed *kanun* or laws with the Sacred Law. In his hands rested the extreme responsibility of pronouncing that a sultan had transgressed the Sacred Law and ought to be deposed. He exercised a function similar to that of a Supreme Court. In reality, the muftis occupied the most influential position in the Muslim Institution and perhaps the Ottoman state. They constituted the conservative, regulative force in the Ottoman state. They were to contribute very largely to the empire's durability, which despite frightful shocks, disasters and losses was to continue far beyond the expectation of the world. The Ulema accomplished much toward building the Ottoman state into a solid structure and toward maintaining it against enemies without and within.

The issue of objectivity is raised when considering the accounts of travellers to the Levant. However, these journeys bring up the essential matter of distance and disparity, ultimately leading to the emergence of a poorly constructed concept of the Orient. It can be argued that the primary motivations behind any voyage are to seek self-discovery and reinforce preexisting beliefs and principles. In the context of a seventeenth-century voyage to the Orient, it was an exploration of European identity. As Chardin claims:

> [...] Asia is not like Europe ... In the Orient ... everything and everywhere is constant.[13]

Chardin emphasises that, in the Orient, only religion has remained unchanged for the last two millennia. Consequently, Europe started rationalising its voyages to a stagnant world that embodied the past, serving as a tangible reminder of history. This mindset undeniably suggested that the Other, representing non-European cultures, was distinct from Europe. However, it is important to recognise that during this period, the Other was still acknowledged and valued for its small acts of kindness, generosity, and overall goodness.

In his play *Bajazet*, the seventeenth century French playwright Racine, endeavours to bring the Orient, specifically the Turks, into the spotlight, despite the absence of any actual royal exchanges between

France and Turkey. Racine exerts considerable effort to bestow dignity upon his Turkish characters during their portrayal on the stage. His frustration becomes obvious: "We have so few points of contact with the princes and other persons who live in the Seraglio, that we regard them, as it were, as people who live in a different age from ours".[14] Hence, Racine considers objectivity as an essential element in his depiction of Turkish characters and society, "The main thing I was concerned with was not to alter anything in the manners of the customs of the nation".[15] He even goes one step further and learns Turkish and inserts it into his play. Racine was undoubtedly aware of the French perspectives on the Turks - a people deemed to be living in a different era. His argument was that Turkey, just like the Ancients, is an integral part of the landscape. By this point, the portrayal of the Orient in literature had become quite common. During this period, it became possible to objectively study the Other, especially as Islam and its ideology were no longer seen as entirely erroneous. Despite the existence of anti-Islamists, anti-Arabists, and anti-Turks, Avicenna's work continued to be highly respected by physicians in Europe.

Orient is the gateway to Europe and Asia

At the political level Gottfried Wilhelm Leibniz (1646-1716) claimed that the Orient must be treated severely, because for him the Orient:

> [...] is the link, the gateway, the barrier, the key the only possible entry point into two parts of the world, Asia and Africa. It is the place where contact is made, the common market of India, on the one hand, and Europe on the other.[16]

Hence, the significance of the Other for Europe was primarily strategic and secondarily economic. Leibniz expressed his disapproval of the Turks and their incapacity to protect Egypt due to its vulnerability. In 1672, he suggested a voyage to Egypt, a remarkable proposal made 126 years before Napoleon. This visionary idea, a century ahead of its time, marked the unsuccessful beginning of the Eastern Question. Leibniz's perspective on the Turkish weakness not only contradicted Chardin but also Thevenot, who acknowledged the Porte's political astuteness.

Nevertheless, Leibniz delved deeper into his observations of the Turks. According to Leibniz:

Though they [the Turks] be the dullest-witted of men, there are to be found a considerable number of renegades [Christians] who might easily instruct them in all divine and human sciences in which the Christians are versed.[17]

Leibniz was judging the Turkish civilisation against that of Christian European culture, "[...] Arts are not honoured; the inhabitants make no effort to improve cultivation of the land, nor do they attempt to build structures that might endure".[18] Leibniz's evaluation of Turkish civilisation in relation to Christian European culture was notably critical, asserting that the arts were undervalued and that there was insufficient effort directed towards agricultural improvement and the construction of enduring structures. This viewpoint embodies the hubristic attitude characteristic of nineteenth-century imperialism, positioning Leibniz more as a forerunner to the subsequent century than as a true representative of the Enlightenment. As a result, by the end of the seventeenth century, a cultural schism had developed, differentiating Europeans from non-Europeans and categorising the so-called 'civilised' against the 'barbarians.' Leibniz was convinced that Europe epitomised global civilisation and culture, in stark contrast to what he perceived as the lack of civilisation among the Turks.

In conlcusion, the concept of the 'Terrible Turk' and its related notions gradually developed within the European consciousness over a span of two centuries. By the end of the seventeenth century, there was an increasing European fascination with travelling, observing, and analysing the political, social, and cultural frameworks of other nations. This burgeoning interest also resulted in political interventions in the affairs of these countries, exemplified by the implementation of Capitulations on the Sublime Porte. These Capitulations functioned not only as an economic strategy for Europeans against the Ottoman Empire from the seventeenth century onward but also as a political tool during the height of European imperialism in the nineteenth century, enabling them to assert their influence in the region.

CHAPTER 8

BIRTH OF MAN'S HUBRIS
THE AGE OF ENLIGHTENMENT

Ahmed Paul Keeler in *Islam & The West: A New Narrative for the Age of Crises* argues that around the year 1000CE, the world was undergoing significant changes. Towns were beginning to form near monasteries, trade was becoming more active, and kings were strengthening their territories and authority. In 1054, the papacy split from Byzantium due to doctrinal differences, leading to the launch of the First Crusade against Islam in 1095. Western Christendom was gaining power and confidence, with its encounter with the Islamic world playing a crucial role in its cultural and intellectual development. The Crusades were occurring in Spain and the Holy Land, and the conquest of cities by the Crusaders resulted in the return of captive engineers and craftsmen to Christendom, contributing to an extensive building program within the Church. This led to the construction of numerous magnificent cathedrals, abbeys, and parish churches in the new Gothic tradition across Europe, symbolising the dominance of the sacred over the secular.[1]

The Church's influence was growing as it amassed vast land holdings and incredible wealth in treasure, blurring the lines between cardinals, bishops, and temporal lords. Tensions arose between the Church and monarchs, exemplified by the murder of St. Thomas a Becket in 1170 in

England. King Henry II's efforts to assert control over the Church were met with resistance from St. Thomas, whose martyrdom elevated him to one of the most revered saints in Western Christendom. This event played a significant role in solidifying the Church's position as the ultimate authority for the next three centuries.[2]

Ultimately, the authority of the Church was seized by the power of kings. In England, Henry VIII assumed leadership of the Church and sought retribution against St Thomas a Becket; his remains were unearthed and burned, and a royal decree declared that he was to be considered a traitor rather than a saint from that point forward. After Henry VIII took control of the Church, he disbanded and demolished nearly a thousand significant abbeys, priories, convents, and friaries. One-third of England's wealth was absorbed into the Royal treasury. The shrines of the saints in abbeys, cathedrals, and churches were dismantled and their remains scattered. Entire social structures of education, labour, and assistance for the poor and sick were eradicated along with the structures. There had never been a self-inflicted destruction by a society to rival it. The thousand-year contemplative core of Christianity in England was torn apart.[3]

The kings exceeded their rightful authority, consolidating more power until absolute monarchies took shape. Charles V in Spain, Charles I in England, Louis XIV in France, and Peter the Great in Russia all ascended to this position. The authority of these new sovereign rulers and the dominance of the secular over the sacred were built upon a new political structure that emerged from the conflicts within Christendom during the Reformation - the sovereign state.[4]

The Germanic lands, divided into numerous principalities and bishoprics, were the site of the most intense warfare between Catholic and Protestant forces. The Peace of Westphalia in 1648 marked the end of the Thirty Years War and allowed each state to choose its form of Christianity, with the decision being accepted by other states. This led to the emergence of the sovereign nation state, fundamentally altering the individual's identity. The collapse of Christendom shifted the primary unifying identity from Christian to a quasi-sacred national identity, with other factors such as the relationship between subjects and rulers and local attachment to place also playing a role.[5]

An artificial construct emerged following the decline of Christendom. Within this fresh framework, individual societies that shared a common language, religion, and history, along with defined geographical boundaries, thrived. With the rise of centralised power and advancements in communication systems, a process of standardisation unfolded, leading to a diminishing diversity within regions. Portugal, Spain, France, England, and the Netherlands emerged as the initial sovereign states, ultimately shaping and dominating the global landscape. However, the world they influenced was characterised by its multi-ethnic, multi-lingual, multi-cultural, multi-religious, and highly intricate nature. The enforcement of the European nation-state model would prove to be a catalyst for creating unstable and irrational political entities, perpetuating ongoing conflicts and oppression.[6]

The despotic reign of the absolute monarchs eventually incited uprisings and revolts, leading to the eradication of monarchy or its relegation to a mere ceremonial status with waning influence. Power was then transferred to the populace, with democracy emerging as the new guiding principle. Amidst the fervour of the revolution, the philosophers and scholars of the Enlightenment period envisioned a world where mankind would thrive in a realm of equality, solidarity, and autonomy.[7]

Martin Luther laid the groundwork for the defining features of Western civilisation by empowering the individual with sovereignty. Richard Rex delves into this concept in his book, *The Making of Martin Luther* that Luther's fundamental doctrine of "justification by faith alone" was designed to provide every individual believer with complete assurance of receiving God's grace and favour. The inherent individualism associated with what would eventually be recognised as '"the personal relationship with God" became ingrained in the essence of liberal Protestantism, subsequently influencing various aspects of Western culture.[8]

Immanuel Kant (1724-1804) solidified the concept of individual autonomy in his explanation of the Enlightenment:

> Enlightenment is man's emergence from his self-imposed immaturity. Immaturity is the inability to use one's understanding without guidance from another. This immaturity is self-imposed when its cause lies not in lack of understanding, but in lack of resolve and courage to use it without guidance from another. *Sapere Aude!* [dare to know] "Have courage to use your own understanding!"—that is the motto of enlightenment. [9]

The relinquishment of control was a response to the misuse of authority by tyrannical monarchs and the ongoing religious conflicts within Christianity. Kant's empowerment of the individual with a fundamentally subjective rational authority would lead to significant repercussions in the future. As a Pietist Lutheran, he could not foresee the implications of removing faith from the equation and setting religion, along with its ethical restrictions, aside.[10] Friedrich Nietzsche would later recognise this shift a century later:

> God is dead! God remains dead! And we have killed him! How can we console ourselves, the murderers of all murderers! The holiest and the mightiest thing the world has ever possessed has bled to death under our knives: who will wipe this blood from us? With what water could we clean ourselves?[11]

Nietzsche predicted that during the 20th century, humanity would face wars of unimaginable horror. He also foresaw that in the 21st century, the very mechanisms he proposed would lead to a crisis of nihilism. His radical proposal was for humans to surpass their limitations and supplant God by evolving into Superman. Paradoxically, this concept inadvertently empowered megalomaniacs who, in the 20th century, brought about the very horrors Nietzsche had foreseen.[12] Furthermore, through the act of killing God, humanity has seized control over the power traditionally held by God and has positioned itself as the supreme being in the universe, embodying the Superman ideal it sought to achieve. This hubris displayed by a created being highlights mankind's utter lack of morality, disrespect for his Creator and disregard for its own mortality. Regrettably, this narrative of secularisation has been unfolding in the Western world for the last five hundred years, rendering the ideological clash with Islam intevitable.

Conclusively, over the past five centuries, the Western world has undergone a significant transformation, beginning with the idea of absolute sovereignty in God, then moving to monarchy and the sovereign nation, and finally progressing to the empowerment of the people through democracy, ultimately leading to the sovereignty of the individual. The Enlightenment period experienced in Europe from late 17th through to early 19th century released the human intellect from the shackles of the authority of the Church. With this emancipation human reason, logic and rationality took centre stage, relegating God to the heavens to oversee matters while leaving humanity to address its own challenges. This has led to a clash of civilisational perspectives between the West and Islam, as the empowerment of individual sovereignty and the dilution of Christian religious values and ethics have diverged from Islam's steadfast monotheistic convictions and principles, posing a persistent challenge by Islam to the "quasi-sacred" Christian West. European philosophers and thinkers considered "enlightened" continued to assess and comprehend the Muslim Other within this specific framework, leading to ongoing alienation and apprehension of the unfamiliar. This phenomenon was particularly notable during the 18th-century Age of Enlightenment.

CHAPTER 9

THE AGE OF ENLIGHTENMENT AND THE ORIENT IN THE EIGHTEENTH CENTURY

As the Ottoman threat diminished, the Europeans endeavoured to comprehend the Ottoman Empire from a standpoint of its emerging dominance over the 'Other'. Throughout the Enlightenment period in the eighteenth century, the Ottomans continued to captivate the attention of European intellectuals and philosophers such as Boulainvilliers, Voltaire, Montesquieu, and Gibbon, evoking both admiration and aversion. The criticism of Ottoman society and culture highlighted everything contrary to European 'values'. The emergence of the term 'despot' and the association of exoticism with the Orient further solidified anti-Turk/anti-Islamic sentiments. Antoine Galland's translation of Arabian Nights in 1704 reinforced this exotic perception of the Orient. Lady Mary Wortley Montagu's travels to Turkey in 1717 further fuelled curiosity and interest in the Ottoman Empire. From Mozart's Turkish music and operas to the Turkish Bath and harem paintings by the French artist Ingres, *Turquerie* became a prevailing trend among the elite circles of European aristocracy. This fluctuation between respect and animosity encapsulates the discussed period and serves as the foundation for the discourse in this chapter.

Europe started to view itself as the epicentre of the world as European influence gradually gained dominance across the globe. According to

Hentsch, "Trapped in the past, the Orient stood as hierarchical second in this well-ordered representation".[1] The history of the Orient has been forcefully taken away, making it now under the control of the West. Consequently, Europe not only assumed dominance over the world, but also took charge of shaping the history of other regions. Despite the lack of unity within Europe, the Orient continued to be perceived as a unified and worldwide threat to its growing supremacy. During the enlightenment period in the eighteenth century, the Orient became a subject of intense discussion and analysis.

Understanding the Other

In 1539, Guillaime Postel established the first Arabic chair in Paris, while Edward Pococke founded a similar chair at Oxford in 1683. These early initiatives paved the way for extensive scholarly research on Islamic history, people, and culture, ultimately leading to the emergence of orientalism. As printing techniques advanced, so did the literary exploration of the "Other". Notably, Jacob Golius (1596-1667) and Thomas van Erpe were the first to publish an Arabic grammar text, followed by Franz Meninski's publication of a Turkish dictionary in Austria in 1680.[2] These milestones marked the birth of scholarly interest in the "Other", which would flourish in the centuries to come.

Over the past three centuries, Europe has largely neglected the substantial contributions of Arab civilisation to its own development. It was during the 18th century that a specific group of intellectuals, referred to as the intelligentsia, began to not only rediscover the historical importance of the Arabs but also to appreciate the significant role of Islam in European history.[3] This period, known as The Enlightenment, marked a notable transformation in religious viewpoints, which included a revised understanding of Islam in Europe. The seventeenth century Biblical critic and priest, Richard Simon (1638-1712), for instance, expressed a belief in the valuable insights provided by Muslim moralists.[4] Historically, Europeans have recognised that the roots of civilisation can be traced back to the pagan Greeks and Romans, with the noteworthy involvement of non-Christian Arabs in disseminating this knowledge to Europe.[5] Consequently, the revival of

Arabo-Islamic culture during this period was both timely and essential.

In the eighteenth century, religion ceased to hold sway over people's lives as the prevailing ideology in Europe was one of global supremacy. The enlightened academics of the time rejected the Christian ideology that had once reigned supreme. As Cassirer explains: "It is not supernatural power nor divine grace which produces religious conviction of man; he himself must rise to and maintain it".[6] The scholar of the eighteenth century held great admiration for Islam.

The perceptive observer of the Other during the eighteenth century, noted that due to the Muslims' profound reverence for God and His divine qualities, led them to abandon the notion of Muhammad as a charlatan. Rather, Muhammad came to be regarded as a sagacious figure who diligently communicated God's message to his adherents. But, according to others, like Pierre Bayle, in 1694, in his *Dictionnaire historique et critique* describes Muhammed as "this infamous impostor [who] swiftly inundated with his false dogmas a vast number of provinces".[7] It is interesting to point out here that Maxime Rodinson describes Bayle's biography of Muhammad as "objective".[8] This raises the question of how this can be possible. The answer lies in taking "an advantage of the official faith" of one's country, as Rodinson exclaims.[9] Boulainvilliers and Voltaire would find themselves in a similar situation in the subsequent years. Nevertheless, Bayle primarily focuses on the Ottoman Empire's tolerance towards its religious minorities.

The dominant belief in Europe during this period was that to grasp the historical context of Arabs and Islam, one must possess a deep understanding of Muhammad and his significant relationship with his followers. According to Hourani, "Whatever European Christians thought of Islam [and Muhammad] they could not deny that it was an important factor in human history, and one which needed to be explained".[10] Consequently, the European fascination with the Other continues to endure. This ideology became ingrained in the works of Boulainvilliers and contemporaries like Simon Ockley (1678-1720), a distinguished professor at Oxford University. Ockley made the initial endeavour to disseminate Oriental studies to the wider audience through his publication, *History of the Saracen Empires*, which was released between 1708 and 1718.[11] As noted by Hazard, Ockley "favoured the Muslim East over the Christian West".[12] Ockley recognised that Muhammad was not merely a visionary prophet, but rather a man of extraordinary accomplishments, who not only safeguarded the knowledge and wisdom of earlier civilisations, but also instigated a moral revolution. In *History of the Saracen Empires*, Ockley states:

> 'I believe in one God, and Mahomet, an Apostle of God' is the simple and invariable profession of Islam. The intellectual image of the Deity has never been degraded by any visible idol; the honor of the Prophet has never transgressed the measure of human virtues; and his living precepts have restrained the gratitude of his disciples within the bounds of reason and religion.[13]

Certain Enlightenment thinkers view Arab civilisation as oscillating between heroic deeds and barbaric actions. Boulainvilliers acknowledges the intelligence and bravery of the Arabs; however, he parallels the 'barbarian' invasions of the Western Roman Empire with the Arab conquests of the seventh century CE. From this analogy, he concludes that the Arabs have inflicted greater calamity, contributing to a rise in lethargy and ignorance in the world.[14] His perspective is largely influenced by his fervent religious convictions. It was in 1688 that the term "fanaticism" first emerged in French literature, a term that would subsequently be linked to the entire Muslim community over the next three centuries.

Conversely, Boulainvilliers recognised the pivotal influence of Muhammad in the annals of Arab history. He was convinced that the Prophet was divinely appointed and served as God's instrument. Boulainvilliers posited that Muhammad dismantled the corrupt Christian authorities in the East, eliminated Greco-Roman paganism, and instituted Islamic governance over the Persians. Thus, he asserted that Muhammad spread "the knowledge of the unity of God from India to Spain and … suppress[ed] every other worship besides his own".[15] Throughout his mission, Muhammad firmly established the concept of unity and a shared heritage among Arab nations. The Arabs not only possessed a unique national identity but also conveyed a message that held universal significance.

Boulainvilliers's viewpoint indicates that both European and Oriental cultures contributed to the development of a universal ideology, albeit at different junctures. This suggests that Islam and Christianity are not inherently opposed. Such a perspective underscores a shift towards recognising and valuing the diversity of others. Nevertheless, Boulainvilliers undermines his own argument by criticising the contributions of Arabo-Islamic civilisation to global history, asserting that they obliterated the arts, sciences, and knowledge by demolishing monuments and libraries. This claim can be contested as it appears to stem from a persistent bias within Western interpretations of the Muslim Orient, which often depict Islam as a historical catastrophe. Notably, Boulainvilliers's writings reveal an unintentional Eurocentrism, yet they are influenced by the universalist principles of the Enlightenment, fostering an appreciation for non-European cultures and societies.

Voltaire, similar to Boulainvilliers, faces challenges in maintaining objectivity regarding Islam. He is often viewed as a supporter of Muslim civilisation, recognising Muhammad as a significant political thinker and the originator of a rational faith. However, Voltaire also criticises Muhammad as the quintessential fraud who manipulates religious narratives to dominate people, while simultaneously exploiting the existing beliefs in his own nation. Furthermore, Voltaire stands out as one of the prominent 18th-century authors who vividly portrayed Turkey in his works, despite never having visited the country. He adeptly transported his fictional characters into the rich and dynamic settings of Turkey.[16]

Voltaire, in his capacity as a historian, strives to maintain objectivity in his analyses. Through his writings, he contrasts his own society with that of other nations, drawing attention to the shortcomings present in Europe. He boldly confronts the widespread misconceptions regarding Turkey in the latter part of the eighteenth century. One prevalent belief was that societies governed by the Ottoman Empire were wholly subservient to the Sultan, both in body and spirit.

However, Voltaire argued that "such a state would collapse".[17] According to Voltaire:

> The Turks are independent and free. They have no class distinction. They only have ranks due to their positions in state duties. They have strong characters and are strong headed but they are also modest and patient.[18]

Consequently, Voltaire not only critiques the social hierarchy of the Ancien Régime but also draws parallels between his own society and that of the Turks, akin to the observations made by Busbecq two centuries earlier.

In contrast to Boulainvilliers, Voltaire expresses a profound respect for the Arabs. The distinguished French philosopher appreciates their kindness, compassion, and generosity. However, he contrasts them with the Hebrews, whom he describes as "that dreadful nation ... adversaries of humanity". He acknowledges the Arabs as significant contributors to the development of world history:

> The Arabs brought their refinements upon Asia, Africa and part of Spain until they were subjugated in turn by the Turks, and, finally, expelled by the Spanish; then ignorance covered all those beautiful regions of the earth; harsh and sombre manners made rude the human race from Baghdad to Rome.[19]

Voltaire's ability to commend both the Turks and the Arabs stemmed from his recognition of the significance of historical perspective.

In the eighteenth century, the term 'despot' began to be utilized as a critique of Islam. This era saw a resurgence of interest in Arab history, prompting Europeans to denounce those who had historically subjugated them and who continued to be perceived as a threat: the Other, particularly the Turks. As a result, the idea of despotism became a crucial element in the heated discussions of the time. For Europe, the Ottoman Empire represented a concrete example of this despotic governance, drawing considerable attention and criticism. Consequently, the concept of despotism played a pivotal role in shaping the European view of the Other.[20]

The depiction of the Turk in literary works reinforced the authoritarian characteristics attributed to Ottoman rulers. In Montesquieu's *Persian Letters*, the character Usbek, while in Turkey, observes: "While the other nations of Europe are every day growing more polished, these people remain in their former ignorance".[21] Montesquieu viewed the Ottoman Empire as fundamentally despotic, although it can be argued that he did not consciously seek to create this impression; rather, it emerged from his subconscious biases. In contrast, Voltaire recognised the absolutist tendencies of his own government under Louis XIV. Montesquieu explicitly emphasises European superiority over the Other, stating, "[…] they have gone before us, and we have surpassed them".[22] Voltaire, similarly believed that progress was confined to Europe, with the Orient and its despotic rulers becoming a subject of discourse in the Western world, largely detached from the actual authority wielded by the Turks or Persians. Notably, the concept of "oriental despotism" later transformed into the term "totalitarianism", which now represents the image of the Other. This observation is particularly important as it underscores the diminished vilification of Muhammad as an individual during the seventeenth and eighteenth centuries.[23] Throughout this period, Muhammad received significantly greater recognition for his remarkable qualities and extraordinary achievements.

Several prominent scholars undertook the endeavour of comparing Christianity and Islam during this period. In 1784, Joseph White, a respected Professor of Arabic at Oxford, commenced an extensive examination of the two faiths, concentrating on their origins, supporting evidence, and impacts. According to White, Muhammad was:

> […] an extraordinary character (of) splendid talents and profound artifice…endowed with a greatness of mind which could brave the storms of adversity (by) … the sheer force of a bold and fertile genius.[24]

Another scholar, Edward Gibbon (1737-94) emerged as the eminent English historian who aimed to provide an impartial and equitable portrayal of the Muslim world. His contributions ensured that the Muslim world held a significant position in the annals of cultural and intellectual history. Gibbon's depiction of Muhammad portrayed him as a benevolent ruler and legislator, characterised by his tolerance and wisdom. According to Gibbon, Muhammad embodied both humility and an elevated stature, rendering him truly remarkable. More than Muhammad as a Prophet, Gibbon was strongly attracted to his success, for "He possessed the courage of thought and action; and although his designs might gradually expand with his success, the first idea which he entertained of his divine mission bears the stamp of an original and superior genius".[25] In addition to Muhammad, Gibbon regards the Qur'an as "a glorious testimony to the unity of God".[26] When comparing Christianity with Islam, Gibbon writes:

> The Mohammedans have uniformly withstood the temptation of reducing the object of their faith and devotion to a level with the senses and imagination of man ... The intellectual image of the Deity has never been degraded by any visible idol.[27]

Gibbon's dissatisfaction with the Church is clearly reflected in this assertion. The impartiality of Gibbon and White in their examination of Islamic history and Muhammad can be ascribed to their reliance on two centuries of European scholarship. This substantial corpus of prior scholarship significantly shaped their unbiased perspectives.

In the latter part of the 18th century, there was a notable transformation in the understanding of the 'Other' narrative, evolving towards a more objective discourse. The Orient was often perceived as stagnant; however, Muslims were not distinctly identified as being different from other cultures. In fact, some individuals even viewed them as superior to Europeans. For example, Thomas Hope (1770-1831), an Englishman, regarded the Turks as equally charitable and trustworthy as himself. This shift represented the emerging viewpoint of the Enlightenment period. The West began to appreciate the Ottoman Orient for its historical contributions, although it did not admire its contemporary condition. It no longer felt threatened by neighbouring cultures, recognising its own superiority in intellectual and scientific achievements. The Other was to be nothing more than "amusement", "exoticism" and "diversion".[28] Some viewed the Age of Enlightenment as the peak of European understanding of the Orient. For Maxime Rodinson: "The 18th century saw the Muslim East through fraternal and understanding eyes".[29]

Islam and the myth of exoticism

The endeavour to establish a more objective understanding of Muslim civilisations resulted in an outcome that differed greatly from what was initially expected. Numerous writers during the seventeenth and eighteenth centuries acknowledged the value and sincerity of Muslim beliefs, and defended Islam against the intolerance and criticism prevalent during the medieval era. However, the literature of this period faced challenges in breaking away from the medieval worldview. This struggle became apparent through the works of European scholars such as Bayle, Boulainvilliers, Voltaire, and others. Consequently, there was a growing interest in Islam and the Arab world during this time, but with a notable difference. Islam was perceived as less threatening compared to Christianity. The eighteenth century witnessed a fascination among Europeans with Oriental literature. This is evident in Antoine Galland's translation of *The Thousand and One Nights* in 1704. According to Galland the Arabian tales demonstrated "how greatly the Arabs surpassed the other Nations in this manner of composition".[30] Galland's translation of the Arabian Nights arrived at an opportune moment, perfectly aligning with the prevailing ambiance of the era, which ultimately led to its triumph. Consequently, he effectively established the literary essence of the Orient for the Occident. According to Robert Irwin:

> The impact of The Arabian Nights on the eighteenth, nineteenth and twentieth century literature is massive. I think there is no book in the world, except the Bible, that had a bigger influence on British literature.[31]

The Arabs' reputation was restored and they were freed from centuries of neglect through Galland's translation of *The Thousand and One Nights*. The Muslims were no longer seen as the Antichrist, and the impact of the *Arabian Nights* was immeasurably significant. Nevertheless, this gave rise to a romanticised perception of the East and the Muslim world, accompanied by a sense of ambiguity.

European visitors, particularly women, were able to enhance the captivating perception of Islam and the Turks by accessing the inner sanctum of the Ottoman court. This occurred at a time when *The Thousand and One Nights* was widely popular, contributing to the creation of a mythical portrayal of the Orient as a realm filled with intrigue, romance, and a symbol of virtuousness, wisdom, and unjustly harmed innocence.[32] Lady Mary Wortley Montagu accompanied her husband, Edward Wortley Montagu, on his diplomatic assignment to Istanbul in February 1717. She remained in Turkey until July 1718 and documented her observations and experiences through a series of letters. According to Croutier, "Her *Turkish Embassy Letters* are perhaps the most authentic and direct experience of the East any foreigner has articulated".[33] Lady Mary was passionate in her letters about Turkey and was aware of the limits of European knowledge of the East. In her letter dated 1 April, 1717, Lady Mary writes about Europe's relations with Turkey, along with her first impressions of Istanbul:

> Tis certain we have but very imperfect relations of the manners and Religion of these people, this part of the world being seldom visited but by merchants who mind little but their own Affairs, or Travellers who make too short a stay to be able to report any thing exactly of their own knowledge [Istanbul is] situated on seven hills, ... showing an agreeable mixture of gardens, pines and cypress trees, palaces, mosques and public buildings, raised one above the another, with as much beauty and appearance of symmetry as you ever saw in a cabinet adorned by the most skilful hands.[34]

Later, the French envoy, Louis Sauveur de Villeneuve (1675-1745) was amazed by the domes of Istanbul's "mosques, rising from within crowns of fire, while an invisible apparatus strung between the minarets made it possible for verses from the Koran to be inscribed in the sky by letters of fire".[35]

Lady Mary, as a woman, enjoyed the unique opportunity to visit numerous households and gain direct knowledge from Turkish women regarding their everyday experiences. Her journey reached its pinnacle when she was granted access to the harems of the Sultan and other prominent pashas, allowing her to satisfy her deepest curiosities. During one of her numerous visits to a harem, Lady Mary corresponded with her sister, Lady Mar, on 18 April 1717, mentioning a girl named Fatima: "[…] of her beauty I was so struck with admiration that I could not for some time speak to her, being wholly taken up in gazing".[36] In addition to her insights into Turkish daily life, Lady Mary documented her journey from Edirne to Istanbul by providing observations on the provincial governance and rural existence in Turkey. She detailed the role of the ulema within the Ottoman administration and society, alongside the captivating performances of the whirling dervishes. Moreover, she examined the qualities and cleverness of Turkish wives, as well as the formidable character of the Janissaries. She also investigated the complexities of mosques and baths, focusing on their interiors and the congregations that gather within them.[37]

Lady Mary Wortley Montagu played a significant role in shaping the prevailing cultural trend of the time, which later became known as *Turquerie* in Europe. Upon her return to England, she introduced numerous elements of *Turquerie*, such as "harem attire, which soon became chic".[38] The extensive correspondence she maintained with the poet Alexander Pope, in which she described the odalisques of the Seraglio Harem and the Turkish hamams (baths), culminated in a body of Oriental literary works and artworks that extended from the late 18th century into the 19th century. Among the contributors to this collection was the esteemed French painter Jean Auguste Dominique Ingres (d. 1867), who created notable pieces such as *La Grande Odalisque* (The Great Odalisque) in 1814 and *Le Bain Turc* (The Turkish Bath) in 1832, both of which vividly conveyed the charm and exotic nature of the Orient. As Alev Croutier states, "In Paris, *Turqueries* became the rage, influencing everything from theatre, opera, painting, and romantic literature to costume and interior design".[39] Consequently, the depiction of the fictional Orient that developed during the 19th century can be seen as a transformation into a feminine representation of the Orient: "a dreamworld of rapture, ecstatic visions and sensual pleasures, and notably one where the male fantasy of limitless power over the female body was realised".[40]

Europe became obsessed with Turkish fashion, embracing harem pants, turbans, satin slippers, and various other stylish accessories. The European aristocracy started adopting the attire of pashas, sultanas, and odalisques. As Croutier explains, "They posed in Turkish costumes for portraits by the popular painters of the period", like the portrait of James Silk Buckingham and his wife in 1816 by Henry Pickersgill.[41] Nargilehs, low divans, and jewelled scimitars gradually transitioned from the homes of the elite to more commonplace settings throughout Europe. The notion of *keyf* (finding fulfilment in idleness) - *dolce far niente* - gained popularity as a philosophy among Europeans, who developed a fondness for serene bliss. Smoking opium and hashish became a means of artistic and spiritual exploration, expanding the boundaries of the romantic mind. Several renowned poetic works by the prominent romantics of that era were composed while under the influence, such as Coleridge's *Kubla Khan*.[42]

Musicians were deeply captivated by the allure of exoticism and its connection to the Orient. Among these composers, Mozart stands out as one who significantly influenced the perception of the Other, particularly through his depiction of the Turkish harem. Through his compositions and others alike, the Europeans' hidden desires and sexual fantasies were brought to light. In Mozart's renowned German opera, "Die Entfuhrung aus dem Serail" [The Abduction from the Seraglio], the portrayal of various aspects of Oriental culture, including music and dance, was remarkably vibrant and served as a saviour for a captivating odalisque in the Seraglio.[43] As Croutier states, "'It was like a scene out of the *Arabian Nights*' became the cliche phrase used to describe any amazing, rich, peculiar experience".[44] Furthermore, the introduction of Turkish instruments brought about a sense of novelty. Instruments such as the "tambura granda" and "tamburo turco", which are large drums, as well as the "triangoli" or cymbals, were occasionally mentioned by Mozart as "Turkish Music" in his scores. It is worth noting that prior to the influence of "Turkish music," the classical orchestra did not include any unpitched instruments. In contrast to instruments like the timpani, Turkish instruments do not produce specific notes but rather create noise with intricate tonal qualities. As Nikolaus Harnoncourt states:

> When, during the course of the 18th century, the menace of Turkish invasion receded, the dangerous, spicy sounds and wicked, exotic colours became, as it were, succulent morsels to be savoured by connoisseurs.[45]

The influence of the *Turquerie* phenomenon extended from fashion to music, significantly shaping European high culture. When Mozart incorporated Turkish instruments into his opera "Entführung", Croutier noted that it introduced entirely "new elements of humanism and ethics".[46] Mozart's use of percussion instruments not only highlighted the conflicts among his characters but also symbolised the cultural tensions between the Western and Eastern worlds. This cultural clash was characterised by a sense of aggression, as the drums were played continuously to support one faction while opposing another. The escalating intensity of the music amplified the courage and fury of one side, while simultaneously instilling fear in the opposing side. The audience at the premiere of "Entführung" was notably surprised when the Turkish instruments were introduced, especially following eight enchanting and exhilarating bars in C-major that had been played softly. Suddenly, the unrelenting and brutal military power of the Turkish instruments erupted.[47] In Act 3, Selim Pasha, Mozart's Turkish character, astonishes everyone by displaying an act of mercy, allowing the two couples to escape from the Seraglio, thereby challenging the perceptions of those who doubted his benevolence. Selim further conveys his noble intentions by sending a message to Belmonte's father, emphasising that responding to injustice with acts of kindness brings greater satisfaction than retaliating with further wrongdoing.[48] As for Constanze, Selim Pasha hopes that she will never regret rejecting his love. Ultimately, the foreigners start spreading the word about the Turkish Pasha, whom they initially perceived as barbaric:

> *Never will I forget your benevolence;*
> *For ever shall I sing your praises.*
> *In every place, at every time*
> *I shall proclaim you great and noble.*[49]

In the eighteenth century, European public and literary discourse was significantly influenced by a compelling representation of the Orient. This representation conjured an enchanting tableau characterised by vivid colors, harems, seraglios, turquoise domes, and towering white minarets that appeared to ascend towards the heavens. Additionally, the imagery encompassed viziers, eunuchs, and odalisques, alongside women held captive and subjected to the dominance of their captors, motivated by carnal desires.

In conclusion, alongside the encyclopaedists of the Enlightenment, the observers of the Orient maintained a realistic, positive, and universalist perspective. Consequently, the eighteenth century concluded with a deep respect and admiration for the Other, fostering a sense of understanding.[50] This understanding, however, also contributed to bolstering European confidence in their perceived superiority over the Other. Nevertheless, this fluctuation between admiration for Islamic culture and the enigmatic East gave rise to a perilous portrayal of the 'Other'. The final decades of the 18th century and the beginning of the 19th century witnessed a proliferation of Orientalist paintings influenced by the *Tales of the Arabian Nights*. European artists embarked on journeys to the Islamic East, depicting romanticised interpretations that captured its enchanting yet perilous nature. According to Bettany Hughes:

> I think what's fascinating about this time is that the East is either portrayed as very very good or very very bad. So you have these two versions: you have the bloodthirsty Moor or the bloodthirsty Turk. And then you have this romantic idea of this sensuous mystical place where

> everything is wonderful, where the air smells sweet. This is a time of colonialism. It's almost as if the West is saying 'We are now in charge of portions of the East, we're almost unveiling it'. Also, it is a very difficult place to get hold of – it does have its own mystery. I think that's what's being realised in the painting. Even though the West is physically in Eastern lands, it still can't quite grab the essence of what the East is.[51]

The supremacy of the West in the realms of politics, economy, technology, and culture became increasingly apparent with the emergence of Orientalism and the establishment of European global hegemony during the nineteenth century. However, the mysterious allure of the East persisted in captivating the Western imagination.

CHAPTER 10
A CRITIQUE OF ORIENTALISM

Between 1500 and 1750, European culture underwent considerable advancements in social pluralism, economic development, and technological innovation. Huntington notes that during this two-and-a-half-century period, "all of the Western Hemisphere and significant portions of Asia were brought under European rule or domination".[1] However, by the late eighteenth century, populations in the American colonies, Haiti, and much of Latin America began to resist direct European authority. Despite this, the latter part of the nineteenth century witnessed a resurgence of European imperialism, which aggressively established Western governance over nearly the entire African continent and most of the Middle East, with the exception of Turkey. In 1800, Great Britain and France controlled thirty-five percent of the world's land area. This figure increased to sixty-seven percent by 1878, and by 1914, alongside Italy and Germany, Western European nations dominated an astonishing eighty-four percent of the globe. This percentage further increased in 1920 when Britain, France, and Italy divided the Ottoman Empire among themselves. The success of European expansion can be largely attributed to their technological innovations and military strength, which enabled them to establish dominance and conquer vast territories. The advancements in warfare during the period from 1500 to 1750 facilitated the West in creating the world's first global empire, exerting control over extensive regions.[2] As Samuel P. Huntington observes:

> The West won the world not by the superiority of its ideas or values or religion (to which few members of other civilisations were converted) but rather by its superiority in applying organised violence. Westerners often forget this fact; non-Westerners never do.[3]

Edward Said's book, *Orientalism*, clearly expresses the idea that European dominance and understanding of the Other stemmed from a sense of superiority.[4] This concept gave rise to Orientalism in the nineteenth century. The term Orientalism was first used in English in 1779 and later in French in 1799. Nevertheless, it is crucial to recognise that European awareness of the Other dates back to the Middle Ages, predating the nineteenth century.

Hentsch observes that there is a "correlation between the construction of orientalism as a systematic, specialised science, and the European conquest of the Orient".[5] Critics of Edward Said argue that *Orientalism* encapsulates the entirety of the West. However, Said refutes the accusations that he portrays "the entire West as an enemy of the Arab and Islamic peoples who endured Western colonisation and prejudice".[6] He defends his perspective by emphasising his interest in the "extension of post-colonial concerns to the problems of geography".[7] Said regarded Orientalism as a discipline that involved "re-thinking what had for centuries been perceived as an unbridgeable chasm separating East from West".[8] Bernard Lewis, a prominent critic of Edward Said, contends that Said manipulates both the geographical and historical aspects of Orientalism to substantiate his argument. Lewis argues that Said prioritises the contributions of British, French, and American scholars over those of their German, Italian, and Russian counterparts.

According to Said, the German input in Oriental studies merely served to refine and elaborate upon the methodologies developed by Britain and France, which were responsible for gathering texts, myths, ideas, and languages from the Orient.[9] In contrast, Lewis finds this assertion to be absurd, stating that any account of Arabic studies in Europe that excludes German contributions is as illogical as a history of European music or philosophy that omits them.[10] In response, Said critiques Lewis for perceiving Islam as "an anti-Semitic ideology" rather than simply "a religion".[11] This is because:

> [...] according to Lewis, Islam does not develop, and neither do Muslims; they merely are, and they are to be watched, on account of that pure essence of theirs, which happens to include a long standing hatred of Christians and Jews.[12]

Said and Lewis express mutual criticism towards each other. What is significant is that, according to Edward Said:

> Orientalism at least had the merit of enlisting itself openly in the struggle, which continues of course in "West" and "East" together.[13]

Is Orientalism a valid concept? Maxime Rodinson argues against its existence. He views Orientalism, along with Sinology, Turkology, and related fields, as "scientific disciplines defined both by the object of their study and by the direction that study takes, such as sociology, demography, political economy, linguistics, anthropology, ethnology or the various branches of general history".[14] Consequently, these disciplines can be employed to analyse cultures and regions across various historical contexts. For Edward Said, however:

> [...] without examining Orientalism as a discourse one cannot possibly understand the enormously systematic discipline by which European culture was able to manage - and even produce - the Orient politically, sociologically, militarily, ideologically, scientifically, and imaginatively during the post-Enlightenment period.[15]

Said firmly emphasises that Orientalism is a construct rooted in a political doctrine imposed upon the Orient, which was perceived as weaker than the West, thereby conflating the Orient's distinctiveness with its vulnerability.[16] For Said, Orientalism represents a discourse of control, specifically reflecting the European subjugation of the Mediterranean Orient. He argues that the foundational concepts of Orientalism can be understood through this origin and its instrumental role, which disregards the culture and history of the oppressed peoples and overlooks the resistance they have mounted against such domination. The principles of Orientalism serve to further this agenda of control or imperialism.[17]

Fred Halliday in his article, *Orientalism and its Critics*, states that Orientalism as a discourse is contestable. He cautions any scholar or student of History not to accept this ism "which identifies such a widespread and pervasive single error at the core of a range of literature".[18] Halliday critiques Edward Said's application of the term, suggesting that Said endows it with "an almost metaphysical power to pervade very different epochs and genres of expression".[19] In doing so, Halliday recognises that Orientalism loses its analytical and explanatory effectiveness.[20]

Halliday asserts that Said's Orientalism offers a unique portrayal of the Middle East, characterised by imperialist and oppressive narratives. However, he also points out that such racist and imperialist discourses are prevalent regarding "all subject peoples, whether they are Islamic or not, and there is nothing to choose between them".[21] In his critique, Halliday implies that Said's analysis is overly subjective, allowing his personal feelings regarding Palestine to overshadow his academic impartiality, particularly in his assertion that the injustices faced by one group are more significant than those experienced by others. To illustrate his point, Halliday references the indigenous peoples of America, highlighting that the European "conquest was also presented as a crusade" and this conquest "was far worse than that of the people of 'Islam'".[22]

Furthermore, Fred Halliday acknowledges that a significant portion of contemporary social science concepts originates from Western Europe and the United States, emerging from the historical contexts of imperialism and capitalism. Consequently, he critiques Edward Said's approach to analysing texts generated within this framework, including journalism, travel writing, and literature. According to Halliday:

> Of course, there are similarities and mutual influences; but while one is necessarily fictional activity, without controls in reality or direct links to the acts of administration, domination, exploitation, the former is so controlled. To assume that the same critique of discourses within literature can be made of those within social science is questionable; it may indeed reflect the hubris, rather too diffuse at the moment, of theorists deriving their validation from cultural studies.[23]

By analysing the Middle East through an orientalist lens, Halliday argues that a distorted narrative of the region is created. He asserts that "many of the phenomena analysed in this way are seen elsewhere in the world", emphasising that the Middle East does not possess any unique characteristics that warrant such analysis, "except possibly in the context of myths that are propagated about it, from within and without".[24] Halliday ultimately concludes that the notion of Western hostility towards the Orient, the Arab world, and Islam is a fabricated myth.

It is essential to recognise that the literature and writings produced during the periods of imperialism and capitalism were significantly shaped by these prevailing ideologies. Nevertheless, it is crucial to highlight that the works of orientalists have been instrumental in fostering misunderstandings regarding the Middle East. These misunderstandings continue to endure, reinforcing a negative perception of the Orient among Western audiences. Ignoring Halliday's claims regarding the 'myth' would entail overlooking the profound influence of European imperialism on the destabilising issues currently confronting Middle Eastern countries.

In his review titled "The Critique of Orientalism", Clement Dodd explores whether orientalism, along with its associated cultural and racial perspectives, is primarily responsible for the Western misinterpretation of the Muslim Middle East. He contends that "orientalists have indisputably achieved much by making oriental societies known to the West".[25] The essential inquiry is how this was accomplished. Dodd refutes the idea that orientalists were complicit in an imperialist mindset. According to Dodd:

> This is because, often living and working in universities, they have grown up and participated, first and foremost, in the general tradition of scholarship, a tradition which, inter alia, subjects its own society to critical and evaluative enquiry.[26]

Furthermore, Dodd asserts that any critical assessment and analysis of the Middle East inevitably reflects Western values. He posits that orientalists have become "too immersed in the values of those they are studying. At best an orientalist keeps a foot in both camps, interpreting, however, imperfectly, the East to the West."[27] From an Islamic perspective, this is viewed as an extension of imperialist social science and is seen as a form of racism that serves to reinforce and justify political dominance.[28]

Muslim scholars, such as Asad in his article "Two European Images of Non-European Rule", contend that foreign conquests have inflicted significant damage upon Islam.[29] Conversely, Dodd offers a differing perspective, claiming that the Ottoman Turks caused greater harm to Islam than the imperialist forces. He argues that during Atatürk's leadership, transformative changes were enacted, including the dissolution of the Caliphate, the disbandment of the Ulema, the substitution of Islamic shari'a with European civil law, the closure of dervish orders, and the prohibition of religious education in schools.[30] However, one might challenge Dodd's viewpoint, positing that he fails to recognise the broader implications of Atatürk's reforms, which arguably did not inflict more damage on Islam than the actions of European imperialists. The reforms initiated by Mustafa Kemal illustrate that Islam possesses the capacity for adaptation and can coexist with modernisation, countering the long-held views of numerous Western and Orientalist scholars. Turkey exemplifies a distinctive case in the Middle East, where a largely Muslim nation has adeptly integrated secularism, Western ideals, and modernity while maintaining its Islamic heritage. In recent decades, there has been a shift towards embracing the Turks'

Islamic heritage, yet existing social and political institutions ensure a balance between the Muslim identity and the Western perspective of the nation.

B. A. Roberson, in his article titled "Islam and Europe: An Enigma or a Myth", aligns with numerous other scholars on the topic by asserting that the conclusion of the Cold War and the decline of the communist threat have resulted in a "perceived threat 'vacuum'".[31] He argues that it has become increasingly evident that Islam is viewed as the emerging 'threat'. Since the Iranian Islamic Revolution in 1979, Islam has remained a focal point of attention, highlighted by events such as the American hostages in Iran, the Iran-Iraq War (2003-2011), the assassination of Egyptian President Sadat, the kidnappings of Western hostages by Hezbollah in Lebanon, the Gulf War of 1991, and the Iraq War (2003-2011) aimed at enforcing compliance with United Nations resolutions. Given this context, it is not surprising that Western historians foreshadowed a clash of civilisations between Islam and the West in the new millennium. This perspective, however, tends to reinforce Eurocentrism and does little to foster genuine cultural understanding. Roberson further notes the challenges in defining the concept of 'threat', suggesting that any definition would inherently be subjective. He explains that "the validity of a threat is measured by what could be described as the probabilistic evaluation of intent, capability, and vulnerability, and the process itself does not remain fixed or static".[32] In other words, while the interpretation of threat may be complex, it can be directed towards specific areas, such as personal safety, family, community, nation, state, or the international order.

Roberson, similar to his fellow historians, reflects on the historical encounters between Western civilisation and Islam throughout the Middle Ages. He emphasises the perceived 'threat' that Western civilisation experienced, starting with the Arab incursions and later the Ottoman Turks. This threat posed by Islam to Europe was twofold: physical, particularly in South and Central Europe, and intellectual, pertaining to the ideological influence of Islam.[33] The influence of Islam diminished as the Ottoman threat subsided. Nevertheless, in the late twentieth century, with the resurgence of Islam, the concept of an

'Islamic threat' has reemerged. Roberson claims that, "Exactly what constitutes this threat is not obvious. The form it has taken is multifarious".[34]

In the early 1980s, the Islamic Revolution in Iran and the fatwa issued by Ayatollah Khomeini against Salman Rushdie raised alarms in Europe about the rise of Islamic radicalism. This concern extended beyond Europe, resonating globally, particularly in Britain where Rushdie was forced into hiding. Consequently, discussions surrounding Islam became increasingly sensitive within Western political circles. For example, during the Rushdie Affair, the British government publicly expressed its respect for the Islamic faith through the BBC's World Service, while also reaffirming its steadfast dedication to freedom of expression. However, the Iranian Revolution was perceived by the West as a considerable threat to regional security, stability, and Western interests. Roberson notes, "While Islam formerly was viewed in the West as one of the ideological bulwarks against atheistic communism, in communism's absence Islam is seen as expansionist".[35] Even decades after the Islamic Revolution, the Western world remains apprehensive about the potential spread of this revolution to other Middle Eastern countries. This situation underscores the prevalent misconceptions in the West regarding the true nature of Islam in the region, as well as a tendency to view Islam through a negative lens.

The impact of European presence in Islamic regions throughout the twentieth century has undoubtedly fostered feelings of discomfort, suspicion, and hostility towards the Western world. This phenomenon can be linked to several pivotal events, including the disintegration of the Ottoman Empire, the secularisation of Turkey, and the dissolution of the Caliphate. Furthermore, the mandates established by Britain and France in the former Ottoman territories underscored their strategic interests, often at the expense of the welfare of local populations and political entities. According to Roberson, this period also saw "the emergence of a variety of military, monarchical, and socialist governments girded with and Arab nationalism often adorned with Islamic pretensions".[36] The Arab-Israeli conflict continues to be an unresolved legacy for Middle Eastern governments, which have struggled to attain stability and order while contending with the borders and states delineated by European imperial powers.

The Islamisation of Muslim societies was also witnessed as a result of the politicisation of a certain segment of the Islamic trend during the 1980s and 1990s. Notable examples include the Muslim Brotherhood in Egypt and Jordan, the Islamic Salvation Front in Algeria, and the Welfare Party in Turkey. As regards to the question of threat in this period, Roberson claims:

> [...] if the region gives the impression of volatility, it is not because of the growth of Islamist activity. Rather, this increased Islamist activity is a manifestation of deeply rooted underlying problems in the region that have contributed to this type of response. In the post Cold War era, the basic problems of Third World countries remain ... They still live largely with systems of rule that are, on the whole, strongly dominated by the military and where the traditional distance between the ruler and the ruled has been maintained.[37]

Hence, Roberson argues that rather than viewing Islamist political entities as a 'threat' to the West, it is more beneficial to contextualise them within this framework. As Middle Eastern governments grapple with both internal and external challenges, Islamist groups are gaining traction by proposing alternative solutions to the daily challenges encountered by the populace.

In the late 1990s, immigration surfaced as a significant challenge with social ramifications for Europe. The multicultural character of Europe had become increasingly evident since the conclusion of the Cold War. Both then and now, there exists a prevailing sense of 'fear' among European communities concerning the continually evolving demographics of their nations. For example, Islam ranks as the second largest religion in both France and Germany, and the third largest in Britain, where an Islamic Parliament has also been established since 1992. This functioning political entity aims to improve the circumstances of Muslims and to fundamentally change the societal norms that govern life in these countries. It is crucial to recognise that these

Muslim immigrants relocated to the West primarily to escape economic difficulties or conflict. Over the past four decades, they have demonstrated themselves to be law-abiding residents or guest workers in their new countries. Consequently, the idea that they represent an Islamic 'threat' to Europe in a political context is unfounded.[38] Roberson asserts that Islam does not pose a threat to Europe, as the Islamists represent a fragmented political force within the Middle East:

> There is little chance of a regional Islamic unity being forged because the modern state has become deeply rooted in the region, nor is it likely for numerous Islamic states to combine into a fundamentally hostile bloc against Europe or the West.[39]

Rather, there is a strong possibility that Islam will align more closely with Western economies and enhance its collaboration with the West in order to effectively engage with the globalisation of the world's economies. The initial years of the 21st century have already witnessed this economic trend, although one could contend that the Global South is currently seeking to reduce its dependence on the dollar and diminish its reliance on the West.

The concepts of East and West have their origins in orientalism. However, Rodinson contends that the East should not be regarded as a separate entity. He underscores that the world consists of individuals, nations, societies, and cultures.[40] Similarly, Marshall Hodgson asserts:

> [...] we must leave behind the Westward pattern of history and the "East and West" dichotomy ... and go onto developing means of organising the various types of interregional history, particularly within literate times ... and studying from a consciously interregional point of view [...][41]

This method of historical inquiry is crucial for deepening our understanding of the overall trajectory of human development.

CHAPTER 11

THE ERA OF IMPERIALISM AND THE SUBSERVIENCE OF THE OTHER

EUROPE'S SUPREMACY OVER THE MUSLIM OTHER

The Treaty of Karlowitz, which followed the Ottoman Empire's failed attempt to capture Vienna in 1683, did not significantly alter the power dynamics between Europe and the Ottoman Empire. While it was the first setback for the Ottomans in eastern Europe, it had minimal impact on their borders. However, according to Lewis, "this treaty marked a crucial turning point, not only in the relations between the Ottoman and Habsburg empires, but, more profoundly, between Europe and Islam".[1] For centuries, the Ottoman sultans had been the dominant force in Islam, but this defeat forced them to sign a peace agreement on terms dictated by their enemies, signifying a significant shift in power dynamics.[2] With the waning power of Islam in Europe, the threat of encirclement loomed as the eastern European advance across the steppes from Russia and the western European expansion across the oceans closed in on the Islamic heartlands. These converging forces set the stage for the empire's eventual downfall in the following century. These pincers were in place to close in on the empire in the century to follow.[3] Consequently, the era of new imperialism and European global dominance in the 18th and 19th centuries aimed to eliminate the geographical divide that had long separated Islam and Europe since the Middle Ages. The intention was to educate the "Other" in accordance with Western ideals, thereby reviving the ideological contrast between the two civilisations once colonialism came to an end in the 20th century.

Following the Ottoman defeat in the Russo-Turkish War of 1764 and the signing of the Treaty of Küçük Kaynarca in 1774, the Sublime Porte was compelled to relinquish territory. Catherine II of Russia hailed the unprecedented success of her country.[4] The war proved to be a catastrophic outcome for the Ottomans. Their initial intention was to safeguard Polish independence and maintain the balance of power in Europe, but they were now abandoning Poland to its fate among expansionist neighbours such as Russia, Prussia, and Austria. Furthermore, they were surrendering the Crimea, along with its 1.5 million Turkish inhabitants, to Russia. Naturally, Russia could not have absorbed Poland without offering a portion to its neighbouring powers, as it risked facing a formidable alliance consisting of Turkey, Sweden, Prussia, Austria, and France. Consequently, the Ottoman Empire was reduced to a state confined to the Balkans, having withdrawn from Eastern Europe. In 1783, Prince Potempkin annexed the Crimea to Russia, prompting a revolt among the Crimeans who had anticipated independence. However, Potempkin swiftly quelled the uprising, resulting in the deaths of approximately 30,000 individuals within a matter of months.

The Crimean Peninsula witnessed a tragic fate as numerous Crimeans who possessed vast lands were mercilessly killed and had their properties seized. Subsequently, the first wave of Russian settlers began to arrive in Crimea, leading to a mass exodus of hundreds of thousands of Muslim Crimeans who sought to flee the region. Unfortunately, half of these individuals perished due to diseases and famine, while some were pursued and massacred by Russian soldiers. Those fortunate enough to escape found refuge in the Balkans, Anatolia, and other Ottoman territories. Consequently, the 356-year-long history of the Crimean Khanate came to a sorrowful end. Throughout its existence, Crimea had served as a homeland for Turkic peoples for 15 centuries, including the Huns, Avars, Bulgars, Khazars, Pechenegs, and Kipchaks. Despite Turkey's inability to intervene militarily, it acknowledged the Russian annexation; nevertheless, preparations were intensified to reclaim Crimea. The territorial gains acquired by Russia through treaties significantly influenced European policies regarding future Russian expansions. The Austrians had acquired vast territories from the Turks in previous conflicts, but those lands were predominantly inhabited by Christian communities. However, the situation was different in the Crimea, as the population consisted of Turkish-speaking Muslims who had been living there since before the Mongol conquests of the thirteenth century. This loss was particularly significant for the Ottoman government because it marked the first time they had lost a Muslim territory inhabited by Muslims, which dealt a blow to Muslim pride. On the other hand, the Russians benefited from this situation in terms of trade. They gained the freedom to navigate and engage in commerce in the Black Sea and through the Straits into the Mediterranean.[5]

Russian annexation of Crimea held great significance as it represented a crucial milestone in the Ottoman Empire's commercial integration, with the participation of various European powers throughout the nineteenth century.[6] The territorial changes that occurred during this period were a clear acknowledgment of Russia's newfound influence in a region where the Ottomans had previously held undisputed control for over two centuries.[7] As part of these changes, Russia was granted certain privileges, such as the right to maintain a permanent embassy in Istanbul, alongside the French and Austrians. These concessions facilitated Russia's ability to send agents to regions in southeastern Europe, particularly Greece, where there were disaffected provinces.[8] Additionally, Article 7 of the Treaty of Küçük Kaynarca granted the Russians permission to construct a Russian Orthodox church in Istanbul and allowed representatives of the Russian imperial court to advocate for the interests of the church in the Ottoman capital. Unfortunately, misinterpretations of Article 7 eventually expanded into a perceived right of intervention and protection for all Orthodox Christians within the Ottoman Empire, including those in Arab lands and the majority of Ottoman subjects in the Balkan Peninsula. It is evident that this treaty played a significant role in shaping the patterns of European expansion and penetration in the Middle East during the nineteenth and early twentieth centuries.[9] The Treaty of Küçük Kaynarca is widely recognised as the starting point of the "Eastern Question", a pressing concern for European chancelleries regarding the fate of the Ottoman Empire.

Catherine the Great had formed alliances with Austria in the event of a potential conflict with Turkey. If successful, several territories including Wallachia, Bessarabia, South Podolia, and Bukovina would be united to establish a Romanian state under Russian safeguard. Additionally, Russia would acquire the land between the Dneiper and Dneister rivers, as well as the Aegean islands. Austria would gain control over Serbia and Bosnia-Hercegovina, while Dalmatia would be taken from Venice and given to Austria. In return, Venice would receive the Turkish provinces of Morea, Crete, and Cyprus. To secure the agreement of other European powers, Egypt would be granted to France, Algeria to Spain, and Libya and Tunisia to Great Britain. France could also potentially acquire Syria, Palestine, and Lebanon. In Asia, the Caucasus and West Georgia would be annexed by Russia. If Istanbul were to be captured, the Byzantine Empire would be revived, with Catherine's grandson, Grand Duke Constantine, assuming the role of Emperor. The Prince had already been educated in Greek for this purpose. This new Byzantine Empire, under Russian protection, would encompass Tsargrad (Istanbul) as its capital, along with Bulgaria, Dobruja, Thrace, Greece, Macedonia, Albania, and Montenegro. Turkey would have received Asia Minor, Iraq, Jordan, Arabia, and Yemen through generous means. However, it was evident that as long as the Ottoman lands were being divided, European powers could cooperate temporarily but would eventually engage in conflict over the spoils. Ultimately, Russian manipulations in Eastern Europe, driven by Pan-Slavism and Pan-Orthodoxy, would eventually lead to Pan-Germanism as a defensive measure, ultimately resulting in World War I. To execute their plan, the Czarina arrived in Crimea in 1787 with a 60,000-strong army, accompanied by Emperor Joseph II of Austria. They embarked on strategizing under an arch labeled "The

Road To Byzantium". However, Great Britain and Prussia vehemently opposed this project. Emperor Joseph, due to a revolt in the Belgian province, decided to postpone the war. Nevertheless, when the Sublime Porte discovered this plan, they declared war on Russia. The Ottoman Empire's survival beyond this war and into the twentieth century can be attributed not to its own military prowess, but rather to the envy, balance of power, and rivalry among the European powers. Consequently, Turkey would be confined to the Balkans and would not play a significant role in Eastern European affairs.

During the late 18th century and the beginning of the 19th century, European modernity dominated the era. The Orient, which was not only a tangible idea during this time but also portrayed as an exotic and alluring place by musicians, poets, writers, and travellers, as mentioned earlier. Simultaneously, Europeans in the 19th century developed a feeling of Western superiority characterised by practicality, imperialism, and a complete disregard for other civilisations. They also cultivated a specialised knowledge focused on the glorious periods of the past.[10] Hentsch describes this era as being "less clearly defined historical period than a state of mind from which we have not yet managed to escape".[11] Consequently, the impact of Europe extended beyond military dominance and encompassed cultural aspects as well. The longstanding barrier between Europe and the Orient was successfully overcome, marking a significant turning point. The construction of the Suez Canal (1859-69), half a century following Napoleon's expedition, solidified this breakthrough.

Following Napoleon's occupation of Egypt in 1798-1801, the vulnerability of the Ottoman Empire became even more apparent to the Western world. Both the Ottoman Empire and the Mediterranean Orient were coveted and sought after, ultimately becoming a contested arena for European powers. Napoleon's Egyptian expedition was not aimed at establishing a French empire in the East, but rather to confront England's growing influence in the region. According to Kappert, "from the point of view of the West, it appeared that Napoleon ... had decided that with his invasion of Egypt he was after world domination ... and dreamed of establishing a great Oriental empire, including India".[12] Napoleon's oriental expedition inadvertently set in motion the plan conceived by Leibniz in 1672 for Louis XIV. Although Egypt served as the battleground for this confrontation, it swiftly transformed into the focal point of the initial European colonisation effort in the region since the Crusades.

Volney (1757-1820) and the Orient

In Volney's 1787 publication, *Le voyage en Egypte*, we encounter an individual characterised by reason and progress. As a European, he possessed a deep-rooted belief in the superiority of his own civilisation, which he felt obligated to extend to other peoples. Volney argued that the declining Orient could only be revitalised through the intervention of Western science, leading to a renewed prosperity befitting its illustrious past. Within this context, Volney expressed his concern over Egypt's governance under Turkish rule, asserting that the Orient deserved a more favourable destiny. According to Volney:

> He [Bonaparte] instituted schools where the people might learn ... French, geography, mathematics and the exact sciences and with the help of the French army the miraculous instrument of the decrees of the Providence ... will reawaken the power of the ancient empire of the Arabs and deliver them from the yoke of the barbarous Osmanlis, purify the law of the Prophet ... and usher Asia into a new century of grandeur, service and glory.[13]

The authoritative dominance over the Other has thus been replaced by a commitment to science and advancement. Volney contended that only Europeans had the capacity to restore the grandeur of Arab history and even assert the ability to purify the teachings of the Prophet. Hentsch considers this stance to be profoundly hypocritical, while Maxime Rodinson views Volney as an individual who genuinely values objective analysis and exhibits remarkable understanding of political and social issues.[14]

Volney's merging of Enlightenment ideals with imperialism resulted in a belief in the superiority of Europe over other cultures. Rather than accepting the Other on its own merits, Europe sought to reshape the image of the Orient to align with its Euro-Christian ideology, thus asserting the superiority of its civilisation over Islamic societies. This perception of alterity legitimised European intervention in the Levant and contributed to a heightened sense of self-importance among Europeans. Although Volney was a well-informed scholar with proficiency in Eastern languages, his primary focus was on contemporary affairs. He believed that understanding the present was crucial for comprehending the past. In this way, Volney anticipated the methodologies adopted by modern European historians and the ensuing obligation of Europe in narrating global history. Any notion of universality was contingent upon adhering to the European paradigm, which not only shaped the narrative of world history but also rationalised political interventions in other cultures. In his quest to revive the grandeur of the Arab empire, Volney proposed a solution to overcome the Turkish predicament by casting them aside, because there was nothing Europe could extricate from the Turkish mindset. To Volney, the Ottoman Empire signified not only the eradication of past achievements but also the shattering of future aspirations.

Volney's message contained contradictions. While he praised the Muslims, he also observed that the Qur'an does not provide any guidance on societal duties, political organisation, or principles of governance. Instead, it portrays an absolute despotism in the commanding figure. Additionally, Volney did not view Muhammad as a visionary figure, as he believed that Muhammad's intention was not to enlighten but to rule and gain subjects. Unlike Voltaire, Volney did not display intellectual curiosity towards the Qur'an. What becomes apparent from Volney's passage is the ethnocentrism inherent in the Western perception of Islam.

The Image of the 'Terrible Turk'

Sultan Abdulmecid (r. 1823-1861), positioned amid the competing influences of Russia and France, promulgated a decree that recognised the Christian religious sites in Jerusalem, which are of profound importance to both Christians and Muslims, as equally sacred to adherents of both religions. This unexpected announcement took both Paris and St Petersburg by surprise. The Tsar, infuriated by this diplomatic move, coined the term "Sick Man of Europe" for the Ottoman Empire and proposed to Great Britain that they should once again partition the empire. However, Britain, concerned about Russia's expansion towards the Mediterranean, chose to only inform the Turkish authorities of the offer. When the offer was rejected, the Tsar resolved to take direct action. Ambassador Menchikov presented an ultimatum to Turkey, demanding certain rights for the Orthodox community. Regrettably, the Sublime Porte rejected the ultimatum. Tsar Nicholas I (r. 1894-1917), perceiving this rejection as a serious affront, used it as justification for war, leading to the outbreak of the Crimean conflict.

On July 3, 1853, Russia commenced its invasion of Romania, which was at that time a *vilayet* (province) of the Ottoman Empire, deploying a contingent of 35,000 soldiers. The Tsar asserted to the international community that this action was not a declaration of war, but rather a provisional occupation that would conclude once the Ottoman Empire recognised the "special rights" of Orthodox Christians. However, on March 12, 1854, Britain and France, concerned about Russia's expansionist ambitions in the Mediterranean and the resulting instability in the region, signed a treaty with Turkey to form an alliance against Russia for the duration of the conflict. This announcement came as a major surprise to the Tsar, as he had unknowingly fallen into a strategic trap. Rather than seeking diplomatic resolutions, he committed a diplomatic error by accusing the British and French of betraying the Christian cause and siding with non-believers against Christians. In light of this, it can be posited that European interactions with the Orient had transformed following Napoleon's Egyptian campaign. According to Andrew Wheatcroft, European engagement with the Orient post-Napoleon's expedition "did little to alter the stereotypes so deeply entrenched in Western culture".[15]

The Europeans were profoundly unsettled by the harsh treatment inflicted by the Turks upon their subjects, which included impalement and various forms of torture. This negative perception of the Ottomans was reinforced by the impactful works of Delacroix's paintings and Byron's poetry, which illustrated themes of Turkish lust and cruelty.

Furthermore, the unfavourable depiction of the Turks was sustained by Western media propaganda, notably in the English comic magazine, *The Punch*. It is noteworthy that during Lord Charlemont's visit to Istanbul in 1749, he did not observe any acts of torture in the streets, although he did learn of one execution.[16] This suggests that while instances of brutality and cruelty did exist, they were not as widespread as believed in the West.[17] Additionally, Robert Curzon, who held the position of joint British Commissioner in Erzurum from 1842 to 1843, contended that arbitrary power was not exclusive to the Ottoman Empire, referencing the United States as "a land of liberty, where every free and independent citizen had the right to beat his own nigger".[18]

Since the early 1800s, particularly following the distressing events of the Greek War of Independence (1821-29), Europe witnessed the plight of Christians and the emergence of the pervasive notion of the 'Terrible and Lustful Turk'. From a Western viewpoint, the Turks were portrayed as barbaric and uncivilised, while they regarded themselves as tolerant yet capable of fierce retaliation when challenged.[19] As Halil Halit, a young liberal Ottoman observer noted that, "Westerners ... always reacted with fury at the ill treatment of Christians by Muslims".[20] The Europeans perceived the conflict between the Greeks and Turks as a component of the broader 'war of liberation' for humanity, aligning with cosmopolitan notions of progress.[21] Turkey was regarded as a representation of outdated systems within Europe, resulting in the Turks being characterised as the 'enemies of humanity' due to their actions against the Greeks during the Greek War of Independence. The horrific acts attributed to the 'terrible Turk' against Christians circulated widely across Europe. In contrast, the tragic slaughter of 20,000 Turkish individuals, including men, women, and children, in southern Greece in 1821 received little attention.[22] The Greek rallying cry 'Not a Turk shall remain in the Morea' was effectively a "call for genocide".[23] According to the historian Charles A. Frazee:

> The Turks of Greece left few traces. They disappeared suddenly and finally in the spring of 1821, unmourned and unnoticed by the rest of the world ...

150 PERCEPTIONS OF THE OTHER

> Upwards of 20,000 Turkish men, women and children were murdered by their Greek neighbours in a few weeks of slaughter. They were killed deliberately, without qualm and scruple ... Turkish families living in single farms or small isolated communities were summarily put to death, and their homes burned down over their corpses. Others, when the disturbances began, abandoned home to seek the security of tire nearest town, but the defenceless streams of refugees were overwhelmed by bands of armed Greeks. In the smaller towns, the Turkish communities barricaded their houses and attempted to defend themselves as best they could, but few survived. In some places they were driven by hunger to surrender to their attackers on receiving promises of security, but these were seldom honoured. The men were killed at once, and the women and children divided out as slaves, usually to be killed in their turn later. All over the Peloponnese roamed mobs of Greeks armed with clubs, scythes, and a few firearms, killing, plundering and burning. They were often led by Christian priests, who exhorted them to greater efforts in their holy work.[24]

Furthermore, Steven Runciman, in his work *The Great Church in Captivity: A Study of the Patriarchate of Constantinople from the Eve of the Turkish Conquest to the Greek War of Independence*, contends that the revered Church fathers, such as Basil, would have been deeply disturbed by the audacious actions of the Peloponnesian bishops who initiated the uprising in 1821. Contrary to widespread assumptions, this conflict was not merely a quest for Greek independence or self-determination; rather, it was a ruthless campaign aimed at the extermination of the Turks and other Muslim populations. The principal architects of this violent struggle were, in fact, the Greek Orthodox Christian clergy.[25]

From this moment onwards, European religious prejudice began to manifest itself, despite the Ottoman government's response of suppressing the Greeks in other parts of the empire, dismissing them from governmental roles, and executing the Greek patriarch of Istanbul for his role in the rebellion. The government's actions were met with indifference towards the massacres suffered by innocent Muslim villagers, while any defensive measures taken by Muslims were exaggerated throughout Europe as instances of Muslim savagery.[26] The acts of violence known as the "Bulgarian atrocities" in 1875 gained significant attention in Europe and the United States due to the severe mistreatment inflicted upon Bulgarian Christians. However, amidst this focus, the equally horrific killings of Muslims were disregarded. It is crucial to recognise that there were occurrences of massacre and retaliation between Christian and Muslim communities, with the Ottoman regular forces striving to restore peace and security for all.[27] Regrettably, by the time they intervened, anti-Turkish propaganda in Europe had already gained significant traction. According to Shaw and Shaw:

> While no more than 4000 Bulgarian Christians had been killed (and considerably more Muslims), the British press trumpeted the charge of 'Bulgarian horrors', claiming that thousands of defenceless Christian villagers had been slaughtered by fanatical Muslims.[28]

American estimates put the total Christian dead at 15,000 while the Bulgarians inflated the figures up to as high as 100,000.[29] With the support of William E. Gladstone, the British Prime Minister from 1868 to 1894, his influential pamphlet titled "Bulgarian Atrocities" achieved impressive sales of 40,000 copies in 1876, effectively highlighting the violence perpetrated by the Turks. Notably, this same anti-Turkish propaganda was employed during the Cretan Revolt of 1866-1869, during which there was no acknowledgment of the Muslim population in Crete or the fact that over one million Muslim refugees had fled to Istanbul after losing their lands in Greece, the Balkans, and southern Russia. Gladstone, a staunch opponent of Turkish rule, vigorously advocated for the expulsion of Turks from Europe and the substitution of the crescent with the cross. As a result, he began to support the Armenian cause, motivated by the ambition to exert influence and supplant Russian dominance in a potentially independent Armenia. Furthermore, Gladstone expressed apprehensions regarding Sultan Abdul Hamid II's (r. 1876-1909) authority as the Caliph of all Muslims, particularly concerning Britain's Muslim population in India. In the 1890s, Armenians intensified their militant actions against the Ottoman government in their pursuit for an independent homeland. As Wheatcroft explains:

> When Armenians used violence to secure an independent Armenia, the killings of Turks were ignored by the Western states, while the Ottoman response was condemned as mindless racial murder.[30]

The government of the Sultan was accused of giving the order to destroy 25 villages in Sasun and to execute 20,000 Armenians. Once again, the response from Europe mirrored previous reactions. Europe failed to address the brutal killings of numerous Armenians by Kurds with personal vendettas, nor did it recognise the over one million Turks who perished during the First World War (1914-18).[31] In contrast, when Tsarist Russia perpetrated pogroms against the Jewish population during the same timeframe, the European response was markedly different. The British publication, *The Times*, expressed disapproval of the actions taken by the Russians and urged the British government to take action, at times by inciting public demonstrations.[32] It was during this period that the French historian Albert Vandal labelled Sultan Abdul Hamid II as "Le Sultan Rouge" (The Red Sultan). Abdul Hamid was universally reviled, more so than any other Ottoman sultan before him. He was denounced as 'Abdul the Damned' or 'the Red Sultan', with his hands represented in the media as stained with blood. By 1907, he had come to symbolise, in the eyes of the Western world, all the negative traits attributed to the Ottomans—cruelty, cowardice, and, to a lesser extent, lust.[33]

Abdul Hamid II and the Ottoman Empire were regarded by Europe as a declining monarchy. In 1853, Tsar Nicholas I articulated his apprehensions regarding this situation during a conversation with Sir Hamilton Seymour, the British minister in St Petersburg:

> [...] we have a sick man on our hands, a man who is seriously ill; it will ... be a great misfortune if he escapes us one of these days, especially before all arrangements are made.[34]

Nicholas I's objective was undoubtedly the fragmentation of the Ottoman Empire by the European powers. As a result, strategic maneuvers were being put into effect.

An Englishman Observes Turkey

Sir Adolphus Slade (1802-1877) was an English traveller who explored Turkey in the nineteenth century, and his insights into the region have often been neglected. According to Lewis:

> The most probable reason is that in general his attitudes were thoroughly out of accord with the commonly accepted opinions of nineteenth century Europe.[35]

Slade maintained a divergent stance from the widespread European belief that the Christian subjects of the Ottoman Empire were suffering under oppression and were in desperate need of aid from a harsh regime. Furthermore, he contested the idea that the Tanzimat reform program, initiated under Sultan Selim III (r. 1789-1808), was ineffective in its implementation. In reality, Slade observed that these reforms had been effectively implemented across various sectors. According to Slade's observations, "no peasantry in the whole world are so well off".[36] He further questioned, "Where is the tyranny under which the Christian subjects of the Porte are generally supposed to groan? Not among the Bulgarians certainly".[37] Slade not only recognised the flourishing Christian peasantry but also noted the rise of a prosperous Greek middle class that had made considerable economic and cultural progress under Ottoman governance. He criticised European observers for making flawed comparisons between Turkey and Europe, arguing that they assessed Turkey through their own biased standards.[38] Slade rejected the notion of an authoritarian Turkish government, viewing this characterisation as a distortion propagated by certain European commentators.

Colonialism & Conquest

Colonialism encompassed more than mere conquest; it embodied a distinct type of appropriation and control. European dominance over other cultures according to La Ronciere La Noury was due to "the superior causes, its elements, its influences on human destinies".[39] According Noury, European imperialism "will be a beautiful study for future historians".[40] Europe's mistreatment of the indigenous populations it colonised and its dismissive attitude towards their perceived inferiority compared to other civilisations is clearly demonstrated by its acknowledgement that the remarkable civilisations of western Asia were part of the history of the western world. Furthermore, Europe believed that it was the responsibility of the West to showcase the true magnificence of these civilisations through the unveiling of the monuments that had been unearthed by Western archaeology after being buried for centuries.

As societies attain a significant degree of maturity and strength, they frequently embark on the colonisation of other cultures.[41] This phenomenon underpinned Europe's rationale for asserting its superiority over various civilisations. In the nineteenth century, Europeans endeavoured to evaluate the accomplishments of the Arab-Muslim civilisation through their own cultural lens. Consequently, to validate its dominance over other civilisations, Europe may have invested considerable effort in portraying itself as the heir to the ancient civilisations of the Near East, while simultaneously being hesitant to acknowledge its legacy from the more recent Arab-Muslim civilisation. Ironically, within the European discourse of the nineteenth century, the task was to accurately appraise the contributions of the Arab-Muslim civilisation.

Ernest Renan (d. 1892) significantly contributed to the accurate understanding of Arab-Muslim civilisation. He recognised the exceptional originality of Arab philosophy, particularly during the 11th and 12th centuries. This era exemplifies a highly developed culture that has, regrettably, been overlooked by its own progenitors. Renan attributed this oversight to the Arabs and Persians succumbing to the relentless influence of various barbarian factions, such as the Turks and Berbers, who redirected the course of Islam.[42]

As the eighteenth century drew to a close, France began to witness a decline in its economic supremacy, particularly in North America, alongside the loss of Egypt to England. To recover its lost influence, France recognised the necessity of employing gunboat diplomacy and engage in direct military conflict to capture Algeria from the Ottoman Empire. This strategic action enabled France to symbolically restore its status and reaffirm its importance. Subsequently, European colonisation commenced with the French capturing Algiers in 1830 and the British establishing themselves in Aden in 1839. This initiated a sequence of events in which the British extended their control over India and Malaysia, while the Dutch asserted dominance in Indonesia. The French and British further broadened their colonial reach with the occupation of Tunisia and Egypt from the Ottomans, respectively, after 1881. As a result, unconditional colonialism began to proliferate. It can be posited that the East seemed fated for European subjugation, as it was internally crumbling due to neglect. This presented an opportunity for the long-awaited dream of Europeanising the world to be realised by the West.

Volney's dominant authority over the Other, which has now been replaced by the impact of science and advancement, belongs to a bygone era. The foremost priority, as it has consistently been, remains self-interest. Meanwhile, the French sought to mold the Other to reflect their own identity and cultural values, unlike the Ottomans, who permitted each *millet* (ethnic group) to exercise self-governance in accordance with their religious and cultural traditions. According to the poet Alphonse Marie Louis de Prat de Lamartine (d. 1869):

> Orient, land of powerful memories, cradle of the world, source of divine belief, the Occident wishes to possess you; we shall conquer you, shall bring freely to you our homage, like pious children who crave only to honour and glorify their mother. Long ago, you received our warlike peoples ... now take the holiest, best-loved of our poets, for it is by allowing you to contemplate our great men that we wish to consummate our modern-day crusade.[43]

According to Lamartine, the recognition of the Orient was contingent upon European perspectives, as the Eastern regions were perceived as the remnants of a once-magnificent civilisation in decline. As a result, the Western world found contentment in the exotic cultures of the East, which remained in a state of deterioration and political subjugation. The turmoil within the Muslim world created an opportunity for Christian missionaries. In their efforts within Islamic territories, these missionaries credited the achievements of European nations to Christianity, while attributing the challenges faced by the Muslim world to Islam. Thus, the dominant view was that Christianity represented progress and modernity, whereas Islam was seen as inherently fostering cultural and developmental stagnation.

The emergence of passing allusions to the satanic origins of Islam marked a significant shift in perspective. To a nineteenth-century observer, Muslims, alongside Protestants and Jews, were collectively perceived as adherents of Satan. It is particularly interesting to highlight that during the era of Voltaire and Gibbon, nearly a century prior, Islam was regarded as a civilisation founded on the ideals of intellectual freedom, the veneration of reason and beauty, and as a contributor to European advancement. However, as European animosity towards Islamic principles intensified—especially concerning intolerance, rigid doctrines, blind faith, fatalism, and a lack of appreciation for the visual arts—this perception underwent a significant alteration. With the rise of colonialism in the Near East, a victorious Europe interpreted any opposition to its supremacy as a conspiracy. Anti-imperialist movements among the subjugated populations of the Orient were labelled as actions of pan-Islamist insurgents. The term itself suggested aspirations for dominance, an aggressive ideology, and a coordinated international scheme. This perspective, propagated through popular media, literature, and even children's literature, profoundly influenced the attitudes of many Europeans.

Europe has consistently struggled to abandon its self-assumed responsibility of civilising and revitalising the East. Europeans viewed the adverse effects of colonialism as mere unintended occurrences within a broader narrative of progress, in which they and their bourgeois class were unwittingly involved.

After Turkey's loss in the Russo-Turkish War of 1764 and the Battle of the Pyramids (1798) against Napoleon, the primary concern in

European diplomacy from 1774 until the conclusion of the First World War in 1918 revolved around the fate of the Ottoman Empire. European diplomats were intent on preventing the Empire from falling under Tsarist control. Various proposals were considered, including the potential partitioning of the Empire. However, there were also those who advocated for the revitalisation and modernisation of the Empire, aiming to aid its recovery and preserve the existing balance of power in the region. Despite the decline of the Ottoman Empire, Lewis notes that, "Turkey remained an important factor in the European balance of power, but it was now the problem of Turkish weakness, not of Turkish strength".[44]

It is noteworthy that in the fifteenth and sixteenth centuries, the formidable presence of the Ottoman Empire and its potential threat to Europe led to the characterisation of the Islamic Other as a "menace" by Europeans. Despite the subsequent decline of the Ottoman Empire, this perception of the Turkish "menace" endured. This time, instead of military conflict, it was the Ottoman Empire's weakness and inefficiency that posed a risk to European financial operations and investments in the Near East. From the nineteenth century onwards, European pressure on the Ottoman Empire's debt compelled the Sultan to accept European intervention in the management of its customs houses and finances. As Turkish military power waned, Islam, which had already ceased to be seen as a significant religious adversary by Christian churches, no longer posed a serious military threat either.[45] Hence, Europe ceased to perceive the Other as a mere spectator; rather, it transformed into an aspiring dominator that exhibited little regard for the values and culture it had displaced and held in disdain, regardless of any alluring aspects it might have acquired. Consequently, it is evident that the beginning of the nineteenth century witnessed the rising European powers interfering in the matters of the Other, thus initiating the process of global dominance that unfolded throughout the century.

The Orient according to Hegel and Goethe

In the nineteenth century, German philosophers like Georg Wilhelm Friedrich Hegel (d. 1931) and Johann Wolfgang (von) Goethe (d. 1832) incorporated the Orient into their philosophical frameworks. The German philosophers perceived the Orient not simply as a mere reflection but as a vital counterpart to Western civilisation. These thinkers posited that a synthesis with the Orient would enable Western civilisation to achieve a state of wholeness and cultural richness. In their historical philosophy, they pursued a vision of unity and continuous advancement, drawing upon the ancient pre-Hellenic period to bolster the principles of European universalism.

Hegel asserted that Europe initiated a quest for global dominance, and in response to this cultural hegemony, the German philosopher depicted the Orient as "instinctively refusing to evolve".[46] However, it is important to recognise that the Orient did not represent stagnation. Just as Bodin (d. 1596) had earlier positioned Europe as the leader of the Universe, Hegel similarly places the West at the pinnacle of Reason's development in his Universal History. For Hegel, Reason, equated with God, is regarded as the ultimate destination of modern Europe.

Hegel aimed to steer the course of history towards a predetermined goal: the realisation of self-awareness and the freedom that accompanies it. For Hegel each civilisation was on a journey of the spirit:

> World history travels from East to West, for Europe is the absolute end of history, just as Asia is the beginning ... for although the earth is a sphere, history does not move in a circle around it, but has a definite eastern extremity, i.e., Asia. It is there that the external and physical sun rises, and it sets in the West, but it is in the West that the inner sun of self-consciousness, which emits a higher radiance, makes it further ascent.[47]

Hegel posited that the progression of world history occurs through specific developmental phases. The first phase, referred to as the Orient, included Asia and the Near East, symbolising a state of infancy. This was succeeded by Greece, which epitomised youth and was compared to a transient flower. The subsequent phase, represented by Rome, denoted adulthood. Ultimately, the "Germanic nations" signified the apex of universal history, indicating the final stage of "complete maturity".[48] Consequently, Hegel argued that the civilisation of Muhammad was destined to fail from its inception due to the inherent incompatibility of Islam with European ideals. According to Hegel:

> Their object was to establish an abstract worship ... for an abstract thought which sustains a negative position towards the established order of things ... In its spread, Mohametanism founded many kingdoms and dynasties ... Those dynasties were destitute of the bond of organic firmness.[49]

Hegel opted to overlook and dismiss the Orient, resulting in the unsuccessful integration of Eastern thought with European universality. However, it is imperative to reintegrate the Orient into the historical narrative, as its exclusion is untenable. If required, this reintegration may necessitate the use of force. This theory, which underscores the notion that diverse civilisations develop within their own contexts and possess unique and intrinsic characteristics, has gained significant traction. Karl Marx proposed that societies must independently discover a path towards transitioning from a communal existence to socialism; failure to do so would lead to the repercussions of the bourgeoisie's global dominance.

Conversely, from the viewpoint of Islam, Goethe is seen as an embodiment of the enlightened individual. At the age of 70, he articulates his desire to honor with profound respect the moment when the Prophet Muhammad received the entirety of the Qur'an from the Divine in his piece entitled "Notes and Essays to the Divan" (WA I, 17, 153):

> How strange that in every special case one praises one's own way! If Islam means: surrender into God's will" it's in Islam that we all live and die.[50]

> However often we turn to it [Qur'an] at first disgusting is each time afresh, it soon attracts, astounds and in the end enforces our reverence. Its style, in accordance with its contents and aim is stern, grand, terrible - ever and anon truly sublime. Thus this book will go on exercising

through all ages a most potent influence ... Whether the Koran is of eternity? I don't question that! ... That it is the book of books I believe out of the muslim's duty".[51]

He [Muhammad] is a prophet and not a poet and therefore his Qur'an is to be seen as a divine law and not as a book of a human being, made for education or entertainment.[52]

Goethe documented various verses from the Qur'an that instruct individuals on how to perceive nature in all its manifestations as indications of divine laws. The multitude of these manifestations signifies the existence of a singular God. The Qur'an's depiction of the connection between humanity and nature, as transcribed by Goethe from the verses of Surah Baqara, establishes the foundational tenets of his respect and connection to Islam. He highlighted the significance of acknowledging "God's greatness in the small", referencing verse 25 of Surah Baqara, which employs the metaphor of a fly.

Goethe was profoundly moved by the notion that Allah conveys His message to humanity through prophets, which led him to express his respect for the Prophet Muhammad. In a letter addressed to A. O. Blumenthal on 28 May 1819, Goethe cites Surah Ibrahim, verse 4: "It is true, as God states in the Qur'an: We did not send a prophet to a people except in their own language".[53] Goethe reiterates this point in a letter to Carlyle, citing the same verse: "The Qur'an states: God has sent a prophet to every people in their own language".[54] Despite not converting to Islam, Goethe, as a freethinker, concluded the nineteenth century with profound admiration and veneration for the religion of Islam, the Qur'an, and the teachings of the Prophet Muhammad.

In conclusion, during the nineteenth century, Europeans exhibited a lack of genuine curiosity regarding the civilisations of the Orient. Instead, the allure that the Orient held for Europeans was predominantly based on myths and fantasies. Despite its historical inaccuracies, the Orient wielded influence by captivating the imagination of Europeans. It is crucial to recognise that the European perspective of superiority and detachment towards a region perceived as "not

Europe" has endured throughout history. As a result, the identity of the Orient has come to represent the antithesis of Europe, inadvertently assisting Europe in reinforcing its position as the preeminent world civilisation.[55] By this period, Europe was distinctly Europe, while the East was unequivocally the East. This subconscious dichotomy had already taken root, contributing to the cultural alienation fostered by imperialism.

CHAPTER 12

FROM THE IMAGINED ORIENT TO THE ORIENT EXPRESS

"AWFUL, DISAPPOINTING AND DIRTY ORIENT"

The Occident's fascination with the Orient, which, for many centuries Ottoman Istanbul represented, continued into the twentieth century with the introduction of the Orient Express in 1883, which ran services from Paris to Istanbul for the next 80 years (1883-1977), briefly pausing during World War I.[1] The original service, which ran from 1883 to 1889, took passengers from Paris to Munich, Vienna, Budapest, Bucharest, and Varna (Bulgaria), before being ferried across the Black Sea to Istanbul. English, French and German advertising posters of the time entice the occidental appetite with the exoticism and fantastical world of the Ottoman Orient (*Figures 294a-b*). The blue waters of the Bosphorus with its skyline adorned with domed mosques and minarets, the Topkapı Palace of the sultans and his harem, veiled women dressed in colourful garments, all play on the inquisitive mind of the European traveller to discover during a brief sojourn in Istanbul to become a part of the exotic orient, just as the stories from the *Arabian Nights* did in the 18th century.

Figures 1a-b. Posters advertising the Orient Express. Left, WL Diffusion, 19th century poster advertising a trip to Istanbul on the Orient Express travelling via European capitals. Photograph reproductions.

Following the Crimean War (1853-56), it was decided to build a train link between Europe and Istanbul. After some signed and prematurely terminated contracts, the concession for the Rumeli Railway was awarded to a Bavarian-born banker from Belgium named Baron Hirsch (Moritz Freiherr Hirsch auf Gereuth) in the spring of 1869. The project envisaged a route from Istanbul to the Sava River's banks via Edirne, Plovdiv, and Sarajevo. After considering several options, a temporary terminus in Sirkeci was built in 1873.

The construction of the new building began in early 1888. The terminus, originally known as Müşir Ahmet Paşa Station, opened on 3 November 1890, replacing the station that had been in operation since 1873. Sirkeci Station (Sirkeci Gar) was Istanbul's historic terminus for trains from Edirne and Europe. It was designed by Prussian architect August Jasmund, known for his oriental architecture and opened on February 11, 1888, during Sultan Abdülhamid II's reign. August Jasmund was sent to Istanbul by the German government to study Ottoman architecture.

The coming of the railway technology to the Ottoman Empire signalled the arrival of one of the prerequisites of civilisation for the ruling elite. The U-shaped architecture of the Sirkeci railway station has become one of the best-known examples of European Orientalism. Influenced by Ottoman architecture, Jasmund desired to create a fusion of East and West in Istanbul, a city that represented the gateway to the Ottoman Orient for centuries, stirring European fascination for everything exotic. This way the Sirkeci station became the last stop on the route of the Orient Express. Jasmund designed the station in a combination of Art Nouveau and Oriental styles. The station's main building has remained unchanged since 1890. At this 19th century Orientalist station near Seraglio Point beneath the walls of Topkapı Palace, right next to Eminönü, its ferry docks, and Galata Bridge, the famed Orient Express ended its run from Paris (*Figures 294c-d*).

Figures 1c-d. Left, the façade of the main entrance to Sirkeci Station in Istanbul, 1888-90; right, the interior of the main hall of the Sirkeci Station. Photograph reproductions.

The first Orient Express made its maiden journey to Istanbul on October 4, 1883, departing from Gare de l'Est in Paris, to the tune of Mozart's *Turkish March*. The route covered an approximate 3,094 km taking 80 hours to arrive at its destination, passing through the cities of Strasbourg (France), Karlsruhe (Germany), Stuttgart (Germany), Ulm (Germany), and Munich (Munich), before concluding its journey in Sirkeci (Istanbul).

While the 1867 *L'Exposition Universelle* was deemed successful by the Ottomans in representing the Orient to European audiences, historically speaking, popularising the exotic Orient for centuries had been at the hands of European writers and travellers.[2] One writer that exoticised the Orient in the early decades of the 20th century was Agatha Christie in her crime fiction novels that took place on the Orient Express to Istanbul and the former Ottoman territories, Cairo, Jerusalem and Baghdad. Writers like Christie use to present the Orient as the Other to the Occidental self. Pramod Nayar, in *The Transnational in English Literature: Shakespeare to the Modern*, defines exoticism as a "representational strategy through which difference is highlighted, sentimentalised, and morally adjudicated ..." focusing on the "foregrounding of cultural difference and foreignness".[3] Christie frequently employed this method in her narratives.

Stories written by Agatha Christie in the early 20th century represent a meeting point between the West and the East. These fiction stories allow for encountering, observing, and addressing differences among people, in this case from the perspective of the imperial superior, that by the close of the 19th century occupied most of the Ottoman territories. The Orient in Christie's novels serves as a backdrop without contributing to plot development. Using it as a backdrop to her setting, Christie exoticises the Orient for the Westerners. Since Mesopotamia was a British Mandate from 1918 to 1932, Agatha Christie's Western characters are merely observers who view everything through Eurocentric prisms. The early to mid-20th century writings of Christie, such as *Appointment with Death* (1938), *Murder in Mesopotamia* (1936), *They Came to Baghdad* (1951), *Destination Unknown* (1954), and *Murder on the Orient Express* (1934), nevertheless capture the dominant orientalist and imperialist mindset of the previous century. Fictional stories that depict the imagined Orient for Westerners, but this time with all its squalid, backwards, and uncivilised characteristics.

The romanticised and fantastical lands of the Orient that the Europeans encountered in the *Arabian Nights* since the early 18th century shattered the 'civilised' occidental traveller to Istanbul and former Ottoman lands in the early decades of the 20th century. The word "disappointment" is frequently used when Western characters first describe their first impressions of the Orient because it differs from what they had anticipated. When asked by the French Dr. Gerard how she feels about Jerusalem in the novel *Appointment with Death* (1938), young English doctor Sarah replies:

"You like Jerusalem, yes?" asked Dr. Gerard, after they had exchanged greetings.

"It's rather terrible in some ways," said Sarah, and added: "Religion is very odd!"

The Frenchman looked amused. "I know what you mean." …

Every imaginable sect squabbling and fighting!"

"And the awful things they've built, too!" said Sarah.[4]

Similarly, when Mr. Cope and the Boynton family discuss the Holy City, Mr. Cope asks,

"Well, Lennox, and what do you think of King David's city?"

"Oh, I don't know." Lennox spoke apathetically – without interest.

"Find it kind of disappointing, do you? I'll confess it struck me that way at first."[5]

The hospital nurse Amy Leatheran from *Murder in Mesopotamia* (1936) writes in her letter:

> *The dirt and the mess in Baghdad you wouldn't believe—and not romantic at all like you'd think from the Arabian Nights! Of course, it's pretty just on the river, but the town itself is just awful—and no proper shops at all. Major Kelsey took me through the bazaars, and of course there's no denying they're quaint—but just a lot of rubbish and hammering away at copper pans till they make your headache—and not what I'd like to use myself unless I was sure about the cleaning.*[6]

When Victoria Jones, a young English woman, first arrives in Baghdad, she is "unfavourably impressed by Baghdad" in the book *They Came to Baghdad* (1951).[7] She immediately scorns the location utterly and thinks to herself:

> Victoria sat down on the bed and passed an experimental hand over her hair. It felt clogged with the dust and her face was sore and gritty. She looked at herself in the glass. The dust had changed her hair from black to a strange reddish brown. She pulled aside a corner of the curtain and looked out on the river. But there was nothing to be seen of

the Tigris but a thick yellow haze. A prey to deep depression, Victoria said to herself: 'What a hateful place.'[8]

Furthermore, in *Murder on the Orient Express* (1934), Istanbul is described by Mrs. Hubbard in the following words:

> I sailed right to Stamboul, and a friend of my daughter's – Mr. Johnson ... met me and showed me all round Stamboul, which I found a very disappointing city – all tumbling down. And as for those mosques and putting on those great shuffling things over your shoes – where was I?[9]

The passages, thus, draw attention to the Orient's passivity because it is the Westerner that evaluates the Orient from his perspective of what the Orient ought to be like. From this viewpoint, the Orient can never prevail, and will remain subservient. The vacillation between the dominant imperial centre – Europe – and its submissive colonial periphery – the Orient – serves as a reminder that the real Orient, like the imagined Orient of the previous centuries, continue to satisfy Westerners' desires and expectations.

The search for this fleeting, dreamy Orient of *A Thousand and One Nights* permeates Christie's novels. Having come to terms with the dirty, dusty and dilapidated environment, the characters continue their search for oriental exoticism and fantasy. Hassanieh is described as "standing up quite white and fairy-like with minarets" in *Murder in Mesopotamia*.[10] Petra is an ancient historical and archaeological city that Sarah describes in *Appointment with Death* as "wonderful and just a little horrible ... The 'rose-red city' has always struck me as dreamlike and romantic. However, it is much more genuine than that; in fact, it is as genuine as raw beef".[11] She discusses the conflict between fantasy and reality when it comes to a Westerner's conception of the Orient and depicts Petra as a real-world location. Here, the site is exoticised and presented as being peculiar and out of this world, though, when she later refers to it as "a strange and unbelievable country unparalleled anywhere".[12] Victoria hopes to wake up in London and realise that she is only "dreaming a wonderful melodramatic dream about dangerous Babylon" when she is embroiled in international intrigue in

Babylon at one point in *They Came to Baghdad*.[13] Christie once again associates the Orient with an improbable and dreamlike situation. In the book *Destination Unknown*, Hilary describes her first visit to the "untouched" city of Fez as being "like stepping into another world" and "living and walking in a dream world".[14] She continues by referring to Morocco as "a land of mystery and enchantment" and saying that she finds it to be "quite enchanting".[15] In addition, Christie's books make reference to the *Arabian Nights*, whose characters have become iconic figures in Western culture. When Hilary says: "It's unbelievable..., Here in the middle of the desert ... It's an Arabian Night fairy tale", she makes a connection between the *Arabian Nights* and her own experience of being in the middle of a desert in the Orient.[16] Murchison, who is with her, concurs and adds, "It exactly looks as though it has come into being by conjuring up a djinn!"[17] It draws attention to the dreamlike and fanciful notions of the Orient, which is consistent with the way that the Western characters arrive there with their own preconceptions and visions of the East. They go there in search of a mystery and a fairy tale that resembles the tales from the *Arabian Nights*. These accounts demonstrate how the West consumes the idea of the Orient as being mystical, ethereal and fanciful, while simultaneously disgusted with its dirty and messy surroundings that further confounds the Westerner.

All aspects of the Oriental world are described as peculiar, such as water, currency, names and religions. While Christie does bring the Orient more into dialogue with the West, describing its cities, monuments, archaeological sites, people and objects, and sometimes incorporating local language, she does so mainly in a derogatory manner, emphasising the peculiarities of the Oriental world and its distinctiveness from the Western world. Consequently, the overall impression is that she only reinforces Westerners' preconceived notions about the Orient, that the entire Orient is unclean, decaying and infested, and that its people are complacent, uncomplicated, unreliable and undifferentiated, akin to a "human cluster of flies" which Christie refers to the merchants in *Death on the Nile*.[18]

The Orient of the late 19th and early 20th century is just a place that is meant to be seen, admired, and written about by the Occidentals through the imperialist and colonial prisms, or more specifically, the English. It serves primarily as a fixed, unchangeable, passive and captivating environment. The mystery that is the Orient continues to confound the Occident even into the early decades of the 20th century. As in earlier centuries, the Occident has difficulty articulating, defining and comprehending its eastern neighbour. In many cases, Westerners view the Orient as a place they have read about and seen in the *Arabian Nights*. They project their own dreams and visions onto it, expecting it to meet those dreams and expectations. As the Westerner's perception of the East varied from "fairy tale" to "dirty" and "disappointment", for the educated young Ottomans in the closing decades of the 19th century, the superiority of the Occident brought to light the political, social, and economic shortcomings of the Sultan's government, necessitating a re-evaluation of the Ottoman Empire's collective identity in the contemporary era.

ADDENDUM

PART II

CHALLENGE, RESPONSE AND REFLECTION

Indeed, Allah will not change the condition of a people until they change what is in themselves.

Quran, 13:11.

Great spirits have always encountered violent opposition from mediocre minds. The latter are unable to comprehend when an individual does not blindly adhere to inherited prejudices, but instead, bravely and honestly employs their intellect.

Albert Einstein

CHAPTER 13

WHERE DID THE MUSLIMS GO WRONG?

ECLIPSE OF REASON: A RELIGIOUS PERSPECTIVE

The waning of rationality and knowledge in the Islamic world since the 16th century can be traced back to a series of factors, including the impact of centuries-old hadith compilations rife with superstitions and irrational beliefs, the inadequacies of the madrasa educational framework which overlooked the importance of natural sciences, and the disregard for philosophical discourse and investigative approaches that once ignited the inquisitiveness of early Muslim thinkers between the 8th and 12th centuries.

In his 2003 publication *What Went Wrong? The Conflict Between Islam and Modernity in the Middle East*, Bernard Lewis explores the shortcomings present in the Muslim world. In this book, Lewis examines the various factors that contributed to the decline of Muslim states, including European imperialism, military invasions, and the weaknesses within the Muslim states themselves. Within this specific chapter, the aim is to offer a new perspective on the shared vulnerabilities of Muslim nations, with a particular focus on the religious mindset and the challenges they face in harmonising reason, knowledge, and science with the divine revelation. Consequently, this results in the stifling of logical reasoning and failure to innovate new technologies and make significant contributions to the progress of human understanding in order to rival their European peers. In the nineteenth century, the Muslim society was deeply entrenched in superstitions, attributing them to religious practices and the Islamic faith itself. It became imperative to address these practices and empower individuals to embrace free thinking and rationality by reconstructing political thought in Islam.

The Ottoman sultan-caliphs maintained the conviction that Arabic is a sacred language, leading them to ban the importation of the printing press. This prohibition was grounded in a religious fatwa issued by a *sheikh ul-islam*, the highest religious authority in the Ottoman Empire, which forbade the use of the printing press from 1455 to 1727. This restriction lasted for 272 years, encompassing a significant period of 100,000 days across a vast territory that extended from North Africa to Iran, and from present-day Turkey to the Arabian Peninsula. While Europe embraced the exploration of God's signs in nature, spread knowledge through printing presses, and subsequently experienced a period of revival, reform, technological progress, and prosperity, the Ottomans regressed and sank deeper into ignorance. While Europeans engaged in intellectual discussions, the Ottomans simply repeated the holy book without truly understanding its teachings on the significance of learning, questioning, exploration, and the pursuit of knowledge. They were fascinated by handwritten books filled with rumours and superstitions, and admired the arguments presented by Al-Ghazali, who, with the unwavering backing of Sultan Sanjar of the Seljuk Turks (r. 1096-1157), aimed to eliminate philosophy.

Perhaps in no other period of history have the converging paths of two extraordinary individuals, born in different geographies and different times, assuming different roles, had such a profound impact on the destiny of a nation. The first of these is the noble prophet of Islam, Muhammad (c.570-632), and the other is Gazi Mustafa Kemal Atatürk (1881-1938), who reinterpreted Muhammad's teachings with an original perspective and opened new horizons for Muslims of tomorrow. This reinterpretation, grounded in human reason and intellect and consistent with the principles of the Qur'an, continues to serve as a source of inspiration and a framework for tackling modern challenges faced by the Islamic community. The objective of this chapter is to examine this viewpoint and assess its relevance in the contemporary religio-political context.

The "Declaration to the Islamic World" was published in the name of Heyret-i Temsiliye on the day after the occupation of Istanbul on March 17, 1920 by the Allied forces, before the opening of the Grand National Assembly of Turkey (Parliament) in Ankara. The declaration begins with the statement that the occupation of Istanbul is an invasion against the Islamic world, which is the centre of the sacred caliphate of Islam. It is emphasised that the occupation of Istanbul by Christians is a new "Crusade" directed towards the Islamic world.[1] After emphasising the trust that this last miserable act of the ongoing Crusader outcry with its unfortunate cruelty will create a sense of resistance and rebellion in the conscience of our Muslim brothers who are bound by the light of Islamic knowledge and independence and the sacred brotherhood united by the Caliphate, the statement concludes with the following prayer:

> We pray that the divine assistance of the Almighty be sent to all of us in our sacred struggle and that He supports our determination to fight, which is based on the spirituality of the Prophet.[2]

At the core of this message of a new Crusade led by the European powers against the vanquished Ottoman Empire at the end the First World War, lay the centuries long decline and weakness, adherence to illogical, superstitious, and archaic beliefs that associated religious practices with the Islamic faith. Thus, Atatürk was resolute in his mission to eradicate the "superstitious" and "irrational" influences that plagued Turkish society. He firmly believed that the only way to dissipate these obscure influences was by embracing the forces of science and education, while also finding harmony between knowledge and religion. Notably, this aligns with the message of the Qur'an directed towards those who engage in rational thought and understanding.

The inflexible religious curriculum in Ottoman madrassas nurtured an educational approach centred on memorisation and repetition. Even today, numerous regions in the Muslim world persist in prioritising repetition, drilling, and imitation from a young age, discouraging inquiry, curiosity and creativity.

Lessons from History: A society entangled in superstitions

During the establishment and rise periods of the Ottoman Turks, importance was given to reason and science. For example, after the conquest of Istanbul, the Sahni Seman Madrasas established by Fatih Sultan Mehmet in the 15th century placed great emphasis on the natural sciences. However, after the death of Fatih Sultan Mehmet, the Ottoman Empire began to disregard reason and science. From the late 16th century to the late 19th century, reason and science were practically forgotten in the Ottoman Empire. The void created by the lack of science was filled with superstition and falsehood; the Islamic religion was tainted with superstition and falsehood; and even worse, superstition and falsehood came to be mistaken for religion. Education also suffered from this situation, and over time, the primary educational institution, the madrasas, were closed to the teaching of the natural sciences.

Until the time of Kanuni Süleyman, medicine and geometry were taught, and after that, Ottoman madrasas became theological schools that taught Islamic jurisprudence (*fiqh*), Islamic philosophy (*kalam*), Qur'an commentary (*tafsir*), hadith, grammar, and rhetoric. The disciplines were frequently known as the "Islamic sciences," as opposed to the Greek sciences, which were frequently categorised as "foreign" or "alien" sciences. Aristotle's four elements, earth, water, fire, and air, and Ptolemy's astronomy and geography still dominate the curriculum in the madrasas. The written works are mostly explanations of the ancients. The debates among madrasa scholars are only about what will lead people astray from religion. They have strayed so far from intellectual thought that even long after the seventeenth century, there were those among the madrasa scholars who wrote delusions such as "if you bury a thread in fly dung and bury it in the ground, mint will grow".[3]

The above statements are quite thought-provoking as they reveal to what extent science was neglected in Ottoman society and how superstition was promoted under the guise of religion. Just like in medieval Europe, those who called themselves "religious figures" protected superstitions and irrational ideas that had no real connection to religion, all in order to hinder the progress of science. According to them, science is separate from religion and should be suppressed wherever it is found! It should never be allowed to develop. However, what they mistakenly believed to be conflicting with science is not the Islamic religion, but rather a series of absurdities consisting solely of superstition and irrationality.

The madrasas not only closed their doors to the positive sciences but also fell into a great inadequacy in terms of religious education. Under the roofs of madrasas, superstitions and nonsense began to be taught as religion. Those who graduated from madrasas have become defenders of "superstition" and "heresy" in the name of the Islamic religion.

In madrasas, there have been debates on whether wearing fur and silk is appropriate in Islam, whether the fruit of a tree grown in a cemetery can be eaten, whether it is necessary to put papers with verses written on them in pockets to protect clothes from moths, and even whether it is more appropriate for the soldiers tasked with digging tunnels during the siege of a fortress by the Ottoman army to throw the soil to the right or to the left.[4]

In the 17th century, the Ottoman scholars are preoccupied with superstitions. The topics that the scholars, known as "Kadızadeler" in Ottoman history, deal with are as follows:

- Is smoking and drinking coffee forbidden?
- Did Prophet Khidr exist?
- Did Pharaoh attain faith?
- Is it forbidden to learn positive science and mathematics?

- Should the call to prayer, religious hymns, and similar recitations be performed with a beautiful voice and melody?

- Should the Sufi masters rotate while performing dhikr?

- What is the level of faith of Prophet Muhammad's parents?

- Is it permissible to curse Yazid (The Umayyad Caliph)?

- Can voluntary prayers be performed in congregation?

- Is it forbidden to listen to a woman's voice?

- Is it permissible to kiss the hand and the hem of the garment of the elders?[5]

The puritanical Kadızadelis did not hesitate to express that even using a spoon was forbidden and that meals should be eaten with the hands. This clearly demonstrates how much the level of education in the Ottoman madrasas had declined and how superstitions were injected into young minds under the guise of "religion," as stated by M. A. Ubucuni:

> In the madrasas, for example, topics such as whether Abu Bakr, Umar, and Uthman were the true caliphs of the Prophet, whether it is more correct to wash the feet with water when getting out of bed or to perform bare-handed ablution, were taught. They were completely unfamiliar with subjects such as geography, history, and natural sciences.[6]

In a directive sent to the judges and deputy judges of the Anatolian provinces in 1673, it was stated that in those regions, those who serve as muftis, teachers, sheikhs, preachers, and *imam hatip* schools should teach their students religious knowledge according to the "shariah order" and prioritise religious sciences over other unnecessary sciences. It was also emphasised that they should not start studying other unnecessary sciences until they have completed their religious studies, "prioritising religious sciences over other sciences" and "not starting other unnecessary sciences without completing religious studies".[7] This is the mindset of the Ottoman Empire in the seventeenth century! This is the "backward" Ottoman mindset that first led the great empire of Mehmed II and Süleyman the Magnificent to be enslaved by the West and then to finally collapse.

Even in the second half of the nineteenth century, when modernisation efforts reached their peak in the Ottoman Empire, there are still works that transmit "superstitions" to society under the name of "religion". The "So-called Secrets" and "Primitive Remedies" found in the book "Hazar Eser" (Thousand Secrets) published jointly by Mustafa Behcet Efendi and his brother in 1862, serve as a prominent illustration of how superstition was often disguised as religious practice within Ottoman society. According to this book:

- In order to protect children from flower disease, they should be given donkey milk to drink.

- If a guilty person is fed quail tongue, they confess all their crimes during interrogation.

- If cauliflower seeds are planted four years later, and if turnip and turnip seed are planted four years later, cauliflower will grow.[8]

It is possible to provide examples that reveal the prevalence of superstitions in Ottoman society as follows:

- The observatory established by the astronomer Takiuddin in Istanbul was destroyed in 1580 when Ahmet Semsettin Efendi issued a *fatwa* stating that "attempting to learn the secrets of the heavens is an audacity" and that "states that establish observatories will face decline".[9]

- The appropriateness of showing maps in geography lessons was debated in terms of religious law. Sultan Mustafa III sent an envoy named Ahmet Rasim Efendi to Prussian King Frederick, requesting three astrologers.

- The printing of Islamic works in the Ottoman Empire, which reached the Turks in 1727 through Ibrahim Muteferrika's printing press, was banned with a decree published on July 5, 1727.[10]

- When Russian delegates came to sign the Treaty of Küçük Kaynarca in 1774, the Sheikh ul-Islam wrote talismans for them. It was believed that if these talismans were buried in the place where the Russian delegation would go, the mouths and tongues of the Russian delegation would be silenced.[11]

- During a plague outbreak in Istanbul in 1831, when the quarantine of ships was discussed, a fatwa was issued stating that "Quarantine is a Frankish custom; it is not permissible to comply with it in the Islamic religion".[12] Ironically, quarantining contagious patients was prescribed in Ibn Sina's *Canon of Medicine* in 1025.

- In a *fiqh* [jurisprudence] book, there were questions and answers such as "Is it permissible to eat the object known as leek?"[13]

Some of the superstitions that are found in the Muslim culture and in the Qur'an commentary books are as follows:

- The heavens rotate on the shoulder of an angel. The world is either on the horns of an ox or on the back of a fish. Earthquakes occur due to their movements.

- Thunder and lightning are believed by some interpreters to be the angels shouting and the pounding of their hearts. Rain is considered to be the tears of the angels.

- The moon is extinguished with the wing of Gabriel and remains in the form of light.

- Eve was punished with the pain of difficult childbirth.

- The snake was cursed to crawl on its belly.[14]

It is possible to propagate these and similar superstitions. These absurdities, which are incompatible with both knowledge and the Islamic religion, have served no purpose other than to confuse people's minds for centuries. It is clear that many of Atatürk's speeches concerning what he termed "empty beliefs" encompass these types of superstitions and the unfounded notions perpetuated by the ulema (religious scholars) throughout history.[15]

The Ottomans were warned about the weaknesses in their education system preventing them to compete with their European counterparts from seventeenth century onward. Unable to reconcile science, philosophy and religion, the Ottoman historian Katip Çelebi (1609–1657) had alerted the Ottoman administration about the complete failure of the *madrasah* in the study of physical sciences and mathematics by its dismissal of such sciences. But such warnings were bound to fail to produce real concern within the distorted concept system that had been planted deep into the Muslims' minds after the 11th century.[16] Teaching of natural sciences did not enter the madrasa curriculum until the late 19th century. Abdulhamid II realised the significance of the natural sciences in rescuing the Ottoman mind from centuries of superstitious beliefs intertwined with religion. According to Ekmeleddin Ihsanoğlu:

> From the seventeenth century onwards, conditions were no longer conducive to the development of science because of the social and economic condition disruption resulting from the weakening of the centra authority, dissolution of political stability, decreasing conquests, loss of land, influx of abundant American silver into Europe, and the diminishing revenues of the empire. The factors that had encouraged scholars to conduct scientific work disappeared and were replaced by the struggle to make a living. Disputes arose in the seventeenth century between the supporters of *salafi* Islam and mysticism among Ottoman intellectuals. The upholders of *salafiya*, who started the movement known as the Kadızadeli, had a negative attitude to philosophy and science that led to the regression of Ottoman science.[17]

Even, during the Tanzimat period in the 19th century, the Ottoman State showed a practical interest in scientific discoveries, but did not prioritise the three main aspects of modern Western science: theory, experiment, and research. This approach was evident in the educational and scientific policies of the Ottomans, including their attempts to establish a higher education institution called *Darülfûnûn* (House of

Sciences), apart from the *madrasa*, modelled after European universities. However, they failed to recognise the significance of scientific research in their programs, unlike their counterparts in Russia and Japan. It was only in 1900, with the establishment of the Faculty of Sciences as part of Istanbul University by Abdulhamid II, that research became a part of Ottoman scholarly circles.[18]

All these examples better explain why Atatürk felt the need to take steps that could be called a return to the essence of Islam. These examples reveal that in Ottoman society, not only science but also religion was neglected for a long time. In this respect, Atatürk addressed both scientific and religious enlightenment in Turkish society. Believing that a purified Islam free from superstitions would not hinder science, Atatürk recognised that the prerequisite for scientific enlightenment was religious enlightenment and attached great importance on education to combating the superstitions that surrounded Islam for centuries.[19]

A Visionary: Islam for "those who understand" ~ Reconciling the Divine Revelation with knowledge

The Turks are not Arabs, they have a Central Asian Turkic heritage, blended with Arabo-Islamic influence and European inheritance. Kemal knew and understood the Qur'an well. He knew that science and revelation reconciled in the scripture and sought to reveal this to the people. Kemal said:

> •God is a metaphysical issue that the human brain can hardly comprehend.
>
> •I believe in my religion the same way I believe in reality itself. It does not contain any evil that is contrary to consciousness nor prevents progress.
>
> •Our religion is the most reasonable and natural religion and that is why it has become the last religion.
>
> •For a religion to be True, it must be compatible with reason, science, knowledge and logic. Our religion reconciles with these laws.[20]

Despite being accused by both Western and Islamic adversaries of eradicating Islam in Turkey and blaming the religion for the backwardness of Muslims and the Ottoman Empire, it is important to note that Kemal's intention was not to condemn the religion itself. Rather, he aimed to challenge the prevailing interpretation of Islam that hindered Muslims from progressing in knowledge and science for centuries.

Kemal did not reject the Islamic tradition; instead, he opposed the Arabisation of Islam as practiced by the Muslim Turks. The Arabisation of Islam, which started in the seventh century, was widely followed across the Muslim world. During the early days of the Umayyad and Abbasid Islamic Empires, there were dissenting voices against this trend by non-Arab Muslims. Abu Hanifa (d. 767), also known as Imam Azam and a non-Arab, regarded as the Socrates of Islam, faced severe consequences for openly expressing his views on this matter.[21]

Kemal contested the Arabisation of Islam, viewing it as a manifestation of Arab imperialism that undermined the unique identity of Muslim Turks. As the prominent Islamic scholar Bayraktar Bayraklı states: "Islamic scholars do not know what Atatürk struggled with. Atatürk fought against ignorance, not Islam. On the contrary, he elevated Islam. It was Atatürk who commissioned the first Turkish interpretation of the Quran. This is a great revolution".[22] Arabic customs and traditions infiltrated daily life in the guise of religious practice. One of his chief aims was to reintroduce Islam to the Turks in their native tongue. He criticised the conservative ulema by stating: "To say that the Qur'an cannot be translated is to imply that the Qur'an has no meaning".[23] Some of Atatürk's reforms are directly aimed at "restructuring religion" and reconstructing Islamic thought in the modern era. The translation and interpretation of the main source of Islam, the Qur'an, into Turkish, is at the forefront of these efforts and its significance in the historical context of Islam is immense for non-Arab speaking Muslim Turks. The "Religious Turkification Studies" that began with the translation of the Qur'an into Turkish are among Atatürk's most important ideals that were realised during his lifetime.

In 1924, Atatürk took steps to tackle the Arabisation of Islam by establishing the Directorate of Religious Affairs and commissioning the first Turkish translation of the Qur'an himself. His main focus was to make Islam accessible to the Turks in their own language, rather than relying on the interpretation of the religion by local religious figures. These interpretations had often been influenced by superstitions, fabricated *hadiths* (alleged sayings of the Prophet Muhammad outside the Qur'an), and lacked reliance on the Qur'an. In 1927, Kemal attributed the setbacks in his nation's advancement directly to the Ottoman Sultanate, providing justification for his stance. He said:

> Can one consider as a civilised nation, a mass consisting of people subjecting themselves to some sheiks, dedes, masters, disciples, fathers, emirs, or, entrusting their lives to all sorts of fortune-tellers, occultists, sorcerers, healers, soothsayers? Should one have kept in the new Turkish State, in the Turkish Republic such elements and institutions which could misrepresent and which, indeed, have misrepresented our nation for many centuries?[24]

Kemal's approach involved separating religion from politics and placing the responsibility of Islam and faith directly on the individual. Kemal stated, "Religion is the bond between Allah and His servant", believing that religion was a personal connection between Allah and the individual. In 1932, Kemal even introduced the Islamic call to prayer in Turkish. Reciting the call to prayer in Turkish continued until 1950 before the traditional Arabic call to prayer was reintroduced, hence, honouring the universality of Islam.

It is appropriate for Atatürk to have commissioned the translation and interpretation of the Qur'an, as it is in line with the logic of the scripture. By translating the Qur'an into Turkish, Atatürk implemented the ruling of the Qur'an that had been neglected for centuries, which states, "Indeed, We have sent it down as an Arabic Qur'an that you might understand".[25] The Qur'an explicitly mentions that it was revealed in Arabic to ensure comprehension by its intended audience, the Arabs of the time. However, it should not be misconstrued that it must solely be read in the Arabic language. God emphasises this point in Surah Ibrahim:

> And We did not send a Messenger except in the language of his people so that he would explain (God's laws) to them.[26]

When the language of a nation is corrupted, culture of that nation is corrupted. When culture is corrupted, future generations are corrupted. If a nation protects its culture then its language is protected; if a nation protects its language then its culture is protected. This principle is a universal law set by Allah, as mentioned in Surah Ibrahim. Atatürk exemplified this through his reforms, particularly in relation to the translation initiative of the Scripture. This entails ensuring that education, including religious instruction, is delivered in the native language of a nation to effectively convey and comprehend God's message as stated in the above Qur'anic verse. Thus, the sanctity lies not in the language itself, but in the profound message it conveys, as emphasised in another verse in Surah Rum of the Qur'an:

> And one of His signs is the creation of the heavens and the earth, and the diversity of your languages and colours. Surely in this are signs for those of sound knowledge.[27]

Furthermore, Atatürk entrusted the task of Qur'anic interpretation to a master like Elmalılı Hamdi Yazar (1878-1942), fully aware of the importance of this matter. And indeed, the Qur'anic interpretation done by Elmalılı, even after 80 years, remains unsurpassed and is a remarkable interpretation. The Islamic scholar, Yaşar Nuri Öztürk provides the following evaluation on this matter:

> The will that established the Republic (Atatürk), after overturning the signs of superstitions (non-Qur'anic fabricated religious practices) that were eroding the empire from within, took the first and important step in introducing the essence of the ... religion to the masses with admirable insight and courage. That step is the translation and interpretation of the Qur'an prepared by Elmalılı Hamdi Yazar, the greatest

commentator of the era, upon the decision and request of the Grand National Assembly of Turkey ...

In this endeavour, which has always been overlooked but is the starting point of the fundamental solution, Atatürk emphasised that not only his mind but also his heart was involved by personally contributing to the financing of the interpretation ... In Turkey, the most reliable and valuable reference source on the subject of Islam at every level is still the Elmalılı commentary. For over fifty years, the relentless exploitation of religion that has brought the country to tears and the commercialisation of religion that has reached the point of surpassing the inquisition, the era and individuals they constantly criticise have not yet produced even a single work that can be placed next to or even close to this nine-volume masterpiece.[28]

In 1932, Atatürk convened a Ramadan *iftar* (breaking of the fast) dinner and invited the prominent Qur'an reciters and *hafiz* (those who memorise the Qur'an) to attend. Nuri Ulusu, one of Atatürk's library assistants, was present at this gathering and documented the events in his memoirs. Ulusu wrote about how Atatürk meticulously recited the first translated version of the Qur'an, as if he was reciting it to a group of people. After finishing the recitation, Atatürk turned to the *hafiz* and said, "From now on, this responsibility falls upon you. You will recite and explain this Turkish translation of the Qur'an to our people just as I did, slowly and deliberately. Our people will fully comprehend and understand our Qur'an".[29] That same year, Atatürk, ordered the reciting and reading of the Qur'an in Arabic and Turkish in Istanbul's famous mosques including Yerebatan Camii, Aya Sofya (Hagia Sofia), and Sultanahmet Camii (Blue Mosque). These and other examples clearly demonstrate that Atatürk did not ban the Arabic Qur'an. Atatürk's aim is not to ban the original Arabic text of the Qur'an, but to ensure that the Qur'an is fully learned and understood by the Turkish people. In his instructions to the memorisers (*hafiz*), Atatürk requested that the prayers be recited in their original Arabic form and that the prayers be performed in this way, but later he wanted the Turkish translations of the verses and chapters to be explained.[30]

Throughout history, and even in present times, there has been a prevailing belief that the Qur'an, being revealed in Arabic, holds a sacred status. Consequently, it has been widely held that the scripture can only be recited, read, and comprehended in its original language. This belief and practice, particularly among non-Arab Muslims such as the Turks, has hindered their ability to establish a personal connection with God and His Word. However, it is important to note that the scripture was initially inspired to the Prophet Muhammad in his native tongue, with the intention of educating and informing the Arabs of his time in their own language. This parallels how God communicated with Moses in Hebrew and Jesus in Aramaic through the Torah and the Gospel respectively. In essence, it is not the language itself that possesses holiness, but rather the message contained within. This is precisely what Atatürk sought to accomplish through his reforms.

In the same year, during a dinner gathering at Dolmabahçe Palace, Atatürk raised the question of praying in Arabic to a person in attendance. The person responded by stating, "Sir, because the Quran was revealed in Arabic...". Atatürk then replied, "Yes, but the Quran was addressing the Arab nation in their own language in Arabia. Let me ask you, is Allah only the God of the Arabs?" In response to this, the person said, "Sir, we learn their meanings". Atatürk then said:

> If you were to express your love to your mother by saying 'ac chere maman', what would your mother say to you? Wouldn't she call you crazy? A mother is the earthly embodiment of Allah. Allah uses the mother as a means to create humans, giving her not just one, but many things from His own power. Therefore, just as a person speaks to their mother in their mother tongue, they should also speak to Allah in their own language.[31]

Reconciling human reason with the scripture, Atatürk makes his case to the audience at the gathering. In addition, Ziya Gökalp's poem titled "Religion and Science" sheds additional insight on the overall religious perspective that is gradually taking form in Atatürk's new Turkish society of the 1930s:

The first guides of people are who?
Undoubtedly, prophets, saints...
In this era, religion is a guide to wisdom:
Morality, art all take from that light...

But then religion gives way to mere asceticism,
now the fervour diminishes,
The winds of saints blow in place,
The title of guide passes down to jurists.

The guides of jurists are tradition,
They forcibly drag religion down this path...
Wisdom says, "Guide me with reason;
So you go right, I'll go left! ..."

Religion is the educator, wisdom the teacher;
Each pulls the soul in a different direction
While they fight, emerges
Positive knowledge born of experience;

This last master says, "Tradition is history,
Reason is the method of this history;
Both show the same thing,
The desired one: the soul's attainment!"

What is that thing?... a heart full of fervour?
Is everything sacred a language to it?
Then take my final words as well:
Religion is the positive knowledge of fervour in the heart![32]

The poet's adeptness in incorporating the Comtian concept of the three stages of human intellectual progression, namely theological, metaphysical, and scientific, into the religious perspective of Islam is evident in these lines.

In the 21st century, converts, or rather reverts, to Islam from Christianity and other faith systems are offering a defensive perspective on the Islam and the West paradigm, challenging the 'decline' and 'backward' theory put forth by Western historiography on modern Islam. One writer who advocates this theory is Ahmed Paul Keeler in his 2019 book *Islam & The West: A New Narrative for the Age of Crises*. Keeler argues that Islam maintained *mizan* or balance within the hierarchy of knowledge. He states:

> In time, philosophers and theologians were to discover the synthesis in which the four fundamental sources of knowledge: revelation (*naql*), mystical cognition (*dhawq*), reason ('*aql*) and sensation (*ihsas*), were brought into a state of *mizan*, and the unity at the heart of Islam was unveiled ... In this hierarchy of knowledge, those sciences pertaining to the knowledge of God, the spiritual and the metaphysical, were the highest, and those relating to the corporeal, the limited and the material, the lowest. Everything had its place, and when it was in its rightful position, *mizan* was achieved ... This hierarchy in the realm of knowledge and higher educational system that grew up embodying it, ensured that the spiritual sciences were properly protected.[33]

Nevertheless, it is possible to argue that while the preservation of *mizan* in the Islamic epistemological tradition was maintained, the absence of natural sciences in the curriculum of the madrasas in the Ottoman Empire from the 17th century onwards resulted in the spread of irrational beliefs and practices, overshadowing the Qur'anic emphasis on the importance of intellect and reasoning as previously noted. This had significant consequences for the educational system in the following centuries. It could be contended that Muslim theologians failed to address the scientific advancements occurring in Europe when it came to implementing a more cohesive curriculum. This resulted in the emergence of visionary leaders in the early 20th century such as Mustafa Kemal Atatürk, who aimed to modernise and educate the Muslim society. Keeler's defensive argument above offer a distorted view of post-17th century Islamic history by presenting a quasi-utopian perspective of the early and early modern Islamic eras, which is far from accurate and certainly not reflective of the reality of that time.

Secularism versus Shariah

Secularism is enshrined in God's law or pathway. Ignorant minds refuse to acknowledge the significance of this aspect of the Qur'an. Islam does not separate secularism from religion. It provides guidelines for various aspects of life including manners, hygiene, marriage, divorce, prayer, devotion, treatment of children, slaves, and animals, as well as commerce, politics, interest, debts, contracts, wills, industry, finance, crime, punishment, war, peace, and spiritual and ethical behaviours. These guidelines aim to uphold a unified perspective on life. Islam not only illuminates morality and provides the emotional and inspirational guidance necessary for individuals to navigate the righteous path towards heaven, but it also manifests itself in various aspects of life, including economics, politics, science, arts, manners, and norms.[34] Islam is not limited to monasticism or asceticism, nor is it solely a personal relationship between an individual and their Creator. Instead, it encompasses all facets of life. Therefore, both moral and physical, individual and communal, issues related to the body and the soul, sex and economics, morality and aesthetics, coexist alongside matters of worship and spiritual yearnings within the comprehensive system of Islam. In Islam, salvation is not achieved through seclusion in the wilderness, but rather in the midst of the bustling and vibrant life. A person is meant to live their life as God has created them, embracing their true nature. The earth is not a place of torment where inherently wicked humanity is confined due to an original sin. Instead, it is a realm to be inhabited in accordance with the commands of Allah. As Muhammad Iqbal eloquently expresses, "There is no such thing as a profane world. All this immensity of matter constitutes a scope for self-realisation of spirit. All is holy ground. As the Prophet so beautifully puts it: 'The whole of this earth is a mosque'".[35]

Secularism and Religion are not two conflicting forces that cannot be reconciled. According to Muhammad Iqbal, "The ultimate Reality, according to the Qur'an, is spiritual and its life consists in its temporal activity. The spirit finds its opportunities in the natural, the materialism the secular. [Although] the structure of Islam as a religio-political system ... does permit such a view ... All that is secular, is therefore sacred in the roots of being".³⁶ It is the enigmatic essence of spirituality and religion that gives significance and worth to our worldly existence. Islamic life does not involve a division between the spiritual and the secular, which would only result in a painful opposition and fragmentation of life. Instead, it entails a continuous effort by religion to embrace the material world, with the ultimate goal of assimilating it, transforming it into its own essence, and illuminating its entire existence.³⁷

Sharia cannot be equated with Islam or the Qur'an. Sharia can be equated with jurisprudence and legal opinions, but not with Islam. The understanding that seeks to equate Sharia with Islam is a misguided approach that aims to make the customs and traditions that contradict the Qur'an and the changing times into religious practices. By first equating Sharia with religion, and then presenting some outdated rules from jurisprudence books as religious laws, this approach deceives people with a typical manifestation of deceiving Allah.³⁸

Turkey has been waking up and going to bed with the headscarf law in recent years. So much so that this issue is being discussed everywhere. There are those who support the law and those who oppose it. Marmara University Faculty of Theology Professor Bayraktar Bayraklı, who says that those who have two different opinions are actually unaware of secularism, "Secularism is the freedom and friendly coexistence of believers and non-believers, those who wear headscarves and those who do not".³⁹ Numerous verses in the Qur'an reinforce secularism. As the Qur'an states: "Let anyone believe and let anyone deny". (Surah al-Kahf: 29); "There shall be no coercion in matters of faith" (Surah al-Baqara: 256). God clearly does not interfere with freedom of religion; therefore, no state authority can legislate laws to enforce this God given freedom. This is the shariah or Holy Law that Prophet Muhammad had been instructed to teach. The Qur'an is very clear about this matter:

> There is no compulsion in religion. (2:256)
>
> For you is your religion, and for me is my religion. (109:6)

> And had your Lord willed, those on earth would have believed – all of them entirely. Would you [Muhammad] then compel the people until they become believers? (10:99)
>
> And say, "The truth is from your Lord, so whoever wills - let him believe; and whoever wills - let him disbelieve". (18:29)

These verses highlight the distinction between individual religious beliefs and practices, asserting that each person is accountable for their own faith and that it is unnecessary to impose one's beliefs on others.

The significance of a sovereign state's responsibility is evident in this context. The state plays a crucial role in ensuring the safety and security of all its citizens by upholding those guidelines set out by the Qur'an, regardless of their beliefs, in order to establish a fair, equitable, and peaceful society. This embodies the core principles of secularism and represents an ideal state that is consistent with the teachings of the Qur'an. To put it differently, anything that hinders an individual's freedom of choice contradicts the principles outlined in the Qur'an, as each individual is solely responsible for his own decisions. Unfortunately, this is not the case with Muslim radicals who adhere to the rigidity of the dogma which they misunderstand and misinterpret in the name of religion.

No state authority can enforce belief in God, faith, wearing of headscarves or practice of religious rituals. Such state sanctioned laws are against Qur'anic authority. This principle embodies the core of secularism, which upholds the freedom of individual choice—a sacred endowment that God does not interfere with, allowing individuals to be responsible for their actions, for which they will ultimately be held accountable. It is important to highlight that actions performed as a fundamental aspect of religious cultural practices may not always align with the religious teachings outlined in the Qur'an. There is a common misconception of confusing religious traditions with the essence of the religion itself. As God has given free will to individuals in order that He may hold them to account for their actions and choices; He does not interfere with that freedom. This is what the Qur'an repeatedly reinforces, and this is what Atatürk gave the

Turks. Hence, secularism is not antithetical to the teachings of the Qur'an.

Democracy in the Qur'an: A Qur'anic lesson for those who misrepresent the essence of Islam

First and foremost, God deals with humanity through a democratic process. This is clearly elucidated in the Qur'an. The concept of consultation, known as *Shura*, holds great significance in Islamic leadership. Unfortunately, many modern Middle Eastern countries have overlooked this crucial concept, leading to the risk of their governments descending into corrupt and totalitarian regimes. By actively involving the people in decision-making processes, *Shura* serves as a safeguard against such regression.

The concept of *shura* plays a vital role in the Islamic political system as it enables the active participation of ordinary individuals in the decision-making process. By fostering consultation, it facilitates the development of a society that actively engages with its leaders. This practice is crucial in establishing a strong bond between the leader and the people, ensuring that the leader remains accountable and avoids the pitfalls of authoritarianism. The importance of *shura* is emphasised in the Qur'an, where God encourages the Prophet Muhammad to seek consultation and guidance from others in matters of governance and decision-making:

> Those who hearken to their Lord, and establish regular Prayer; who (conduct) their affairs by mutual Consultation; who spend out of what We bestow on them for Sustenance.[40]

This verse highlights the significance of heeding one's Lord, establishing regular prayer, conducting affairs through mutual consultation, and utilising resources for the betterment of society.

If those in power, including rulers and politicians, maintain open lines of communication with the public, they will be embodying a principle aligned with the divine. A political system cannot truly be deemed democratic if the populace's voice remains unheard. A significant aspect that has historically influenced the evolution of democracy is the transparency of communication between the governed and those who govern. In essence, the presence of accessible channels for the populace to communicate their needs, issues, and concerns to their leaders is a fundamental component of democracy. The struggle for citizens to ensure their voices resonate with their leaders has spanned centuries. The establishment of these communication channels and the ability of the populace to articulate their perspectives have been pivotal in realising democratic governance. Even if a regime asserts its democratic nature, it cannot genuinely be classified as such if the voices of the people are silenced. Citizens express their opinions and desires not only through the electoral process but also by articulating their challenges and concerns.

In the administration of the universe, the Supreme Allah attentively hears the prayers, aspirations, challenges, and concerns of His servants, responding by assessing and offering resolutions. Thus, the lines of communication between humanity and Allah remain perpetually open. This continuous accessibility for the troubles, issues, and wishes of His servants is illustrated in the following verse:

> When My servants ask you concerning Me, indeed I am near. I respond to the invocation of the supplicant when he calls upon Me [...] (Al-Baqarah, 186).

This indicates that individuals possess the capacity to express their worries and hopes to the Sovereign of the universe. The Almighty Allah guarantees that these lines of communication are consistently accessible. When leaders foster open communication with their constituents, they reflect divine principles and demonstrate exemplary leadership. In contrast, if they opt to close these channels, they not only contradict Allah's teachings but also risk descending into oppression. A fundamental tenet emphasised throughout the Qur'an is the imperative to neither oppress nor be subjected to oppression. Thus, the foundation for peaceful coexistence and societal harmony rests with those who are prepared to confront social injustices and advocate for the freedom of the oppressed.

The aforementioned verse assures that the Almighty Allah will respond favorably to the sincere requests of those who supplicate. The establishment of open communication channels in a democratic context should begin within the family unit. Spouses ought to maintain transparent communication by actively listening to each other's issues and concerns. Likewise, children should feel encouraged to share their difficulties with their parents, who in turn should be receptive and work collaboratively to find solutions. This dynamic can be characterized as a democratic family.

In the realm of education, it is essential for students to have accessible communication channels to articulate their challenges and needs to their teachers and school administrators. It is imperative that educators and administrators do not obstruct these channels. Failure to do so would undermine the democratic nature of education, transforming it into an autocratic system where teachers assume authoritarian roles rather than fostering a democratic environment. The educator committed to democratic principles maintains open lines of communication with their students, which is essential for fostering a freedom-oriented educational environment.

In a similar vein, democratic governance embodies the principles of virtue. Al-Farabi (d. 950 CE) articulated that "politics is the art of instilling virtues in the people". When the channels of communication between the populace and their leaders are obstructed, the capacity to cultivate virtues dissipates. Political practitioners must be attuned to the grievances, pleas, hardships, and sorrows of the people, actively seeking solutions and offering support. Those who ignore these voices transform the practice of politics into a form of oppression, undermining the foundational integrity of the political art. By extinguishing the virtues inherent in politics, they precipitate societal decline and lead their communities toward irreversible consequences.

The Almighty Allah provides us with various avenues such as forgiveness, acceptance of repentance, mercy, love for His servants, sustenance, and relief from difficulties. He grants forgiveness to those who earnestly seek it, with the exception of those who associate partners with Him: "Allah does not forgive the association of partners with

Him, but He forgives anything else for whom He wills. Indeed, whoever associates partners with Allah has strayed far from the truth" (An-Nisa: 116). Thus, for individuals who commit the sin of associating partners with Allah, the opportunity for forgiveness remains available to those who earnestly appeal to Him for their transgressions.

To improve one's future, the route of repentance is accessible to those who turn to Allah: "Then Adam received certain words from his Lord, and He accepted his repentance. Indeed, He is the Accepting of repentance, the Merciful" (Surah Al-Baqara: 37). Allah welcomes the repentance of those who wish to abandon their previous sinful ways and embark on a new path, keeping the door to repentance perpetually open.

Allah promises to ease the suffering of those who earnestly turn to Him in prayer during their times of hardship, as illustrated in the verse: "And when adversity touches man, he calls upon Us, whether lying on his side or sitting or standing; but when We remove from him his adversity, he continues [in disobedience] as if he had never called upon Us to [remove] an adversity that touched him" (Surah Yunus: 12). This passage highlights that Allah is responsive to the pleas of those in distress and will alleviate their difficulties. Additionally, verse 156 of Surah Al-A'raf conveys that Allah's mercy is all-encompassing, and the pathway to His mercy remains accessible to those who seek it. The revelation of the Qur'an and the mission of the Prophet serve as evidence of Allah's commitment to keeping this channel of mercy open.

Those in leadership roles should embody forgiveness and provide opportunities for individuals embarking on a new chapter in their lives, consistently demonstrating compassion. The Almighty Allah also maintains an open channel of love. As stated, "Say, [O Muhammad], 'If you should love Allah, then follow me, [so] Allah will love you and forgive your sins. And Allah is Forgiving and Merciful'" (Al-Imran, 31). In this verse, Allah affirms that He will extend His love to those who adhere to the teachings of the Prophet, highlighting not only His love but also His willingness to forgive. Consequently, individuals in positions of authority across various fields should cultivate love, foster connections with others, and strive to be beloved in return.

Divine providence from Almighty Allah ensures that sustenance is available to those who labour diligently while expressing gratitude and trust. It is imperative for leaders and politicians to prioritise the economic well-being of their constituents, recognising the efforts of hardworking individuals and advocating for their rights. They must prevent any form of exploitation or infringement upon these rights. In essence, the concerns of the populace must be communicated to and acknowledged by those in positions of authority, rather than being disregarded. Ignored grievances do not vanish; instead, they are assessed by Allah and may return to society as a looming threat. For instance, those who govern with fairness and justice should heed the concerns of both students and parents in vocational education, ensuring that their voices are not silenced. Failing to do so would constitute a violation of their rights, with potential repercussions in the hereafter.

Radical groups often insist on adhering to the cultural traditions associated with the Prophet Muhammad; however, they do not convincingly argue that the Qur'an itself embodies the Prophet's tradition (*sunnah*). The Prophet's primary directive was to guide individuals exclusively through the Qur'an, without reliance on supplementary means. Contemporary Muslim states have deviated from the core principles of the Qur'an. While the Qur'an is among the most frequently recited and read texts globally, second only to the Bible, it remains one of the least comprehended and applied to current realities. This lack of understanding stems from the neglect of the knowledge that God emphasises in the Qur'an, which is often disregarded and insufficiently explored. Readers frequently lack expertise in essential fields such as biology, chemistry, physics, astronomy, mathematics, embryology, optics, psychology, sociology, history, and geology when interpreting Qur'anic verses that pertain to these disciplines, thereby impeding their ability to fully understand the divine message. Traditionally, Muslims have relied on medieval interpretations and commentaries of the Qur'an from esteemed imams throughout history.

Although these interpretations are valuable within their historical context, their limited grasp of modern knowledge highlights the need for ongoing reinterpretation of the text to maintain its relevance in today's society. I believe this represents a critical challenge for contemporary Muslims: their insufficient knowledge and adherence to outdated practices rooted in superstitions that have become intertwined with divine revelation. This frustration is perhaps enunciated by Bayraktar Bayraklı in his weekly Friday sermon in 2020 in the following emphatic words:

> How often does the Qur'an state: "We found our ancestors on this path... their path is sufficient for us..."? The reality is that people historically have followed the beliefs of their forebears, which has hindered them from embracing the true path of God. This is a significant issue facing the Islamic world today. Allah Almighty addresses this in Surah Al-Baqarah 170, Surah Al-Ma'idah 104, Surah Luqman 21, and others, highlighting the phrase "We found our ancestors on this path." Individuals are restricting themselves from progressing, from exploring new ideas, and from initiating change. Faith represents a profound transformation—a revolution within the heart. Yet, many resist this revolution, this innovation, this necessary change. Without collective renewal, a society cannot advance. For fifty years, I have sought to convey this message to the Islamic world. The writings of past scholars have become a barrier for the community. *Who are you to think, to write, to innovate? Their works are deemed sufficient; just comprehend what they have articulated.* This mindset has stifled the Islamic world, leaving it bound by chains that prevent liberation. This contradicts the tradition of our Prophet, who was tasked by Allah to "Relieve them from their burden and break the shackles that are put on them, O Muhammad (Araf 157)". In other words, break the chains and shackles on their minds and hearts. Is it not the responsibility of today's religious leaders to emulate the Prophet and serve as educators for Muslims? You must take action to break these chains! We will dismantle the superstitions, shortcomings, and errors of the past. They will not hold this nation back any longer. We will no longer seek guidance from graves; the dead will not dictate our path. We refuse to compromise the present and future of

our nation and this Muslim generation for the sake of history. While we acknowledge the past, we will embrace only what serves us well and critically examine it. Our focus will be on shaping our will and thoughts towards the future and the hereafter. It is only by doing so that we can progress with the times.[41]

From a religious standpoint, straying from true monotheism (*tawhid*) to seek help and guidance from the deceased, whether they are buried in graves, tombs, or are spiritual leaders, has steered the Muslim community towards *shirk*—an act of idolatry, polytheism, and the association of both living and deceased beings with God.

Knowledge is the foundation of faith. It begins with the intellect (*aql*) and is then embraced by the heart. This is illustrated by Abraham, who intellectually believed in God yet harboured doubts about resurrection in the afterlife. In Surah Baqara verse 260:

> And remember when Abraham said, "My Lord! Show me how you give life to the dead". Allah responded, "Do you not believe?" Abraham replied, "Yes I do, but just so my heart can be reassured".

During the period spanning the ninth to the twelfth centuries, Muslim scholars emerged as pioneers in a wide array of fields, showcasing remarkable intellectual prowess that would leave a lasting impact on the world. Their contributions to science, mathematics, medicine, philosophy, and the arts were not only groundbreaking but also laid the foundation for future advancements in these disciplines. If the Nobel Prize for science had existed during this golden age of knowledge, it is highly likely that these scholars would have been the recipients of numerous accolades, reflecting their unparalleled contributions to human understanding.

This era was characterised by a flourishing of ideas, driven by a spirit of inquiry and a commitment to learning. Scholars such as Al-Khwarizmi, who is often referred to as the father of algebra, and Ibn Sina, known in the West as Avicenna, made strides that would influence generations to come. The translation movement, which involved the translation of ancient texts into Arabic, played a crucial role in preserving and expanding upon the knowledge of previous civilisations, including the Greeks and Romans.

Fast forward to the present day, and we can still observe the echoes of this rich intellectual heritage. The principles and discoveries made by these early scholars continue to inform contemporary science and philosophy. Today, the global community is witnessing a resurgence of interest in the contributions of Muslim scholars, as their work is increasingly recognised for its significance in shaping modern thought. The legacy of this remarkable era serves as a reminder of the importance of intellectual curiosity and collaboration across cultures, inspiring current and future generations to pursue knowledge and innovation. The contrast between that remarkable period and the current state of affairs in the Muslim world is striking.

Throughout history, certain individuals have emerged as leaders who elevate nations toward their destined potential. These leaders possess unique insights and a visionary outlook that fosters meaningful change—not merely for the sake of change, but to empower societies that resist injustices, ignorance, oppression, and enslavement. Frequently, rather than conforming to prevailing norms, these remarkable individuals exhibit the courage and authenticity to apply their reasoning abilities, challenging the status quo and presenting new viewpoints. This departure from conventional thought can be bewildering for those who find comfort in established practices and traditions, resulting in a conflict between innovative thinkers and those who favour familiarity. The subsequent chapter examines one individual's struggles and triumphs against European imperialism and the societal ignorance surrounding the reconciliation of reason with faith—Mustafa Kemal Atatürk (1881-1938).

CHAPTER 14

CHALLENGING IMPERIALISM, EUROCENTRISM & MUSLIM RADICALISM

ATATÜRK'S VISION OF MODERNISATION AND THE FUTURE OF THE MUSLIM WORLD

During the decline of the nineteenth century, Europe rose to a position of dominance worldwide. The European perspective on the Orient underwent a transformation, shifting from medieval Mediterranean perceptions of being heretically confined to being seen as barbaric and exotic, and eventually as despotic. The Orient became marginalised and seen as a forgotten entity, a survivor of history. In the late twentieth century, Islam experienced a resurgence and is observing the Occident closely. The West, now finds themselves uncomfortably aware of this shift. According to Said, for the past two hundred years, "the West [was] the actor, the Orient a passive reactor".[1] Europe must now, for the first time, confront the Other consciously. The backlash of colonisation has made the West realise that the Other is a significant player on the global stage. Europe is uneasy about the rise of Islam because it is not facing a traditional army like it did in the past, but rather Islam is seen as a rebellious and covert enemy. For Europe and the United States, the resurgence of Islam validates its role as the complete opposite of European civilisation - a disruption to the *established order* and stability set up by the West. Since the fall of communism in the 1990s, the Western world has been searching for its ideological adversary or antagonist, which has been found in the

Middle East. Marxist ideology no longer poses a genuine threat to Western liberal philosophy, as the West has already triumphed over communism and emerged victorious in the Cold War. Therefore, Islam is the only ideology capable of presenting a radical challenge to Western dominance in the present day.

The refusal of the Orient to join the Occident in its pursuit of modernity, and the Occident's desire to incorporate the Other in its universal destiny, continue to exert a strong influence on our projections and attitudes, ranging from the most hostile to the most friendly. Europe, unfortunately, has not learned from its historical involvement in the Middle East, including the painful experiences and crises since 1945, such as the creation of Israel in 1948 and the 1956 Suez Canal crises, ongoing Arab-Israeli conflicts, 1967 Six Day War, 1973 Yom Kippur War, 2008-09, 2012, 2016, 2021, and 2023-2024. As a result, with each new crisis, the same old stereotypes resurface. This has led to a growing wave of anti-Muslim and anti-Arab sentiments in the West. It is evident that these sentiments have now become a successor to anti-Semitism. In the past, the Jew was seen as the repulsive element in society, but now the Arab and the Muslim have taken on that role. This shift can be attributed to the Jews, under the banner of rampant Zionism, being assigned the dubious mission of defending the West in the eastern Mediterranean and cleansing Europe of its historical crimes against Judaism. Consequently, the prejudices of Europeans and Americans have been further reinforced by this inversion.

Decline of Europe

Western thought, once confident in its superiority and dominance over other civilisations, gradually shifted towards a counterattack against its own triumphant nationalism and the scientific foundations of universalism. The immense impact of World War I exposed Europe's failure and paved the way for a surge of disillusionment. Post-World War I, Europe embarked on a path of political and economic decline. The war shattered the self-assured belief of European civilisation in the uninterrupted and boundless nature of its progress, thereby shaking European ethnocentrism. Humanity, or the traditional notions of a universal human being, was no longer solely evaluated based on Greece, Rome, and Europe.

Nevertheless, Europe faced great challenges in moving on from Greece and Rome, as it was incredibly arduous to leave them in the past where they rightfully belonged. In his renowned publication *Mohammad and Charlemagne* (1939), Henri Pirenne (1862-1935), a Belgian scholar, presented the Pirenne thesis, which has subsequently become widely recognised. This thesis reflects the prevailing European perspective that the abrupt emergence of Islam on the opposite shores of the Mediterranean permanently shattered the cohesion of the "Roman Lake". According to Pirenne:

> With Islam a new world was established on those Mediterranean shores which had formerly known syncretism of the Roman civilization. A complete break was made, which was to continue even to our own day. Henceforth, two different and hostile civilizations existed on the shores of Mare Nostrum. And although in our own days the European has subjected the Asiatic, he has not assimilated him.[2]

The Europeans continue to feel forlorn over the demise of Mediterranean harmony, which they had once considered their own. Whether it was the German 'barbarian' or the Arab invader who caused this disintegration of unity, it holds no significance. According to Pirenne, this notion of Europe's imagination still persists. For Pirenne, this has remained in the imagining vision of Europe.

The devastation of World War I and the subsequent disillusionment led to the decline of European civilisation, which faced a significant challenge in dealing with the beginning of its downfall. This line of thinking gave rise to a compelling rationale for action. Instead of attempting to address the shattered state of affairs and restore European cohesion, the solution was found in the complete dismantling of the six hundred year old Ottoman Empire and the division of its territories among the European powers.

At the onset of the First World War, European colonialism had firmly taken root in the Middle East. Algeria and Tunisia were under French control, while the British had established their presence in Aden and Egypt. These nations also held significant sway over the affairs of the Ottoman Empire, with their foreign ministers Sykes and Picot clandestinely devising a plan to dismantle it in 1916. According to Said:

> [...] as a result of World War I, Asiatic Turkey was being surveyed by Britain and France for its dismemberment. There, laid out on an operating table for surgery, was the Sick Man of Europe, revealed in all his weakness, characteristics, and topographical outline.[3]

The British and French were designated to divide the Ottoman Empire once the war concluded, and that is precisely what occurred. Syria and Lebanon were taken over by the French as mandates, while Transjordan, Iraq, and Palestine were acquired by Britain. In 1918, Jerusalem was captured by the British, effectively resurrecting the Crusader spirit of the medieval era. After 1,280 years of Muslim rule, the "city of peace" transitioned into Christian hands, eventually leading to the transfer of power to the Zionists within the next thirty years. As Said states, "In England numerous committees were empowered to study and recommend policy on the best way of dividing up the Orient.[4] However, the division of the Arab lands of the Turks was not the sole outcome. It was now the turn of mainland Turkey itself, the very country that had both threatened and fascinated Europeans for the past six centuries.

The British, French, and Italians divided Turkey among themselves, while the Greeks were granted the authority to occupy Izmir and the Anatolian interior. The Allied forces gained control over the Straits, and eventually occupied Istanbul in 1920. Consequently, Europe succeeded in acquiring the coveted 'jewel of the East' after its previous failed attempts to defend it centuries ago. With the restoration of Christendom in 'Constantinople', Europe's consciousness finally found solace. The seat of orthodox Christianity had been reclaimed. The collapse of the Ottoman Empire at the conclusion of World War I, along with the final distribution of spoils between Britain and France, marked the pinnacle of European colonial dominance. According to Edward Said, "by the end of World War I Europe had colonised 85 percent of the earth".[5] According to Shaw and Shaw, when the Allied forces entered Istanbul on 12th (French) and 13th (British) November 1918 it was with an:

> [...] unshakeable belief in the truth of their own propaganda, that the Turks had slaughtered millions of Christians for no reason whatsoever, forfeiting their right to rule even themselves and demonstrating once again the essential superiority of Western civilisation over that of Islam.[6]

The Allied high commissioner, Admiral Calthorpe stated that "it has been our consistent attitude to show no kind favour whatsoever to any Turk ..." and "[a]ll interchange of hospitality and comity has been rigorously forbidden [...]".[7] With the inclusion of Jerusalem and Constantinople within Europe's sphere of influence, the Orient undeniably lost its most valuable possessions. The final objective was to eradicate any opposition to European supremacy.

Mustafa Kemal Atatürk: Challenging European Imperialism and Muslim Radicalism

There is indisputable evidence of the European intellectual impact on Turkey following the French revolution. The *Tanzimat* reform movement during the 19th century serves as a testament to this influence.[8] Ottoman Turkey, starting from the beginning of the 1800s, witnessed the emergence of a distinct generation known as the Young Turks. These individuals not only played a pivotal role in the downfall of the Ottoman Empire but also witnessed the ascent of their most influential leader from within their own ranks, who staunchly resisted Western imperialism.

Mustafa Kemal (1881-1938), the sole individual who obstructed European imperialism in Turkey, emerged as a revered figure among his compatriots and a source of inspiration for countless Muslims residing in the Middle East and India, who were subjected to British and French dominion. By triumphing over Britain and France, Kemal propelled Turkey to become the inaugural nation to overthrow European imperialism in the aftermath of the war. The East, marked by the emergence of Nationalist movements, started to turn to Nationalist Turkey as a model and guide. Thus, Turkey became the first Oriental country to take a firm stance against Western imperialism and reject subjugation. According to Kinross:

> The name of Mustafa Kemal spread throughout Asia, as that of Garibaldi had once spread throughout Europe, firing the imagination of all those peoples in whom the First World War had kindled a spark of national consciousness and awakened the desire for freedom. The news of his struggle had its repercussions throughout Syria and Egypt, as far as Persia, India and China. Here surely was the prototype, for others to emulate, of the eastern Nationalist Revolution.[9]

Kemal emerged as a role model for those engaged in their endeavour to topple the foreign and non-believer imperialist regimes.[10] Iraq, Iran, India, and Egypt all followed Turkey's lead in overthrowing their European rulers one after another. This led to a surge in nationalism and self-awareness in the Middle East, the effects of which can still be felt today. As a result, European dominance in the region was shattered. However, the period between 1911 and 1922, marked by numerous wars such as the Tripolitanian War in 1911, the Balkan Wars from 1912 to 1913, the First World War from 1914 to 1918, and the War of Independence from 1919 to 1922, resulted in the decimation of an entire generation of Turkish elites. Thousands of Turkish soldiers lost their lives in distant lands like the Dardanelles, Caucasus, Galicia, Macedonia, Dobruja, Yemen, Hijaz, Libya, Sinai, Palestine, Iraq, and Iran. The valuable Turkish heartland, Anatolia, which had never experienced invasion before, suffered long-lasting damage.

The Treaty of Sevres, signed by the Ottoman government in 1920, signified the formal surrender and subsequent partitioning of the once-mighty empire. In the aftermath of this treaty, British forces assumed control of Istanbul, the empire's capital, as well as the strategically vital Bosphorus Straits and eastern Thrace, in collaboration with the Greeks. Concurrently, Greek forces occupied the Aegean coastline, including the city of Izmir and its surrounding areas. The Italians established their foothold in the southwestern region of Turkey, while the Armenians took control of the northwestern territories. The French expanded their influence over southeastern Anatolia, Syria, and Lebanon. Furthermore, the British extended their authority to encompass Iraq, Transjordan, Palestine, and the Suez Canal.

Confronted with an existential crisis stemming from imperialist occupation, Mustafa Kemal founded and organised a nationalist movement that actively opposed this foreign domination, launching the Turkish War of Independence in 1919. After expelling the Greeks from Izmir in 1922, negotiating with the Italians and the French to withdraw, Kemal challenged the British to leave Istanbul, eastern Thrace and the Straits by threatening to cross the Dardanelles and march on to the capital. This situation, known as the Chanak crisis, escalated when the British refused to comply and bolstered their defenses on the Asian side of Çanakkale, effectively obstructing the Turkish army. In an interview featured in the Daily Mail on September 15, 1922, Mustafa Kemal, expressed his demands:

> Our demands remain the same after our recent victory as they were before. We ask for Asia Minor, Thrace up to the River Maritsa and Constantinople ... We must have our capital and I should in that case be obliged to march on Constantinople with my army, which will be an affair of only a few days. I much prefer to obtain possession by negotiation, though naturally I cannot wait indefinitely.[11]

With the public opinion against another conflict following the First World War, the British capitulated on 23 September by accepting Kemal's terms. Over the course of four years, Kemal achieved a decisive victory against the Allied Powers, which ultimately forced the imperialist nations to engage in negotiations for a new peace treaty with the nascent Turkish government. The culmination of these efforts was the signing of the Treaty of Lausanne in 1923, which allowed Kemal to restore the territorial integrity and sovereignty of Turkey, successfully resisting both imperialism and foreign occupation. Historically, Kemal's victory against imperialism represents the first significant assertion of self-determination by a Muslim Other resisting subjugation that inspired other Muslims under colonialist rule to resist foreign occupation.

Mustafa Kemal possessed a visionary mindset and had a clear vision for the path he wanted to guide the new independent Turkey towards. I have decided against categorising Mustafa Kemal as a reformer of religion because this label suggests modifying the sacred scripture itself. He did not aim to reform Islam, the religion set out in the Qur'an, but rather to modify the religious customs and cultural traditions that had been followed for centuries, which involved people relying on religious scholars (*mufti*) who only possessed knowledge of the Qur'an in Arabic, in order to access information about their faith. It is significant to emphasise that a notable distinction exists between the religious principles revealed by God in the scriptures and the cultural customs and traditions that arise from those divine teachings, often through outdated interpretations that have become irrelevant and intertwined with superstitions over time—a concern that Kemal's revolutionary vision sought to address.

Out of the ruins of the Ottoman Empire, Kemal created a new Turkey. His aim was to modernise and Westernise at the same time. For Kemal one could not be achieved without the other. To achieve his aims Mustafa Kemal had to reject his peoples' past - that is their Ottoman past, heritage, superstitious customs not associated with Islam and institutions that rejected the natural sciences. With the stroke of a pen, Kemal proclaimed the abolishment of the Ottoman Sultanate and Empire on 1 November 1922, declared a republic on 29 October 1923, and abolished the Caliphate five months later on 3 March 1924. When the 37th Head of the Imperial House of Osman, the last Ottoman Caliph, Abdulmecid II, (r. 1922-1924) wrote Kemal asking for increased privileges, the President of the Republic reacted:

> Let the caliph and the whole world know that the caliph and the caliphate which have been preserved have no real meaning and no real existence ... The position of Caliphate in the end has for us no more importance than a historic memory.[12]

The Ottoman Empire had come to an end, yet a free nation-state of Turkey had emerged in Anatolia under the leadership of Mustafa Kemal, who had steered its progress towards modernisation. The nation was no longer bound by the outdated financial and economic restrictions of capitulations imposed on it by Europe, and was prepared to embark on a renewed and independent spirit. Following a decade of perseverance between 1911 and 1922, the arduous journey had finally concluded - Turkey had achieved its freedom.[13]

With the formal declaration of the dissolution of the Ottoman Empire on 1 November, 1922, Mustafa Kemal in an address to the Grand National Assembly of Turkey declared:

> New Turkey has no relation with the old one. The Ottoman Government has disappeared into history. A new Turkey has now been born.[14]

Making a complete break from its Ottoman past, Kemal created a new secular Turkish identity for the Turks by separating religion from the state with the aim of fashioning a modern Turkish identity along European lines while maintaining its unique Islamic traditions and traits. In 1923 Kemal stated:

> Every nation has its own traditions, mores and national traits. No nation should imitate exactly another. Because if it does, it will really neither attain that identity nor preserve its own. Such imitation would, doubtless, lead to disappointment.[15]

The Ottoman Turks' imitation of Europe in the past had the unintended consequence of undermining the Islamic identity of the Turks.[16] Kemal's cultural and institutional reforms were designed to tackle the complexities of Turkish-Muslim identity. Kemal aimed to address this issue by implementing a language reform (1929) and translating the Qur'an into Turkish (1935) in order to understand "the true essence of Islam".[17] In addition, he established the Directorate of Religious Affairs (Diyanet İşleri Başkanlığı) in 1924, which aimed to educate and promote Islam without any superstitious beliefs. These reforms were just a few of the measures taken to confront this challenge. By replacing the Arabic script with the Latin alphabet, adopting civil and legal codes from Europe, and blending Western and Eastern political and cultural institutions with a uniquely Turkish-Muslim character, Mustafa Kemal's new Turkey sought to create a distinct identity.[18] It is crucial to recognise that Kemal did not eliminate Islam from the lives of the populace; rather, he championed religious freedom as a fundamental individual right, which aligns with the religious tenet expressed in the Qur'an: "Let there be no compulsion in religion".[19] He empowered his citizens by promoting their understanding of Islam, becoming the first leader of a Muslim nation to translate the Qur'an into Turkish, thereby enabling them to grasp their faith in their own language. Consequently, Kemal emerged as the first leader in the Islamic world to challenge the Arabisation of Islam and restore the religion's inherent universality.

Kemal was lauded by his contemporaries for reforming the religious culture and making Islam more accessible, encouraging individuals to engage with their beliefs through their own reasoning. By providing the Qur'an in Turkish, Kemal facilitated a personal connection between the people and God. Mahmut Esat Bozkurt (1892-1943), the Minister of Justice of the Turkish Republic between 1924 and 1930, in his book entitled *Atatürk Ihtilali* (*The Atatürk Revolution*) compared him to Martin Luther, the sixteenth century German Protestant Reformation leader, because both leaders nationalised their respective holy books.[20] A notable contemporary and admirer of Kemal was the nationalist poet Ziya Gökalp (1876-1924). In his 1918 poem "Vatan" (Fatherland), he articulated his nationalist vision on the evolving religious culture in Turkey:

> A country where in Turkish call to prayer is said,
>
> The meaning of his prayer the villager can understand ...
>
> A country is whose schools the Turkish Qur'an is read,
>
> Everyone, young and old, understands the Guide's command,
>
> Oh Turkish son, there is your homeland![21]

The essence of the Qur'an lies in its divine message, which encourages individuals to derive lessons from it and incorporate them into their own lives. To do this one has to understand what one reads and hears. The essential message of Gökalp's intentions above is conveyed in the poem through the phrases "Turkish Qur'an is read" and "everyone ... understands", emphasising the importance of providing access to the Qur'an and Islam for those who engage their intellect in comprehending the faith in their own language rather than blindly adhering to it. Furthermore, the poet's perspective on religion and language, as depicted in these lines, shapes his stance on the role of Arabic within Turkey's educational system under Atatürk.

Additionally, the alteration of the dress code, which prohibited men from wearing the turban and fez—representing Arabic culture and outdated Ottoman customs, respectively—alongside the granting of voting rights to women in 1934, the right to divorce, and the absence of specific clothing restrictions, allowed Kemal to elevate his vision of a "new Turkey" to a position among the civilised nations of the world. With hindsight as historians' guide, according to Huntington, by rejecting Turkey's Islamic past "Atatürk made Turkey a 'torn country'", a claim that has been rejected by Turkish historians and writers.[22] A critique of Huntington's views and Turkish response to it will be examined in chapter fifteen.

Ironically, late twentieth century Muslim radicalists look unfavourably at the Turkish hero of the 1920s. According to Lewis, by creating a secular society out of the Ottoman-Islamic remains:

> Atatürk occupies a prominent place - not as the valiant defender of his people, who confronted the Europeans and beat them, but, rather, as the miscreant who, in his moment of victory, joined them and was thus guilty of the ultimate surrender and betrayal.[23]

Radical Muslims exhibit a deep-rooted commitment to their sectarian divisions and distortions of the Islamic religion. They do not represent Islam, nor do they come close to reflecting the true interpretation of Islam as outlined in the Qur'an. They lack the intellectual nuance to acknowledge the historical context in which Mustafa Kemal fought tirelessly. His primary objective was to liberate his people from the oppressive rule of the Ottoman sultan, freeing them from the status of mere subjects or "reaya" (slaves, *kul*- Turkish, and *reaya*-Arabic). Kemal bestowed upon individuals the freedom to think independently, rather than blindly following a leader like a flock of sheep, as the term *reaya* explicitly implies in the Qur'an, "O believers! Do not say, "Râ'ina." [Herd us!] But say, "Unẓurna," [Tend to us!] and listen attentively".[24] Additionally, Kemal vehemently opposed any form of foreign domination, refusing to succumb to external subjugation. Radical Muslims, in their criticism of Kemal, tend to overlook the fact that the last Ottoman Sultan, Mehmed VI, effectively surrendered his nation through the Treaty of Sevres in 1920, a decision imposed by the victorious powers following the conclusion of the First World War.

The extremist voices among Muslim radicals foresee a day when the Caliphate is restored. The dissolution of the Caliphate in 1924 marks a significant milestone in a continuum of historical transitions that have predominantly influenced the realms of politics, bureaucracy, and public service. It serves as a reminder that the past is irretrievable. Each community is assigned a specific period of existence, much like every culture, civilisation, and institution created by humanity, including the Caliphate, which follows its own unique timeline. For those Muslims who advocate for the restoration of the Caliphate, the Qur'an offers relevant guidance. In Surah Yunus 49, it is stated:

> For each community, there is an appointed term. When their time arrives, they cannot delay it for a moment, nor can they hasten it.[25]

From a secular perspective on history, once empires have fallen, they do not rise again. This principle applies to the Caliphate as well. Furthermore, this notion is also reflected in a divine decree from Allah in the aforementioned verse, which radicals would do well to consider. Moreover, the more fervently radicals strive to restore the Caliphate, the more the historical forces at play impede its revival.

Voice of Reason ~ Contextualising Atatürk's Reforms: Muhammad Iqbal and Atatürk's Turkey in 1930

Offering a fresh new perspective requires the process of independent thought combined with an understanding of the Qur'an. This is called *ijtihad* in Arabic, literally meaning, effort, to strive, to persevere, to endeavour. Kemal's reforms in Turkey falls under this religious context. At the height of Mustafa Kemal's visionary reforms in Turkey in the late 1920s and early 1930s, a contemporary of Kemal, Muhammad Iqbal (1877-1938), educated in Lahore (Pakistan), England and Germany, published *The Reconstruction of Religious Thought in Islam* in 1930. Like Kemal, Iqbal advocated strongly for the overall political and spiritual rejuvenation of the Muslim world. In his publication, *The Reconstruction of Religious Thought in Islam*, Iqbal emphasised the need to reassess the intellectual underpinnings of Islamic philosophy. This book represents a notable addition to modern Islamic thought and exemplifies the dominant perspectives of the era on the necessity of reform in religious thinking and mindset. Moreover, its core message continues to resonate within the Muslim world.

During the pre-decolonisation era of South-East Asia, Iqbal expressed his aspirations for the future independence for Muslims in the region from the shackles of European imperialism and colonisation. He emphasised that Turkey is unique among Muslim nations today, having successfully awakened from its dogmatic slumber and attained self-awareness. Kemal and the Turkish Nationalists adopted the concept of the separation of Church and State from the historical development of European political thought.[26] According to Iqbal:

> The point of supreme interest with the Nationalist Party [led by Kemal] is above all the State and not Religion. With th[is] think[ing] religion as such has no independent function. The state is the essential factor in national life which determines the character and function of all other factors. They, therefore, reject old ideas about the function of State and Religion, and accentuate the separation of Church and State. Now the structure of Islam as a religio-political system, no doubt, does permit such a view […].[27]

Under Kemal's reforms, Turkey has embraced intellectual freedom and transitioned from the ideal to the real through rigorous intellectual and moral struggles. Turkey is poised to face new challenges and perspectives as its society evolves, unlike other Muslim countries that remain stagnant in their traditional values. Iqbal notes that the English philosopher Hobbes astutely noted that having a succession of identical thoughts and feelings equates to having no thoughts and feelings at all. Muslim countries lack innovative and creative thinking, to put it differently. Iqbal argues that this is the predicament faced by most Muslim countries, while Turkey is forging ahead to establish new values. Through profound experiences, the Turkish people have discovered their true selves and embarked on a journey of growth, change, and innovation. The crucial question that lies ahead for Turkey, and potentially other Muslim nations, is whether Islamic law can evolve.[28] From this perspective, the Muslim nations have found themselves at a crossroads for centuries, facing a challenge in their intellectual, technological, and economic progress.

Let us examine the reforms of Kemal from Iqbal's perspective. The Grand National Assembly has exercised its authority of *ijtihad* in relation to the establishment of Caliphate. According to Sunni Law, the appointment of a Caliph is absolutely essential. The initial query that arises in this context is whether the Caliphate should be entrusted to a single individual. Turkey's interpretation of *ijtihad* is that, in accordance with the essence of Islam, the Caliphate can be vested in a collective body or an elected Assembly by the will of the people.[29] This is in accordance with the Qur'anic authority, "O you who believe! Obey God and obey the Messenger, and those from among you who are invested with authority".[30] As Iqbal states:

> Personally, I believe the Turkish view is perfectly sound. It is hardly necessary to argue this point. The republican form of government is not only thoroughly consistent with the spirit of Islam, but has also become a necessity in view of the new forces that are set free in the world of Islam.[31]

For the sake of national sovereignty, Kemal and the Grand National Assembly took an unprecedented action by abolishing the Caliphate in 1924. In order to understand the Turkish view, Iqbal looks at the fourteenth century Muslim historian Ibn Khaldun's views on the Universal Caliphate.[32] According to Khaldun, the Universal Caliphate can be viewed in three different ways: firstly, it is considered a Divine institution and therefore, it is believed to be essential. Secondly, some argue that it is merely a matter of expediency. Lastly, such an institution is unnecessary.[33] The Turks contend that their political thinking should be influenced by their historical political background, which clearly indicates that the concept of Universal Caliphate has proven to be unsuccessful in reality. This concept was feasible when the Ottoman-Islamic Empire was unified. However, with the fragmentation of the Empire, separate political entities and nation states have emerged. The concept, therefore, is no longer applicable and cannot function as a relevant element in the structuring of contemporary Islam. Instead of being beneficial, the Caliphate has hindered the potential reunification of independent Muslim nations.[34] Taking the argument a step further, the idea of a Universal Caliphate is eclipsed or supplanted by Arabian imperialism from the earlier centuries of Islam, which persists in shaping the religious mindset today.[35] Iqbal believes that Muslim unity is based on independence and sovereignty, while also respecting the unique social traditions of each nation. Considering Kemal's reforms from this perspective, they are deemed justified within the historical and religious contexts. Moreover, their enduring relevance as a contemporary model for establishing an egalitarian society in line with the principles of Islam cannot be overlooked. According to Iqbal:

> It seems to me that God is slowly bringing home to us the truth that Islam is neither Nationalism nor Imperialism but a League of Nations which recognises artificial boundaries and racial distinctions for facility of reference only, and not for restricting the social horizon of its members.[36]

The Qur'an reinforces this message: "O mankind! We created you from a single (pair) of a male and a female, and made you into nations and tribes, that ye may know each other (not that ye may despise (each other). Verily the most honoured of you in the sight of Allah is (he who is) the most righteous of you. And Allah has full knowledge and is well acquainted (with all things)".[37]

1933 ~ Contextualising Higher Education Reform of Atatürk and the Transfer of Western Knowledge to Turkey

In 1949, Albert Einstein encounters a young international student named Münir Ülgür during his time at Princeton. Upon discovering that Ülgür hails from Turkey, Einstein's enthusiasm becomes evident as he exclaims, "Did you know that your country gave birth to the most exceptional leader of the entire century?" Einstein proceeds to recollect an invitation he received from Atatürk in the early 1930s, urging him to impart his knowledge at one of their universities. However, as destiny would have it, this opportunity did not come to fruition.[38]

Reforming the higher education sector was imperative in order to embrace intellectual freedom. Atatürk remained resolute in his stance on this issue, considering it a crucial step towards the modernisation of Turkey. The process of university reform was initiated when the government of Turkey received a letter from Albert Einstein in 1933. Western historians frequently overlook the important contribution made by Jewish scholars from Germany and Austria in the advancement of the Turkish higher education system, who were brought in by Atatürk's administration during the 1930s. The task of rebuilding a nation from the remnants of an outdated empire, entangled in superstitions and devoid of reason, logic, and science, demanded unwavering determination and a visionary outlook for the future. Despite facing criticism from his staunch opponents in the West, as well as conservative and radical Islamic religious factions both within and outside of Turkey, Atatürk's detractors fail to recognise that Islam, as guided by the Qur'an, cannot be truly embraced without the pursuit of education and the utilization of intellect. A poignant example of this is the current suppression of education for girls and women in Afghanistan in the name of religion.

Following the collapse of the Ottoman Empire and a prolonged struggle for independence, Turkey established itself as a Republic in 1923. In terms of higher education, the Republic inherited more than 300 Islamic madrasas, one of which was converted into an early university in the early 1900s. Furthermore, there were three military academies, one of which was expanded to incorporate a civil engineering school in 1909. As the 1930s began, the government acknowledged the necessity of modernising its higher education system and implemented measures to tackle this matter. Due to the limited number of well-educated Turkish citizens available to implement Turkey's medical and educational reforms, the new government seized the opportunity presented by Europe's tragedy. Approximately 190 distinguished intellectuals, who were unable to pursue opportunities in America due to immigration restrictions and anti-Semitic hiring practices, were welcomed to Turkey to contribute to the development of higher education.[39] Some of these academics that helped transform the higher education landscape of Turkey include: Hans Reichenbach (1891–1952, philosopher, mathematician), Richard von Mises (1883-1953, applied scientist, philosopher, mathematician), mathematicians and applied scientists William Prager (1903–1980) and Hilda Geiringer (1893–1973), astronomer E. Finlay Freundlich (1885–1964), physicist Arthur Von Hippel (1898–2003), archaeologists Benno Landsberger (1890 - 1968) and Hans Güterbock (1908 - 2000), economist and economic sociologist Wilhelm Röpkec (1899 –1966) and Alexander Rüstow (1885– 1963) respectively, architects Margarete Schütte-Lihotzky (1897–2000) and Bruno Taut (1880-1938), zoologist Kurt Kosswig (1903-1982), and public dentistry innovator Alfred Kantorowicz (1880–1962).[40] Einstein personally knew and continued to correspond with his colleagues working in Turkey.[41]

This initiative not only saved the lives of over 1000 individuals, including their family members and staff, but also highlighted Turkey's significant yet often overlooked role during the Shoah (Holocaust), with notable figures like Albert Einstein involved. Unfortunately, this historical event remains largely unknown outside of Turkey and has received minimal attention from historians.[42]

By the early 1930s Einstein had already been a visiting scholar at Christ Church in Oxford while trying to seek permanent employment elsewhere. Like other Jewish scholars persecuted in Hitler's Nazi Germany at the time, Einstein sought to further his academic career and his livelihood in other countries. As Princeton University was the first to accept his theory of relativity, Einstein chose his place of academic residency in the United States in 1933. In the year mentioned, he dispatched a letter to Atatürk, specifically dated 17th September. Nevertheless, the letter ended up being delivered to the Office of the Prime Minister, İsmet İnönü, in which he sincerely requested Turkey to extend an invitation to "forty skilled experts and distinguished scholars ... to establish themselves and contribute their expertise in your nation". The letter reads:

> Your Excellency (Atatürk),
>
> As Honorary President of the World Union "OZE" I beg to apply to your Excellency to allow forty professors and doctors from Germany to continue their scientific and medical work in Turkey. The above mentioned cannot practice further in Germany on account of the laws governing there now. The majority of these men possess vast experience, knowledge end scientific merits and could prove very useful when settling in a new country.
>
> Out of a great number of applicants our Union has chosen forty experienced specialists and prominent scholars, and is herewith applying to Your Excellency to permit these men to settle and practice in your country. These scientists are willing to work for a year without any remuneration in any of your institutions, according to the orders of your Government.
>
> In supporting this application, I take the liberty to express my hope, that in granting this request your Government will not only perform an act of high humanity, but will also bring profit to your own country.
>
> I have the honour to be, Your Excellency's obedient servant,
>
> Prof. Albert Einstein[43]

Sami M. Günzberg, a Jewish Turkish dentist, was the one who encouraged Einstein to write the letter. They had met at an International Conference in Paris organised by the Union for the Protection of the Well-Being of the Jewish Population (OSE), where Einstein held the position of honorary president. Günzberg, who was also Atatürk's dentist, possessed extensive knowledge regarding the Turkish leader's aspirations to modernise Turkey.

The handwritten Turkish annotations are highly compelling in the original letter sent. The notation in the top right corner reveals that İnönü sent the letter to the Ministry for National Education, also known as Maarif Vekaleti, on October 9, 1933. The remaining annotations can be attributed to Reşit Galip, the current Minister. One of them states that, "It is not possible to accept the proposal with the existing legislation",[44] while another one declares that "These are not acceptable according to today's law",[45] indicating that the Ministry initially rejected the proposal. However, it must be noted that with over 40 German scientists of Jewish ancestry appointed to the position university professorships under the University Reform program suggests that Atatürk personally intervened in this matter.[46]

It may pose a challenge for historians specialising in higher education to find a comparable qualitative shift that occurred on a national scale within such a brief period, particularly in a Muslim country. The migration of intellectuals to Turkey during the war resulted in a significant loss for one country, a gain for another, and a delay in benefits for a third country, as many of these intellectuals eventually settled in the United States.

Arnold Reisman in the article "Turkey's Invitations to Nazi Persecuted Intellectuals Circa 1933: A Bibiliographic Essay on History's Blind Spot", argues that in 1933, Turkey embarked on an urgent process to reform its legal and healthcare delivery systems, as well as its higher education system, by utilizing refugees escaping from the Nazis. Through official government invitations, these individuals found a safe refuge. Due to strict immigration laws and prevalent anti-Semitic hiring practices in American universities, many found America inaccessible. However, seizing other opportunities, most of these distinguished intellectuals migrated to the West and played a crucial role in advancing America's academic landscape. What is neglected in the West, however, is the fact that English-speaking historians are still unaware of this significant chapter in the history of the 20th century.[47]

The idea of establishing a fully modern higher education system, inspired by universities in Western Europe, originated from the "Rapport sur l'universite' d'Istanbul" written by Swiss educationalist Albert Malche in 1932. This report was commissioned by Atatürk's government. Following Malche's recommendations, the government of the Republic of Turkey officially shut down *Dar'ül fünun* (Ottoman House of Science opened in 1865) on July 31, 1933, thereby terminating all existing faculty contracts. The very next day, Istanbul University was inaugurated, utilizing the physical infrastructure of *Dar'ül fünun* and employing a small portion of its original faculty, along with more than 30 internationally renowned German professors who had sought refuge in Turkey.[48]

The majority of expatriate professors specialised in medicine, mathematics, and natural science, with fewer expatriates found in the fields of law and the arts. From the academic year 1933-1934 onwards, professors exiled from Germany took on leadership roles in eight out of twelve fundamental science Institutes, along with six directors of the seventeen clinics at the Faculty of Medicine in Istanbul. Nevertheless, a report presented in the autumn of 1933 by Professor Philipp Schwartz highlighted the deficiencies in equipment and facilities faced by the Faculty of Medicine. Across all seven fundamental science disciplines, there were merely 30 antiquated microscopes available. The clinics were found to be in poor condition, lacking proper maintenance and adequate resources. This assessment made by a professor who had emigrated was partially corroborated by other sources.

Ankara had a limited number of academics who chose to settle there. This was primarily because the University of Ankara was still in its early stages of development, with only a few institutes and scientific organisations in existence. Unlike in Istanbul, where the disciplinary boundaries were clearly defined, Ankara lacked such clarity. The majority of scientists, architects, and artists who came to Ankara did so under the sponsorship of the official German and Austrian legations, rather than being invited by the Notgemeinschaft to the University of Istanbul. Among the emigrants in Ankara, the state school of music had the highest number, followed by the faculty of arts and the medical institutes.

Two decades following the collapse of the Ottoman Empire and amidst the mass departure from Germany which stripped the country of its top educational institutions, the University of Istanbul that Atatürk helped elevate to world class rank. Surprisingly, classes commenced in November of 1933.[49] On 20 October 1933, *Le Journal d'Orient*, reports with the headline: "Les nouveaux professeurs de l'Universite" (The new professors of the University):

> The University has begun welcoming new professors from Europe who have been invited to teach. Professor Hirsch, who will be instructing maritime commerce at the Law Faculty, arrived at the university the day prior. During his visit, he engaged in discussions with the dean and his fellow colleagues. Professor Hirsch expressed his intention to immerse himself in the Turkish culture while residing in Istanbul, with the goal of learning the language within three years. Furthermore, he expressed a strong sense of belonging to Turkey, considering it as his own country. It is expected that all foreign professors will assume their positions by the 25th of October.[50]

Germany's top universities experienced a significant loss of scholars, resulting in a mass exodus. This depletion was so severe that the University of Istanbul earned the well-deserved title of "the best German University in the world".[51] The profound influence of these scholars on Turkey's higher education system, healthcare delivery, and the arts cannot be overstated. Their contributions are highly valued within Turkey and among its intellectual community worldwide. Present-day Turkey boasts an impressive number of 72 universities, many of which are on par with or even surpass most American universities. Today, Turkey is several decades ahead of western countries, particularly the United States, in terms of percentages of women working as physicians (26%), engineers (27%), architects (33%), lawyers (30%), and university professors (42%). This is also true at the senior level administration of universities, government agencies, and management of private sector companies.⁵²

The impact of professors who immigrated and their valuable contributions to Turkey's modernisation still have a lasting effect on the country and the educated Turkish Diaspora. This topic is particularly significant given Turkey's current circumstances. While Turkey aims to become a member of the European Union, it also faces difficulties in preserving its secular identity within a democratic system. Moreover, Turkey has a predominantly traditional Islamic population and is surrounded by hostile theocratic nations. Nevertheless, in the current political climate, the fluctuation between secularism and religious lifestyle in Turkey has sparked renewed fervour among supporters and opponents alike. In an article published in the widely circulated *Hürriyet* newspaper on 29 October 2006, journalist Murat Bardakçı commemorated the 83rd anniversary of the Republic by drawing a comparison between the Turkey established by Atatürk and the present-day Turkey:

> We celebrate the 83rd anniversary of the Republic by discussing women-only parks, religious sect members' robes, or whether shaking a woman's hand is a sin. Here is the difference between Turkey in the days when the Republican regime was only ten years old and the Republic Turkey that is 83 years old: German physicist Albert Einstein, one of the world's greatest geniuses, sent a message to Ankara to the Prime Ministry on September 17, 1933, saying, "I am honoured to be your loyal servant." In his letter, he requests employment from Turkey for 40 scientists from different professions who were not able to work in Germany after Hitler came to power. Einstein's request was accepted by Atatürk and all of these scientists came to Turkey and took part in the University Reform.
>
> Turkey is commemorating the 83rd anniversary of the proclamation of the Republic by discussing the Mayor of Bağcılar's attempt to open a park only for women, whether a man performing prayer without a

robe provokes a man praying in the row behind him during prostration, or whether shaking a woman's hand is a sin. Happy birthday!

Today, I am publishing a document that is extremely important as it shows where Turkey has gone instead of where it should have gone in the years since the proclamation of the Republic: German physicist Albert Einstein, who is considered one of the greatest geniuses of the world, wrote to the Turkish Government 73 years ago. A request letter he sent to Turkey to provide job opportunities to 40 leading German scientists [...].[53]

The term "philosophy" encompasses a well-defined field of study, but can also be applied to various frameworks within different areas of knowledge, such as "philosophy of science", "philosophy of economics", and "philosophy of art". Therefore, a change in an established framework within any field indicates a shift in philosophical approach across disciplines. Paradigm shifts are often met with resistance, as noted by philosopher Sir K. Popper, who suggests that they require a revolution. Theoretical physicist and Nobel laureate Max Planck (1858-1947) famously stated that a fresh scientific discovery does not prevail by persuading its adversaries and enlightening them, but instead by the passing of time until its adversaries perish and a new generation emerges that embraces it.[54] Arguably, those who introduce new paradigms or bring about paradigm shifts can be considered as philosophical innovators or reformers within their respective fields. As Albert Einstein once stated, "Great spirits have always encountered violent opposition from mediocre minds. The latter are unable to comprehend when an individual does not blindly adhere to inherited prejudices, but instead, bravely and honestly employs their intellect".[55] Mustafa Kemal Atatürk and all other visionaries and reformers throughout history including those fighting against social justice, oppression, inequality, rights of women, ignorance, messengers of God from Abraham to Moses, Jesus and Muhammad, all fall into this category of "great spirits" who did not "blindly" follow "inherited prejudices", but, chose to use their God-given intellect for the betterment of humanity.

This crucial migratory event has transformed Turkey's higher education and shaped the history of Western science and knowledge in the country after the creation of the Republic in 1929. Numerous notable anthologies, monographs, and other publications exist where one would anticipate discovering information on this topic. Regrettably, there is nothing but a resounding absence of any such material. The Princeton University Press published *Political Modernization in Japan and Turkey* in 1964, a project funded by the Social Science Research Council and the Ford Foundation. In a detailed thirty-page chapter on "Education in Turkey", Frederick W. Frey, a Princeton PhD and author of *Turkish Political Elite* (1965), fails to recognise the important role of German émigré professors in the development of Turkish higher education. This significant aspect of the introduction of Western knowledge into Turkish society is surprisingly not discussed elsewhere in the 500-page book. Moreover, other books including, *Jewish Immigrants of the Nazi Period in the USA* by H. A. Strauss published in 1979, *Lifeline To A Promised Land* (1948) by Ira A. Hirschmann, the 1990 publication of the *Encyclopedia of the Holocaust*, edited by I. Gutman, do not mention *Notgemeinschaft deutscher Wissenschaftler im Ausland* (German scientists abroad) nor the work of Philipp Schwarz.

Given the internal divisions among the Turks regarding their identity and representation, it is understandable why the Western world may not prioritise showing them and Islam respect. Once again, in the 21st century, Euro-American historiography demonstrates its bias and prejudice against the Muslim Other. As a Muslim nation, Turkey was simply outside the scope of Europe-centred academic research. In general, historians tend to view the East through the historical perspective of Europeans, portraying it as an infidel, menacing, morally corrupt place and backward. The Turkish display of enlightened self-interest and a degree of generosity towards individual Jews and non-German non-Jews appears to be considered by many who are not Islamic scholars or Turkologists as peculiar exceptions within a broader context. These motives and actions are often perceived as crude and self-serving, despite the fact that the Turkish historical record is actually quite commendable. Due to its geographical distance and the historical divide between Christianity and Islam, Turkey is often given little attention, if any.[56]

Atatürk's confrontation with European imperialism ultimately secured a future for the nascent modern nation-state of Turkey. By resisting European domination and preventing the West from seizing the core of Anatolia, he became a beacon of hope for millions of Muslims globally, who remained under the influence of European powers in the newly established Middle Eastern protectorates of the former Ottoman Empire, as well as in Southeast Asia, including the Indian subcontinent and the Dutch East Indies (Indonesia). Recognising education as a fundamental reform to elevate Turkey to a higher level of civilisation, Atatürk instilled in the youth of his nation a profound sense of national identity through the application of reason and intellect. Furthermore, his initiative to translate the Qur'an into Turkish not only allowed Turkish Muslims to understand their faith through rational thought but also strengthened their identity as Turks within the broader Muslim community. Atatürk regarded education as the fundamental element for modernisation and progress. Contrary to the claims of his opponents, he believed that this approach to modernisation was not in opposition to the teachings of the Qur'an; instead, he viewed these reforms as aligned with the essence of both the Qur'an and Islam.

Can Atatürk's vision continue to be a model for the Islamic world today?

Atatürk strongly opposed the politicisation of Islam and its evolution into an ideological framework, viewing this shift as a significant factor contributing to the decline of Islamic societies. He argued that Pan-Islamism, which had been a prominent intellectual movement during the Ottoman Empire and peaked under the rule of Abdulhamit II (r. 1867-1909), lacked substantial relevance even in the context of 1921 during the Allied occupation of Istanbul, aside from its aspiration for the welfare and happiness of Muslims globally. Atatürk expressed this sentiment with the following words:

> I interpret Pan-Islamism in the following manner: our nation, along with the government that represents it, inherently desires the well-being and prosperity of all our religious citizens in the world ... This brings us immense joy and satisfaction. We observe that these citizens share a similar concern for our happiness, a sentiment that is evident on a daily basis [...].[57]

Atatürk's statements suggest that in the New Turkey, the dedication to the Islamic world will persist through political, economic, and cultural connections that diverge from the traditional concept of the "umma" or Muslim community.

Atatürk's comprehensive approach to foreign policy led him to take a keen interest in the Islamic world. During the War of Independence (1919-1922), he fostered strong ties with Islamic nations and facilitated cooperation among countries such as Turkey, Afghanistan, Iran, and Iraq through the establishment of the Sadabad Pact in the Republican era. This initiative underscores Atatürk's commitment to fostering "cultural" and "political" connections with the Islamic world, prioritising national interests over the concept of "umma". Additionally, he cultivated relationships with figures like Afghan King Amanullah Khan and Iranian Shah Reza Pahlavi. The pursuit of a homogenous Islamic cultural identity based on religious traditions was not compatible with the national interests of the newly established Turkey, as it would necessitate compromising its sovereignty over cultural and religious practices. This perspective remains relevant today, as the collective foreign policy of the European Union often clashes with the individual policies of its member states.

Despite the launch of the Global Strategy in 2016 and the introduction of the Strategic Compass in 2022, the European Union's approach to foreign and security policy has primarily advanced in theory rather than in practical application. Much like the Muslim world during Atatürk's era and also in contemporary contexts, the European Union faces a similar challenging dichotomy between its core values and strategic interests, as well as the need to present a unified EU stance while also considering the diverse perspectives of its 27 member states.

Additionally, Paul Taylor contends that the presence of multiple, often conflicting, power centers in Brussels further complicates the situation.[58] Consequently, the consensus that does form tends to be a sluggish and inadequate response to policy challenges, and at its worst, it results in a dissonance that is both embarrassing for Europeans and confusing for the international community.[59]

The EU's initial reaction to the Hamas-Israel conflict (2023-) serves as a prime example of ineffective practices. Rather than recognising the enduring conflict that has persisted since 1948, the European Union appears to be supporting the Israeli right-wing government's Zionist agenda by confronting its historical responsibility for past atrocities committed against humanity. This strategy merely strengthens and underscores the conflict instigated by Hamas on 7 October. Critics argue that this demonstrates the Union's inability to become a significant geopolitical player, as member governments are unwilling to relinquish sovereignty on foreign affairs in the same manner they do for trade, business regulation, or monetary policy, where the EU collectively acts through institutions such as the European Commission and the European Central Bank.[60]

While democracy in the United States faces challenges under Trumpian politics; concurrently, similar authoritarian trends have been observable in the Global South, particularly within Muslim-majority nations, where they have persistently undermined the democratic desires of the populace for decades. From a historical perspective, it is essential to revisit the visionary goals and achievements of Mustafa Kemal Atatürk, especially in light of Turkey's recent struggles with its identity over the past two decades under the leadership of Recep Tayyip Erdoğan and his Justice and Development Party (AKP), which has been in power since 2002. Maria Chiara Cantelmo argues that Erdoğan's movement has consistently upheld the Kemalist approach to the State, leading some scholars to interpret the AKP's experience as a manifestation of a novel or post-Kemalism, particularly considering its recent embrace of the national Islamic discourse.[61] For Cantelmo, there exist significant connections between Kemalism and Islamism that extend beyond a mere ongoing conflict or a straightforward cause-and-effect association.⁶² Taking into account the uncertainties surrounding Kemalist ideology in a majority Muslim nation and the complex nature of Turkish secularism, one could even argue that political Islam has effectively utilised Kemalist principles and establishments (such as the Directorate of Religious Affairs) and repurposed them for religious objectives.⁶³ The current ruling party's approach of politicising Islam to secure the backing of traditional rural Anatolian Muslims contradicts the foundational principles established by Atatürk, particularly through the Directorate of Religious Affairs and his Turkish translation of the Qur'an. Erdogan's strategy effectively reverses historical progress by dictating to the populace not only what to believe but also how to think and vote, prioritising religious convictions over national interests. On the matter of politicising religion, Atatürk said:

> Those who use religion for their own benefit are detestable. We are against such a situation and will not allow it. Those who use religion in such a manner have fooled our people; it is against just such people that we have fought and will continue to fight.⁶⁴

The relationship between Islam and democracy in contemporary Turkey is presently a multifaceted challenge, particularly since secularism has not been widely accepted as a shared principle, despite its establishment through the reforms of Mustafa Kemal. Cantelmo contends that the "Turkish model" of Islamic liberalism, which gained traction during the Arab Spring, has not successfully disseminated to other Muslim countries and has diminished in relevance within Turkey following the events of 2013. The current trend of Islamisation in Turkey may be utilized as a strategy to navigate the political turmoil confronting the AKP and to bolster institutions that have been jeopardised by the unsuccessful coup attempt in 2016.⁶⁵ Moreover, the escalating authoritarian inclinations exhibited by President Erdogan and his ruling party pose a significant threat to the democratic institutions that have been strengthened in Turkey since the death of Mustafa Kemal Atatürk in 1938, despite the four military coups (1971, 1980, 1997, 2016). This troubling trend encompasses the erosion of an independent judiciary, the imposition of constraints on press freedom, and the systematic suppression and imprisonment of individuals who express dissenting opinions against Erdogan or his administration, as exemplified by the arrest of Ekrem İmamoğlu, the popular mayor of Istanbul and a potential presidential candidate, on March 23, 2025. Collectively, these actions undermine the fundamental democratic rights of citizens, adversely affect Turkey's reputation in the international arena, and reduce its credibility on the global stage. The implications of these developments are profound, as they not only challenge the principles of democracy within Turkey but also raise concerns among international observers regarding the country's commitment to upholding human rights and democratic norms. These concerns are central to the European Union's stance, which hinders Turkey's aspirations for permanent membership. Thus, attributing the ongoing clash of civilisations debate solely to Western influences can be misleading; Turkey itself promotes this cultural conflict by failing to adhere to the collective standards set by the EU, which it aspires to join. Political instability is not unique to Turkey; it reflects a broader trend observed in many Muslim-majority countries worldwide, spanning from the Gulf States and Saudi Arabia to Egypt, North Africa, Central Asian Turkic Republics, Pakistan, Afghanistan and beyond.

Furthermore, one could argue that Atatürk's stance against the politicisation of Islam was a progressive move for his time, reflecting his innovative and visionary mindset. In light of the current upheaval within the Muslim world, his principles and reformative actions remain a guiding framework for breaking free from the cycle of extremism and radicalism that has historically influenced various aspects of Muslim political discourse. While it may seem that I am endorsing the ideology of 'Kemalism' or Atatürk's views, this interpretation is misleading. There is no such thing as 'Kemalism' as this indicates a personal ideology he was forging in Turkey. For those who persist in their criticism of him in the Muslim world, it is important to note that Kemal did not wage war on Islam, the religion, nor did he attemt to eradicate Islam in Turkey; rather, he fought against the ignorance of the mind. On this matter, Kemal said:

Know that whatever conforms to reason, logic, and the advantages and needs of our people conforms equally to [Islam]. If our religion did not conform to reason and logic, it would not be the perfect religion, the final religion [...].⁶⁶

It is this very ignorance that continues to dominate many Muslim nations, which are often governed through authoritarian and autocratic regimes that restrict women's rights, access to education, and political representation.

In a speech presented to the Turkish Grand National Assembly on April 10, 2025, Indonesian President Prabowo Subianto highlighted the significance of Mustafa Kemal Atatürk not only to Indonesia and his personal convictions but also to the wider Global South, a perspective that continues to hold relevance in contemporary discussions. His remarks regarding Atatürk were met with applause from the assembly members:

> I am an admirer of Turkish history; I study and learn from it. Your history inspires me. In my youth, I had an icon, someone I greatly admired; my hero and icon was Mustafa Kemal Atatürk. Fatih Sultan Mehmet was also one of my idols and heroes. If you were to visit my office or home in Jakarta, you would see a statue of Atatürk. This is not just in Indonesia; I refer to the global south, particularly developing countries. In all these nations, Mustafa Kemal is regarded as an idol and a model, representing courage, leadership, patriotism, and perseverance. This is why the current state of the world, particularly its geopolitical situation, demands strong leadership—courageous and wise leadership. Turkey and Indonesia must take the lead and be strong. If we collaborate, we will be more powerful. Our voices will resonate more strongly and be heard more clearly by the rest of the world.⁶⁷

Mustafa Kemal Atatürk remains a figure of respect and admiration among Muslim nations globally and those of the Global South. His vision for the Muslim community continues to resonate, even in the face of radical critiques and opposing voices that seek to hinder the progress of the Islamic world. Atatürk's exemplary leadership and resilience serve as a model for contemporary Muslim leaders who are navigating growing geopolitical challenges, a sentiment echoed by the Indonesian President, who advocates for a more unified and assertive voice for the Global South on the global stage.

From a global and objective perspective—if such a standpoint exists—there appears to be no viable alternative for achieving progress and liberation from the destructive patterns that have ensnared the Islamic world, largely due to its own (in)actions and the historical interventions of Christian-secularist-Western imperialist powers. Education continues to be the fundamental element necessary for lifting the Muslim world out of the self-imposed suffering exacerbated by Western interference.

Modern Turkey and the West

The perception of the Turkish people today still carries negative associations. While Europe and America, representing the Western world, have accepted Turkey as a member of the North Atlantic Treaty Organisation (NATO), a military alliance that played a crucial role in countering Communism during the Cold War, Turkey's efforts to join the European Union have been delayed for decades. This delay is primarily due to concerns over Turkey's human rights record, particularly regarding its treatment of the Kurdish minority and the ongoing Cyprus issue, which has faced strong opposition from the Greek lobby within the EU. In contrast, the European Union has already approved the membership of most of the the former Eastern bloc countries, Poland, Hungary, Czech Republic, Slovakia, Bulgaria, and Croatia.

Turkey's aspiration for full membership in the European Union, alongside its position as NATO's second-largest military force, presents certain challenges. However, it is likely that Turkey will continue its NATO membership unless the current ruling party intentionally renounces its Atatürk heritage and seeks to position itself as a leader of the Islamic world. Huntington suggests that such a shift could be advantageous for Turkey, although it remains unlikely in the near future. In the context of the post-Cold War landscape, Huntington anticipates that Turkey will persist in playing a crucial role within NATO, as well as in the Balkans, the Arab region, and Central Asia.[68]

In contemporary Turkey, the Turkish populace is engaged in a process of introspection regarding their national identity, contemplating their alignment with either Eastern or Western cultural influences. Educated and affluent segments of society often view themselves as adherents of European values, a legacy of Atatürk's vision for the nation. In contrast, a significant portion of the rural population in Anatolia continues to uphold a religious and conservative perspective.

The populist narrative argues that in order to move forward, Turkey in the 21st century needs to confront its historical legacy. For over a thousand years since embracing Islam in the 10th century, the Turkish people have been shaped by an Islamic cultural, social, and political perspective. However, his critics, both conservative Turks and Arab Muslims, argue that Atatürk's revolution severed the country from its religious past, heritage, traditional attire, and written language, resulting in a void of identity that is only now starting to be acknowledged.[69]

The European Union's hesitance to bestow complete membership upon Turkey underscores the sentiments expressed by the late Turkish Prime Minister Mesut Yilmaz (d. 2020). In his remarks, the former Prime Minister asserted that the European Union wants a "Christian club based on Christians values" and would never extend membership to a Muslim nation, emphasising the exclusivity of the organisation.[70] By characterising the EU as a "Christian club", the Turks emphasise the notion of a conflict between rival religious ideologies, each viewing itself as superior to the other. According to Ziya Onis of Bosphorus University:

> Apart from economic considerations, it should be remembered that the EU is ultimately a political project. What the EU's founders desired was an eventual political union among states that shared similar cultures, ideals, and institutions. It is also important to emphasise that EU members are predominantly Christian populations. Would they view Turkey, with a predominantly Islamic population in spite of its secular

character, with suspicion? This depends on many factors. Current acts of violence against Turks in Germany, however, are an indication that tensions are not entirely economic.[71]

Hence, the Christian-Muslim debate has once again resurfaced. Is it Islam that prevents Turkey from being a part of Europe? However, when we examine history, the answer is more political rather than religious. During the Concert of Europe in Vienna in 1815, the Ottoman Empire was invited to participate and collaborate with the rest of Europe in order to suppress the rising wave of liberalism and nationalism, which posed a threat to the monarchical governments of the major European powers at that time. A similar situation occurred during the Cold War era, when communism began to challenge the dominance of capitalist Europe and North America. Turkey was embraced as a member of NATO to ensure containment of communism in the Caucasus Mountains and the northern region of the Black Sea. The Western powers had no objections to Turkey's role in NATO when it served their own political and ideological agenda against Bolshevism. However, they raised concerns about Turkey's poor economic management, human rights issues, and the ongoing Cyprus problem (which Europe has maintained a bipartisan stance on since 1974 by accepting Greek Cyprus into the EU and leaving out the Turkish Cypriots) as a pretext to impede Turkey's accession into the 'Club'. As Onis states in his article, *Turkey In The Post Cold War Era: In Search Of Identity*, to base Turkey's inability to full EU membership solely on the Cyprus problem, human rights and further democratisation would "rest on faulty analysis", because:

> Clearly, one can identify the more immediate EU concerns and short-term constraints on Turkey's graduation to full membership, including the Greek veto over Cyprus and Turkey's human and minority rights records.The suggestion that resolution of these problems would guarantee EU membership, however, rests on faulty analysis... the Cyprus issue as a key obstacle to Turkey's admittance as full member is a mistake. Similarly, further democratisation and an improved human rights record are central objectives in their own right. To argue,

however, that further democratisation in Turkey will automatically secure full membership envisions yet another simplistic scenario.[72]

Ziya Onis believes that Turkey will not be admitted to the European Union for decades because Turkey's levels of industrialisation and economic development are significantly below the Western European average. Similarly, Turkey's inflation and unemployment figures compare unfavourably with even the least-advanced EU members, namely Portugal and Greece.[73] Another important constraint on Turkey's full membership is its size and population. As Onis perceives:

> Turkey's level of development and population size, free labor mobility constitutes a very sensitive issue from the perspective of the Union, and probably constitutes the single most important barrier to Turkey's graduation to full membership.[74]

Awarding full membership to Turkey, a nation with a population surpassing 85 million, would lead to Turkish representatives occupying a majority of the seats in the European Parliament. It is improbable that any member state of the EU would consent to granting such significant influence to a country with a Muslim majority. While the Ottoman Turks failed in their historical efforts to conquer Europe, it is similarly unlikely that they would gain supremacy through full membership in an organisation that might be viewed as a 'Christian Club'.

Europe's bipartisan stance on the Cyprus issue has, in effect, placed the entire responsibility on Turkey. European nations and Western allies often fail to use the correct political language when addressing the presence of Turkish military forces on the island. While Turkey maintains that its troops are stationed there to uphold peace, a role they have fulfilled since the 1974 Peace Operation, the West views this military presence as an invasion. The historical justification for Turkey's 1974 intervention was rooted in the independence granted to Cyprus by Britain in 1960. The Treaty of Guarantee allowed Britain, Turkey, and Greece to intervene on behalf of Greek or Turkish Cypriots to ensure their protection. This is exactly what Turkey did in 1974, intervening to safeguard the Turkish Cypriot community from potential ethnic cleansing orchestrated by the Enosis movement, which sought to unify Cyprus with Greece under the leadership of Greek Cypriots.

The double standards prevalent in the West and the European Union are evident in the context of the Cyprus issue. While the West professes to value the democratic freedoms of all peoples, it conveniently overlooks the sovereign rights of the Turkish Cypriots, who constitute more than one-third of the island's population. The international community exclusively recognizes the Greek government of Cyprus as the representative of all Cypriots, a stance that is fundamentally flawed. In the northern part of the island, the Turkish Republic of Northern Cyprus has been managing its democratic processes, including multi-party elections and an independent judiciary, for over fifty years, relying solely on Turkey for recognition. If Europe is genuinely committed to fostering stability in the region, it has failed to resolve the deadlock between Greek and Turkish Cypriots. The EU's decision to grant full membership to the Greek Cypriots as the sole representatives of the island has significantly contributed to the political stalemate, particularly following the overwhelming rejection of reunification with the Turkish Cypriots in the 2004 referendum.

In the context of contemporary political dynamics between Turkey and the West, it is evident that double standards persist in the foreign policies of Western governments regarding Turkey and the Muslim World. The European Union's hesitance to integrate Turkey into a predominantly Christian union has posed significant challenges for the Muslim-majority nation. Paradoxically, as a member of NATO, Turkey stands as the second-largest military force within the alliance, following the United States, and is regarded as a key military contributor to defend Europe against a potential invasion, likely from Russia. Despite the double standards, amid the ongoing conflict in Ukraine and the steadfast backing from Western nations, Turkey seeks to uphold equilibrium in its foreign policies by fostering a balanced relationship with Russia, all the while continuing its membership in NATO. While Europe criticises Turkey for alleged human rights abuses and the undermining of democratic institutions, it simultaneously maintains a hypocritical position regarding the genocidal actions of Zionists in Palestine. Furthermore, in the context of the Cyprus conflict, the alignment of Western support is unmistakably evident, favouring the Christian Greek Cypriots over the Muslim Turkish Cypriots.

In conclusion, following Britain's defeat by the Turks during the 1922 Chanak crisis and the ongoing Arab dissatisfaction due to unfulfilled wartime promises in the former Ottoman territories now controlled by Britain and France in the Middle East, Europe faced a new competitor that jeopardised its supremacy. This context allowed for the emergence of Bolshevism as a formidable adversary, setting the stage for the Cold War between superpowers. Communism became the primary ideological foe of the West until its dissolution in 1991. The fall of communism was succeeded by the advent of George Bush's 'New World Order', a development some critics aptly referred to as the 'New World Disorder', which proclaimed the victory of freedom over authoritarianism, and the United States as the sole superpower in the world. On 2 September 1990, Saddam Hussein's invasion of Kuwait led to the United States initiating Operation Desert Storm just six days later by invading Iraq. Concerned about losing its influence over the oil-rich Kuwait and the potential threat posed to Saudi Arabia's oil fields by the Iraqi leader, the United States deployed troops in a region that houses Islam's holy sites. This unprecedented 'unholy' and 'sacrilegious' action by a Christian power, coupled with the invasion of Kuwait, marked a resurgence of the ideological and impending military conflict between the West and Islam, echoing the civilisational rift established by the partitioning of the Ottoman Empire nearly a century earlier by European imperial powers, which resulted in the occupation of Istanbul, the seat of the Ottoman Muslim Caliphate for over four centuries.[75]

The political ramifications of the Ottoman Empire's disintegration and subsequent division are still felt in the volatile region today. The establishment of Israel in 1948, coupled with the consequent displacement of the Palestinian people from their homeland, along with ongoing Western backing of Israel to the detriment of the displaced Palestinians, has contributed to the instability in the Middle East. This scenario has intensified the religious and civilisational divide, prompting radical reactions from Muslim groups, as evidenced by the attacks on New York and Washington on September 11, 2001. The military interventions in Muslim territories following the first Gulf War of 1990-91, along with the conflicts in Iraq (2003-2011) and Afghanistan (2001-2021), have reinforced the perception of a clash of civilisations, redirecting global attention to Islamic radicalism and the troubled Mediterranean region, which chapter fifteen further explores. Consequently, Islamic ideology has emerged as a formidable challenge to Western dominance in contemporary times, just as it did in the past, reminiscent of historical conflicts dating back to the Crusades. The West continues to grapple with the integration of Islam into its values, presenting an ongoing dilemma. It is also essential to recognise the importance of the 'Pirenne thesis' in influencing European and Western interests throughout history.

CHAPTER 15

RE-AWAKENING OF ISLAM
DOUBLE STANDARDS OF WESTERN REPRESENTATIONS OF RESURGENT ISLAM: 1970-1995

Following the end of World War II, the Orient was no longer under the control of Britain and France. Instead, the United States emerged as the dominant power in the region. During the height of the Cold War, the countries in the Orient became pawns in the rivalry between superpowers. They found themselves entangled in the Arab-Israeli conflict, with the USA providing financial and military support to Israel, while the USSR did the same for Arab nations such as Egypt, Syria, and Iraq. The United States viewed its efforts to protect Israel as an essential part of its ongoing battle against world communism. Simultaneously, it saw itself as the leading force in the Islamic world, a position that had previously been held by Britain and France.

The Palestinian issue is filled with such intense emotions that no one would be pleased to avoid discussing it. However, it is impossible to escape the necessity of addressing it. The presence of the state of Israel in the former State of Palestine plays a crucial role in shaping the political beliefs of the majority of educated Muslims today. It has been the cause of numerous troubles that have plagued the Arab world for over six decades and has remained a constant source of instability in the Middle East. From a Western perspective, Israel represents the establishment of a homeland for the Jewish people, serving as just compensation for centuries of persecution endured at the hands of Europeans. On the other hand, Muslims perceive Israel as a settlement of European and American colonisers in a Muslim land, supported by former imperial powers and sustained by American military might. Many Muslims view Western support for Israel as nothing more than sheer hypocrisy. Moreover, Muslims who have experienced European dominance during the era of colonialism can clearly see that the idea of settling people from elsewhere in a developing country against the wishes of the native inhabitants could only have emerged within the context of colonialism and as a manifestation of a colonialist mindset. Therefore, for Muslims, the creation of Israel is seen as parallel to the Crusades, with Westerners once again occupying the Holy City of Quds (Jerusalem) in Palestine.

Following the 1967 Six Day War, the portrayal of Arabs in the media underwent a significant transformation. Initially, they were depicted as vaguely defined stereotypes, often portrayed as nomadic camel riders. However, after the Yom Kippur War of 1973, a new caricature emerged, portraying Arabs as incompetent and easily defeated. This image was reinforced through cartoons in the media, where Arabs were consistently shown standing behind gasoline pumps. During this period, Arabs were perceived as disrupters of both Israel's and the West's existence. These stereotypical images even found their way into Hollywood productions, further perpetuating these portrayals.[1] As Morroe Berger exclaims:

> The modern Middle East and North Africa is not a center of great cultural achievement, nor is it likely to become one in the near future.[2]

Since World War II, Arab nationalism has emerged as a movement openly expressing its opposition to Western imperialism, indicating that Islam has not been easily dominated by the West politically.[3] According to Edward Said in *Covering Islam - How the Media And The Experts Determine How We See The Rest Of The World*, American view of Islam:

[...] has become a subject familiar to every consumer of news in the West, have almost entirely domesticated the Islamic world, or at least those aspects of it that are considered newsworthy.[4]

For example the news coverage of Iran during the Khomeini's revolution in 1979 and the twenty-four hour coverage of the Gulf War (1990-91) crisis "never before has an international trouble spot ... been covered so instantaneously as so regularly as it has by the media".[5]

In the 1970s, Muslim radicalism demonstrated its unwavering commitment to its core principles and its refusal to embrace any form of political ideology, as exemplified by Iran. The revival of Islamic values in the 1990s was characterised by a clear disinterest in aligning its ideology with either democratic liberalism or Marxism. As Dilip Hiro has shown:

> The success of Islamic forces in 1979 in Iran, where they toppled the powerful pro-Western monarch, Shah Muhammad Reza Pahlavi, and ten years later in Afghanistan in securing the withdrawal of the Soviet troops (stationed there since 1979), established that Islam was capable successfully confronting both Western capitalism-imperialism and Marxist socialism. It thus established its credentials as an indigenous third way, wedded neither to East [Communist East] nor West.[6]

Not only did Iran base its existence on religious doctrine, but just a few miles to the west in Menachim Begin's Israel, there existed a regime that fully embraced religious authority and a highly conservative theological doctrine, emphasising a backward-looking perspective.[7] After the Gulf War, the Saudi society and its perceived lack of freedom became the central focus of the Western media's attention.[8] According to Hippler and Lueg:

> Ideologues from East and West are enjoying a vogue. In almost all forms of the media, 'experts' seek to enlighten us on the new dangers from the East: holy wars, fanatical masses, the revenge of the Middle Ages on modernity and of religion on the Enlightenment. Islam is sometimes a 'challenge', sometimes a threat. The conquest of Vienna by

the Turks is apparently once again imminent. With Khomeini, Gaddafi, Saddam Hussein, Arafat and the Algerian fundamentalists, the anti-Western wave is rolling on, at any rate splashing across popular magazines and television screens.[9]

The portrayal of the Islamic world in the 1990s by the Western media often depicted a grim picture, with headlines filled with tragic news stories and doomsday scenarios. The looming spectre of a potential 'religious war' in the former Yugoslavia was particularly alarming to many in Europe. At the height of the Bosnian conflict (1992-1995), the German news magazine Der Spiegel wrote, "Soon, Europe could have a fanatical theocratic state on its doorstep."[10] Not only Europe but America is also feeling the 'threat' from Islam on its soil, with the bombing of the World Trade Center in New York. In news footages Muslims are seen shaking their fists and screaming anti-Western slogans. Thus aggression is often made out to be a characteristic of Islam and its followers. For many people in the West, Islam is hardly ever seen as a cultural category, but as a religion, one which is threatening. At this juncture, it is historically significant to highlight the genocide of Bosnian Muslims perpetrated by Christians in the very centre of Europe.

The Forgotten Genocide of Bosnian Muslims

The narrative surrounding the genocide of Bosnian Muslims represents the first instance of genocide in Europe since the Holocaust, which occurred before and during World War II. This tragic event is frequently neglected and remains largely unacknowledged, contributing to what can be termed a European Amnesia regarding this atrocity. During this period (1992-1995), Muslim populations were systematically targeted by Christian forces, resulting in the execution of individuals across all age groups, including women, children, and infants. Similar to the heinous acts perpetrated by the Nazis against the Jewish population during World War II, there are numerous documented images illustrating the violence inflicted upon Bosnian Muslims by Orthodox Christian militias. These images reveal the horrific nature of these events, many of which are profoundly distressing.[11]

The situation in Palestine today bears a striking resemblance to another instance of genocide, this time occurring in Europe, specifically within predominantly white European regions. The perpetrators of this violence were fervent Christians, while the victims were predominantly indigenous Muslims of European descent. This represents a profoundly tragic event that unfolded approximately 30 years ago.

For the Orthodox Serbian Christian participants in Europe, the Bosnian War (1992-1995) represented a deeply religious experience, profoundly rooted in their Christian faith. Conversely, among European Muslims and a notable, albeit small, non-Muslim audience globally, there exists an uncomfortable acknowledgment that the atrocities committed during the war were significantly more severe than those of September 11. This troubling amnesia is viewed as an unacceptable attempt to obscure the sectarian nature of these crimes, which must not be overlooked. It is important to clarify that the Muslims in question are not from Pakistan, India, Saudi Arabia, or the Middle East; rather, they are indigenous white Europeans. This distinction is crucial, as Muslims in Europe are often perceived as outsiders or immigrants, a characterisation that, while flawed, does not apply in this context. The Muslims involved in this situation are all white Europeans who have practiced Islam for over six centuries, and Bosnia is recognised as an indigenous white European Muslim nation.[12]

Concentration camps resurfaced in Central Europe during the Bosnian War, where Muslims were imprisoned in facilities that echoed the historical persecution of Jews, particularly the experiences of European Jews in Nazi concentration camps. These camps were managed by individuals who identified as Christians, motivated by their religious convictions. It is crucial to note that not all Christians endorse these perspectives; nevertheless, this scenario can be described as a Christian-led pogrom against Muslims in Europe, leading to the internment of Muslims in concentration camps. According to documents from the UNHCR, over 8,000 Bosnian Muslims lost their lives in the Srebrenica camps in 1995, while mass expulsions of 25,000 to 30,000 Bosnian civilians were carried out by units under the command of General Ratko Mladic, all under the watchful gaze of the United Nations Dutch peacekeeping forces.[13]

The documented and internationally recognised figures regarding the Bosnian genocide indicate that the number of murders significantly exceeded those who perished during the events of September 11. This is not intended to create a comparison of tragedies, as both the Holocaust and the Bosnian Genocide are profoundly tragic events in their own right. However, it is noteworthy that the impact of September 11 resonates deeply within the European consciousness, with the loss of approximately 2,000 to 3,000 lives being a focal point of remembrance. In contrast, the genocide in Bosnia resulted in the deaths of three to five times that number, yet it remains largely unacknowledged in public memory. This is particularly striking given that these atrocities occurred within Europe, rather than in the United States, highlighting a troubling aspect of collective memory regarding war crimes and genocide.

Europe and America appear to have overlooked the most recent genocide on the continent, while simultaneously, we are witnessing an ongoing genocide in Palestine by Israel since 2023. Many in the West continue to deny that it constitutes genocide, or, more disturbingly, they are actively providing financial support, legal protection, and military resources to those perpetrating this atrocity, namely the Zionists. Consequently, all Western governments share complicity in these actions. Thus, it can be asserted that Europe, often regarded as a civilised and advanced region, is currently implicated in bloodshed and genocide, even as it neglects its historical responsibilities.[14] According to Abdal Hakim Murad (Tim Winter):

> One of the most disturbing features of the war which devastated Bosnia between 1992 and 1995 was the widespread refusal of Western politicians, churchmen and newsmen, to acknowledge the role which religion was playing in the conflict. It was only mentioned, indeed, during periodic denunciations of the risks of Islamic extremism - a phenomenon that, when pressed, journalists working in Bosnia

conceded was rather elusive. The reality, which was frequently one of militant Christian extremism, was never, to my knowledge, frankly discussed. The war was, we were told, a contest between 'ethnic factions'; and the fact that its protagonists were divided primarily by religion, and shared a race and a language, was deemed insignificant. Anti-Muslim prejudice was no doubt at work here: one may assume that if the Serbs and Catholics had been Muslims, and their victims Christians, then the Western mind would immediately have characterised the war as a case of violent Muslims murdering secular, integrated, democratic Christians. Since in Bosnia the favoured stereotypes were reversed, the memory has largely been dismissed, censored and forgotten as an annoying anomaly.

That official characterisation, by and large, persists. Generally it is the case that the European and American popular consciousness has forgotten about Bosnia although only ten years have elapsed since almost eight thousand Muslims were pushed into mass graves at Srebrenica, while the local UN commander accepted a glass of champagne from the victorious Serbian general, who then went off to church. And where Bosnia is still remembered, there is a dogged resistance to defining it as what it was: a war which, at least for its Christian participants, was an intensely religious experience.[15]

Thus, as Michael Sells argues, the violence that occurred in Bosnia can be characterised as a religious genocide in multiple ways: the victims were selected based on their religious affiliations; the perpetrators received endorsement and support from leaders within the Christian church; and the violence was rooted in a religious narrative that depicted the targeted individuals as traitors to their race, framing their extermination as a holy endeavour.[16]

The Media and Representations of Islam in the 1990s

During the peak of the Bosnian conflict in the 1990s, several critical inquiries arose in the West: Is there a real possibility that the Western world faces a 'holy war' instigated by Muslims? Furthermore, does the resolution of the tensions between the Eastern Bloc and the West, along with the rise of unpredictable theocratic states on the outskirts of

Europe, present a potential risk of a new religious conflict for us?[17] The German newspaper is clearly referencing the medieval Crusades. During the first Gulf War (1990-91), the Western powers showcased their overwhelming military dominance over a well-equipped nation that had extensive experience in warfare and was influenced by Islam. However, it is worth considering whether the threat posed by Islam is primarily psychological or religious, possibly stemming from a clash of cultures. The religious and cultural symbols of Islam have the potential to evoke strong emotions, as demonstrated by the continuing "headscarf affair" in France. In one of these incidents, several Muslim girls were suspended from school for wearing headscarves and refusing to remove them. The headmaster justified this action by stating that their insistence on wearing headscarves was seen as provocative and militant, alluding to Muslim militancy.[18] The act of wearing headscarves is immediately perceived as a threat to Western culture.

Muslim radicalism is often associated with hostility towards progress, reactionary political ideas, and a longing to revert back to the Middle Ages. This notion of resisting modernity has been perpetuated by the media, leading to a division between Western modernity and Islamic antiquity.[19] Unfortunately, the Western media rarely highlights movements within Islamic societies that strive for democratisation. The level of democracy in Islamic countries has largely been of little concern to the West.

The portrayal of Islam in Western media often revolves around the Middle East, with a focus on bearded radicalists who shape the perception of a militant interpretation of Islam. This portrayal associates Islam with concepts such as 'Holy War', fanaticism, violence, intolerance, and the oppression of women. However, it is important to differentiate between these extremists and the broader Islamic religion. By equating terms like Muslim, Islamic, fundamentalist, and fanatic, Western media tends to attribute all these characteristics to Islam as a whole, when in reality they are more applicable to a specific form of fundamentalism. It is crucial to make a clear distinction between Islam as a religion and political extremism carried out in the name of religion. These are two distinct entities with significant differences. When the term 'Islamic' is used to describe political extremism, the Western media tends to merge religion with other aspects such as lifestyle and faith. Ironically, Western thinking claims to combat foreign irrationality through the principles of European enlightenment, but in reality, it often reverts to pre-Enlightenment stereotypes that it claims to challenge.

The Western media's persistent portrayal of Islam as hostile has sparked cultural comparative analysis. This analysis reveals that traits such as misogyny, aggression, fanaticism, and irrationality exist not only in Islamic countries but also in the West. The racist attacks and riots that occurred in Europe during the early 1990s serve as a stark reminder of the underlying issues within Western civilisation. Particular events, including the violent assaults on African street vendors in Florence, Italy, in 1990, the vandalism of Jewish graves in Carpentras, France, also in 1990, and the racially charged attacks on asylum seekers in Hoyerswerda (1991) and Rostock (1992) in Germany, reveal a disturbing trend of racial violence in Europe during this era. Furthermore, the racially motivated murder of Turkish residents in Mölln (1992) by neo-Nazis emphasises the seriousness and frequency of such hate crimes. These incidents not only illustrate the entrenched racial, but also highlight the religious prejudices that persist in European society.

Interestingly, an increasing number of individuals in Europe and the United States are turning to religion, including white Christian fundamentalism. However, the West tends to view these occurrences as separate from its own culture, rather than as integral parts or expressions of it. Even historical events like National Socialism, fascism, and Stalinism are often regarded as mere 'accidents' and not associated with Christian-Western culture. For example, the Catholic Church required nearly fifty years to issue an apology for the Holocaust, culminating in Pope John Paul II's acknowledgment in 2000 of the injustices perpetrated by the Christian community against both Jews and Muslims throughout the last two thousand years. Furthermore, the West tends to employ varying criteria when addressing comparable or distinct issues in other cultures, especially those of an Islamic nature. As Esposito explains:

Many failed to make the same distinctions with regard to Islam and Islamic organisations between the actions of a radical minority and the mainstream majority that were made so easily when ... the world watched the Branch Davidian sect, an extremist 'Christian' group in Waco, Texas, kill FBI agents and, protected by an astonishing arsenal of weapons, hold off federal authorities for weeks.[20]

The Western world holds the belief that it has successfully removed religion from the public sphere and confined it to the private realm, thus triumphing over it. However, incidents like the one referenced above suggest otherwise. Islam, on the other hand, continues to instill fear in the West as a religion. This very religious dimension, which the West tends to interpret narrowly, exacerbates the existing divide between Eastern and Western societies.

CHAPTER 16

THE CLASH OF CIVILISATIONS OR DIALOGUE OF CULTURES?

THE MUSLIM RESPONSE

With the publication of Francis Fukuyama's *The End of History and the Last Man* (1989) and Samuel P. Huntington's *The Clash of Civilizations and the Remaking of the World Order* (1993 / 1996), the focus on Islam in modern historiography has been reignited, leading to a renewed European fascination with the Muslim world. Fukuyama acknowledges the universal appeal of Islam, asserting that it has even surpassed liberal democracy in various regions, thereby challenging Western dominance to some extent. However, he argues that Islam's cultural conquests have reached their conclusion. According to Fukuyama, Islam's current resurgence lacks the ability to attract followers beyond its own sphere of influence. He believes that Islam is more inclined towards embracing liberal ideas rather than actively spreading its own global agenda. Fukuyama emphasises that, if anything, it is fundamentalism that poses a threat to Western hegemony. This once again highlights the Eurocentric approach to determining historical outcomes. Fukuyama's thesis emerged at the end of the Cold War in 1991 with the demise of the Soviet Union, coinciding with the Western conflict against Saddam Hussein in the Gulf War (1990-91). Samuel P. Huntington, in *The Clash of Civilizations*, builds upon this notion of a New World Order that emerged after the collapse of the Soviet Union. Huntington essentially continues where Fukuyama left off, suggesting that Islam is the civilisation most likely to clash with the West. This clearly aims to portray Islam as incompatible and incapable of coexisting with other world civilisations. Thus, as the millennium drew to a close, Europe found itself once again searching for its identity and seeking ways to reestablish its authority, much like it did a thousand years ago.

Atatürk on the Clash of Civilisations

It is of considerable historical significance to recognise that seventy years prior to Samuel Huntington's publication of *The Clash of Civilizations*, Mustafa Kemal Atatürk, the architect of modern Turkey, delivered a poignant address to the youth of Konya on March 20, 1923. In his speech, Atatürk contended that the perceived conflict between civilisations plays a significant role in the stagnation experienced by Muslims. He emphasised that the protracted strife between Muslims and Christians, marked by deep-seated prejudice and animosity, has led Muslims to neglect the cultural and scientific advancements made in the West, ultimately impeding their own development. Atatürk expressed this perspective in the following manner:

> We also know that there is an unforgiving enmity between the society belonging to the Islamic world and the masses of Christian world. Muslims became eternal enemies of Christians, and Christians became eternal enemies of Muslims. They looked at each other with infidel and fanatical views. These two worlds have lived with this fanaticism and enmity towards each other for centuries. As a result of this enmity, the Islamic world remained distant from the progress of the West, which had been certain in every century and had its own flowering. Because the people of Islam were unwilling to rise to that progress, they looked at it with hatred. At the same time, there was a long-standing enmity between the two masses. It is the result of the feelings of enmity that our attachment to weapons, indifference to the innovations of the West, became one of the reasons for our decline [...].[1]

Atatürk identified that the conlflict between Muslims and Christians obstructed Muslims from reaping the benefits of the modern civilisation associated with the West. He highlighted that this conflict adversely impacted Muslims in two significant ways:

> a. The sense of "otherness" created by historical enmity and the hatred towards everything associated with it.
>
> b. Constant vigilance and readiness in the face of never-ending Crusader (Christian) attacks; thinking of nothing other than weapons and war.

Thus, from Atatürk's perspective, the preparedness for conflict depleted the resources of Muslim nations and hindered their ability to develop into thriving, dynamic, and economically prosperous societies. His message resonates strongly with contemporary Islamic nations: robust economies are essential for fostering prosperous and productive societies.

Other Muslims' Response to Huntington

In the past few decades, subsequent to the release of Huntington's contentious publication, the Muslim world responded by offering a counterargument. The release of *Medeniyetler Çatışması* (Clash of Civilisations) by Murat Yılmaz in 1995, which came two years after Huntington's original article was published in the Foreign Affairs journal on June 1, 1993, established the framework for a clash or dialogue of cultures in the new millennium. Many scholars from the Muslim world, Asia, and the West answered the call by Murat Yılmaz to challenge Huntington's contentious and polarising thesis. This chapter predominantly focuses on the Turkish and other Muslim responses to Huntington's work. It is important to note that the reactions of Muslim scholars occurred prior to the September 11 attacks, and their perspectives should be understood within the historical context of their time.

In contemporary times, the dislocation caused by the influence of the modern Western world on beliefs and cultural norms that were unable to withstand the encounter is evident everywhere. Entire communities now find themselves in a state of spiritual and psychological emptiness. The Islamic world, although shaken to some extent, has managed to endure with its fundamental principles largely intact. In this particular instance, one could describe it as an unstoppable force encountering an immovable object. It serves as the sole remaining example of an alternative lifestyle, thought process, and approach to various aspects of life. Its link with the past has not been broken. Seyyed Hossein Nasr's chapter titled "From Indonesia to Morocco" in the book *Islam and the Plight of Modern Man*, argues that:

> [...] for the overwhelming majority, Islamic culture must be referred to in the present tense and not as something in the past. Those who refer to it in the past tense (like Fukuyama) belong to a very small but very vocal minority which has ceased to live within the world of tradition and mistakes its own loss of centre for the dislocation of the whole Islamic society.[2]

Islam continues to thrive as a civilisation and a way of life. For Muslims, Islam remains an integral part of their daily existence.

Ahmet Davutoğlu, a Turkish intellectual and parliamentarian, argues in his article "From Fukuyama to Huntington" that both Fukuyama and Huntington have drawn inspiration from past historians for their theories. Fukuyama's ideas are rooted in the principles of Hegel, while Huntington's clash of civilisations theory is based on Toynbee's work. However, unlike Huntington, Toynbee believed that the West, along with other civilisations, was in decline. Davutoğlu suggests that if Toynbee's analysis of dying cultures and civilisations, including the West, is correct, then there is no reason or means for a clash between cultures.[3]

Davutoğlu provides historical examples to support his argument. He points out that prior to the widespread influence of the West in the nineteenth century, Islamic and Orthodox Christian civilisations coexisted harmoniously for almost five centuries. Similarly, in India, Islam and Hindu cultures were more tolerant of each other until British occupation. In Andalusia, or Muslim Spain, the dynamic Muslim, Christian, and Jewish cultures coexisted for seven centuries until the fall of Grenada in 1492. According to Davutoğlu, these examples demonstrate that Islam has a history of coexisting with the West and other civilisations.[4] He criticises Fukuyama's theory as an attempt to conceal the social, cultural, and spiritual disintegration of the West. He argues that both Fukuyama and Huntington advocate for the triumph and continuation of Western hegemony.[5]

In his article "Is it a Clash of Civilisations?", journalist Kemal Kahraman asserts that during the First and Second World Wars, Germany was the primary adversary. The First World War resulted in the destruction of the Ottoman State, while the Second World War led to the creation of Israel. Kahraman suggests that these events were orchestrated to maintain division in the Middle East. Furthermore, he argues that the United States revived the weakened Soviet Union after the Second World War to initiate the Cold War. When the Soviet Union eventually collapsed, the West proclaimed its victory over communism and anti-democratic ideologies. However, it soon became evident that the West needed a new opponent. This gave rise to Francis Fukuyama's *The End of History* and Samuel Huntington's *The Clash of Civilizations*. Kahraman poses several thought-provoking questions:

- Did the Age of Enlightenment not signify the end of History when the West embraced its ideals?

- Did the West not declare its supremacy during the Industrial Revolution, when it transformed into an industrialised and modernised civilisation?

- Did the Western democracies not triumph over fascism at the end of the Second World War?

- And finally, did the collapse of the USSR not mark the end of History?[6]

According to Kahraman, it appears that the West continually seeks to reinvent itself in order to justify its perceived superiority. Following the demise of communism, the world witnessed the Gulf War, conflicts in the Caucasus between Azerbaijan and Armenia, and the dissolution of Yugoslavia. Kahraman argues that the West views these events as an offensive against Islam. Consequently, Islam remains the only viable opponent for the West, making the notion of a clash of civilisations in the next era of human history seem justifiable.[7]

In her article titled "Huntington and Western Supremacy," Binnaz Toprak argues that the conflict between Armenians and Azeris is not rooted in Islam's violent history, as some Western historians claim. Rather, the Armenian-Azeri conflict stems from the Soviet Union's failure to address the national interests of both ethnic groups and serves as a form of retribution against Leninism. Toprak predicts that the next millennium will be characterised by confusion and instability, contrasting Huntington's vision of a bipolar world divided between the West and Islam. According to Toprak, the concepts of the "West" and the "East" are no longer relevant, and books on "Islam and the West" belong to a bygone era dominated by orientalist perspectives. She believes that the future global order will be shaped by economic outcomes and must include the perspectives of diverse civilisations, including Islam. Human rights, equality, peace, regional security, and globalisation will significantly influence the development of these civilisations. Toprak also emphasises the significant role that national, ethnic, and religious identities will play in shaping future historical outcomes. In contrast to Huntington's view, Toprak argues that clashes between religions and ethnicities are already evident, citing examples such as the ethnic cleansing of Bosnian Muslims by the Serbs, the destruction of mosques and churches by Hindus and Indonesians, neo-Nazi attacks on Turkish "guest-workers" in Germany, and the racial disparities between Afro-Americans and white Americans. Therefore, Toprak rejects the notion that Islam will be the primary obstacle to Western hegemony in the formation of George Bush's post-communist New World Order, deeming it an oversimplified perspective.[8]

The European bourgeoisie formulated the concept of class struggle. Sociologists of a liberal persuasion, such as Mignet, Thierry, and Guizot, attributed the progress of societies to this struggle. However, Marx, in his correspondence with his friend Weygenmeyer, expressed a contrary view, stating that history cannot be determined solely by class struggle. According to Huntington, humanity is transitioning from a clash of ideologies to a clash of civilisations. In Huntington's theory, as explained by Doğu Perinçek in the article "Hiristiyan - Müslüman Çatışması" (Christian-Muslim Clash), class struggle has been supplanted by cultural differences as the primary challenge of the new era. Nevertheless, one may argue that ideology is an integral part of culture. Perinçek does not see this paradox as problematic. In his perspective, the emergence of a New World Order will only come about through struggle, thus rendering any confusion or conflict in semantics and terminologies inconsequential.[9]

Huntington's civilisations are religious entities as well, but they cannot be dissociated from their political agendas. Initially, all religions and belief systems - Buddhism, Christianity, Islam, Confucianism, and Hinduism - are essentially manifestations of a single human culture. They all represent different forms of capitalism, and before that, feudalism and slavery. The only distinction lies in their perceptions of themselves and others. According to Perinçek, Huntington's concept of a clash of civilisations is an attempt to conceal the class struggle. In today's world, there is a clear division between the North - the privileged - and the South - the underprivileged. This division, as emphasised by Perinçek, underscores the ongoing struggle between social classes.[10]

The Western, Japanese, and Slav-Orthodox civilisations are merely cultures driven by imperialism and capitalism. There are no discernible cultural differences between Clinton and Yeltsin. Perinçek argues that America, Japan, Germany, and Russia all belong to the same capitalist cultural groups. Their conflicts will not be rooted in culture, but rather in political and economic hegemony. Therefore, Huntington views the New World Order through the lens of religio-cultural terms. Consequently, the 'civilised' North justifies its oppression of the 'religious' South using ideological justifications. The impoverished masses in the South, lacking a strong ideological foundation, inadvertently aid the affluent North in formulating theories about the course of history. Imperialism spreads religion to the South, but it is the Hindus, Confucians, Muslims, Latin Americans, and Africans who suffer the consequences.[11]

The collapse of the Soviet Union resulted in an ideological void, leading to a global quest for a new global order. This led to the emergence of a non-polarised world system when Iraq invaded Kuwait, triggering the Gulf War. The Gulf War, in turn, gave rise to Fukuyama's theory of the end of History, which proclaimed the triumph of Western liberal democracy over this new world system. However, Fukuyama believes that the current resurgence of Islam will not pose a threat to the West's hegemony. In Ibrahim Kiras' article, "Islam delays the 'End of History,'" it is argued that Muslim nations should avoid escalating conflicts with the West, as both civilisations are interdependent, as outlined by Huntington.[12]

In his article titled "Islam - the Only Solution," Huseyin Hatemi raises the question of whether any Muslim nation(s) have the potential to challenge the dominance of the West. The response remains unchanged: none. Until now, there has been no coalition or even consideration among Muslim nations to address this matter. Hatemi goes as far as excluding Turkey, which holds the strongest military power among Islamic nations in the region, from taking on such a formidable task.[13]

Hatemi argues that Islam is not the main obstacle to Turkey's entry into the European Union (EU). He points out that if this were true, Turkey would not have been allowed to apply for membership or have a seat in the European Council. Instead, he believes that the world political situation has pushed Islam to the forefront, leading to Turkey's exclusion from the EU. Hatemi identifies Zionism as the problem for Islam today. He believes that the Judeo-Christian world, which shares a common heritage, feels excluded from the Muslim Mediterranean inheritance. According to Hatemi, the instability and division in the region are caused by the West, influenced by Zionism, aiming to prevent Islam from attaining its rightful place in the sun. This situation is likened to cutting out Ishmael from Abraham's inheritance.[14]

The present-day Europe is increasingly recognising its disgraceful history - a history marked by racism and the legacy of capitalist-imperialism. Muzaffer Ozdağ, in his work "Medeniyetler Çatışması," highlights the profound spiritual turmoil experienced by the Western world, as eloquently identified by Samuel P. Huntington. The pervasive anti-Semitism, the deep-rooted hatred towards Jews, stands as a shared spiritual and conscious guilt of Christian Europe. This serves as a lasting testament to the modern Europe's historical inheritance.[15] In a gesture to commemorate Christianity's second millennium in 2000, the Vatican extended apologies to the Jewish community for past transgressions, including the Inquisition and the Holocaust. Additionally, apologies were offered to the Muslim community for the Crusades and the exploitative practices during the era of colonialism. On 13 March 2000, from the altar of St Peter's Basilica, Pope John Paul II stated the following words:

> We forgive and we ask forgiveness. We are asking pardon for the divisions among Christians, for the use of violence that some have committed in the service of truth, and for attitudes of mistrust and hostility assumed towards followers of other religions.[16]

Ozdağ believes that the evidence of this culpability is evident in Huntington's publication. Huntington's deliberate act of singling out Islam and Sinic civilisations as the primary contenders for conflict with the Western world can be viewed as a provocative psychological manoeuvre that he devised towards the conclusion of the Cold War.[17]

Ozdağ perceives the underlying idea behind Huntington's theory as follows: the Christian-White-Western nations colonised the world and subjected it to their control. Unsatisfied with their achievements, these 'superior' nations engaged in two world wars, which ultimately led to the liberation of the oppressed peoples from imperialism. To prevent history from repeating itself, Ozdağ argues that the West must unite and establish a common front with the goal of economically exploiting others in order to succeed once again. Consequently, the globalisation of world economies heavily relies on the economies of the West, particularly America. Currently, the dominance of the European Union, along with China and Japan, poses a challenge to the markets of the world.[18]

Huntington categorised Mexico, Russia, and Turkey as "torn countries." Ozdağ, on the other hand, believes that Mexico has the potential to overcome its challenges and emerge as a major power. He attributes the unity of Mexico to the influence of Anglo-American culture and economy. In the case of Russia, Ozdağ suggests that instead of viewing its Orthodox-Slavic civilisation as a threat to the West, it would be more appropriate to unite Russia with the West and consider it as one entity. Regarding Turkey, Ozdağ blames the ineffective political leadership in post-Atatürk Turkey for its torn state. He believes that it is premature to judge Turkey as intellectually or politically torn, considering that it has only been a secular, democratic country for seventy-five years, in contrast to the British and American journeys to their current positions.[19]

Turkey's diverse culture should not hinder its development or divide it, as Huntington suggests. Instead, Turkey should embrace both Eastern and Western influences to shape its identity. This does not mean that Turkey is a divided nation; rather, it highlights the fact that Turkish identity extends beyond Europe. Turkey should leverage its strategic geographical position to maximise economic benefits by forging stronger ties with major global powers, while avoiding any economic or political unions. Furthermore, Turkey should embrace its heritage from both the East and the West, including the significant role of Islam in its cultural identity. The emergence of independent Turkic Central Asian Republics following the collapse of communist Russia, which share common cultural, religious, and linguistic ties with Turkey, further reinforces the notion that Turkey's identity transcends Europe. Rather than viewing this broader identity as a weakness, it should be seen as an asset. The challenge lies in accepting and embracing this identity as Turkey moves towards the future and celebrates the 100th anniversary of the founding of the Republic by Mustafa Kemal Atatürk (29 October 1923). The concept of 'civilisation' has been historically associated with the orientalist agenda. Initially, the term 'civilisation' was strategically employed by orientalists, much like in the Middle Ages. Over time, it acquired a universal significance. This was evident in the case of Muslim civilisation, which had to confront its Western counterpart that held economic and technological dominance over the world. In his article titled "Medeniyetler Arası Çatışma Teorileri ve Tarihin Sonu Üzerine" (On Theories of Conflict Between Civilisations and the End of History), Sami Şener highlights the universality of the term 'civilisation' as the West, starting from the sixteenth century, sought to impose its norms and beliefs on other cultures. By the nineteenth century, the Islamic world, in particular, endeavoured to emulate its adversary in order to achieve 'modernisation'.[20]

Şener argues that Arnold Toynbee did not perceive any connection between race and geography as the determining factors for the development of civilisations. He believed that technological superiority did not necessarily correlate with the progress of civilisations. This theory was supported by the examination of twenty-one cultures. According to Toynbee, civilisations bring about their own downfall; they are not destroyed by external forces. The Western world has made significant efforts to uphold its political and economic dominance globally. Consequently, it has adopted a confrontational approach towards other civilisations, as described by Huntington as the 'clash of civilisations'.[21]

Spengler, however, argues that prior to the decline of a civilisation, it experiences a resurgence in religious or spiritual beliefs. This can be observed in various cultures such as those that worshipped Mithra, Isis, and the sun, as well as Ancient Rome during a mystical phase before the rise of Christianity. During this period of religious revival, the culture not only anticipates its own demise but also witnesses the birth of a new civilisation. An example of this is the pagan Arab society, which witnessed the emergence of Islamic civilisation following Prophet Muhammad's revelations.[22]

Şener perceives Huntington not as a historian examining the ebb and flow of civilisations, but rather as someone who approaches the subject with a militaristic mindset. Both Fukuyama and Huntington endorse Hegel's theory of isolationism, failing to acknowledge the interconnectedness of civilisations. Hegel discussed the end of History when he observed the events in Napoleonic Europe and America during that time. While Fukuyama champions the triumph of Western philosophy, Huntington regards Islam and Sinic civilisations as the primary adversaries in the New World Order. According to Şener, Fukuyama's theory merely emphasises the West's ethnocentricity, as the author believes that the liberal-democratic ideology represents the unquestionable culmination of History.[23]

The portrayal of the 'Other' in a subordinate position to the West is a common tendency among Western scholars. Şener argues that this psychological distress still persists. When America first encountered the rest of the world through Columbus, it created a dichotomy of backwardness/advancement, barbarism/civilisation, and an 'us/them' mentality. The West has always viewed itself as a universal entity. As Fukuyama acknowledges, a continuous historical philosophy from the Ancients to the Middle Ages' Christendom has fostered the principles of ethnocentrism and the universality of the West. However, Wallerstein argues that this is not entirely true, as European imperialism, which went unchecked for the past four hundred years, has now witnessed a reversal of fortunes. The rise of political systems in the Third World and the liberation from colonialism define the era in which we currently live.[24]

Mustafa Özcan, the foreign affairs correspondent for the New Light Newspaper in Turkey, highlights the significance of Fukuyama and Huntington's theories emerging after the Cold War in his article titled "Meş'um Teori, Barbar ve Medeni" (Ominous Theory, the Barbarian and the Civilised). The appearance of both Fukuyama's *The End of History* and Huntington's *The Clash of Civilizations* was not a mere coincidence. Rather, it was a natural consequence of the ideological struggle between capitalism and communism that unfolded during the Cold War era. These theories emerged as a result of the ideological void left behind by the end of the Cold War. Consequently, what was once Fukuyama's philosophical speculation has now transformed into Huntington's political reality in *The Clash of Civilizations*. The responsibility of implementing this theory now lies with NATO. European politicians, such as De Micheles (Secretary General of NATO between

1994-95), have already recognised the necessity for NATO to remain prepared for potential conflicts with countries in the South. Even the NATO General Secretary in 1995, Willy Cleas, explicitly stated that fundamentalism has become the new adversary for the West, replacing communism.[25] Although he stopped short of explicitly mentioning Islam, his words echo those of William Gladstone, who, a century earlier, held the Qur'an in his hand and proclaimed that "So long as there is this book, there will be no peace in the world".[26] Gladstone directed his anger towards the Ottoman Turks, who were challenging the dominance of Christian Europe at the time. It is evident that prejudices persist and thrive on animosity, influencing even the judgements of the most well-intentioned individuals. With Cleas's words, it becomes clear that Huntington's interpretation of history has already started to shape Europe's political ideology in the early 1990s. The NATO General Secretary was criticised by The TIMES newspaper, which accused him of being influenced by Huntington's theory. The newspaper's headline read, "In search of a new enemy, the new Secretary".[27] According to Huntington, Islam is considered an adversary of the West and should not receive military technological assistance. He also viewed Pakistan as a dangerous opponent due to its nuclear weapons production with Chinese technology. However, Huntington failed to acknowledge that Israel was selling American weapons technology to China.[28]

Özcan argues that throughout history, various civilisations have often viewed other cultures as inferior or uncivilised. The ancient Greeks considered all non-Greek peoples as barbarians. Similarly, after Christopher Columbus discovered America, the indigenous Red Indians were deemed backward and uncivilised. The French and English, upon occupying Africa, regarded its inhabitants as barbarians and embarked on a mission to civilise them. The West has consistently seen itself as the only positive influence on these supposedly uncivilised "Others." Ronald Reagan further perpetuated this mindset by derogatorily labelling the Soviet Union as the "evil empire" and communism as a "disease that spreads." However, times have changed. Today, the Red Indians in America are recognised as the true Native Americans, just as indigenous peoples in other countries are considered the "Natives" of their respective nations. Currently, according to Özcan, the Islamic world is portrayed as the "evil empire" and becomes NATO's new enemy.[29] This idea of a cold war strategy against Islam is unleashed by Huntington. Edward Said argues that this theory is not new and traces its origins back to Orientalist and Turcolog, Bernard Lewis. Both Lewis and Huntington are criticised by Said for elevating Western civilisation above all others. Their critical studies of civilisations do not seek democratic pluralism, but rather provide a justification for Western cultural imperialism.[30]

Zeyneb B. Sayın asserts that Islam's emergence as an enemy of the West did not occur in the 1990s; rather, its origins can be traced back several centuries when European borders were forcibly imposed at the expense of Muslims and other non-European peoples during the era of European colonisation. Consequently, the subjugated peoples have been compelled to adopt the concept of modernisation. After suffering defeats at the hands of the West, Islam began to seek and reaffirm its cultural and ideological identity in the 19th century. In the 20th century, Islamic Resurgence movements emerged in countries such as Iran, Algeria, Chechnya, and other Muslim nations, marking a significant turning point. According to Sayın's article titled "Western Modernism, Islamic Fundamentalism", it was during this time that the West, fearing the loss of its hegemony, started perceiving Islam as a threat. An illustration of this can be seen in the West's reluctance to assist the Bosnian Muslims, as it did not wish to establish a Muslim state in the heart of Europe. Sayın also allluded to a similar scenario that was unfolding in Kosovo at the time.[31]

Sayın cautions against the potential danger of Islam falling into a trap of succumbing to a second era of western dominance. The West, in its efforts to prevent Islam from redefining its identity and ideology, may advocate for the westernisation of Islam, which Sayın perceives as a ploy to once again subjugate Islam. However, if the West intends to "westernise" Islam, it will face an arduous task. The only instance where this approach was somewhat successful was when Japan was coerced into adopting an open door policy. Nonetheless, such endeavours by the West will primarily serve its own interests. Sayın firmly

THE CLASH OF CIVILISATIONS OR DIALOGUE OF CULTURES? 265

believes that Islam is not the "Other," but rather a distinct and unique civilisation that should be comprehended without misconceptions, prejudices, and ignorance. In Sayın's perspective, Islam strives to preserve its distinctiveness amidst the diverse civilisations of the world.[32]

In his article "The New World Cultures," Ömer Laçiner argues that Islam and Christianity, as well as the Islamic East and the West, need to find a way to resolve their differences. Throughout history, these two worlds have constantly vied for universality, resulting in clashes. However, Laçiner believes that Islam's claim to universality is not based on asserting its superiority like the West does. He points out that Islam hindered itself by not pursuing a policy of conversion in the Christian lands it conquered. Unlike the Ottomans, who allowed Christians and Jews to freely practice their religions in the Ottoman Empire, the outcome would have been different if they had converted the Slavs and Greeks to Islam during their five-century rule in the Balkans.[33]

Laçiner holds a different viewpoint regarding the notion that societies attempting to westernise in the 20th century have faced identity crises. He argues against the idea that Turkey is a divided country, as this was not the case throughout its history until the late 19th century. Turks, Orthodox Greeks, Armenians, Albanians, Arabs, and Kurds all identified themselves as Ottoman citizens and enjoyed the benefits of this status. Each ethnic group, known as a 'millet', practiced their own religion, spoke their own language, and respected the cultural and traditional differences between one another, all while coexisting within a specific geographic region. This was the perspective of the Ottoman Empire and the Islamic State. Interestingly, the European Union is currently attempting a somewhat similar system.[34]

Following the partition of the Ottoman Empire by the British and the French, except for the Arabian Peninsula, a series of semi-quasi nation states were established based on European principles. Consequently, national identities were formed along ethnic lines, as per the European model, and were demarcated by European-drawn borders. This factor is cited by Saddam Hussein as one of the reasons why he deemed

Kuwait's claim to independence as illegitimate, arguing that it had always been a part of Iraq and was unlawfully created by Britain due to its abundant oil reserves. Therefore, Laçiner perceives this as the underlying cause for the ongoing disunity in the Middle East today.[35]

Yasin Aktay viewed Fukuyama's declaration of the end of History as a momentous event, akin to the arrival of the kingdom of God. Fukuyama believed that humanity would now experience eternal bliss, having achieved ideological perfection. However, Aktay, in his article "From the End of Eschatology to the Continuation of Conflict", dismisses Fukuyama's perspective as a harsh reflection on the past two centuries. He perceives Fukuyama's *The End of History* as a mere analysis of historical conflicts. On the other hand, Huntington's objective was not solely to glorify European civilisation, but rather to examine the potential adversaries Europe might face. Aktay argues that this theory was not groundbreaking, as the Turks and other Muslims were already aware of it.[36]

In his article "From a Clash to Destruction of Civilisations," Murat Yılmaz highlights the connection between liberalism and the emergence of socialism and anarchism. Yılmaz argues that if liberalism represents the culmination of all ideologies, then Huntington's war of civilisation can be seen as justified. However, Yılmaz views this perspective as pessimistic when it comes to determining the outcome of history.[37] This perspective sheds light on the constant fear of the 'Islamic threat' and how it is mirrored in the concept of the 'Christian West' as the enemy. Westerners claim this concept, which serves the purposes of Islamists. Muslim writers have accused the West of being aggressive, expansionist, and intolerant. They argue that the West is characterised by spiritual decadence, declining morals, and the degradation of women as sex objects. Interestingly, this stereotypical image of the West bears striking similarities to the West's stereotypical image of Islam. In recent decades, many Muslims have felt compelled to defend their culture and beliefs against Western accusations, which often stem from a simplistic view of Islam. Consequently, the Western perception of Islam as hostile plays a significant role in Islam's defensive posture and the creation of a hostile counter-perception of the

West. The danger lies in the potential deterioration of dialogue between these two cultures. If this occurs, it would only strengthen the position of those who believe in an unbridgeable divide between the East and the West.[38] In the words of the leading German intellectual Franz Nuscheler (b. 1938) in a lecture given at Cologne, in September 1991:

> I am not as afraid of the new threats being built up there as I am of the reactions in the North, in our own societies. What goes on daily before our eyes as regards policies on asylum seekers and refugees gives me a greater reason for fear than Islamic fundamentalism or the growing number of asylum seekers. The image of the South as 'the enemy' does not only strengthen prejudice but also breeds racism and gives wide and effective support to sealing off fortress Europe. It is not Europe's military security, not its affluence are threatened, it is its humanitarianism.[39]

It is regrettable that certain scholars from the Western world, instead of addressing the flaws within Western societies and their policies, apply the same standards when criticising other civilisations. This approach only serves to create a divide between cultures, hindering the establishment of mutual understanding and coexistence. One particular criticism from the West is that Islam is incompatible with democracy and secularism.

The assumption that the intertwining of religion and politics inevitably leads to fanaticism and extremism has played a significant role in concluding that Islam and democracy cannot coexist. However, failing to distinguish between moderate Islamic movements and those that are violent and extremist is overly simplistic and counterproductive. Furthermore, Islamist movements or parties that actively participate in the political and social spheres do not necessarily pose a threat to the political system itself. Instead, they may be perceived as a threat by entrenched rulers and political elites who view them as an appealing alternative.

It is worth noting that the United States government, as well as the media, does not equate the actions of extremist leaders or groups within Judaism and Christianity with the religions as a whole. Whether it is the bombing of abortion clinics, the massacre of Muslims at prayer in the Hebron Mosque, or the genocidal policy of ethnic cleansing by Bosnian (Christian) Serbs, these actions are not attributed to Judaism and Christianity in their entirety. Similarly, the American government does not condemn or view the mixing of religion and politics in countries like Israel, Poland, Eastern Europe, or Latin America as an inherent threat. Unfortunately, a comparable level of fairness and impartiality is often absent when it comes to Islam.[40] This lack of even-handedness distorts the perception of Islam among Westerners.

CHAPTER 17

THE NEW MILLENNIUM AND THE MUSLIM OTHER

9/11 AND THE CLASH OF CIVILISATIONS DEBATE REVISITED

At the beginning of the new millennium, a familiar pattern emerged with the revival of tensions between Christianity and Islam, as well as between Islam and the Western world. This situation mirrored an event that took place nearly a thousand years earlier, which had significant repercussions across the Mediterranean region and continues to impact the collective consciousness of Muslims today. In 1095, Pope Urban II called for a Crusade, a holy Christian campaign against the Muslims in the Levant, undertaken in the name of God and Christ.

In 1095, Pope Urban II delivered a significant address that initiated the call for a Crusade against Muslim forces. This call was prompted by a request from Emperor Alexios I Komnenos of the Byzantine Empire (r. 1081-1118), who sought aid from Western powers to combat the Seljuq Turks, who had taken control of a substantial portion of Asia Minor. During the council held at Clermont, Pope Urban II spoke passionately to a large assembly, encouraging them to assist the Greeks and to reclaim Palestine from Muslim dominion. Although the official records of the council's discussions have not been preserved, there exist four written accounts of Urban's speech, authored by those who were in attendance. One notable account comes from the chronicler Fulcher of Chartres (d. 1127). It is important to recognise the connection between the principles of the peace and truce of God, which aimed to foster harmony within Christendom, and the subsequent call for a Crusade. Nonetheless, one might ponder whether this represents an endorsement of violence and contributes to the ongoing discourse regarding the clash of civilisations. According to Fulcher of Chartres, Pope Urban II spoke the following words:

> O sons of God, you have promised more firmly than ever to keep the peace among yourselves and to preserve the rights of the church, there remains still an important work for you to do. Freshly quickened by the divine correction, you must apply the strength of your righteousness to another matter which concerns you as well as God. For your brethren who live in the east are in urgent need of your help, and you must hasten to give them the aid which has often been promised them. For, as the most of you have heard, the Turks and Arabs have attacked them and have conquered the territory of Romania [the Greek empire] as far west as the shore of the Mediterranean and the Hellespont, which is called the Arm of St. George. They have occupied more and more of the lands of those Christians, and have overcome them in seven battles. They have killed and captured many, and have destroyed the churches and devastated the empire. If you permit them to continue thus for awhile with impurity, the faithful of God will be much more widely attacked by them. On this account I, or rather the Lord, beseech you as Christ's heralds to publish this everywhere and to persuade all people of whatever rank, foot-soldiers and knights, poor and rich, to carry aid promptly to those Christians and to destroy that vile race from the lands of our friends. I say this to those who are present, it meant also for those who are absent. Moreover, Christ commands it. "All who die by the way, whether by land or by sea, or in battle against the pagans, shall have immediate remission of sins. This I grant them through the power of God with which I am invested. O what a disgrace if such a despised and base race, which worships demons, should conquer a people which has the faith of omnipotent God and is made glorious with the name of Christ! With what reproaches will the Lord overwhelm us if you do not aid those who, with us, profess the Christian religion! Let those who have been accustomed unjustly to wage private

warfare against the faithful now go against the infidels and end with victory this war which should have been begun long ago. Let those who for a long time, have been robbers, now become knights. Let those who have been fighting against their brothers and relatives now fight in a proper way against the barbarians. Let those who have been serving as mercenaries for small pay now obtain the eternal reward. Let those who have been wearing themselves out in both body and soul now work for a double honour. Behold! on this side will be the sorrowful and poor, on that, the rich; on this side, the enemies of the Lord, on that, his friends. Let those who go not put off the journey, but rent their lands and collect money for their expenses; and as soon as winter is over and spring comes, let him eagerly set out on the way with God as their guide.[1]

Similarly, at the dawn of the twenty-first century, in 2001, Osama Bin Laden (1957-2011), at the beginning of the U.S.-led war in Afghanistan (7-17 December, 2001) said, "This war is similar to the previous crusades led by Richard the Lionheart, [Frederick] Barbarossa and Louis of France. In the present age they rally behind Bush".[2] Bin Laden references the Crusades, where Christian armies fought against Muslims in the Middle Ages. By incorporating Huntington's thesis, Bin Laden highlights the clash of civilisations as a continuous and enduring conflict between the two cultures throughout history. For more than twenty years, the assault on New York City on September 11, 2001, has remained a subject of ongoing scholarly and political deliberations and conversations.

Jeffrey Haynes in his essay entitled, "Twenty Years of Huntington's 'Clash of Civilizations'" argues that the significance of Huntington's article does not lie in the fact that his argument was 'correct' or 'right'. Instead, he proposes two points: Firstly, Huntington's article holds importance as it accurately encapsulated the prevailing spirit of the post-Cold War era, a perspective that has persisted during the uncertain era of 'globalisation'. Secondly, it has stood the test of time as a lasting declaration on globalisation, encompassing both the aspirations and anxieties associated with it.[3]

The 9/11 attacks highlighted the impact of cultural and religious differences, particularly fundamentalist Muslims, on global conflict. Some saw it as the start of a clash of civilisations between the Christian West and the Islamic world. However, others argued that it marked the decline of transnational Muslim radicalism. The attacks brought culture to the forefront, reinforcing Samuel Huntington's clash of civilisations thesis. This led to a simplistic division of the world based on essentialist characteristics of the Christian West and Islam. Huntington famously said, "Islam has bloody borders", suggesting that these borders explained global divisions.[4]

David A. Welch argues in the essay "Enemy Wanted: Apply Without", about the surprising end of the Cold War that left many individuals in a state of uncertainty, as they tried to comprehend the future of global politics. While some were still grappling with this uncertainty, others had already made their predictions. John Mearsheimer anticipated a return to the chaotic multipolarity reminiscent of the 1930s. Charles Krauthammer, on the other hand, declared that the United States was experiencing a unique "unipolar moment." Francis Fukuyama envisioned the triumphant spread of liberal democracy worldwide. Lastly, President George H. W. Bush enthusiastically advocated for a "new world order" founded on the principles of law and effective global governance.[5]

The end of the Cold War left people uncertain about the future of global politics. Some, like John Mearsheimer, an American political scientist, predicted a return to chaotic multipolarity, while others including the political columnist Charles Krauthammer, believed the United States was in a unique unipolar moment. For Francis Fukuyama, there were also visions of the spread of liberal democracy and the establishment of a new world order, according to President George W. Bush.[6]

Huntington focused on culture, defining civilisation as the broadest form of culture. He believed conflicts within a civilisation were battles within the same cultural framework. Culture held utmost significance, surpassing all other factors. In an interview, Huntington expressed the importance of shared cultures, languages, and values for a sense of belonging. However, globalisation posed a challenge to this longing. In 1993, he identified Islam as a threat due to perceived animosity towards the Western world.[7]

Since 9/11, Western nations have become increasingly concerned about "home-grown terrorism". This involves young individuals, often second or third generation Muslim immigrants, becoming radicalised. Shockingly, individuals born and raised in Western societies have been involved in acts of terrorism, like the Madrid train bombings in 2004, the murder of Theo van Gogh in Amsterdam in 2004, and the London bombings in 2005.

The categorisation of identity into opposing Western culture and Islam overlooks the various forms of Islam seen throughout history and today. Furthermore, individual identity is often viewed as a singular concept, disregarding the existence of multiple identities within a person. Hence, it is entirely possible for someone to identify as a Muslim, a Western citizen, a proponent of democracy, and someone who values diversity and human rights simultaneously. Additionally, culture is not static; it transforms and adjusts as circumstances evolve.[8]

Like the centuries before, Islam today is often seen as intolerant and violent, influenced by a long-standing 'orientalist' tradition. However, this perception is based on selective interpretations. Islam actually celebrates diversity and requires followers to accept other religions. The early sayings of Muhammad and Ali show inclusiveness. Devout Muslims must reject racism, not hate Judeo-Christian civilisation, and embrace tolerance. Dislike towards the West may stem from perceived injustices. Historically, Muslim countries have shown more tolerance towards other religions than Europe until the 19th century, as seen in Medieval Spain and the Ottoman Empire.[9]

Evidence suggests that the "clash" thesis has been politically employed in a surprising way, contradicting the typical narrative of neoconservative ideas. Former President George W. Bush, known for his neoconservative foreign policy, surprisingly incorporated elements of liberalism in his use of the clash of civilisations concept. In a 2007 Presidential Address, Bush rejected Huntington's idea and stated that the "war on terrorism" was actually a "struggle for civilization." This rejection was reiterated by Bush's administration, including Secretary of State Colin Powell and Condoleezza Rice.[10]

Bush rejected Huntington's idea but still found value in it. He redefined "civilisation" to align with liberal principles, shifting from a clash *of* civilisations to a clash *for* civilisation. His foreign policy emphasised universal freedom and democracy. The "war on terrorism" framed the conflict as ideological, not religious.[11] Huntington argues for openness, learning, and innovation, but contradicts himself by acknowledging the clash of civilisations. The practical implementation of his plea is unclear.

The implications of adopting a perspective that avoids oversimplifying cultures and acknowledges their complexity are significant. By recognising that cultures are not monolithic or identical, individuals can approach intercultural conversations with a positive outlook on mutual comprehension. This perspective allows for a deeper understanding of the diverse entities involved, including their complex histories. It promotes a more nuanced and respectful dialogue that fosters genuine understanding and appreciation for different cultures. Additionally, by avoiding essentialisation, individuals can avoid perpetuating stereotypes and biases, leading to more inclusive and equitable interactions. Overall, adopting this perspective enhances intercultural communication and promotes a more inclusive and diverse society.[12]

Al-Qaida's Challenge to Orientalism and Imperialism

The Islamic faith upholds the principle of religious universalism, which centres around the belief in the singular existence of Allah as the supreme deity and the acceptance of Muhammad as his chosen messenger. The divine message conveyed to the Prophet Muhammad by the Angel Gabriel is meticulously recorded in the sacred scripture, the Qur'an, which is regarded as the ultimate and definitive revelation from God to all of mankind. However, when certain Muslim extremists claim to represent the entire Muslim community, the Western media often seizes upon these assertions and associates them with the religion of Islam. According to Sheikh Saaed Shaaban, the former leader of Muslims in Tripoli summed up the views of political Islam in the following words:

> We must reject democracy in favour of Islam, which is the unique [political] perfect system worked out by the Almighty [...] Our march has just begun, and Islam will end up conquering Europe and America [...] For Islam is the only [path to] salvation [...] It is our mission to bring salvation to the entire world.[13]

It is contradictory to the true nature of Islam and the teachings of the Qur'an to politicise Islam using provocative language. Muslim leaders worldwide should no longer tolerate the representation of Islam by any individual as if it represents the beliefs of all Muslims. This kind of rhetoric only serves to perpetuate misunderstandings and misinterpretations of Islam in Western societies.

A discussion exists regarding the perspective that Al-Qaida depicts the West in a negative light, positioning it as the aggressor and framing the Islamic community (ummah) as the victim. They consider the struggle for media influence to be vital in their resistance. Nevertheless, while their attempts to disseminate their narrative against the West have attracted attention, they have also rendered themselves more vulnerable to scrutiny. The availability of Western translations, critiques, and analyses of primary sources has fostered an academic environment where this counter-narrative is recognised, understood, and even immunised against criticism.

The idea of Occidentalism is the construction of a Western identity that the Orient uses to distinguish itself. Occidentalism can be employed to bolster narratives of defiance against Western intervention. Egyptian philosopher Hassan Hanafi argues for the necessity of a scholarly examination of Occidentalism (*istighrab*) to be established in the developing countries to advance the process of decolonisation. This field would seek to offer a structure for comprehending the West, ultimately fostering a more robust sense of independent Islamic (specifically, Arab Muslim) self-identity.[14]

Eastern depictions of the West have a long history. Russia, Asia, and the Middle East have all considered the West as an external other for at least a century before it became a significant concept in the West itself. According to scholar Sadik al-Azm, if Orientalism exists, there is also a reverse Orientalism that favours Islam and the East.[15] In this reverse perspective, Islam plays a central role in perpetuating this prejudice. Al-Azm argues that the Islamic aspect of resistance has transformed political literature by emphasising the opposition of East against West instead of the more familiar national liberation against imperialist domination.[16]

Edward Said argues that the discourse propagated by those who are not Palestinians hinders the Palestinians from finding a platform to express themselves. Literature serves as a means to justify and represent their cause.[17] However, if discourse promotes violence, the creation and dissemination of literature itself becomes a conflict. This is a particular concern for Al-Qaida ideologues, as they believe that the subaltern's voice is not being heard. Osama bin Laden claimed that George W. Bush's simplistic interpretation of the war on terror led many countries unable to speak for themselves to align with the powerful world terrorism of the USA.[18] Furthermore, Bin Laden stated that in the past, the Americans had complete control over them, and the victims were not even allowed to voice their grievances.[19]

Beside the physical resistance, there is a continuous battle over the historical and cultural narrative.[20] Therefore, discourse and the literature it stems from can offer a structure for reconstructing an independent historical path. Colonialism manipulates the history of the oppressed, distorting, mutilating, and erasing it.[21] Consequently, the process of decolonisation involves the rediscovery of lost and suppressed histories, the revival of the numerous pasts silenced by colonial rule.[22] Edward Said takes it a step further by suggesting that resistance has the potential to shape an alternative modernity; it is not just a response to imperialism but a different way of understanding human history.

The Al-Qaida organisation's narrative is an attempt to create an alternative modernity that is separate from the West. By drawing on early

Islamic generations and traditions, the organisation aims to establish a foundation that predates colonialism and develop its own unique history. This strategy, common among pan-Islamic narratives, serves the dual purpose of seeking legitimacy through tradition and is not exclusive to jihadist groups.[23] As Karl Marx noted in the nineteenth century, revolutionaries often look to the past for inspiration, borrowing names, battle cries, and costumes to give a sense of historical continuity to their movements.[24]

The "jihadists" believe that an uncorrupted form of Islam embodies the correct set of values. Their goal is to revive the lost Caliphate which serves as a blueprint for reclaiming Islamic territory from Western control.[25] The Caliphate serves as a concrete symbol for identification. Lawrence argues that Bin Laden sees the conflict not as one between Al-Qaida and the global Crusaders, but as a struggle between Muslims and the global Crusaders.[26] This viewpoint aligns with Huntington's the clash of civilisations theory, explicitly supported by Bin Laden in an interview with al-Jazeera reporter Taysir Alluni.[27] Jihadists believe that only Islam has the ability to liberate them from Western dominance. Strategist Abu Mus'ab al-Suri argues that the current world order, led by the United States, would never accept a state governed by Islamic law because it represents a civilisation and ideology separate from the World Order.[28] According to this interpretation, Orientalists and Muslim radicals are viewed as collaborating, highlighting the fundamental and decisive role of the Islamic faith.[29]

The concept of a unified people based on religion is not solely a creation of jihadists. Frantz Fanon argued that the struggle for national freedom in the Arab world is accompanied by a cultural awakening of Islam, shaping the narrative.[30] Al-Qaida presents its conflict as an ongoing struggle of Islam, drawing inspiration from historical events like Saladin's re-conquest of land from the Crusaders.[31] This narrative emphasises the importance of learning from Muslim ancestors who successfully fought against the Crusaders, providing the necessary conditions for resistance.

The Muslim community (*ummah*) needs an opposing civilisation to define its identity, often portraying the West as enlightened and virtuous. However, this narrative reinforces Orientalism, perpetuating victimisation and positioning the West as dominant. The human continuum is divided into friend and foe, with Orientalist literature creating a polar distinction between the Orient and Occident.[32] This negative framing dehumanises the enemy and can lead to calls for violence, creating destructive stereotypes between the West and the Islamic World.[33]

The beginning of Occidentalism according to Bin Laden

Individuals in Muslim nations have observed the consequences of diminishing political authority among rulers, along with considerable socioeconomic and identity issues, following the collapse of the Ottoman Empire in the early 20th century and the advancing European imperialism. Mustafa Kemal identified a critical weakness within Muslim nations, choosing not to attribute their challenges to external adversaries. Instead, he pointed to the clerical interpretations of the Qur'an and their enduring effects, which obstructed the integration of reason, logic, science, and Divine revelation necessary for elevating societies from poverty to economic prosperity through education. In the 1920s and 1930s, he sought to educate and rejuvenate Islam in Turkey, aiming to dispel superstitions and myths that had shaped religious practices for generations, while also enacting significant reforms. In contrast, individuals like Bin Laden and other radicalists preferred to blame an external enemy for the difficulties confronting Islam. Kemal recognised that a nation's progress depended on economic and technological development, alongside active political participation from its citizens. Nevertheless, Arab nation-states have faced significant challenges in adapting to modernity, achieving economic growth, and establishing political legitimacy. For radical groups, engaging in violent conflict with perceived external threats appeared to be a viable solution.

In 1990, the invasion of Kuwait by Iraq marked the beginning of the Gulf War. A coalition consisting of Muslim Middle Eastern countries, as well as American, British, and other nations, united to expel Saddam Hussein's army. This period, known as *al azma* or the crisis, held significant importance for certain Arab Muslims, including Bin

THE NEW MILLENNIUM AND THE MUSLIM OTHER 279

Laden. The crisis was deemed as such for two main reasons: firstly, it involved Muslim Arabs fighting against fellow Muslim Arabs, and secondly, it entailed the entry of American and other non-Arab forces into Saudi Arabian territory. To comprehend why the latter reason was viewed as problematic, one must grasp the fact that the Saudi city of Mecca, the birthplace of the prophet Muhammad, holds immense religious significance for Muslims. In fact, it is considered so sacred that non-Muslims are prohibited from entering it. Some Muslims perceive this sacredness to extend throughout the entirety of Saudi Arabia. Non-Muslim soldiers entering a Muslim country, especially to support one Muslim nation against another, was seen as offensive. Some radical Muslims saw America and its allies as incompatible with Islam, which they believed stood for unity among Muslim communities, moral integrity, obedience to Allah and the teachings of the Qur'an, and the traditions of Muhammad. The presence of troops from a country that represented the opposite of the Muslim way of life was viewed as an "invasion" of Saudi Arabia, fuelling Bin Laden's animosity towards America and the West.[34]

Bin Laden identifies the United States' backing of Israel in its conflict with the Palestinian people as a significant factor contributing to his animosity towards the nation. He critiques the U.S. for its willingness to enforce United Nations resolutions related to Iraq while neglecting those pertaining to Israel. In particular, he questions the lack of action regarding the United Nations Resolution 242, which demands Israel's withdrawal from the West Bank. These grievances led Bin Laden and others to issue a *fatwa* (religious edict) in 1998, grounded in Islamic law, calling for Muslims around the globe to kill Americans and their allies. In 1998, he outlined three reasons for war with America:

1. The US has stationed troops in Saudi Arabia

2. Second, the US led economic embargo on Saddam Hussein's Iraq killing a million Muslims

3. Third, these wars are economic and religious to keep the Jewish state secure and to direct attention from the occupation of Jerusalem and the killing of Muslim Palestinians

According to Bin Laden,

> To kill Americans and their allies, both civil and military, is an individual duty of every Muslim who is able, in any country where this is possible, until the Aqsa Mosque [in Jerusalem] and the Haram Mosque [in Mecca] are freed from their grip and until their armies, shattered and broken-winged, depart from all the lands of Islam, incapable of threatening any Muslim.[35]

Bin Laden witnessed the desecration of Saudi Arabia and perceived the policies of the United States and the Western world as hypocritical when it came to the Palestinian issue. Additionally, he recognised the contradictory stance of the West, which claimed to uphold values such as freedom, democracy, and justice, while supporting authoritarian regimes and dictatorships in the Arab world, including Saudi Arabia, Libya, Egypt, and Syria, solely to serve American interests in the region. This led him to interpret the conflict with the US and its allies through a religious lens:

> The people of Islam [have] suffered from aggression, iniquity, and injustice imposed on them by the Zionist-Crusaders alliance and their collaborators, to the extent that the Muslims' blood became the cheapest and their wealth was loot in the hands of enemies. Their blood was spilled in Palestine and Iraq. The horrifying pictures of the massacre of Qana, in Lebanon, are still fresh in our memory. Massacres in [Tajikistan, Burma, Kashmir, Assam, the Philippines, Somalia, Chechnya, and Bosnia-Herzegovina] took place, massacres that send shivers in the body and shake the conscience.[36]

Bin Laden urged Muslims to protect their faith in the context of the Afghanistan conflict, characterising it as a "crusader campaign" against Islam. His main driving force was his religious convictions, viewing the conflict as a holy war initiated by Western powers. Although President Bush Sr. and Prime Minister Blair held contrasting opinions, Bin Laden and his supporters steadfastly maintained this viewpoint.

Since 2002, in the aftermath of the September 11 attacks in 2001, Western media has consistently reported on assaults conducted by Muslim militants in Israel, particularly those executed by Hamas and Islamic Jihad. These incidents frequently involved suicide bombings, leading to devastating casualties, including the deaths of 22 young Jewish individuals at a Tel Aviv nightclub in 2001, 15 at a pizza restaurant in Jerusalem, 10 in a bus ambush in Emmanuel, and 15 in a bus attack in Haifa. The cycle of violence persisted, resulting in 20 fatalities across four separate attacks in Jerusalem, 15 in a snooker hall in Tel Aviv, and 39 in a series of bus attacks. Following these events, both the attacks and subsequent retaliations continued to escalate. The Arab-Israeli conflict has remained unresolved since Israel's establishment in 1948, with the ongoing apartheid faced by the Palestinian population indicating that a resolution is unlikely. Consequently, Osama bin Laden has characterised the Western world as the epicentre of "oppression, falsehoods, moral decay, and decadence".[37] Bin Laden continued to provoke America:

> Go ahead and boast to the nations of man, that you brought them AIDS as a Satanic American Invention" [and that] you have continued to sink down this abyss from level to level until incest has spread amongst you ... [a country with] the Giant corporations and establishments [which are created] under the name of art, entertainment, tourism, and freedom, and other deceptive names that you attribute to it.[38]

The West is perceived as an aggressive imperial force, positioning Islam as the victim of its actions. This perception fosters the conviction that a defensive jihad is essential to combat the invading adversary, advocating for unwavering resistance until death rather than capitulation.[39] This defensive posture is deemed crucial due to the barbaric laws of warfare instituted by the American-led global order. Al-Suri contends that, in contrast to the savagery exhibited by Western military forces, Islamic nations demonstrate compassion. The coalition forces in Iraq are likened to the "new Mongols", regarded as equally barbaric as their historical counterparts.[40]

Following the September 11 attacks, President George W. Bush spoke to a global audience, asserting that "Freedom itself was attacked this morning by faceless cowards".[41] This notion of cowardice extends beyond Western perspectives, as those in resistance movements also perceive their opponents as feeble and lacking in Islamic values. Abu Bakr Naji condemns the fear and frailty of the enemy, even in light of their technological superiority.[42] He argues that the American and Western military forces are now incapable of enduring prolonged conflicts.[43]

Al-Qaida strategically employs Western rhetoric to its advantage, leveraging the perceived hypocrisy of its adversaries to promote its own narrative of truth. Anwar al-Awlaki notes that this approach is not novel; hypocrisy has posed a challenge to the Muslim community since the era of Prophet Muhammad.[44] As Naji indicates, by revealing and denouncing hypocrisy, one can diminish the influence of wrong-doers and potentially lead to their downfall.[45]

Western nations employed rhetoric in their counter-terrorism efforts to assert universal principles, effectively criminalising any opposition. Carl Schmitt posited that waging a war in the name of humanity negated the adversary's claim to humanity itself. He contended that concepts like peace, justice, progress, and civilisation could be strategically manipulated to claim them for oneself while simultaneously denying them to the enemy.[46] Bin Laden acknowledged this dynamic and the West's exclusive control over values in the aftermath of the September 11 attacks:

> Western civilization, which is backed by America, has lost its values and appeal. The immense materialistic towers, which preach Freedom, Human Rights, and Equality, were destroyed. These [Western] values were revealed as a total mockery as was made clear when the US government interfered and banned the media outlets from airing our words (which don't exceed a few minutes), because they felt that the truth started to appear to the American people.[47]

Bin Laden openly acknowledges the effectiveness of these non-Western media platforms and the double standards of his adversaries.

The Pan-Islamist narrative challenges Western dominance but paradoxically gains traction in the West due to the limited understanding prevalent in Eastern contexts. Existing power structures maintain their legitimacy by permitting controlled opposition and by studying and developing defenses against dissent. As Edward Said posits, knowledge confers authority. The allure of Al-Qaida has waned as it became more accessible through the Internet and platforms like al-Jazeera, initially existing outside the purview of Western discourse. It was perceived as a singular theory associated with incarcerated individuals. A significant risk for the West lay in oversimplifying Al-Qaida's ideology without comprehensive analysis. Nevertheless, contemporary Western scholarship now engages in a critical examination of this discourse. It is plausible to assert that Al-Qaida's ideology has been integrated into the Western intellectual landscape.[48]

The contemporary conflict between Western and Islamic civilisations is fundamentally rooted in the tension between secularism and religion as a guiding principle for life. The universalist aspect of Christianity is founded on the belief in a singular God, the notion of Jesus as the saviour for humanity, and the commandment from Jesus to disseminate his teachings across all nations.[49] According to Bassam Tibi, secularism has eclipsed Western Christianity, leading to a prioritisation of concepts such as universalism, human rights, democracy, and free market principles over traditional religious teachings.[50]

The political landscape represents the primary sphere in which the West can mitigate the perceived conflict. The West's stance on the Palestinian issue carries considerable symbolic weight. This issue acts as a catalyst for figures like Bin Laden and the al-Qaeda organisation, fostering a sense of betrayal among Muslims towards the West. While it is essential for America and the West to ensure the security of the Jewish population, they must also champion justice and prosperity for the Palestinians. The statements made by US Secretary of State Colin Powell in November 2001 likely provided encouragement to Muslims in the Middle East. Powell articulated a vision of a future where Israel and Palestine exist as two independent states with secure and recognised borders.⁵¹ He proposed that the principles enshrined in UN Security Council Resolutions 242 and 238 should underpin any prospective resolution in the region. The ongoing conflict in Palestine remains a significant obstacle to achieving genuine peace. Extremist factions within both Islam and the West will continue to perceive a clash of civilisations, particularly as the West unconditionally supports the Jewish State. Without a meaningful resolution to this issue, enduring peace and security will remain elusive.⁵²

The concept of world order put forth by Bin Laden and other Muslim radicalists is fundamentally flawed, a fact that remains unaddressed by any intellectual discourse. While they effectively underscore the deficiencies, stagnation, and challenges faced by contemporary Islamic societies, they fail to propose viable solutions. There is an absence of a practical Islamic framework that aligns with the demands of the modern world. The Islamic Republic of Iran cannot serve as a model due to its Shia identity, which distinguishes it from its Arab and other Muslim neighbours. Additionally, the political doctrine of the rule of the religious jurisprudent, introduced by Ayatollah Khomeini, represents a novel aspect of Shia ideology that has encountered persistent difficulties since his passing in 1989. Although Usama Bin Laden, his adherents, and other Muslim radicalists may provoke chaos and strife with the West and its allies within the Islamic realm, they are unlikely to create an alternative order that poses a substantial threat.

PART III

RECOGNISING THE OTHER IN THE 21ST CENTURY

Imperialism as a political project cannot sustain itself without the ideas of empire, and the idea of empire, in turn, is noursihed by a philosophical and cultural imaginary that justifies the political subjugation of distant territories and their native populations through claims that such peoples are less advanced, cognitively inferior, and therefore naturally subordinate.

Amy Allen

You are in no position to dictate.

Donald Trump to Volodymyr Zelenskyy (28 February 2025)

CHAPTER 18
DECOLONISING ORIENTALISM
CRITIQUING EURO-AMERICAN INTELLECTUAL HEGEMONY IN ACADEMIA

One area where Muslims have failed to catch up to the West is in the area of knowledge. Since the Middle Ages, particularly after the twelfth century, the Muslim world faced challenges in reconciling religion and science, leading to a shift towards focusing on the *hadiths* as the supposed tradition of the Prophet Muhammad, superstitions and cultural practices. They have forgotten that the tradition of the Prophet Muhammad is the Qur'an itself. This shift resulted in a decline in the intellectual contributions made by Muslim scientists since the end of the golden age of Islam, which came to a halt by the end of the 12th century.

Despite the destruction of the Istanbul Observatory in 1580 by a decree from the *sheikh al-islam*, scholarly contributions persisted beyond the 12th century. In the following centuries, Muslims started adopting ideas and technological advancements from Europe. What led to this phenomenon? What hindered the development of new ideas and technologies within the Muslim intellectual tradition? Why has Islam not been able to make significant and innovative contributions to the advancement of human knowledge over the past millennium?

One potential avenue to explore this intellectual void in the Islamic world in the modern era is by examining the distribution of Nobel prizes in science since 1901. A comparison of the Jewish and Muslim population figures worldwide reveals significant disparities. While there are approximately 15 million Jews, there are 1.3 billion Muslims in the world today. Surprisingly, Jewish scientists have received 25% of the total Nobel prizes in science awarded since 1901, with 49 out of 196 in biomedical, 28 out of 158 in chemistry, 45 out of 189 in physics, and 28 out of 66 in economics. This amounts to a total of 150 awards out of 609.[1] In contrast, the number of Muslim individuals who have been awarded the Nobel prize for science in the past century is only 0.5% of the total prizes given. Out of the 609 recipients from 1901 to 2011, there have been three Muslim awardees: Mohammad Abdus Salam from Pakistan received the Nobel Prize in Physics in 1979, Ahmed Zewail from Egypt received the Nobel Prize in Chemistry in 1999, and Aziz Sancar from Turkey also received the Nobel Prize in Chemistry in 2015.[2] These three awards represent a small fraction of the total prizes, with no Muslim recipients in the field of biomedical science, one in chemistry out of 158, one in physics out of 89, and one in economics out of 66. However, if we include the most recent Muslim recipient of the Nobel Prize in Chemistry in 2023, Moungi Bawendi from Tunisia, the total number of Muslim awardees increases to four out of a total of 965 individuals.[3] Daron Acemoğlu, a Turkish-American economist of Armenian descent, stated that he would not have received the 2024 Nobel Prize in Economics had he chosen to advance his academic career in Turkey. Acemoğlu, who was awarded the Nobel Prize for his studies on the impact of societal institutions on economic success, expressed his concerns regarding Turkey's academic and judicial frameworks. He emphasised that the limitations on academic freedom in Turkey would have precluded him from achieving such an honour there. Acemoğlu remarked, "If you tell a scientist what they should research, that scientist is not going to win a Nobel prize".[4] Acemoğlu is only the third Turkish citizen to win a Nobel award, following novelist Orhan Pamuk (2006) and molecular biologist Aziz Sancar (2015). Nobel laureate physicist Steven Weinberg has noted that "Though there are talented scientists of Muslim origin working productively in the West, for forty years I have not seen a single paper by a physicist or astronomer working in a Muslim country that was worth reading".[5] Surprisingly, Spain and India each make a greater contribution to global scientific literature than the collective output of several Muslim countries. Spain, although not typically viewed as a major intellectual hub, manages to translate a higher number of books in a year than the entire Arab world has translated over the course of a thousand years.[6]

The statistics are remarkable and elucidate the absence of originality, inventiveness, imagination, and inquisitiveness. The educational syllabus in Muslim countries relies heavily on memorisation without placing significant importance on analytical and critical thinking, devoid of any form of inquiry. If individuals who follow the Islamic faith genuinely delve into the Qur'an with great attention to detail, they will discover that God implores humanity to actively pursue knowledge, inquire, question, and employ rationality to arrive at conclusions regarding His creation of the universe.

If the Nobel Prize is considered the highest achievement in intellectual contributions to the advancement of human knowledge, it is also essential to reflect on the representation of Black recipients of this esteemed accolade. From 1901 to 2022, a grand total of 954 individuals have been honoured with the prestigious international prize, spanning across six distinct categories: Physics, Chemistry, Medicine, Literature, Economics, and Peace. Out of these recipients, only 17 have been Black, making up 1.7% of the total number of recipients.

An article published in Forbes Magazine on 28 January 2025, Duncan Madden reports that World of Card Games undertook a comprehensive study to identify the most intelligent countries in the world. This research methodology utilised data from several esteemed sources, including Nobel Prize Organisation, World Population Review, U.K. Office for National Statistics, and U.S. Census Bureau, assessing metrics such as Nobel Prize nominations, university rankings, average national IQ scores (using the Lynn-Becker scale), and higher education attainment levels. Each metric was standardised on a scale of 0 to 100, with 100 indicating the highest-performing country in that category. The overall Smart Capital Score was calculated as a weighted average of these scores, giving slightly more weight to Nobel Prize nominations and educational attainment. In cases of limited data, the most recent information was used, and adjustments were made to ensure fair comparisons among all countries.[7]

According to the study, Switzerland is ranked the most intelligent country globally by World of Card Games, scoring 92.02 out of 100. With a population under nine million, it is also one of the wealthiest and most beautiful nations. The Swiss have 1,099 Nobel Prize nominations and an average IQ of 99.24. Notably, 40.02% hold at least a bachelor's degree, and 18.05% have a master's degree. Additionally, 32 Swiss universities have received Nobel Prize nominations.[8]

European nations dominate the ranking, with the United States as the only non-European in the top ten, holding third place with a score of 89.18, just behind the United Kingdom at 89.40. The U.S. leads in Nobel Prize nominations with 5,717, compared to the U.K.'s 2,392, and has 256 universities with nominations, double the U.K.'s 128. However, the U.K. has a higher average IQ of 99.12, compared to the U.S.'s 97.43. The Netherlands ranks fourth with an IQ of 100.74, while Finland, in tenth place, has an average IQ of 101.20.[9]

The concentration of Nobel nominees and laureates in a few countries, particularly Germany, the UK, and the US, stems from their long-standing support for educational institutions since the mid-20th century. Experts highlight that fundamental research, which the Nobel Prizes emphasise, is crucial for significant scientific advancements. According to Duncan:

> Marc Kastner, a physicist in California and founding president of the Science Philanthropy Alliance, told the American Institute of Physics that Nobel Prizes are a "lagging indicator" explaining that "They show us what we were doing right decades ago".[10]

It is essential to contend that although rankings can offer insights into intelligence and the ways in which nations cultivate talent, they should not be regarded as conclusive. Intelligence manifests in various forms that extend beyond mere academic achievement and accolades. Factors such as culture and society, along with the availability of opportunities, significantly influence approaches to problem-solving and innovation. As highlighted by the study, this ranking should encourage dialogue regarding the diverse methodologies and experiences that contribute to a more intellectually advanced global community. For Muslim countries, this study not only validates their concerns about their failings behind in innovation and research relative to their Western peers but also highlights the limited government funding available for independent researchers and the deficiencies present in secondary and higher education curricula, thereby reinforcing the observations made by Marc Kastner.

Can the Muslim world afford to lag behind the West in the 21st century?

Education plays a crucial role in shaping a prosperous and knowledgeable society. A high level of literacy, combined with groundbreaking research and original ideas, is essential for staying competitive on a global scale. This shift in mindset is a positive development, as Muslim scholars are now engaging in intellectual debates with their Western peers, particularly in the field of religious studies. However, Joseph Lumbard's optimistic perspective on the revival of Muslim scholars in countering Euro-American intellectual dominance is primarily focused on Islamic theology and Qur'anic studies. The scope of scientific research contributions by Muslim scholars warrants further exploration and discussion.

The Islamic civilisation boasts the distinction of having the world's oldest university that has been functioning without interruption. Established in Fes, Morocco, in AD 859, the University of Qarawiyyin marked the commencement of the Islamic Golden Age. However, despite this promising start, universities in the region are currently facing severe challenges. The 57 countries belonging to the Muslim world, which includes those with a Muslim-majority population and are part of the Organisation of Islamic Cooperation (OIC), collectively accommodate nearly a quarter of the global population. Hillel Ofek, in the 2011 article titled "Why the Arabic World Turned Away from Science?" published in *The New Atlantis*, states that:

> The Arab world consistently demonstrates a stark contrast in various aspects when compared to other regions. Despite comprising only 5 percent of the global population, Arabs contribute a mere 1.1 percent to the world's book production, as outlined in the U.N.'s 2003 Arab Human Development Report. In the time frame from 1980 to 2000, Korea generated 16,328 patents, while a total of nine Arab nations, including Egypt, Saudi Arabia, and the U.A.E., collectively issued a meager 370 patents, with a significant number going to non-nationals. A study from 1989 showed that the United States published 10,481 highly cited scientific papers in a single year, whereas the entire Arab world managed only four. Despite the somewhat comical nature of the situation, a 2002 article in Nature magazine pointed out that Islamic countries excel in only three scientific fields: desalination, falconry, and camel reproduction. The ongoing efforts to establish new research and scientific institutions in the Arab world ... underscore the substantial progress that still needs to be made.[11]

Establishing new research and scientific facilities in Muslim countries is crucial in maintaining competitiveness with the West. Research and Development (R&D) activities are characterised as innovative endeavours aimed at advancing current knowledge, resulting in original, experimental, scientific, and technical contributions. Design activities focus on enhancing and optimising product functionality, thereby generating added value and fostering competitiveness within the industry and other pertinent sectors.[12]

As of 2012, Muslim contribution to the world's patents was only 1.6%, to academic publications 6%, and to global research expenditure 2.4%. As noted above, Nobel laureates in the sciences from OIC countries have been limited to three: Egypt in 1999, Turkey in 2015, and Tunisia in 2023. The winning recipients ironically conducted their research in the United States. Presently, these nations, have less than twelve universities in the top 400 of global rankings, with none in the top 100 indicated in reports like the *Royal Society's 2014 Atlas of Islamic World Science and Innovation.*[13] That is not much to brag about! For instance, OIC nations typically allocate less than 0.5% of their GDP towards research and development. Turkey is the only exception investing 1.4%

of its gross GDP (2021) in research and development R&D). In 2021, Turkey is home to over 1,500 research and development (R&D) and design centres, which collectively employ more than 70,000 individuals.[14] Malaysia comes second investing slightly over 1% (compared to the global average of 1.78%; with most developed countries investing 2-3%).[15] Other Muslim countries including Saudi Arabia spend 0.45% (2021), Algeria 0.53% (2017), Egypt 0.91% (2021), Azerbaijan 0.21% (2021), Pakistan 0.16% (2021), Iran 0.79% (2019), Iraq 0.04% (2021) and Jordan 0.7% (2016). Comparing these low statistics to the United States' spending on R&D 3.46%, United Kingdom 2.91% (2021), European Union 2.28% (2021) and Israel 5.56% (2021), Muslim countries have much to learn to raise their standard of education and research to the level expected of them at the international level.[16] Furthermore, students from Muslim-majority countries perform significantly lower in standardised international science assessments compared to their global counterparts, indicating a deteriorating trend.

In order to emerge as guiding lights in society, OIC universities must rejuvenate their instructional approaches and blend scientific knowledge with humanities disciplines like history and philosophy. To achieve genuine meritocracy, universities should devise innovative methods to evaluate faculty members, acknowledging their significant contributions in research, teaching, and community engagement. However, for this transformation to occur, governments must grant universities greater autonomy.

The scientific productivity of the 20 OIC countries has accounted for more than 90% of their overall science production in the last twenty years. During the period from 1996-2005 to 2006-2015, most countries within the OIC doubled or even tripled their output of scientific papers. Notably, Qatar experienced a remarkable increase of 7.7 times, while Iran's output grew by 7.6 times. However, despite these advancements, the number of scientific papers produced by OIC countries still falls below the average of countries with similar GDP per capita. In the most recent decade, the OIC research output averaged 4.2 papers per dollar of GDP per capita, whereas a group of four peer countries including Brazil, Spain, South Korea, South Africa, and

Israel averaged 8.6 papers per dollar of GDP per capita.[17] Furthermore, papers originating from OIC countries tend to receive fewer citations compared to those from other countries. The average number of citations per paper for the period of 2006-2015 was 5.7, whereas South Africa and Israel, countries with similar GDP per capita, received 9.7 and 13.8 citations per paper, respectively. Interestingly, none of the 100 most-cited papers since 1900 had a lead author from a Muslim-majority nation.[18] At another level, according to the Scopus database, which is the largest abstract and citation database of peer-reviewed literature, Iran holds the 16th position, Turkey holds the 19th position, and Malaysia holds the 23rd position in terms of global publication data as per Scimago (SJR) 2014.[19] It is interesting to note that these countries are ranked higher than Scandinavian countries, Switzerland, Taiwan, South Africa, Israel, and Singapore. Saudi Arabia holds the 35th position, while Pakistan holds the 43rd position.

Scientific research should prioritise its relevance and responsiveness to the intellectual and practical needs of society. Unfortunately, this essential objective appears to be overlooked and disregarded by the majority of academic institutions in Muslim countries. In order for scientists and engineers to foster creativity, innovation, and a deep understanding of ethical, religious, and societal implications of their research, it is crucial for students to receive a comprehensive education that encompasses liberal arts. While only a few institutions strive to connect their students' learning with their cultural backgrounds and contemporary knowledge, Tehran's Sharif University of Technology took a pioneering step in the early 1970s. They introduced a comprehensive program that integrated Islamic history, philosophy, and culture with science and engineering. Notably, their graduate program in the philosophy of science stands as the sole program of its kind within the OIC. It is worth noting that Sharif University's commitment to this holistic approach may have played a role in its recent recognition as the top Iranian university and the eighth-ranked university in the OIC, according to the Times Higher Education world university rankings. It is one thing to be ranked in the top ten universities in the OIC and another to be ranked in the top 500 or 1000 in the World University

Rankings by Quacquarelli Symonds (QS) or Times Higher Education (THE).

University education in the Islamic World

Universities in the Muslim world often struggle to rank highly in global university rankings. However, some of these institutions are actively addressing this issue by improving their research and development capabilities, hiring internationally qualified faculty, reducing student-faculty ratios, and upgrading facilities. As developing societies invest more in higher education, it is important to consider whether the Western-centric education model, as promoted by rankings, should be the only measure of competitiveness. Should Muslim countries prioritise standardisation over diverse educational approaches? Additionally, does an increase in research output always equate to high-quality research and teaching? By asking these questions, we can challenge conventional wisdom and take steps towards enhancing the competitiveness of universities in the Muslim world.

In 2016-2017, only seven universities from the Islamic world were included in the top 500 World Universities. However, as per The Times Higher Education World University Rankings 2018, a total of ninety-six universities from Muslim countries have made it to the top 1102 universities globally. This indicates a positive trend towards the advancement of higher education in the Islamic world, even though only 18 Muslim countries are represented on the list in 2016-17. It is hoped that more Muslim countries will be featured in upcoming reports. Among the 96 universities listed in 2016-17 rankings, Turkey has 22, followed by Iran with 18; Pakistan with 10; Malaysia and Egypt with 9 each; Saudi Arabia with 5; U.A.E. and Indonesia with 4 each; Jordan and Morocco with 3 each; Tunisia with 2; and Algeria, Bangladesh, Kuwait, Lebanon, Nigeria, Oman, and Qatar with 1 each.

In THE 2025 world university ranking, Turkey's Council of Higher Education (YÖK) has reported that Turkish universities have demonstrated notable performance in several disciplines, with 35 institutions securing positions within the top 1000 for education sciences, which is the country's most successful area.[20] Nevertheless, these outcomes are considerably less impressive when evaluated against the stringent academic rankings of the world's leading universities.

In the field of education sciences, a Turkish university has achieved a position within the top 100, while six others are listed among the top 500, and 35 are included in the top 1,000. Middle East Technical University (METU) is ranked 89th worldwide, Boğaziçi University falls within the 151-175 range, Hacettepe University is categorized in the 251-300 range, and Anadolu University, Bahçeşehir University, and Bartın University are all ranked between 401-500. YÖK President Erol Özvar highlighted the significant achievements of Turkish universities in education sciences and engineering, attributing their success to extensive experience and human resources. He stated, "We take great pride in our universities' accomplishments, particularly in education sciences. These rankings show that we are aligned with global advancements and at the forefront of international trends. While we celebrate these results, we recognize our universities have even greater potential".[21] It is appropriate to mention that Universities in the Muslim world, much like their Western counterparts such as Cambridge, Oxford, and Harvard, face significant challenges in competing and sustaining consistent positions in global rankings.

Ellen Hazelkorn, serving as the Dean of the Graduate Research School at the Dublin Institute of Technology in Ireland, examines the significant ranking publications and the performance of various global regions in her article titled "Striving for World Class Excellence: Rankings and Emerging Societies," published in 2012. North America and Western Europe stand out as the top performers, housing prestigious universities with ample resources, including medical schools, predominantly located in English-speaking countries. While these rankings highlight the quality of these institutions, they also reveal the inherent bias in the criteria used for ranking. The Academic Ranking of World Universities (ARWU) places significant emphasis on bibliometric databases and citation practices, giving priority to research published in internationally recognised peer-reviewed journals in the English language. This inclination towards English publications creates a disadvantage for non-English language communities, irrespective of their research output. Even when reputation is evaluated through impartial surveys, rankings such as QS and THE tend to favour individuals who are native English speakers, thereby impacting the ultimate rankings. Hazelkorn asserts that due to the limited knowledge about institutions, faculty and peers "tend to rank high those departments of the same type, and with the same emphases, as their own universities or those with whom they are most familiar".[22] This supports Lumbard's evaluation of the prevalence of "intellectual colonialism" and "intellectual hegemony" by maintaining the Other in a subordinate position, where the "presumed intellectual superiority of Euro-American analytical modes has become a defining and enduring characteristic".[23]

Revamping the curriculum to encourage innovation

In 2024, an extensive evaluation was conducted by THE ranking body, examining over 134 million citations from 16.5 million research publications. Additionally, valuable insights were gathered from 68,402 scholars worldwide through survey responses. The comprehensive data collection process encompassed 411,789 datapoints, originating from a diverse range of 2,673 institutions that willingly submitted their data.[24]

While rankings consider various performance indicators, there is a significant dependence on research capacity. However, it is important to note that knowledge creation and dissemination are not the sole objectives of a university. By prioritising research over quality instruction, we conveniently overlook one of the main responsibilities of training and producing capable and accountable individuals. This approach has a detrimental effect on educational institutions and discourages emphasis on teaching. Furthermore, rankings that rely on a limited set of criteria undermine the diversity of institutions, ultimately monopolising and distorting the true essence of a competitive university.

In the 2024 THE ranking, no university from Muslim country made it into the top 100 list.[25] Why? We need to look at the curriculum and the existing university structures in place. First, there are notable challenges in science education, particularly in OIC universities where textbooks are often imported from Western countries like the United States or Europe. While these textbooks are of high quality, they are presented in English or French and reflect a Western perspective disconnecting many students from their cultural background. To bridge this gap and promote the creation of locally-produced academic resources, universities should provide incentives for staff to develop these materials, offering rewards similar to those for research publications.

Certain fundamental truths are often met with controversy and pushed to the fringes. Take the concept of evolution, for instance, which is typically limited to biology students and presented as a mere "theory", seldom integrated with other branches of knowledge. It is crucial to promote widespread education on evolution and demonstrate its compatibility with Islam and its cultural values. Additionally, incorporating the teachings of philosophy and the history of science would prove beneficial.

Second, the global consensus is that enquiry-based science education fosters the deepest understanding of scientific concepts and laws. But in most OIC universities, lecture-based teaching still prevails. Exceptions are rare. One is the Petroleum Institute, an engineering university in Abu Dhabi, UAE, where the faculty has created a hands-on experience with positive results on student interest and enrolment, particularly of women.[26] Additionally, faculty members in OIC countries rarely receive pedagogy training or assessment due to government regulations and centralised administrative systems, making it difficult for universities to implement curriculum changes or introduce innovative practices.

What is the solution?

OIC universities need more autonomy to become merit-based institutions leading transparency and meritocracy in their societies. Universities need to promote the right metrics, so that they do not inadvertently encourage plagiarism and junk science through pressure to publish. The region needs consistent data on science student and faculty profiles, curricula, pedagogy, language of instruction and so on, akin to what the Institute of Statistics of the United Nations Educational, Scientific and Cultural Organisation collects — but at a fine-grained, university level. This is a task that must be undertaken by national or transnational bodies, such as the Islamic World Academy of Sciences (IAS) or the Islamic Educational, Scientific and Cultural Organisation (ISESCO).

The Muslim nations seek recognition from the Western educational system. Numerous universities in the Muslim world are striving for US accreditation in order to gain global recognition. For instance, the renowned US business accreditation organisation, Association to Advance Collegiate Schools of Business (AACSB), has granted accreditation to a minimum of five universities in the UAE (Abu Dhabi, American University of Sharjah, UAE University, University of Dubai, Zayed University), three in both Turkey (Bilkent, Istanbul, Sabanci) and Saudi Arabia (Prince Sultan, King Abdulaziz, King Fahd), two in Malaysia, and one each in Qatar, Lebanon, Egypt, and Kuwait, with none in Pakistan. Likewise, the US Accreditation Board for Engineering and Technology (ABET) has accredited at least twelve universities in Saudi Arabia, eleven in the UAE, five in Turkey, two in both Qatar and Bahrain, one in Oman, and even one in the Palestine State, while there are no ABET-accredited engineering universities in Pakistan.

Epistemological unity and Muslim academia

At this juncture in our discussion, it is crucial to address relevant inquiries: Are Eurocentric biases still dominant in today's academic sphere? In what ways do modern orientalist perspectives hinder the inclusion of marginalised, conquered, and oppressed voices in intellectual discussions? Why must the intellectual traditions of diverse cultures adhere to Euro-American academic norms in order to gain acknowledgement?

It is an undeniable historical fact that imperialism by major powers throughout history has contributed to the marginalisation of the conquered and the oppressed. Colonisation of the former Ottoman territories by the European powers at the end of the First World War contributed to the further deterioration in the decline of learning in the Muslim world. As John Henrik Clarke states:

> To control a people, you must first control what they think about themselves and how they regard their history and culture. And when your conqueror makes you ashamed of your culture and your history, he needs no prison walls and no chains to hold you.[27]

The majority of Arab nations attribute the lack of intellectual progress in the modern era to colonialism. However, can the same be said of the Turks? Throughout history, Turkey, unlike many other nation states that emerged after the fall of the Ottoman Empire, managed to maintain its independence and avoid foreign imperial control. Under the leadership of Mustafa Kemal, Turkey successfully resisted all European attempts to exert dominance, as mentioned in earlier chapters. The Muslim nations are united by their unwavering faith in the Islamic tradition that has been established over the past fourteen centuries. However, the lack of self-criticism and the reluctance to question existing intellectual traditions, mindsets, and practices hinder any potential intellectual advancement.

European colonisation and imperialism cannot be the sole blame for the decline of learning in the Muslim world. There have been two notable instances in world history where nationalist imperialist attitudes have resulted in similar outcomes. The first of these occurred during the Umayyad dynasty, shortly after the passing of Prophet Muhammad in 632CE, when Arabisation of Islam took place. As Arabic became the dominant language in the Islamic world, all scholarly works in various fields such as theology, philosophy, mathematics, physics, biology, chemistry, medicine, history, and others were written mostly in Arabic. The remaining significant languages in the Muslim world, namely Farsi (Persian) and Turkish, were limited to literature, military, political discourse, and administrative works. Historians often overlooked the ethnicity of Muslim scholars who contributed to these major works during the medieval period of Islam, and their significance was diminished. Both Arab and non-Arab scholars were collectively recognised as 'Muslim' scholars. Furthermore, as Islamic knowledge spread to medieval Europe, the names of these scholars were Latinised, erasing any indication of their religious background when their names are read. Consider if today, recipients of the Nobel Prize for science from America, Britain, Germany, France, and other countries were labelled as 'Christian'. Such a classification would undoubtedly spark controversy and show disrespect towards the nation responsible for their education.

The second factor, and possibly the most relevant one, contributing to this phenomenon is the widespread use of the English language in academic circles, which has led to the eradication of an entire knowledge system and the reshaping of the cognitive framework of Islamic studies. Boaventura de Sousa Santos has aptly termed this as "epistemicide", referring to the destruction of knowledge.[28] Unfortunately, contemporary Muslim scholars who approach their research from the perspective of epistemic unity according to Qur'anic methodology, often face neglect from the Euro-American academic community like Steven Weinberg, due to their deviation from established standards.

Understanding the distinction between Islamic and modern perspectives on verifiable knowledge is crucial. While modern thought emphasises scientific method and material evidence, Islamic belief encompasses knowledge from the unseen, human, and material realms, obtained through Revelation and sound reasoning. This fundamental difference sets Islam apart from Christianity, where some doctrines may conflict with reason.[29] Joseph E. Lumbard's substantial contribution to this field of study offers valuable insights and serves as the foundation for the subsequent discussion in this chapter. According to Lumbard:

> Epistemology and noetics have, therefore, been analyzed extensively from the time of al-Kindı (d. 256/870) up to the present. Central to these discussions lies the question of the relationship between revelation and reason as stated by some and the relationship among revelation (*wahy*), reason (*aql*), and inspiration (*ilham*) or unveiling (*kashf*) as stated by others. In the pre-modern period, this debate was developed

by Muslim thinkers in part because the recognition of prophethood as a phenomenon experienced by all human collectivities required that Muslim philosophers and theologians explain not only the knowledge possessed by the Prophet Muhammad (SAWS), but also that possessed by the prophets before him. Since this time, the need to reconcile prophetic knowledge with knowledge obtained through philosophical investigation has led to robust epistemologies wherein prophethood, inspiration or unveiling, and philosophical investigation (with all of the empirical manifestations we would today call "science") have been conceptualized as various modes of knowing God and knowing creation (*khalq*) in relation to God, the Creator (al-khaliq).[30]

Although Muslim territories are not currently under direct colonisation, the influence of intellectual colonialism persists through the prioritisation of Eurocentric knowledge production systems. This preference often disregards and even excludes modes of analysis that originated in the Islamic world, which have been developed and refined over a span of more than a thousand years.[31] Consequently, this intellectual hegemony leads to a complex form of "epistemological reductionism" that undermines the effectiveness of analytical tools derived from the classical Islamic tradition.[32] The assumed intellectual dominance of Euro-American analytical approaches has become an inherent and enduring characteristic of Qur'anic Studies, impacting every facet of the discipline. This enduring nature hinders certain scholars from engaging with, let alone utilizing, the analytical methods of the classical Islamic tradition, thereby impeding a more inclusive dialogue within the global community of Qur'anic Studies scholars.[33] Muzaffar Iqbal argues that Western scholarship on Qur'anic studies frequently disregards or deems insignificant the concept of revelation (*wahy*) as interpreted in Islam.[34] Another factor to consider in the lack of Muslim contributions to academia is coloniality.[35] The systems and frameworks that guarantee the perpetuation of imperial dominance endure.[36]

Scholarly works in European languages often overlook the valuable research conducted in Arabic, Persian, Turkish and other languages. Additionally, sources that have shaped the Islamic tradition for centuries are frequently disregarded in Euro-American academic studies of the Qu'ran. This disregard is apparent in Nicloai Sinai's 2017 publication, *The Qur'an: A Historical-Critical Introduction*, where works by Muslim academics on the Qur'an are excluded.[37] In addition, Western academics have disregarded and failed to acknowledge recent Qur'an commentaries by Muslims of non-English speaking backgrounds. The release of Bayraktar Bayraklı's *Interpretation of the Quran in the Light of a New Understanding* in 2022, a renowned Turkish Qur'an scholar, Islamic theologian, and *hafiz*, brings forth a fresh perspective on this sacred text. This groundbreaking work, spanning 22 volumes and encompassing over ten thousand pages, represents a significant accomplishment in illuminating God's revelation in the context of the modern world. Bayraklı's emphasis on God's pedagogical method and epistemological unity underscored in the Qur'an offers a unique perspective on comprehending the sacred scripture. Regrettably, these valuable contributions made by non-English speaking Muslims also expose the academic prejudice that reflects the elitism prevalent in Euro-American academia. This bias disregards Muslim scholarship and favours Western scholarship as the primary and authoritative source for Qur'anic studies.

The existing orientalist perspectives towards Islam in contemporary times, primarily held by the educated elites who are predominantly white and affiliated with the Euro-American academic community continue to persist. As Amy Allen argues, the prevalent perspective within postcolonial scholarship is the progressive and developmentalist interpretation of history, where the West or Europe is viewed as more advanced or enlightened compared to other regions.[38] This viewpoint is closely linked to the civilising mission of the West, which served as a rationale for imperialism and colonialism, and still supports the neocolonialism evident in today's political, legal, and economic global structure.[39]

Numerous academics' intense preoccupations with linking their traditions to Western hegemonic universal exacerbate the issue, leading to the development of Eurocentric biases when applying theories to comprehend a specific culture instead of referencing the culture's own traditions. Even if the text and the individuals analysing it share the same cultural or religious background, the theoretical framework used is derived from outside the culture. Conversely, Eurocentric and Anglo-American theories rarely face the same scrutiny, as they generate their own self-reflective theories believed to be immune to external perspectives from beyond the Euro-American academic sphere. Utilizing foreign theoretical frameworks simultaneously can lead to intellectual confusion and create illusions about the subject under examination.[40]

Due to the absence of discrimination that defines the contemporary society, and particularly prevalent among Westernised Orientals, Muslims, and others, intellectual communication and the study of philosophy and metaphysics have been hindered by various extreme behaviours. These behaviours have prevented a meaningful exchange of ideas and a comprehensive examination of these subjects. The comparison between great gnostics and saints with skeptics has often led to a complete confusion of different levels of inspiration.[41]

Systemic institutional racism has led to the continued dominance of the Western philosophical tradition over marginalised philosophical traditions. As Jay Garfield argues, disregarding the philosophical customs of diverse cultures, regardless of our personal preferences, perpetuates the colonial endeavour of imposing our own culture over theirs. This endeavour was rationalised by the notion that it was the white man's duty to enlighten the ignorant non-believers and introduce them to civilisation. To uphold this belief, we must disregard the evident intellectual traditions of these cultures and refuse to acknowledge their epistemic value, which we readily attribute to our own traditions. Placing the Western philosophical tradition at the forefront as the sole definition of "philosophy" while neglecting other traditions within our academic departments or personal lives directly contributes to institutional racism. Acknowledging our involvement in this system and choosing not to alter our personal behaviours or advocate for change within our institutions, even in a passive manner, ultimately perpetuates individual racism.[42]

The modern field of Islamic Studies is deeply rooted in the developmentalist and progressive interpretation of history. This perspective has long been used to justify the civilising mission of the West and still supports the informal imperialism of the neo-colonial world. Despite condemning colonialism and imperialism on moral and political grounds, numerous scholars in Euro-American academia and beyond maintain an epistemological allegiance to the very structures they criticise.[43] This results in a significant hermeneutical imbalance as it refuses to acknowledge the epistemic legitimacy of the sources under examination. The relegation and dismissal of specific methods of investigation and understanding ostracises numerous cognitive and interpretive approaches that hold significant importance for Muslims across various regions. When treated merely as a subject of examination, Islamic intellectual customs are deprived of complete participation in their own interpretation. Regrettably, numerous individuals unknowingly contribute to this phenomenon of hermeneutic marginalisation by embracing Euro-American interpretations of their cultures and a global humanism that disregards, diminishes, or even rejects the cognitive superiority of these cultures. In the pursuit of advancement, this method sustains systemic epistemic biases that marginalise their own cultures, preventing them from engaging in addressing current challenges, and demanding that they be altered in order to be acknowledged.[44]

The Western modes of thought that have been passed down should be thoroughly examined and evaluated through an Islamic lens, rather than from a standpoint of intellectual inferiority and modern narratives of oppression. It is essential to comprehend the cognitive framework that gives rise to Islamic sciences and in which they are embedded. Embracing scientific facts exclusively, from a secular and Western perspective without recognising the convergence of knowledge through the incorporation of religious sciences, only serves to maintain ignorance within the minds of scientists and rationalists. As Max Planck in *Where is Science Going?* states:

> Science cannot solve the ultimate mystery of nature. And that is because, in the last analysis, we ourselves are a part of the mystery that

we are trying to solve ... This is one of man's oldest riddles. How can the independence of human volition be harmonized with the fact that we are integral parts of a universe which is subject to the rigid order of nature's laws? ...

There can never be any real opposition between religion and science; for the one is the complement of the other. Every serious and reflective person realizes, I think, that the religious element in his nature must be recognized and cultivated, if all the powers of the human soul are to act together in perfect balance and harmony. And indeed it was not by any accident that the greatest thinkers of all ages were also deeply religious souls, even though they made no public show of their religious feeling. It is from the cooperation of the understanding with the will that the finest fruit of philosophy has arisen, namely, the ethical fruit. Science enhances the moral values of life, because it furthers a love of truth and reverence—love of truth displaying itself in the constant endeavor to arrive at a more exact knowledge of the world of mind and matter around us, and reverence, because every advance in knowledge brings us face to face with the mystery of our own being.[45]

The Muslim scholars of the medieval period are widely recognised for their significant contributions in reconciling religion with science. It is believed that without drawing inspiration from Qur'anic teachings, scientific progress would not have been possible. Celebrating the contributions of individual scholars such as Ibn Sina (d. 1037), Ibn Rushd (d. 1198), or Ibn Khaldun (d. 1406) has its place, but failure to understand the metaphysical and epistemological universe that gave rise to them risks relegating their contributions to artefacts or mere symbols and allows them to be treated as "exceptions". Therefore, considering the great achievements of these scholars as anomalies enable their remarkable accomplishments to be utilised as a discreet method to distort the vibrant intellectual environment from which they originated. These distortions are crucial in colonialism, as they sustain the false belief that contemporary thinking is more refined, intricate, and lively compared to that of ancient civilisations.[46] Therefore, once academia acknowledges epistemic unity by reconciling religion with science, then progress towards reconciliation with the Muslim Other can begin.

Yaşar Nuri Öztürk: Challenging Euro-American intellectual hegemony

In the discipline of Islamic and Qur'anic Studies modern Muslim scholarship is challenging the secular Western academic hegemony. Yaşar Nuri Öztürk (1951-2016) served as a faculty member and dean in Turkish universities for 26 years. He also taught 'Islamic Thought' courses as a visiting professor at The Theological Seminary of Barrytown in New York, USA. He gave numerous conferences on Islamic thought, human rights, and humanity in Turkey, the USA, Russia, Europe, Africa, the Middle East, and the Balkans. Öztürk's extensive writings, including articles like "Islam and Europe,"[47] "Islam and Democracy,"[48] and "İslam-Batı İlişkileri ve Bunun KEİ Ülkelerindeki Yansımaları"[49], numerous interviews have left a significant impact in the Western and Islamic spheres. His publications number more than thirty and have been translated into Turkish, English, German and Farsi. One of his most influential works, *Kur'an'daki İslam* ("The Islam of the Qur'an") stands out as a cornerstone of the back to the Qur'an movement. Öztürk's involvement in and contributions to this movement, coupled with the breadth of his intellectual endeavours, have become key focal points within many scholarly theses across Turkish, German, English, and French academic institutions including the The University of Edinburgh and Columbus State University.[50] Between 1993 and 2003 his Turkish translation of the Qur'an went into 126 printings in Turkey, holds the distinction of being the most widely printed book in the history of the Turkish Republic. In 2000, Öztürk was nominated by TIME magazine as one of the most influential thinkers of the 20th century.[51]

Other scholars including Muhammad Mustafa al-Azami and his 2020 publication of *The History of the Qur'anic Text: From Revelation to Compilation A Comparative Study with the Old and New Testaments*, Ahmad Dallal's *Islam, Science, and the Challenge of History*, Miri Shefer-Mossensohn's *Science Among the Ottomans*, Khaled El-Rouayheb's *Islamic Intellectual History in the Seventeenth Century*, and Asad Q. Ahmed's *Palimpsests of Themselves: Logic and Commentary in Muslim South Asia* demonstrate how the Islamic civilisation in the post-classical period (ca.1200–1900) continued to prioritise the pursuit of various forms of knowledge.

Conclusively, the process of decolonisation holds the promise of fostering fresh and varied knowledge ecosystems that recognise the significance of multiple viewpoints.[52] It is evident that the Euro-American academia, predominantly composed of individuals of white ethnicity, holds significant influence over the global narrative. Academic knowledge from non-English speaking regions, such as countries with Christian dominance like Russia, communist China, and Muslim nations including Arab, Turkish, Iranian, Malaysian, and Indonesian, tends to be disregarded.

Contemporary Muslim scholars, although their voices may not resonate prominently within current academic and scholarly circles in the West, are nonetheless making significant contributions to the discourse, regardless of prevailing Euro-American biases. Their serious efforts to advance knowledge through various epistemological methodologies, including Qur'anic methodology, highlight a lack of recognition from the West. This oversight not only demonstrates a misunderstanding but also represents a missed opportunity to appreciate the richness inherent in diverse forms of knowledge.

Boaventura de Sousa Santos argues that by embracing diverse knowledge systems, there is a possibility of altering the criteria for validating hierarchies, ensuring that newly established or revised hierarchies conform to the appropriate structure, without favouring any single methodology solely due to historical intellectual colonisation.[53] From this perspective it is crucial to promote counter-hegemonic strategies that promote "equity between different ways of knowing and different kinds of knowledge".[54] Consequently, no single methodology would emerge as the prevailing approach to knowledge acquisition.

CHAPTER 19

RELIGION, POLITICS AND THE EMERGING WORLD ORDER

Today, humanity engages in a variety of conflicts including religious wars, moral wars, wars of civilisation, wars of progress, ideological wars, and cultural wars. Physical conflict is not always necessary; sometimes, a smaller nation that opposes a larger and more powerful country may face international embargoes affecting its economy, culture, technology, and more. Even within the realm of Christianity, there is a holy war being waged. The Russian Orthodox Church, under the leadership of Patriarch Kirill, has distanced itself from the Western Christian Church by initiating a religious war against its Christian counterpart in Ukraine. As the Global South asserts itself against religious extremism and white supremacist movements, questions arise about the future of American supremacy and the shape of the international order in the years to come. Humanity must navigate these cultural conflicts to determine its destiny.

Three opinion pieces published in international media between 2022 and 2024 offer diverse perspectives on the current global narrative. These include an article by Australian journalist Stan Grant titled "Vladimir Putin's invasion of Ukraine is not just a war of politics – it's a holy war" (2022), a piece by former Member of the House of Representatives of the Netherlands, Joram Van Klaveren, titled "Can Western liberalism tolerate anything at all but itself?" (2023), and an article by Anton Fedyashin, an Associate History Professor at the American University in Washington, DC, titled "End of Wilsonianism: Ukraine, Gaza wars will shape new global order" (2024).

Stan Grant in his article "Vladimir Putin's invasion of Ukraine is not just a war of politics – it's a holy war" argues that faith is a topic that often causes controversy and debate in our society. Typically, these discussions revolve around scandals within the church, instances of abuse by priests, or issues related to morality and discrimination. Unfortunately, these conversations often oversimplify the complexities of faith. However, it is crucial that we delve deeper into the profound impact that faith can have on our world. When faith is misused or exploited, it can lead to devastating consequences. This is an aspect that we often overlook.[1]

Jocelyn Cesari argues that religion plays a significant role in the formation of nation states. Nations are not simply random entities; they are built upon a foundation of shared beliefs and values.[2] Religion can serve as a powerful tool for shaping collective identity. Cesari uses political Islam as an example of how faith can be utilised as a modern technique of governance.[3]

Faith should not be dismissed as a mere weapon for controversy or division. It has the potential to shape societies and influence the course of history. It is essential that we engage in thoughtful discussions about faith, recognising both its positive and negative impacts when misused for personal and political advantage.[4]

The Islamic world has embraced Western ideas of the modern state, whether willingly or under coercion, yet religion continues to play a crucial role in public life and identity. Extremist Islam, on the other hand, goes a step further by retaliating against the West. The terrorist attacks on September 11 orchestrated by Osama bin Laden jolted the West out of its belief that religious wars were a thing of the past. In his own manner, Putin shares similarities with Osama bin Laden, both using faith as a tool.[5]

Bin Laden and Putin, despite being products of the modern world, have responded to it in different ways. Bin Laden referenced the Crusades from the 11th century, while Putin sought to revive the concept of holy Russia from the 10th century. Both individuals aimed to reshape the world according to their ideologies. Bin Laden romanticised warfare and frequently posed with a gun, while Putin glorified Russia's history of war and its symbols of military power. The church plays a significant role in both cases, with Russian Orthodox priests even blessing nuclear weapons. Russian Orthodoxy has its own version of *jihad*, known as *podvig*, which encompasses a spiritual struggle. This concept has defined wars in Russia from the 1300s to World War II and the conflicts in Chechnya.[6]

Religion misused can sometimes lead to extreme actions. In 2020, Patriarch Kirill conducted a liturgy in a newly constructed cathedral within the Russian Armed Forces complex in Moscow. This cathedral, one of the tallest in Russia, is situated in Patriot Park and is decorated with military imagery, commemorating Russian military victories. Th interior decorative aesthetics suggest it focuses more on glorifying war rather than serving as a place of worship for Christ, as if the paintings reflect a "cult of victory".[7] Despite numerous priests condemning the violence in Ukraine, Patriarch Kirill views Putin's military actions as a holy "crusade". He often speaks of the harmonious relationship between the Church and the State, referring to it as the "kingdom and the priesthood".

Patriarch Kirill, similar to Putin, upholds traditional and conservative values, and has shown support for Putin's measures against homosexuality and Western cultural influences. According to Cesari, the West is viewed as an adversary that threatens national identity and opposes the "Western imperialist project".[8] Cesari also draws parallels between Putin's call for Christians worldwide and the call to arms by radical Islamic groups, suggesting similarities in their approaches.[9] The conflict in Ukraine cannot be comprehended without acknowledging the weaponisation of faith. Whether it is Vladimir Putin, Osama bin Laden, the Islamic State, or Christian white nationalist terrorism, religion as an identity can possess a lethal grip.[10]

The secular West must reflect on how it has belittled and ridiculed faith, relegating it to the personal sphere and leaving a void that can be exploited politically and spiritually by others. Western mainstream media tends to oversimplify the world into good and evil terms, overlooking how modern religious conflicts are a response to secularism. Putin's actions in the name of religion contradict the faith core values of peace, humility, mercy, and forgiveness.[11]

Joram Van Klaveren, the former member of parliament in the Netherlands, in the article "Can Western liberalism tolerate anything at all but itself?" argues that the traditional values that governed the old world for centuries are now being systematically marginalised in the contemporary Western society. Francis Fukuyama's book *The End of History* represents the prevailing spirit of the early 1990s. Following the conclusion of the Cold War, the world was poised to embark on a new era where Western liberal democracy (and its accompanying economic system) would stand as the sole and everlasting benchmark for all matters. Although there are numerous criticisms regarding the universal applicability of this theory, it is evident that a trend towards "general liberalisation" did indeed take hold in the Western world. The aforementioned reality is an immediate consequence of secularisation, the diminishing impact of religion on individual existence as well as society at large.[12] The traditional values and moral principles that once prevailed for centuries in the old world are now being systematically marginalised in the contemporary Western society. Religion no longer aligns with the prevailing narrative of the Occident. Individuals are educated to embrace notions of "freedom" and "progressiveness," which in turn leads them to exhibit intolerance towards what they perceive as "intolerant".[13] However, the Global South (also known as the 'Other', 'Third World', or 'developing countries') now has an opportunity to contribute to shaping the world order as blindly adhering to the US's commands has proven to be a hindrance for its allies in terms of economic impact.

Anton Fedyashin's piece titled "The Decline of Wilsonianism: Ukraine, Gaza conflicts to influence emerging global structure" (February 2024) delves into the ideological similarities between Leninism and Wilsonianism, which played a significant role in shaping the post-World War I global order, providing context for the current evolution of the global landscape. In the article titled "The Decline of Wilsonianism: The Impact of Ukraine and Gaza Wars on the Emerging Global Order" (February 2024), Fedyashin delves into the ideological similarities between Leninism and Wilsonianism, which played a significant role in shaping the post-World War I global order. This historical context serves as a foundation to understand the current trajectory of the world order. Notably, amidst this ongoing evolution, the voice of marginalised groups is gradually gaining prominence and becoming more audible.[14]

A century ago, the deaths of Soviet leader Vladimir Lenin and US President Woodrow Wilson occurred in close succession. This milestone presents an opportune moment to reassess the impact of their respective geopolitical strategies, namely Leninism and Wilsonianism. During the tumultuous period of the Great War in April 1917, both leaders put forth contrasting visions for a new global order, each imbued with messianic and universalist ideals. Their ideologies injected a novel dimension into foreign policy, aiming to rescue Europe from its own turmoil and safeguard the rest of the world from Europe's influence. It is worth noting that significant shifts in geopolitical thinking have historically emerged from the crucible of warfare, such as the establishment of the Westphalian system following the Thirty Years' War, the Congress System in the aftermath of the Napoleonic conflagration, and the bipolar system that emerged after the Second World War.[15]

Revisionist statesmen have consistently established new geopolitical paradigms at crucial turning points. The ongoing Ukraine and Gaza crises in 2024 are currently challenging the Western global dominance, thereby providing an opportunity for the Global South to actively contribute to shaping the world order. Can we expect visionary leaders akin to Lenin and Wilson to emerge and shape the new international system?

In his renowned speech to Congress on April 2, 1917, Wilson presented a fresh interpretation of the Great War, framing it as a struggle between "free and self-governed peoples" and "selfish and autocratic power." He passionately advocated for creating a world that is "safe for democracy," laying the foundation for what is now known as the "democratic peace theory" in American foreign policy. Wilson's belief was that an American-led global order would dismantle the European tradition of clandestine agreements, secret treaties, and covert operations. Instead, transparency would become the cornerstone of a progressive liberal world order.[16]

Upon his arrival in Petrograd two weeks later, Lenin presented his renowned "April Theses," denouncing the Great War as an imperialist conflict driven by the capitalist nature of colonial bourgeois governments. He advocated for the formation of a new International consisting of liberated worker and peasant democracies. The Bolshevik ideology also included the promise of a peaceful golden age. Lenin emphasised the importance of internationalism in socialism and, similar to Wikileaks, the Bolsheviks exposed European diplomacy by revealing secret agreements between the Russians and their allies, particularly at the expense of the Ottoman Empire. Lenin aimed for a transparent revolutionary world order that prioritised peace without territorial gains or annexations, challenging the traditional European diplomatic practices.[17]

Both individuals influenced global affairs through narratives that organised and directed broad public dissatisfaction. Lenin and Wilson shared the belief that ideology could free humanity from imperialism and reshape international relations following centuries of domination by the Old World. Recognising a systemic crisis through the emergence of alternatives from diverse geographic and political backgrounds is a crucial skill. Wilson and Lenin sought to move past the geopolitical effects of the "long nineteenth century" by promoting the spread of similar ideological systems as a means to establish peace. The interconnected nature of their visions would ultimately shape the course of world events up to the present day.[18]

Since the collapse of the USSR in 1991, Wilson's vision has prevailed during the US's unipolar moment, but the liberal globalist project is now unravelling due to self-inflicted wounds. A drift towards regionalism has increased the influence of small powers amidst the chaos of a profound geopolitical transformation. The world beyond the West seems to be transitioning towards a post-ideological era. With no clear diplomatic plan to handle the diminishing hegemony of the US, President Joe Biden's administration has embraced a Wilsonian binary approach.[19]

Rather than viewing global affairs through the perspective of power balance and pursuing agreements with rivals, Washington has reframed the current Ukraine conflict since 2022 as a clash between democratic and autocratic systems. However, the achievements have been minimal. Despite the sanctions imposed by NATO allies (excluding Turkey) and their allies in the Pacific region, more than 80 percent of the global population resides in nations that have not taken such actions. In the meantime, Russian President Vladimir Putin has effectively reached out to the countries of the Global South by presenting an anti-colonial storyline that bears a resemblance to Leninism in its structure.

However, a significant distinction lies in the substance—Moscow's discourse lacks any socialist elements, instead promoting capitalism and socio-cultural conservatism. Despite Washington's continuous attempts to portray the Russian invasion as a colonial land-grab, this approach has been successful thus far. The Global South, while denouncing the invasion of Ukraine and refusing to acknowledge the Russian annexations of Ukrainian land, views this conflict as a response to a NATO expansion that mirrors colonialism.

The 2014 regime change in Kiev, which was backed by Western powers, and the Biden administration's unwavering support for Israel during its operation in the 2023-25 war in Gaza, have revealed a clear double standard among Western nations when it comes to annexations, occupied territories, and civilian casualties. This discrepancy highlights the inconsistency in Western foreign policy. Furthermore, the spread of democracy, as championed by Wilsonian ideals, would have faced greater challenges if the US dollar had not become the global reserve currency following World War II.[20]

The United States has gained unprecedented power to influence both allies and adversaries. However, the staggering debt of $34 trillion currently burdening the US, along with the focus on weaponising the dollar and Western financial institutions, has spurred the development of economic and financial institutions that operate independently from the West. The Shanghai Cooperation Organisation (SCO) and the BRICS (Brazil, Russia, India, China, South Africa) economic group are now the fastest-growing international organisations, surpassing NATO. The effectiveness of their economic goals is yet to be determined, but blindly adhering to American directives has proven to be a hindrance for Washington's allies.[21]

Throughout the Cold War, aligning with the Western ideological camp led to economic prosperity, as seen in the comparison between North and South Korea, as well as West and East Germany. However, since the war in Ukraine (2022-), joining the trend of imposing economic sanctions on Russia is causing de-industrialisation and financial ruin in Europe. The Biden administration's (2021-24) proposal to seize $300 billion from Russian financial reserves held by Western institutions will only hasten the decline of Western financial and economic supremacy. A century after Wilson's passing, his vision is perhaps facing its final moments. Reviving it will require a level of innovative and charismatic American leadership that has yet to be demonstrated.[22] Considering this, Donald Trump's re-election for a second term as US president in 2024 may represent a significant threat to the integrity of American democracy and erosion of international law. The true impact of this situation will become apparent over time. The extent to which the nations of the Global South, including Turkey, will assert their influence in light of the declining role of the United States on the global stage is yet to be determined. The following chapters will explore in greater detail the growing importance of the Global South in international affairs.

CHAPTER 20

THE GLOBAL SOUTH IN THE 21ST CENTURY

THE VOICE OF THE OTHER IN THE MULTIPOLAR WORLD

The Professor of International Politics, Daniel Drezner argues that in the last ten years, the term 'Global South' has emerged as the new Other in the global narrative, signifying a convergence of various trends. Firstly, the nations located in the southern hemisphere have become increasingly diverse. For instance, including countries like Singapore or the United Arab Emirates in the definition of the Global South is a mischaracterisation. Secondly, the term has shed its previously condescending connotation.[1] Furthermore, the significance of these nations in international relations has reached unprecedented levels. In an era characterised by intense competition among great powers, these powers must vie for influence over the global community. The escalating tensions between China and the United States, Russia's military actions in Ukraine, and the surge of violence in the Middle East have rendered countries such as India, South Africa, Brazil, and Indonesia crucial players in the geopolitical landscape.[2] Additionally, the coalition of Global South countries aimed at challenging the dominance of the dollar as the primary currency in the global economy is starting to contest the hegemony of the United States.

The Bretton Woods Conference, also known as the United Nations Monetary and Financial Conference, convened 730 delegates from 44 allied nations at the Mount Washington Hotel in Bretton Woods, New Hampshire, USA. Its objective was to establish regulations for the global monetary and financial system post-World War II.[3] July 2024 will commemorate the 80th anniversary of the 1944 Bretton Woods conference, held amidst the turmoil of World War II. Held from July 1 to 22, 1944, the conference led to the signing of agreements that, once approved by member governments, established the International Bank for Reconstruction and Development (IBRD) and the International Monetary Fund (IMF). These institutions laid the groundwork for the Bretton Woods system, which governed international commercial and financial relations.[4] The Articles of Agreement aimed at stabilising exchange rates, regulating financial flows, and supporting post-World War II reconstruction and economic growth. Additionally, various suggestions for enhancing international economic collaboration were formalised in the Final Act of the conference. More significantly, the exchange rates were fixed to gold and the American currency that continues to dominate the global markets today and causing enormous economic inequity in the developing economies.

Countries have been making efforts to enhance their financial systems in recent times. The implementation of fast payment platforms has had a major impact on the financial scenarios of countries such as Brazil and India. Additionally, nations have started integrating their financial frameworks, allowing for almost instant settlement between different countries. The BRICS initiative has successfully linked central and commercial banks from China, Hong Kong, Thailand, Brazil, South Africa, India, and the United Arab Emirates, reducing dependence on the dollar. Saudi Arabia became a part of the project earlier this month, and it is anticipated that several more countries will join in the upcoming year.[5]

The former German Foreign Minister and Vice Chancellor, Joschka Fischer, in an article titled "Will Europe be the world's biggest loser?" posted on the Project Syndicate: World's Opinion Page website on 23 May, 2023, argues that the era of global stability that followed 1945 has come to an end. The world transitioned from the bipolar dynamics of the Cold War to a unipolar world dominated by America, which provided a sense of strategic order. Despite various conflicts, both small and large, such as those in Korea, Vietnam, the Middle East, and Afghanistan, the international system managed to maintain a level of stability and coherence.[6] Fischer states:

> Since the beginning of the new millennium, however, this stability has increasingly given way to a renewed rivalry between major powers, chief among them the United States and China. Moreover, it has long been clear that India, Brazil, Indonesia, South Africa, Saudi Arabia, Iran, and other emerging economies' political and strategic influence will increase, as will their role within the global system. In the context of a deepening conflict between China and the US, these rising powers will have many opportunities to play one of the twenty-first century's two superpowers off against the other. Indeed, many of these opportunities seem too good to miss.[7]

With the raging war in Ukraine that decisively put an end to the era of peace in Europe, the genocide in Gaza occurring before the eyes of the world powers and the growing rift between US-China relations, Europe, therefore, faces a significant disadvantage. It exists in a region that is becoming increasingly perilous, yet it continues to be a collection of independent nation-states that have never been able to come together to achieve genuine unity, even in the aftermath of two global conflicts and the lengthy Cold War. In a global landscape where powerful nations with expanding military expenditures hold sway, Europe still lacks the status of a true influential force.[8]

William R. Rhodes and Stuart P. M. Mackintosh argue that the world is witnessing a phase of worsening relations between the United States and China, as both nations are supported by their respective allies and engage in separate international platforms.[9] Although the exact consequences of this shifting geopolitical landscape are uncertain, it is evident that it is hindering efforts to tackle the most critical challenges faced by humanity. The post Cold War global order is failing and has failed at solving humanity's most pressing problems. A new global order is taking shape, one that is not primarily influenced by the US-led West. This emerging framework seeks to reduce the dependence of the global economy on the US dollar.

BRICS and New Multipolar World

The global economic supremacy of the West, led by the United States and the European Union, is changing fast with the emergence of alternative economic system - BRICS+, an emerging counterweight in a multipolar world.[10] BRICS, initially known as BRIC and later rebranded as BRICS in 2010 upon South Africa's inclusion, is an abbreviation representing Brazil, Russia, India, China, and South Africa. Its establishment in 2009 aimed to cultivate economic, political, and cultural collaboration among its constituent nations. Now, other countries are lining up to join this alternative emerging economic superpowerhouse to counteract the West's dominance in global economy.

China is leading the way in expanding the BRICS+ forum to challenge American dominance, particularly as the United States faces the Thucydides Trap - the inclination towards conflict when a rising power poses a threat to replace a regional or global hegemon.[11] The new BRICS line up, which now includes Egypt, Ethiopia, Iran, and the United Arab Emirates alongside the original members, aims to establish a different global order that empowers the Global South, the marginalised Other. The combined economies of the BRICS+ member countries are valued at over $28.5 trillion, which currently constitutes approximately 28 percent of the global economy.[12] By 2024, BRICS+ nations are projected to represent a significant portion of the global economy and population - "36% of global GDP and 45% of the world's population".[13] Despite not always seeing eye to eye, these countries are reshaping the balance of power in international institutions like the IMF, World Bank, G20, and UN in favour of China's interests.[14] The ultimate goal of these economic alternative systems is to reduce the reliance on the US dollar in the global economy, diminishing American economic supremacy.

The New Development Bank established by BRICS in 2015, the Asian Infrastructure Investment Bank, and substantial resource transfers, estimated at around $1 trillion, through China's Belt and Road Initiative, are strengthening the expanded group. These initiatives are integral to China's endeavour to establish its own worldwide financial framework, which will bolster its objectives and rival the European-led IMF and the US-led World Bank. The outcome of China's efforts to coordinate the Global South remains uncertain, with the United States expressing its hope for failure. However, some view BRICS+ as a fresh global economic model. The reality lies somewhere in between, although the US appears to be losing its popularity.[15]

The supremacy of the dollar is slowly waning as countries endeavour to decrease their dependence on this currency. According to data from the Atlantic Council, the share of dollars in global reserves has fallen by 14 percent since the start of the 21st century. In 2002, the dollar accounted for 72 percent of global reserves, but it now makes up roughly 58 percent. Although this trend does not indicate an imminent downfall of the dollar, it underscores a gradual transition away from its dominance as nations strive to reduce their reliance on the currency and lessen the influence that the United States wields through its monetary policies to advance its foreign policy goals. More than 40 additional nations have expressed interest in joining BRICS. The expanded BRICS coalition now represents a total population of around 3.5 billion people. Furthermore, BRICS nations account for about 42 percent of worldwide crude oil production.[16]

In the case for Turkey, as the Muslim Other in the eyes of the Europeans, its inclination to join BRICS+ signifies a change for Europe and the Western alliance. Turkey, a NATO member is making a historic move by distancing itself from the European Union and aligning its future with China and the BRICS Alliance. This shift is indicative of a larger trend unfolding across Europe, especially as the conflict in Ukraine continues to escalate, further undermining European dominance. What is the reason behind Turkey's keenness to join BRICS and what implications would this have on European countries?

Turkey's recent initiative to join the BRICS coalition highlights its strategic objective to enhance its global influence and broaden its international partnerships beyond its conventional Western allies. As

President Recep Tayyip Erdogan's government adapts to a changing geopolitical environment, the decision to forge closer ties with BRICS —an entity that encompasses some of the largest emerging economies —demonstrates Turkey's wider ambitions within a multipolar framework.

Originally formed by Brazil, Russia, India, China, and South Africa, BRICS has gained increasing appeal for nations seeking alternatives to Western-centric global institutions such as the International Monetary Fund (IMF) and the World Bank. Turkey's potential membership would represent a further significant expansion of the bloc, thereby augmenting its global influence and reach.

Turkey's engagement with BRICS is, in part, a response to the frustrations stemming from the slow progress of its protracted efforts to join the European Union (EU). Despite years of negotiations, Turkey's aspiration for EU membership remains unfulfilled, prompting Ankara to seek alternative pathways to enhance its global influence. Additionally, Turkey's relations with NATO allies have become increasingly strained, particularly due to its ongoing interactions with Russia following the latter's invasion of Ukraine in 2022. This situation has further propelled Turkey to pursue new alliances that resonate with its independent foreign policy objectives.

From an economic perspective, Turkey stands to gain considerably from BRICS membership. The New Development Bank established by the group provides alternative financing avenues that could facilitate Turkey's ambitious infrastructure and development initiatives. In 2022, Turkey's GDP was approximately $906 billion, positioning it as one of the largest economies in the region. By becoming a member of BRICS, Turkey could strengthen its trade ties with other member countries, potentially leading to an increase in exports and overall economic growth.

Turkey became a NATO member in 1952 and possesses the second largest military in the alliance, underscoring its importance to NATO. While many Western countries were focused on the 34 criminal charges against Donald Trump in late May 2024, a crucial meeting took place in Beijing during Fidan's visit from 3-5 June 2024. Turkish Foreign Minister Hakan Fidan held talks with Chinese Foreign Minister Wang Yi to discuss Turkey's economic prospects. Despite waiting for EU membership for twenty years, Turkey faces the grim prospect of never achieving it. Their strategic positioning along the Black Sea was the main factor behind their NATO membership at first. Nevertheless, the idea of integrating a predominantly Muslim nation into the EU has been met with significant resistance from the majority of Europeans. Following years of disappointment and unfulfilled pledges from the EU, Turkey is now looking to shift its focus towards China and other BRICS nations in search of better economic opportunities. The Turkish Foreign Minister explicitly stated that the China BRICS Alliance might offer Turkey a more promising option than the European Union.

The potential of Turkey, a NATO member with the second largest NATO Army, joining the BRICS alliance is likely not something the West desires. When news of this broke, the Kremlin promptly expressed support for Turkey's decision. Following this, China's Minister Wang Yi announced China's readiness to enhance strategic alignment with Turkey to counter power politics on the global stage. China is prepared to further strengthen coordination and cooperation with Turkey within the frameworks of the United Nations and the Group of 20 to oppose hegemony and power politics, as well as to uphold global supply chain stability. This statement reflects China's government stance, viewing Turkey's entry into the BRICS alliance as a strategic move.

The Turkish foreign minister attended a BRICS meeting in Russia during the block's meeting in Moscow on June 10, 2024. Foreign Minister Hakan Fidan emphasised Ankara's desire to become a member of BRICS.[17] During his meeting with the Russian President Vladimir Putin, the Russian leader gave his support for Turkey to join the BRICS Alliance:

> We welcome Türkiye's interest in the work of BRICS. Of course, we will strongly support this desire to be together with the countries of this association, to be together, closer, to solve common problems.[18]

What has sparked Turkey's interest in the BRICS Alliance remains a point of curiosity. BRICS is expected to have a significant impact on the global economy, leading many countries of the Global South to view it as an alternative to the G7 bloc and a representation of shifting power dynamics on a global scale. Additionally, analysts believe that Turkey's desire to join BRICS is influenced by the changing power structures in the world. If Turkey becomes a member, it will be the first NATO Ally to join the bloc. Turkish officials have also emphasised that the stalled accession process to the European Union has played a role in their decision. It is crucial to consider the implications and conditions that come with joining such an alliance.

The sanctions levied against Russia following its invasion of Ukraine in 2022 have instilled fear among numerous nations in the Global South, who are concerned that the West may utilise global financial mechanisms as instruments of coercion against them. Aslı Aydıntaşbaş, an expert in Turkish foreign policy, made remarks to the Brookings Institution, a think tank based in Washington, DC.

In the aftermath of the war in Gaza, Russia and China have more effectively harnessed this anti-Western sentiment, capitalising on frustrations over Western double standards as well as the use of sanctions and economic coercion by the West. It doesn't mean that middle powers want to trade US dominance for Chinese, but it means they are open to aligning with Russia and China for a more fragmented and autonomous world.[19]

Joining BRICS does not demand the same level of political and economic obligations as joining NATO and the EU. Despite concerns from the West about Ankara's interest in a bloc led by China and Russia, Turkey's leadership remains determined. With Russia's support for Turkey's membership, it appears inevitable that Turkey will eventually become a BRICS member. The invitation extended to various West

Asian nations by the bloc last year has caused unease among the US and European countries.

The assembly of BRICS+ nations alongside other countries including Turkey, meeting in Kazan, Russia (22-24 October 2024) highlights an increasing alignment among nations that aspire to alter the global power dynamics. For certain countries, such as Moscow, Beijing, and Tehran, this alignment serves as a direct challenge to the influence of the United States and its Western allies. The BIRCS meeting in Kazan conveyed the notion that it is the West that finds itself in a position of isolation due to its sanctions and alliances, while a "global majority" of nations backs their efforts to contest American dominance on the world stage. On the final day of the Kazan summit, thirteen nations were designated as "partners" of the BRICS+ alliance. This status falls short of full membership but offers the possibility of complete admission in the future. The nations recognised as partner countries within the alliance include Algeria, Belarus, Bolivia, Cuba, Indonesia, Kazakhstan, Malaysia, Nigeria, Thailand, Turkey, Uganda, Uzbekistan, and Vietnam.

The establishment of the partner status category during the Kazan summit appears to be a strategic measure by BRICS to mitigate the recurrence of conflicts in the future. A government aspiring to join the organisation must initially be recognised as a "partner" for a designated period prior to full membership. This procedure bears resemblance to that of the Shanghai Cooperation Organisation, which includes China, Russia, India, and Iran among its members. As for Turkey's full membership into the BRICS economic alliance, according to Haluk Direskeneli:

> India's firm stance reflects its concerns over South Asian regional security and what it describes as Turkey and Pakistan's roles in promoting instability in areas such as Jammu and Kashmir. This incident underscores the complex regional dynamics influencing BRICS' expansion decisions and highlights the challenges Turkey faces in balancing international relations in its pursuit of multilateral partnerships.[20]

However, as partner countries, Turkey and the other countries will have the opportunity to represent themselves at select BRICS events and engage in certain international initiatives of the bloc. Full membership, on the other hand, confers voting rights on BRICS matters and allows for comprehensive participation in all BRICS events.

The Kazan meeting of the BRICS member countries and those interested in joining the economic alliance has turned it into a major geopolitical and economic force, representing over one-third of global GDP (PPP), more than 40% of the world's population, and about 30% of global oil production. In contrast, the G7 comprises less than 10% of the global population and under 30% of GDP (PPP), with their economic share steadily declining as BRICS grows.

On 23 October, BRICS members released the Kazan Declaration, advocating for peace, a fair international order, multilateral reform, sustainable development, and inclusive growth. The declaration aims to establish a "more equitable, just, democratic, and balanced multipolar world order," emphasising that multipolarity can benefit *emerging markets and developing countries* (EMDCs).[21]

Contrasting with the West's "rules-based international order," the declaration highlighted the UN's central role and the importance of international law. It called for comprehensive UN reform, particularly of the Security Council, to ensure equitable representation of EMDCs and least developed countries in global decision-making.[22]

The declaration also urged reforms in Bretton Woods institutions to enhance EMDC representation in leadership roles, recognising BRICS's role in improving the international monetary and financial system. Additionally, it condemned unlawful unilateral coercive measures, including illegal sanctions, and called for their elimination.[23]

For centuries, the Global South has been viewed as the Other by Euro-American hegemony. However, they are now rising to confront the US-led world order and the global financial system that has predominantly benefited the West since the conclusion of the Second World War. This dynamic is shifting as the Global South asserts its sovereignty by promoting the use of their national currencies as the primary means of trade with other nations. The future transformation of BRICS into a defensive alliance akin to NATO is uncertain. Currently, the Global South is prioritising the transition of global economic power from the dollar to the utilisation of national currencies among member and partner nations for trade. Its effectiveness to curtail the dominance of the U.S. dollar in international transactions hinges on the cohesion and resolve of the organisation, should it genuinely aim to transform the global economy.

The Voice of the Other: Criticism of the Western world order and the need for reform

Turkey, historically regarded as the Muslim Other by Europe and the West for many centuries, continues to be perceived in this manner. However, it has experienced a significant transformation, evolving from a passive participant in European matters related to Turks. The responsibility for changing alliances does not solely rest on Turkey's shoulders. Europe has experienced a noticeable decline in recent times and is currently grappling with the challenges of navigating a rapidly changing world. The article "Will Europe be the world's biggest loser?" reinforces this reality by highlighting the conflicts between Russia and Ukraine, the competition between China and the United States, and the emergence of new middle powers. These factors are leading to a significant restructuring of the global order, placing Europe at a clear disadvantage and giving a voice to the marginalised Other on the global stage, which had been suppressed by Euro-American dominance for centuries.

During the annual session of the United Nations General Assembly (UNGA), global leaders convened to voice their apprehensions regarding the ongoing crises and significant challenges confronting the world. In his address at the UNGA on September 24, 2024, Turkey's President Recep Tayyip Erdogan highlighted the hypocrisy and double standards prevalent in the Western-dominated world order in relation to the Global South. Furthermore, Erdogan presented his nation as a proactive collaborator on both regional and global fronts, while advocating for the reform of international institutions during his address at the UN General Assembly.

Initially, the Turkish President reiterated his well-known assertion that "The world is bigger than five," highlighting the dysfunctions and inequities present within the global governance framework. This observation is significant, as the geographic context of crises may shift and their designations may vary; however, the existing multilateral system and the United Nations Security Council (UNSC) consistently fail to address ongoing crises, often exacerbated by the actions of its permanent members. This has been particularly evident in the situation in Syria since 2011.

Furthermore, Erdogan challenged the legitimacy of Western values by stating, "Gaza has become the largest cemetery for children and women in the world".[24] Western nations, spearheaded by the United States and key European Union countries, have positioned themselves as champions of human rights, democracy, and freedoms. Nevertheless, their inaction in response to Israel's treatment of Palestinian children and women, coupled with the steadfast support from the US and EU for Israel, has once again illuminated the presence of double standards and hypocrisy regarding the so-called universal values.

Erdogan appropriately condemned this insincerity in his address; however, his focus on this hypocrisy extends beyond the atrocities occurring in Gaza or the prolonged occupation by Israel. The Turkish president highlights the Eurocentric values system and critiques the reality that the interests of a powerful minority are safeguarded at the expense of numerous other members of the global community. His speech in support of reform targeted the five Permanent Members of the Security Council: the United States, Britain, France, Russia, and China:

> The world is bigger than five ... The Security Council has ceased to be the guarantor of world security and has become a battleground for the political strategies of only five countries.[25]

Furthermore, while Erdogan emphasised the necessity for reform in global governance and criticised the West's hypocrisy regarding human rights and freedoms, he subtly addressed the shifting dynamics of the world order. He underscored Türkiye's historical role and mission as an active, effective, and influential participant in shaping the new global landscape.

Gaza was a focal point in the speech delivered by the Turkish President, who also addressed Türkiye's involvement in foreign policy matters. Erdogan underscored Türkiye's expanding influence on the global stage. He discussed various disputes and conflicts, both in neighbouring regions such as Gaza, Northern Cyprus, Syria, the Balkans, Ukraine, and the South Caucasus, as well as in more distant areas like Latin America and the situation of Uyghur Muslims in China. Additionally, he emphasised Türkiye's proactive role in addressing common challenges such as terrorism, climate change, and xenophobia.

Erdogan's appeal to the international community, particularly to nations that endorse Israel's actions in Gaza, was a prominent aspect of his address. However, a broader interpretation of his proposals for reforming global governance, his critique of Western hypocrisy regarding rights and freedoms of all peoples, and Türkiye's increasing international stature should be considered as underlying themes in Erdogan's impactful and historically significant speech at the United Nations General Assembly.[26] For Erdogan and the nations of the Global South, the importance of reforming the United Nations highlights their dedication to achieving a more influential position and to symbolically eradicate their perceived subordinate status within the international organisation. Furthermore, Turkish President Erdogan has asserted that Muslims, who make up a quarter of the global population, should be adequately represented in international decision-making processes, as they rightfully deserve. During the 16th Traditional Iftar Dinner with Ambassadors held in Ankara on 3 March 2025, he said:

> The presence of an Islamic country with veto power in the UN Security Council is a necessity, rather than a need. Our struggle, guided by the principle that 'the world is bigger than five', is aimed at building a more inclusive structure to replace the global system that perpetuates

problems, … The time has long come for global decision-making mechanisms to adapt to the changing realities of the world.[27]

Erdogan asserts that granting veto power to an Islamic nation at the United Nations Security Council would be a significant move towards rectifying the undemocratic nature of the council, particularly in light of the Western bias against Palestinians in the context of the Gaza conflict. He highlighted that the rise of Islamophobia, anti-migrant attitudes, and trade conflicts is causing a stalemate in the rules-based international system, asserting that such ideologies contribute to a lawless environment.[28] Furthermore, Erdogan cautioned that a more severe and inequitable international order is emerging, one that neglects the vulnerable. He stated, "If this trend continues unaddressed, it will inevitably result in political and military upheavals, the early indicators of which are already apparent", emphasising that humanity cannot afford to overlook these challenges, ignore imminent threats, or postpone addressing critical issues.[29]

Moreover, the urgent matter at hand is the equal accountability of each member state within the United Nations, which includes the five Permanent Members of the Security Council. Therefore, the imperative of upholding international law that applies to all nations, while safeguarding the rights, self-determination, and sovereignty of all countries, as stipulated in the United Nations Charter following the Second World War. This underscores the critical nature of the situation.

What happened to "Rules-based International Order"?

A new concept, the "rules-based international order", has emerged in Western discourse over the past two decades, yet these rules remain undefined, unlike the 1945 United Nations Charter aimed at promoting peace and equality. Instead, Western diplomacy has focused on choosing sides in conflicts, with the term primarily used by a biased coalition led by the U.S. to categorise nations as "with us or against us", echoing the sentiments of George W. Bush.[30] The 21st century has witnessed a significant shift away from traditional diplomacy by Western nations.

Richard Falk, a renowned expert in international law who has previously served as the United Nations special rapporteur for the occupied Palestinian territories (2008-2014) argues that the expanding global nature of policymaking and problem-solving has rendered reliance on state-level governance and national interest calculations increasingly ineffective.[31] According to Falk this is due to the fact that the issues on the political agenda significantly impact the entirety of human lives and the collective future of humanity—particularly for future generations—regardless of geographical location. Notably, these global concerns have not prompted governments to establish more robust frameworks for global governance. The 94 year old international law expert, Falk, tells TRT World in an exclusive interview at the Gaza Tribunal Special Conference in Istanbul:

> World War II created a new framework of international life based on the expectation that behaviour would be much more regulated by law and moral principles. Even though the winners of that war did not accept restraints for themselves, they presented themselves as guardians of moral development ... The law is no longer an authority that applies equally to both the weak and the strong. Instead, it has become a policy instrument—used as a tool against adversaries and as a shield for allies ... From a public policy perspective, what the US has done is a clear interference in the operations of formal UN institutions and international society [...].[32]

The alarming failure to safeguard vulnerable global and human interests might have been anticipated to motivate more responsible governments and their citizens to diligently work towards creating a more autonomous and adequately funded United Nations; however, this has not occurred. Falk argues that successfully addressing global challenges appears unattainable without enhanced institutional capabilities supported by the necessary political will to develop and enforce suitable legal norms. The determination of how these norms will be defined presents a significant adaptive challenge, highlighting the realisation that the Westphalian system, even if bolstered by responsible geopolitical leadership—which is currently lacking—cannot meet the essential requirements for global order. It is particularly disheartening that there is such limited public mobilisation surrounding the pressing challenges of the twenty-first century.[33]

Falk argues that following the dissolution of the Soviet Union in 1991, the United States positioned itself as the inaugural "global state" in history. This was achieved through the establishment of a vast network of foreign military bases, naval presence in all oceans, and the militarisation of both outer space and cyberspace. The objective was to create a global state that overshadowed the sovereignty of other nations, which are generally reluctant to compromise their traditional sovereign rights concerning national security, with the notable exceptions of China and Russia. This American-led global framework operates with the acquiescence of numerous countries, including those in Europe, Canada, and Australia, while simultaneously employing coercive tactics against a select few, such as South Africa and Ukraine, to achieve its goals. This is particularly evident in its approach to counterterrorism and non-proliferation efforts, utilising non-territorial strategies such as drones, cyber sabotage, and elite covert operations, alongside conventional military interventions. The considerable allocation of resources towards achieving global military supremacy is viewed as an endorsement of neoliberal capitalism; however, it concurrently undermines the importance of the Westphalian state, which asserts that each state holds exclusive jurisdiction over its territory and is fundamentally connected to development as well as both internal and external security.[34]

Possible Solution: Rescinding Impunity for the United States Under Article 6 of the United Nations Charter

It is essential for the international organisation, predominantly composed of nations from the Global South, to assert its voice within the United Nations and to uphold the legal frameworks established by this international body. To achieve this, implementing necessary reforms is crucial. A significant reform that could be introduced is the establishment of accountability measures for each country regarding its transgressions against other nations or marginalised communities. It is important to clarify that the Article 6 campaign is not specifically aimed at singling out the United States. Rather, the United States has distinguished itself through its own actions. The primary concern here is the application of international law and the principle of equality before the law for all nations. Every nation should be subject to the law, rather than above it. However, since 1945, following the establishment of the United Nations, the United States has operated as if it is above the law.[35]

This represents a highly selective interpretation of international law, which has never been uniformly applied to all nations. At the heart of the Article 6 campaign lies a demand for justice—specifically, a call for equal justice for all nations, ensuring that no entity enjoys impunity, accountability is upheld, and no one is above the law. Article 6 of the United Nations Charter states:

> A Member of the United Nations who has persistently violated the Principles contained in the present Charter may be expelled from the Organization by the General Assembly upon the recommendation of the Security Council.[36]

Notably, the United States of America stands out as the most persistent violator of the principles enshrined in the United Nations Charter.

The foundation of this perceived power, for lack of a better term, is not rooted in their economic, political, or military strength. Instead, it is the impunity that has allowed the United States to act with disregard for international norms, particularly in the Global South. This impunity has been maintained through their dominance within the United Nations. If, or rather when, they are held accountable and removed from their privileged position in the UN, they will no longer be above the law. The United States will then be subject to the same legal standards as all other nations. The manner in which they have conducted themselves suggests that international law is selectively applied, primarily targeting their adversaries or those they seek to exploit or colonise.[37]

The United Nations General Assembly includes representatives from all 193 member states, but its resolutions lack legal authority. In contrast, the Security Council, with 15 members, is tasked with maintaining international peace and its resolutions are legally binding. The council can direct member states to impose sanctions or take military action. However, the five permanent members— the U.S., U.K., Russia, China, and France—have veto power, which limits the council's ability to address conflicts involving a permanent member or its allies, as seen in the Israel-Hamas conflict (2023-2025) and the Russian invasion of Ukraine (2022-).[38]

The United States has exercised its veto power against resolutions that criticise Israel more frequently than any other member of the council, having done so 45 times as of December 18, 2023, as reported by Blue Marble. Since 1945, the U.S. has vetoed a total of 89 Security Council resolutions, indicating that just over half of these vetoes were directed at resolutions addressing issues related to Israel. Among the vetoed resolutions, 33 specifically dealt with the Israeli occupation of Palestinian territories or the treatment of the Palestinian population.[39] In addition, concerning the shortcomings of the United Nations and the manipulation of its authority within the international organisation, the month after his second inauguration in 2025, U.S. President Donald Trump made a substantial impact on the global arena by disregarding the prevailing consensus of the General Assembly and aligning with Russia on a United Nations resolution aimed at condemning its military operations in Ukraine.[40]

Israel and the United States function as a singular entity, with Israel largely reflecting American policy in the Middle East. This dynamic has been evident since the establishment of Israel and the formation of the United Nations. Addressing the issue of Israel necessitates the removal of the United States from its influential position within the United Nations, as this would eliminate the support that allows Israel to operate above international law, particularly through the veto power held in the Security Council. Historically, global consensus has favoured the Palestinian cause, aligning with principles of justice. Israel's actions have been sustained primarily due to American support; thus, if the United States were to withdraw from the United

Nations, Israel would be compelled to adhere to international law and regulations.[41]

The current state of international justice has reached a level where the concept is not taken seriously by anyone. Institutions such as the International Court of Justice (ICJ), the International Criminal Court (ICC), and the United Nations, along with the broader framework of international law, have lost their credibility. This decline is largely due to the fact that these laws are not enforced against the nation that is the primary violator, which undermines the entire premise of international law and justice. It has become evident that the foundation of America's power, for lack of a more precise term, lies in its impunity, which facilitates its acts of aggression and global oppression. To address this issue, it is crucial to eliminate this impunity, thereby holding the nation accountable under the law.[42]

Regarding the campaign to invoke Article 6, one must consider its potential effects on global governance and the credibility of international law, especially in light of the Universal Declaration of Human Rights, which seems disconnected from the injustices and oppression we witness today. If successful, the removal of the United States from the United Nations will help restore faith in the principles of international law and justice. The United States' dominance over the United Nations, coupled with its ongoing violations of the UN Charter and international law without facing any repercussions, has contributed to this crisis of accountability.[43]

The current situation has severely undermined the principle of international justice, rendering it ineffective. This has also diminished the significance of vital documents such as the Universal Declaration of Human Rights, which have not been enforced in relation to crimes committed by Western nations. For instance, the Nakba (forced removal of Palestinians from their homeland in 1948) is viewed as a crime of Western colonisation, yet there has been no accountability when the United States or its allies have engaged in similar actions. Consequently, the credibility of international law and justice has been called into question among the global populace. It is important to note that the majority of this population does not belong to the Western or white demographic; rather, they are situated in the Global South and have often been victims of American foreign policy, exploitation, and colonisation. In the years following 1945 and 1948, when these foundational documents were established, there was a fleeting hope that the era of suffering, enslavement, and oppression might come to an end. However, it became evident that the architects of these documents had no intention of applying them to themselves; instead, their purpose was to wield these instruments against the oppressed, particularly those in the Global South and the colonies.[44]

If one were to examine any nation globally, including those in the West or Europe, it would be evident that the United States has consistently violated the UN Charter and international law since 1945. A simple point on a world map could illustrate numerous instances of such violations. The United States is acutely aware of its vulnerability to prosecution for crimes against humanity, war crimes, and various other breaches of international law. The absence of accountability for these actions over the past eight decades is a troubling reality that the nations of the Global South have all endured.[45]

The ongoing unilateral actions taken by the United States only intensify the narrative of conflict between the West and Islam from the viewpoint of the Muslim community, thereby undermining opportunities for reconciliation and the establishment of trust. Additionally, these actions diminish the United States' capacity to act as an impartial mediator in the Arab-Israeli conflict. In this context, reforming the United Nations will remain a key objective for the nations of the Global South in the 21st century, ensuring that member states possess a significant voice within the global assembly. The subsequent chapter delves deeper into the stance adopted by the Global South in opposition to neo-American imperialism.

CHAPTER 21

AMERICA: THE LAST BASTION OF WESTERN IMPERIALISM
THE ILLUSION OF GREATNESS

In the 19th century, the United States emerged as a potential power, akin to the established European imperialist empires such as Britain and France, which rationalised their domination of non-European populations through a perceived civilising mission born out of Charles Darwin's intellectual movement. In his seminal work, *On the Origins of Species*, the notion of survival of the fittest within the animal kingdom was prominently emphasised. This concept was subsequently adapted into Social Darwinism, which extended Darwin's theories to the context of human societal struggles. The subjugation of the 'Other' became a fundamental principle of the foreign policies pursued by European imperialist powers, a trend that was significantly shaped by the ideologies of the 19th-century intellectual movement known as Social Darwinism. The conviction of inherent superiority, bolstered by economic strength and technological advancements in military capabilities, provided a justification for European imperialist nations to exert control over diverse populations globally, including Muslims, Indians, and the indigenous peoples of the Americas, Australia, New Zealand, and other regions.

The perception of superiority over the 'Other' significantly bolstered the civilising missions initiated by Britain, France and Spain to educate and Christianise the 'backward' peoples of the world, which included Muslims. From this perspective, the concept of *Manifest Destiny*, advocated by the ruling elites in the United States throughout the 19th century and thereafter, represents a continuation of the European imperialist ideology that appears to recur across the ages.[1] Adherents to this belief system consistently aim to impose their views rather than engage in meaningful dialogue with the 'Other', who is often placed in a subordinate role. This ideology sustains the dichotomies of 'us versus them' and 'the civilised versus the uncivilised', narratives that remain pertinent today and further reinforce Huntington's thesis regarding the clash of civilisations. Analysing our contemporary era through this framework reveals the enduring historical patterns that continue to influence the current global discourse between powerful nations and the Global South.

"Pax-Trumpica", Manifest Destiny and the American neo-Imperialism

The ascension of Donald Trump to power marks a significant shift in American imperialism, signalling a departure from the traditional norms and principles that have long underpinned U.S. foreign policy. Historically, American foreign policy has often been framed within the context of international law, human rights, and multilateral cooperation. However, under Trump's leadership, there has been a noticeable erosion of these principles, as the administration increasingly prioritizes unilateral action and national interests over adherence to established legal frameworks.

This transformation reflects a broader trend in which the United States appears to be discarding any pretense of commitment to international norms. The rhetoric and actions of the Trump administration have often embraced a more aggressive and confrontational stance, suggesting that might makes right. This shift can be seen in various aspects of foreign policy, from trade wars and military interventions to the withdrawal from international agreements and organisations. The implications of this approach are profound, as it signals a move towards a more primal law of the jungle, where the powerful act according to their desires, often without regard for the consequences faced by weaker nations.

In this new paradigm, the vulnerable—be they smaller nations, marginalised communities, or global populations—bear the brunt of the consequences. The disregard for international law and norms not only undermines global stability but also exacerbates existing inequalities and injustices. As powerful nations pursue their interests with impunity, the potential for conflict increases, and the prospects for cooperative solutions to global challenges diminish.

Moreover, this shift in American imperialism raises critical questions about the future of global governance. If the United States, a historically dominant player on the world stage, opts for a more self-serving and aggressive approach, it may embolden other nations to follow suit, leading to a breakdown of the international order that has been in place since the end of World War II. The result could be a more chaotic and dangerous world, where the principles of diplomacy, cooperation, and mutual respect are replaced by a survival-of-the-fittest mentality.

The ascension of Trump to power represents not just a change in leadership but a fundamental reorientation of American foreign policy. The abandonment of international law in favor of a more primal approach to power dynamics signals a troubling trend that could have far-reaching consequences for global stability, justice, and the future of international relations. As the powerful act according to their desires, the vulnerable will continue to endure the harsh realities of a world increasingly governed by might rather than right.

Trump's rhetoric, which mirrors a 19th-century perspective characteristic of European colonial powers, emerges at a time when international allies are already contending with the consequences of his re-emergence on the global stage. Donald Trump's vision of transforming America into "history's greatest civilisation" reflects not a position of isolationism for the United States, but rather an approach characterised by expansionism and territorial acquisition.[2] While there may be room for debate regarding U.S. expansionist desires, Trump's economic policy of imposing tariffs on American trading partners, as well as his inclination to withdraw troops from Syria and decrease troop levels in Germany suggests a different narrative. Nevertheless, his proposals regarding land acquisition carry symbolic weight among the Middle Eastern populace and warrant careful consideration. For the Palestinians, his discourse evokes both historical and contemporary parallels to the establishment of the Crusader kingdoms in Palestine by Christendom between 1098 and 1291, as well as the actions of European Zionist settlers leading to the formation of Israel in 1948.

The term "Pax-Trumpica" superficially underscores the 19th-century American ideology known as *Manifest Destiny*, a phrase first articulated by journalist John O'Sullivan in 1845. This ideology embodies the belief in the unique moral superiority of the United States as an exceptional nation, asserting its mission to reshape the world by advocating for republican governance and, more generally, the "American way of life." It also reflects the conviction that the nation is destined by divine providence to fulfill this mission.[3] This belief system is intertwined with the Christian-Zionist evangelical movement in the United States and contributes to the ongoing American political, military, and economic interventions on the global stage, all framed under the guise of national security and the notion of a divinely ordained American destiny to lead the world. Nevertheless, indications of a U.S. withdrawal from global engagement have become increasingly clear, which warrants careful examination in light of recent developments.

Historically, powerful nations have justified colonialism and territorial domination for economic and security reasons. Trump seems to be making a similar argument. The mention of territorial expansion in his inaugural speech, is particularly noteworthy, considering Trump's expressed intentions to reclaim the Panama Canal, annex Greenland, and incorporate Canada as part of the United States.[4] According to Dan Steinbock from the China and America Institute (US), Shanghai Institute for International Studies (China) and the EU Center (Singapore):

> With 800 military bases in almost 90 countries, plus hundreds within the US, America has the largest collection of defence posts in foreign lands throughout history.

As interventionist military measures replaced political solutions, the US has been at war, engaged in combat, or otherwise employed its forces in foreign countries in all but 11 years of its more than 250 years of existence.[5]

The majority of United States military installations are located in Japan, Germany, and South Korea. This ongoing substantial overseas military presence emphasises the influence of contemporary American imperialism. Furthermore, The World Population Review, a monitoring organisation, reports that the United States military has conducted invasions in approximately 68 countries from the year 1812 to 2024.[6] Of the 194 nations recognised by the United Nations, the United States has invaded a minimum of 84 and has been involved in military engagements with 191.[7] The addition of Gaza to this list reinforces the geopolitical ambitions of Trump's America that are intended to be supported by the establishment of "the strongest military the world has ever seen" alongside its capitalist "entrepreneurs".[8] According to Artyom Lukin at the Oriental Institute, Far Eastern Federal University, Vladivostok:

> Unlike the empire builders of the ancient past, new imperialism does not seek to directly conquer and rule all the peoples and lands it can subjugate. Instead, it focuses on controlling the most valuable pieces of geopolitical real estate—such as strategic waterways and islands — and achieving dominance in the "global commons" including the oceans, space and cyberspace ...
>
> There is little reason to believe that Donald Trump and his allied cohort of capitalist techno-barons are any different in their quest for power and glory. Having consolidated their influence within the US, they now seek a larger stage to enact their ambitions and inflate their egos.[9]

Trump perceives global politics and American exceptionalism primarily through the framework of real estate, profit generation, and the reinforcement of the capitalists capitalists—specifically, the neoconservative ideologues who play a role in the "Make America Great Again" movement.

The significant shift in United States foreign policy was revealed in the presence of Israeli Prime Minister Benjamin Netanyahu at the White House, and it has been characterised as jeopardising decades of initiatives focused on achieving a two-state solution, which envisions a peaceful coexistence between Palestinians and Israelis. On February 4, 2025, during a press conference at the White House, Donald Trump emphasised the importance of taking control of Gaza to avoid repeating historical errors. He stated:

> You have to learn from history. History is – you just can't let it keep repeating itself. We have an opportunity to do something that could be phenomenal.[10]

Trump's proposals to "do what's necessary", assume "long-term ownership"[11] of Gaza, and facilitate the relocation of Palestinians from Gaza to Egypt and Jordan are likely to exacerbate tensions between the West and the Islamic world. On this point, he said:

> Instead, we should go to other countries [reference to Egypt and Jordan] of interest with humanitarian hearts, and there are many of them that want to do this and build various domains that will ultimately be occupied by the million Palestinians living in Gaza, ending the death and destruction and frankly bad luck.[12]

Trump's remarks concerning the destruction in Gaza during the 2023-25 conflict are articulated from viewpoints that align with pro-Israeli Zionist and white Christian evangelical ideologies, which constitute a significant portion of his support base in the United States. If the United States genuinely aimed to act as an impartial mediator in the longstanding conflict between Arabs and Israelis, then learning from history would also necessitate acknowledging the historical injustices faced by Palestinians since 1948, when the State of Israel was established, resulting in the displacement of millions from their ancestral lands.

Trump's suggestion assuming control of the Gaza Strip and undertaking redevelopment efforts in the region transforming Gaza into the

"Riviera of the Middle East" embodies a distinctly American capitalist perspective rather than offering a political resolution to the long-standing conflict.[13] To realise his real estate ambitions for this war-ravaged region, he would need to displace millions of Palestinians from their ancestral lands, an act perceived by the local population as collective punishment. For the Palestinians of Gaza, this displacement, a possible "second Nakba", reminiscent of the mass displacement of Palestinians that occurred after Israel's unilateral declaration of statehood in 1948. Such developments would pave the way for the creation of an American-style utopia, "something really spectacular", envisioned as the "Riviera of the Middle East".[14] This concept aims to accommodate a new wave of settlers, referred to as "the world's people", who would inhabit the region, reflecting the earlier settlement patterns of European Zionist immigrants who ultimately seized control of Palestine. As an afterthought Trump added, "also the Palestinians".[15]

To finance this massive rebuilding and reconstruction project, Trump is relying on the rich Gulf states of Bahrain, Kuwait, Oman, Qatar, Saudi Arabia, and the United Arab Emirates making up the economic union of the Gulf Cooperation Council. His intention for them to fund the rebuilding of Gaza, and then for the United States to simply take over the area and control it withoutany military involvement. According to Trump:

> This can be paid for by neighboring countries of great wealth. It could be one, two, three, four, five, seven, eight, twelve. It could be numerous sites, or it could be one large site.[16]

In Trump's perspective, the establishment of peace for the Palestinians is contingent upon their relocation to different areas:

> They're going to have peace; they're not going to be shot at and killed and destroyed like this civilization of wonderful people has had to endure.[17]

According to Trump, this represents the sole viable option for the Palestinians. The following day, seemingly in alignment with an agreement reached with the Israeli leader, Trump posts on his social media platform, Truth Social:

> The Gaza Strip would be turned over to the United States by Israel at the conclusion of fighting. [Palestinians] would have already been resettled in far safer and more beautiful communities, with new and modern homes, in the region. No soldiers by the U.S. would be needed![18]

To accomplish this vision, Donald Trump must first "clean out that whole thing," which entails not only clearing the extensive debris resulting from continuous bombardment throughout the conflict but also removing its current residents.[19] Such characterisations of the Palestinians as the voiceless 'Other' in his language unintentionally reveal the lingering European biases against Muslims that have existed from the Middle Ages to the present. According to Michael R. Allen from West Virginia Univesity:

> Trump, the real estate developer president, understands better than the ethno-nationalist zealot Netanyahu that the real basis for colonization is dispossession and the creation of new property for the colonizers.[20]

The sole method of perceiving Trump's real estate vision for Gaza is both morally objectionable and unlawful according to international law, clearly exemplifying the current Western colonial agenda. The proposal has faced significant criticism in the Middle East from the Arab League and the Organisation of Islamic Cooperation, which have characterised it as a potential "second Nakba". Additionally, it has faced backlash globally, including from nations such as Canada, France, Germany, and the United Kingdom. In response to Trump's suggestion, Yousef bin Trad Al-Saadoun, a member of the Saudi Shura Council appointed by the Saudi monarch, stated:

He (Trump) should relocate his beloved Israelis to the state of Alaska and then to Greenland – after annexing it.[21]

During a meeting with U.S. Secretary of State Marco Rubio on 11 February, 2025, in Washington, Egyptian Foreign Minister Badr Abdelatty firmly opposed any notion of displacing Palestinians from their homeland. He emphasised the necessity for the international community to unite in support of the Palestinians to rectify the "historic injustice" they have endured and to restore their "legitimate and inalienable rights".[22] In light of the Arab opposition to the removal of Palestinians from Gaza, Donald Trump reconsidered his earlier stance and stated, "No, they [Palestinians] wouldn't" be permitted to return to Gaza after its redevelopment.[23] On the same day, meeting with the Jordanian King Abdullah, Trump once again expressed his stance on assuming control of Gaza and resettling the Palestinian population in neighbouring nations. Without rejecting the president's proposal, the Jordanian king, who was seated beside him, remarked:

> I think we have to keep in mind, there is a plan from Egypt and the Arab countries. I think the point is, how do we make this work in a way that is good for everybody? ... Let's not get ahead of ourselves.[24]

The substantial financial assistance that the United States extends to Egypt and Jordan each year serves as a significant leverage point for Trump, thereby limiting the ability of these two Middle Eastern nations to manoeuvre in this context. Nonetheless, Trump is resolute in his pursuit of a deal regarding the future of Gaza, viewing it as a pathway to establish enduring peace in the region. It is yet to be determined whether this initiative represents a sincere attempt or merely a preliminary phase leading to a different strategy for attaining peace and stability. Whether he can achieve this without the consent of the Palestinians is another matter. According to Kevin Liptak:

> At its root, US officials said, Trump's suggestion was intended in part to spur action on an issue he has viewed as moribund, with no other nations offering reasonable solutions for how to rebuild an area that

has been obliterated by Israeli bombardment following Hamas' October 7, 2023, terrorist attacks.[25]

The elimination of Hamas from Gaza is deemed essential by both the United States and Israel prior to the initiation of any peace initiatives. The Arab League's peace proposal, introduced on 5 March 2025, offered a potential solution for the reconstruction of Gaza while ensuring the current residents are not displaced; however, it was unequivocally dismissed by Israel and the United States for failing to sufficiently tackle the Hamas situation.

Should Trump's scenario for Gaza and the Palestinians materialise, it would constitute ethnic cleansing and a violation of international law, potentially leading to charges being brought against him by the International Court of Justice. A day after Trump's announcement on Gaza, Francesca Albanese, the United Nations Special Rapporteur on the occupied Palestinian territories said, "[…] it's forced displacement, which is an international crime … The international community is made of 193 states, and this is the time to give the Unite States what is has been looking for - isolation".[26]

AI and the neo-Pharaohs of this world!

The culturally insensitive encyclopedists of the 18th century, the accounts of travellers to the Ottoman Orient, the misrepresentations of Muslims by Orientalist artists and scholars, and the subjugation by European imperialist powers have collectively contributed to centuries of degradation, humiliation, and oppression of the Other. This historical legacy has now transformed into the realm of Artificial Intelligence. Donald Trump shared a post on his official social media platform, Truth Social, on February 26, 2025, which featured an AI-generated video, created by an Israeli-American, Solo Avital, a Los Angeles-based filmmaker. Intended as a satire on Trump, this video showcased a dramatically reimagined vision of Gaza, illustrating what the U.S. president envisions as the "Riviera of the Middle East" in the future. The insensitivity depicted in the video constitutes an affront to the Palestinians, who have endured prolonged suffering due to conflict and displacement. In this provocative clip, Gaza is reimagined as a luxurious seaside Dubai-style resort, complete with pristine beaches, palm trees, and opulent yachts. The central to this surreal depiction is a prominent golden statue of Donald Trump, symbolising his influence and presence in this reimagined landscape. Rabbi Ben Hollander, reported in The Times of Israel, said that Pharaoh is a role model for demagogues.[27] The demagoguery of Pharaoh and the demagoguery of authoritarian and egotistical rulers like Donald Trump is captured in the satirical video.

The AI-generated video, which runs for 33 seconds and is titled "Gaza 2025 What's Next?", begins with a dramatic scene where individuals emerge from a dark tunnel, only to find themselves on a beach adorned with palm trees and yachts, that starkly contrasts with the surrounding debris and destruction caused by American made military hardware. The soundtrack accompanying the visuals is a striking blend of upbeat and provocative lines, such as "Donald's coming to set you free, bringing the light for all to see" and "feast and dance, the deal is done, Trump Gaza number one". These lyrics set a tone that is both celebratory and controversial, suggesting a narrative of liberation and triumph in a region fraught with historical tensions. It portrays Trump as a saviour figure of the region.

The video itself is a kaleidoscope of surreal imagery, featuring what appear to be AI-generated depictions of a shirtless Donald Trump and Israeli Prime Minister Benjamin Netanyahu, both lounging by a pool in swimsuits and sipping cocktails. This scene, with its juxtaposition of political figures in a relaxed, almost hedonistic setting, raises eyebrows and invites scrutiny, suggesting a deliberate connection to past controversies and public discourse. The visuals are further enhanced by scenes of billionaire Elon Musk, who is portrayed dancing joyfully beneath a shower of cash on a sun-soaked beach, embodying a sense of wealth and carefree indulgence, and enjoying hummus by the shoreline. As the video unfolds, it introduces a variety of other striking visuals, including belly dancers with beards performing with grace and flair. One particularly notable moment captures the U.S. president embracing a minimally dressed belly dancer, a scene that blurs the lines between political power and entertainment, evoking a sense of spectacle.

A notably impressive scene reflects an AI-generated depiction of an imposing golden statue of Trump, enhancing the surreal quality of the video. This imagery represents a larger-than-life persona, an omnipotent god-like figure that surpasses conventional political boundaries. Additionally, the video features a gift shop filled with miniature figures of Trump seated on thrones, a whimsical yet unsettling representation of idolisation and commodification of political figures. This stark contrast between beauty and devastation is unsettling, as it seeks to convey a narrative of hope and prosperity in a region long associated with conflict and suffering. The visuals, while vibrant and celebratory, also provoke a deeper reflection on the complexities of power, representation, and the ongoing struggles faced by the oppression of the Palestinians in Gaza. The overall effect is a disorienting blend of fantasy and reality, challenging viewers to grapple with the implications of such imagery in the context of contemporary geopolitics. Shahid Bolsen argues that the only option for America is to generate an AI-driven virtual outcome, as the ability to produce a tangible result is beyond their reach. This situation reflects a profound disconnection from any genuine impact or influence in the real world, leading them to rely solely on AI-generated CGI animations to bring their imagined scenarios to life.[28]

Upon its release, the video quickly went viral, amassing millions of views on Instagram and being widely shared on Trump's Truth Social network by morning of that day. However, the response from the online community was overwhelmingly negative. The backlash that the video encountered primarily originated from Trump's conservative Christian support base, as well as from members of the Republican Party. Many users took to social media to express their outrage, labelling the video as "pure evil", "racist", and a disturbing representation of "ethnic cleansing". Lawyer and activist, Shola Mos-Shogbamimu, described the video as "ethnic cleansing rebranded as a real estate deal".[29] The portrayal of Gaza as a resort trivialises the real suffering of its people and reduces a complex geopolitical issue to a mere spectacle.³⁰ One account user with the name, Kainoa P, wrote: "You're doing great Mr President. But don't let it get to your head. God put you in that position for His glory, not yours".³¹ Someone else wrote, "Looks like the Gaz-A-Lago resort already dropped its first official tourism promo".³² Another user on the social platform reacting to the video, wrote:

> Mr President while I appreciate what you do, is not about you. To God be the glory and the honour, for without Him, you couldn't have accomplished anything. The statue is a symbol of the antichrist, please humble yourself to God.³³

Meanwhile, the Palestinian response has been about freedom from oppression and the oppressor. Basem Naim, the Hamas Political Bureau member said, "We are not struggling to improve prison conditions, but to get rid of the prison and the jailer", alluding to the occupying force, Israel.³⁴

The backlash highlights the sensitivity surrounding the Israeli-Palestinian conflict and the ongoing humanitarian crisis in Gaza. By presenting such a starkly altered vision of the region, the video raises questions about the ethics of using AI-generated content to comment on real-world issues, particularly those involving human suffering and displacement. As discussions continue to unfold online in the coming days and months, the video serves as a reminder of the power of media in shaping perceptions and the responsibility that comes with it.

It is perhaps of greater significance that individuals wielding global power and authority, reminiscent of the ungodly Pharaonic figures depicted in the Bible and the Qur'an, emphasise their ability to exert influence through their resources and wealth. They assert that all things in this world are commodified and subject to a price, operating without fear of accountability, much like their misuse of power within the United Nations. The hedonistic references and narcissistic self-portrayal of arrogance in the video serve as a mirror reflecting a nation in turmoil and decline, evoking memories of ancient empires that have long faded into the annals of history. Furthermore, history has shown us the fate of numerous demagogues, megalomaniacs, and avaricious individuals.

The United States cannot persist in promoting the Abraham Accord, which seeks to forge political connections between Arab nations and Israel, while simultaneously adopting a contradictory foreign policy that neglects the continuing struggle of the Palestinians, relegating their situation to historical errors without confronting the fundamental causes of the problem at hand. This continued neglect of the Palestinians' dignity in their pursuit of sovereignty and self-determination within their homeland by the United States further highlights the historical persistence of European and Western attitudes towards Islam dating back to the medieval era. This is the lens through which the Muslim world interprets such comments and intentions from the United States.

Decline of "American greatness"

The U.S. president's vision of international geopolitics equally echoes the new phase of American imperialism that is emphasised in his inaugural address on January 20, 2025:

> America will soon be greater, stronger, and far more exceptional than ever before...We will be a nation like no other, full of compassion, courage and exceptionalism. Our power will stop all wars and bring a new spirit of unity to a world that has been angry, violent and totally unpredictable ...
>
> ... The United States will once again consider itself a growing nation — one that increases our wealth, expands our territory, builds our cities, raises our expectations and carries our flag into new and beautiful horizons.[35]

Phyllis Bennis, a fellow of the Institute for Policy Studies, contends that although colonialism and imperialism are fundamental aspects of American history, the actions of "carrying the flag into new horizons" and "expanding our territory" represent a contemporary manifestation of U.S. imperialism in the 21st century.[36] Is this perspective accurate?

Donald Trump's remarks regarding Greenland, the Panama Canal, and Canada, as well as his suggestions on owning Gaza during the press conference, is to refrain from viewing them as expansionist or indicative of a land-grabbing agenda for the United States. Instead, one might consider a different interpretation of *Pax-Trumpica*. The independent American-Muslim political thinker, Shaid King Bolsen from the Middle Nation argues that the isolation and degradation of America is inevitable; it is a necessary outcome dictated by the inherent logic of Western predatory capitalism.[37] Just as Gorbachev did not single-handedly dismantle the Soviet Union but merely presided over its unavoidable decline, America too has reached the end of its trajectory. When reference to Western predatory capitalism is made, it is crucial to note that the issue extends beyond capitalism itself; it is fundamentally intertwined with the cultural and civilisational characteristics of the West. For Bolsen, the West's behaviour is not solely a product of capitalism; rather, their version of capitalism is shaped by their intrinsic nature. This unique approach to trade and business has given rise to phenomena such as the national and global financial crises. Consequently, their societies now face significant challenges. He argues that, while this is a complex topic deserving of further exploration, the essential point remains: this transformation is not only necessary but also inevitable. It will occur regardless of who is in power, be it Trump or any other leader.[38]

The emergence of a class of anational elites or oligarchs, represented by major corporations, "his [i.e., Trump's] allied cohort of capitalist techno-barons", like Tim Cook (Apple), Larry Page and Sergey Brin (Google), Mark Zuckerberg (Meta), Elon Musk (X, Tesla Inc., Space X), and Jeff Bezos (Amazon), has resulted in private profit motives that are increasingly detached from the broader economy.[39] This detachment means that these entities are not linked to productive activities, national identity, or the well-being of citizens. Their interests do not align with the standard of living, stability, safety, or prosperity of the nation. Consequently, this class of private sector power has effectively become a nation unto itself, one that transcends borders and national interests, driven solely by their own agendas. This is further evident by the appointment of Elon Musk, the proprietor of Tesla, the social media platform X, and SpaceX, to Donald Trump's administration as the leader of the Department of Government Efficiency, commonly referred to as DOGE, in 2025. According to Shahid Bolsen:

> What we are currently observing is not an unprecedented decline of Western power; rather, it represents the inevitable culmination of the imperial project. The actions of the anational entities are now being directed towards Europe and America in a manner similar to what they [i.e., the West] have long inflicted upon the Global South. The machinery of the empire was never designed to benefit the populace of the imperial core; it was established to serve the private interests of those who wielded control over the empire. As the United States retracts from its imperial role, these same private sector elites are now undermining the very system that has sustained them for decades.
>
> For many years, the Global South has been systematically deprived of its sovereignty, with its governments reduced to mere administrators of corporate interests. This corporate imperialism has led to the extraction of resources and the control of populations through mechanisms such as debt, military intervention, and economic coercion. Now, this same process is being applied to the former centers of imperial power. The United States is not merely withdrawing from global hegemony; it is being consumed from within. The institutions that once managed the empire abroad are now being dismantled domestically. Organisations like the National Endowment for Democracy (NED) and the United States Agency for International Development (USAID) are being repurposed to facilitate the exploitation of the American economy and the subjugation of its own citizens under the same neoliberal framework that was imposed elsewhere.[40]

Thus, form this perspective, the entirety of the nationalist rhetoric of Trump and other presidents of the past serves merely as a facade, concealing the impending decline of America's global influence, spanning from Africa to the Middle East and from the Pacific to the Americas.[41] The United States is anticipated to persist as a global power, albeit in a diminished capacity, for the foreseeable future.

Bolsen argues that it is important to emphasise that statements made by Trump should not be accepted at face value, as he often does not convey genuine intentions. His public statements are frequently either strategic bargaining tools or deliberate misdirections. The discussions surrounding Panama, Greenland, and the notion of Canada potentially becoming a U.S. state appear to be tactics aimed at alienating allies and isolating the United States. From this perspective, this is a deliberate strategy, and that achieving this outcome is his true objective.[42]

The perception of American greatness is gradually revealing itself as the final stronghold of Western imperialism, observable to the global audience. The concept of *Manifest Destiny* has proven to be merely an illusion, serving as a means to construct the narrative of a formidable nation, akin to a form of self-aggrandizement and enhancement of national pride.

In "America Will Own Gaza", Bolsen argues that the perception of American supremacy has consistently been a reflection of relative power rather than absolute dominance. The United States was never truly invincible; it simply faced no significant challengers. Following the Cold War, the Soviet Union represented America's primary global competitor, yet even then, the two nations were not truly equal in terms of economic performance, technological advancement, or global influence. Nevertheless, the USSR was sufficient to prevent the United States from achieving global supremacy.[43]

While the Soviet military was indeed formidable, the nation suffered from severe economic and administrative issues. Its collapse was a result of self-inflicted wounds rather than a direct consequence of American power. The downfall of the Soviet Union stemmed from ineffective central planning, poor policy decisions, excessive military expenditure aimed at competing with the United States, internal corruption, stagnation, and unsuccessful economic reforms such as perestroika. Ultimately, the Soviet system did not fall due to defeat by the United States; rather, it simply could not sustain itself in the long run.[44]

The dissolution of the USSR resulted in the United States emerging as the default superpower, not due to its overwhelming strength, but rather because there were no other viable competitors. This period of unipolarity has now concluded. The current U.S. Secretary of State, Marco Rubio, has recognised that America's status as the sole global superpower was a historical anomaly, and that era has now become a part of history. In an interview on 3 February, 2025, the Secretary of States, Marco Rubio, said:

> So it's not normal for the world to simply have a unipolar power. That was not — that was an anomaly. It was a product of the end of the Cold War, but eventually you were going to reach back to a point where you had a multipolar world, multi-great powers in different parts of the planet. We face that now with China and to some extent Russia, and then you have rogue states like Iran and North Korea you have to deal with.[45]

The United States is no longer the unipolar superpower of the world that it assumed by default after the collapse of the Soviet Union. It is now a regional power. The multipolar power landscape is characterised by spheres of influence that are not dominated by a single superpower, but rather shaped by regional powers such as South Africa, Turkey, the BRICS nations, the Gulf Cooperation Council, the United States, Russia, and China.

The perception of the U.S. as an unstoppable force was largely due to the absence of rivals, a situation that has changed. Presently, the United States faces several competitors in a multipower world: China, which challenges it in technology and economic spheres; Russia, which asserts its influence in military and geopolitical matters; and the collective of the Global South, including the BRICS nations, which stand in opposition to U.S. interests. These emerging competitors present challenges that the United States struggles to address. Notably, Russia today wields considerable influence, arguably even more than during its time as part of the Soviet Union. While its economy is significantly smaller than that of the United States, the strategic importance of its economic relationships continues to undermine American dominance.[46]

When one examines the situation objectively, it becomes evident that the narrative Americans hold about themselves does not withstand critical analysis. For instance, regarding World War II, which is often celebrated in American discourse, it was primarily the Soviet Union that played a decisive role in defeating the Nazis. In fact, approximately 80% of Nazi casualties were inflicted by Soviet forces, not by American troops. Much of the perceived strength and power attributed to America has been overstated. Furthermore, this relative power is currently in decline, as it was historically predicated on the absence of competing powers. With the emergence of other global powers, it is crucial to recognise that America was never as powerful as it has been portrayed. Additionally, the power it once possessed has been diminishing for several years. This is the current state of affairs, and it is important to note that the power structure within America is acutely aware of this reality. Their actions, including withdrawal and self-isolation, are not voluntary choices but rather responses to necessity.[47]

The necessity for America to adapt stems from its diminished status in global affairs. The nation no longer possesses the global supremacy it once did, nor does it maintain a competitive edge. The coercive power that characterised its influence in a unipolar world has significantly waned. There are two primary factors that contributed to the perception of American power. First, following the dissolution of the Soviet Union, the absence of a rival made the United States appear formidable. Second, the often brutal and malicious application of its power reinforced this perception, leading many to conflate danger with strength. However, it is crucial to distinguish between being powerful and merely being dangerous. While America has historically exhibited a propensity for violence, it has not demonstrated true bravery. In light of the emergence of China, the rise of BRICS, and increasing regional autonomy, it is evident that America is retreating out of necessity.[48]

The global landscape has shifted away from an America-centric perspective. In fact, even Donald Trump did not embody this viewpoint. Consider the situation in Afghanistan, where the United States maintained a military presence for two decades with the aim of dismantling the Taliban, which now governs the country. Furthermore, the U.S. expressed intentions to remove Bashar al-Assad from power as early as 2011, yet this objective was only recently achieved through the efforts of Turkey, Iran, and Russia. Notably, the current Syrian government comprises individuals previously labelled as terrorists by the United States, a designation that was later retracted.

Moreover, under President Joe Biden and his predecessor Barrak Obama, the U.S. has struggled to influence events in Ukraine, has been unsuccessful in its attempts to oust Nicolás Maduro from Venezuela, and is now engaging in negotiations with him. The U.S. has faced setbacks in Bolivia, Georgia, Kazakhstan, and Hungary, and is barely maintaining its influence in Moldova. Its efforts have also faltered in Niger, Burkina Faso, Mali, Ethiopia, and Guinea. It is evident that it has been quite some time since the United States could assert its authority and dictate global affairs. Therefore, it is perplexing that some continue to perceive America as the dominant force governing the world.[49]

The Global South challenging American neo-Imperialism

The nations of the Global South have become increasingly outspoken regarding the foreign policies of the United States. At the forefront of this movement is South Africa. Following the United States' decision to reduce aid to South Africa on February 11, 2025, citing "unjust racial discrimination" against white Afrikaners, the reaction from Johannesburg has been notably forceful and direct. South African parliamentarian Julius Sello Malema addressed the National Assembly the next day, stating:

> We want to make it very clear that we should not be confused with a generation of cowards who can be bullied by imperial forces and power hungry individuals intoxicated by the wealth of the United States of America [that] has bullied nations before and impose senseless and arbitrary sanctions and threaten wars.

But we are a different generation. We are a generation of economic freedom fighters and will not be bullied Mr President. We agree with you Mr President that we should not be bullied. We stand on the shoulders of the giants who confronted The Establishment with their very lives and we are willing to follow in their footsteps. We are not cowards and they must not try us. We continue to stand with the people of Palestine who remain under siege. We agree as the National Assembly, that the Israeli Embassy must be cleared, yet their flag continue to fly in our country. While Palestinians are threatened with mass deportation to foreign lands, we support the government's case in the International Court of Justice and we must remain Resolute in the face of sanctions and sponsored attacks ... Importantly we must oppose the colonisation of Gaza by the USA. Justice and freedom for Palestine - one day the people of Palestine will know the true meaning of freedom Mr President.

We are not being attacked by Trump administration because [we] did anything wrong. They are attacking us because of our stand on Israel. They are attacking us because of the action the government has taken to ICJ [International Court of Justice] and we are saying to you - do not be misled by people who are saying you are under siege because of expropriation ...

When you say they cannot bully us you must start by removing the Israeli Embassy to show them that we will not be bullied.[50]

The actions of Donald Trump in displacing the Palestinian people from Gaza bear a striking resemblance to the measures taken by the apartheid government against black South Africans in the past. The Global South has reached a point where it will no longer accept the erosion of the sovereignty of independent nations or the coercive tactics of affluent and influential countries with imperialistic ambitions, which were once tolerated. Furthermore, the Global South is becoming more vocal in asserting their stance against the injustices of the West.

A coalition referred to as the Hague Group has been formed, consisting of nine nations from the Global South, with the aim of supporting the decisions of the International Court of Justice (ICJ) and the International Criminal Court (ICC), restricting arms sales to Israel, and challenging the impunity endorsed by the United States.[51] Inspired by South Africa's initiative to bring Israel before the ICJ on charges of genocide against the Palestinians, the Global South is asserting itself as an active and vocal player in international relations.[52] The Hague Group faces significant challenges, including the endorsement of impunity by powerful nations, the weakening of international legal frameworks, and backlash against countries seeking to hold Israel accountable. Recent geopolitical events have highlighted the urgency of the Hague Group's mission. President Trump's proposal to annex Gaza not only supports Israel's actions but also undermines international law, which the global community must uphold. Additionally, the Hague Group advocates for the Global South, challenging the dominance of Western, particularly US-led, institutions in enforcing international rulings. The geopolitical events in the Middle East between Israel and Hamas (2023) have further underscored the critical nature of the Hague Group's objectives. The proposal by US President Donald Trump to annex, ethnically cleanse, and "take over" Gaza not only represents a blatant endorsement of Israel's genocidal actions but also undermines the very principles of international law, which the global community is obligated to protect. Regarding the breakdown of international diplomacy, South Africa's Minister of International Relations and Cooperation, Ronald Lamola, stated, "injustice anywhere is a threat to justice everywhere".[53] Additionally, the African Union member states and the Carribean countries are collectively pursuing reparations from European nations, which may include financial compensation and formal recognition of historical wrongs.[54] Between the 15th and 19th centuries, at least 12.5 million Africans were forcibly taken, transported under duress mainly by European traders, and ultimately sold into slavery.[55]

The United Kingdom and the European Union no longer act as neutral facilitators but pursue victory against perceived adversaries, as seen in the Ukraine-Russia conflict (2022-) and the U.S. and UK's tepid response to Israel's actions in Gaza, which resulted in over 48,000 civilian deaths. President Trump has even sought to protect Netanyahu from accountability. In fact, the recently elected President Trump for a second term of office (2025) has attempted to protect Netanyahu from facing consequences by implementing sanctions against the International Criminal Court, which determined that both Benjamin Netanyahu and his defense minister, Yoav Gallant, were guilty of committing war crimes against humanity, alongside the late Hamas leader Ismail Haniyeh, and issued warrants for thier arrest.[56] Furthermore, Trump threatened repercussions for anyone who might pursue legal action against Israel's Prime Minister.

When Trump makes statements regarding his vision for global affairs, or if Joe Biden were to express similar sentiments, it is important to recognise that such declarations do not constitute a Divine mandate that all nations must follow. Those times have passed. In fact, Trump's assertions do not differ significantly from Biden's; both have expressed a desire for Egypt and Jordan to accept Palestinian refugees, only to be met with rejection. Trump wields no more authority than former President Biden did when he was in office (2021-2024); they occupy the same position. While Trump may envision expelling Palestinians and attempt to manifest this idea, it remains an unrealistic proposition. It can be construed that Trump is aware that the Palestinians are not going anywhere. It is crucial to note that the implications of his suggestions, whether made in earnest or not, amount to calls for genocide and ethnic cleansing, which are crimes against humanity. Any actions he might pursue to garner support for such proposals should lead to his prosecution at the International Court of Justice.[57]

As discussed in previous chapters, the post-Soviet period saw the West confronting Islam, which emerged as the sole enduring ideology following the collapse of communism. This ideological confrontation, coupled with over a thousand years of strife between Christendom and Islam, ultimately culminated in the September 11 attacks on the United States. Beyond the ideological dichotomy of "with us, or against us", the attacks on New York can be viewed as a direct challenge to the United States' pro-Israel foreign policy in the Middle East from a political standpoint. While U.S. foreign policy in the region may not have undergone substantial changes, it has indeed become more intransigent. From this historical standpoint, Trump's perspective on the Palestinians embodies the long-standing patterns of Western political, economic, cultural, and psychological imperialism over the Muslim Other. His ambition to own and reshape Gaza into the "Riviera of the Middle East" suggests a desire to mould the region according to Western ideals, simultaneously disregarding the local population's inherent right to dignity, self-determination, and liberation from oppression and occupation—principles for which the United States itself struggled during its War of Independence against British colonial rule.

'America First' - Division in the Western Alliance

There seems to be a division regarding unity within NATO, the Western defense alliance. NATO has provided security for the Europe for nearly 80 years, but this assurance can no longer be taken for granted. Established by the United States in the aftermath of the Second World War, NATO was created as a strategic response to the geopolitical landscape of the time, primarily aimed at countering the spread of communism and providing a collective defense framework for democracies around the globe. The alliance was built on the principles of mutual defense, shared values, and cooperation among member states, fostering a sense of solidarity in the face of external threats. In this context, the formation of NATO in 1949 marked the tangible manifestation of the ideological struggle between democracy and freedom versus tyranny, autocracy, and authoritarianism, thereby positioning the Western alliance against any forces that threaten its core values. Given the current global landscape, the shift in ideological and political alignment raises concerns for Western democracies.

For nearly eight decades, NATO's foreign policy evolved through various global challenges, adapting to the changing dynamics of international relations. The alliance played a crucial role in maintaining peace and stability in Europe during the Cold War, engaging in various military operations and partnerships to address emerging threats. However, this carefully crafted foreign policy framework faced significant disruption within a month of Donald Trump's inauguration in 2025.

AMERICA: THE LAST BASTION OF WESTERN IMPERIALISM 361

Trump's presidency marked a departure from traditional U.S. foreign policy, characterised by an "America First" approach that prioritised national interests over multilateral commitments. His administration's rhetoric and actions raised questions about the United States' commitment to NATO and its collective defense obligations, leading to a palpable sense of uncertainty among member states. This shift not only strained relationships within the alliance but also emboldened adversaries who sought to exploit perceived divisions among NATO members.

As a result, the unity that had been a hallmark of NATO's existence began to fray. Member countries found themselves grappling with differing perspectives on defense spending, military engagement, and the overall direction of the alliance. Some nations expressed concerns about the reliability of U.S. leadership, while others sought to strengthen their own military capabilities in response to a perceived withdrawal of American support. This fragmentation threatened to undermine the very foundation of NATO, raising fears about the alliance's ability to respond effectively to emerging security challenges.

In this context, the future of NATO became a topic of intense debate, with calls for a reassessment of its strategic priorities and operational frameworks. The need for a renewed commitment to collective defense and a unified approach to global security became increasingly urgent as member states navigated the complexities of a rapidly changing geopolitical landscape. The division regarding unity within NATO not only highlighted the challenges facing the alliance but also underscored the importance of fostering collaboration and solidarity among its members in order to address the multifaceted threats of the 21st century.

Stephen Collinson in his news article to the CNN titled "How the world changed in a month" (22 February, 2025) argues that Donald Trump dedicated the initial month of his second term to an unprecedented endeavour — the disassembly of the international framework that the United States has constructed over the last 80 years.[58] Collinson argues that while the West's decline was a theoretical possibility, few expected a president to take such drastic actions. After

Trump's election win the second time in 2024, some Western diplomats felt they could manage his social media-driven foreign policy. However, the urgency of an emergency meeting among European leaders in Paris on 3 February 2025 shows they underestimated the potential impact of Trump's second term.[59]

Trump has shifted the U.S. stance on the Ukraine conflict, siding with the aggressor and echoing the Russian President Vladimir Putin's rhetoric while undermining the Ukrainian President Volodymyr Zelenskyy's leadership. His Vice President, J. D. Vance, criticised European leaders as "tyrants" during a Munich visit (14 February 2025) and urged Germany to dismantle safeguards against fascism, allowing hard-line, extremist, and conservative groups to access political representation. Meanwhile, Defense Secretary Pete Hegseth told European nations to take on conventional security responsibilities, raising concerns about NATO's mutual defence principle.[60] Collinson asks the pertinenrt question: "So, what can Europe do now that America — the country that rebuilt the continent from the ashes of World War II — seems to be becoming an openly hostile power?"[61] The answer for the European politicians is that the United States has become an "unreliable partner".[62] The response from European politicians indicates that the United States is perceived as an "unreliable partner" despite British Prime Minister Sir Keir Starmer's rejection of such a perspective.[63] This perception of unreliability was notably highlighted in a press conference held in the Oval Office of the White House on February 28, 2025, featuring the U.S. President Donald Trump and Ukrainian President Volodymyr Zelenskyy, which included Vice President JD Vance.

In the Oval Office meeting, in front of the world media, disagreements quickly surfaced, particularly concerning the terms of a proposed minerals agreement that would grant the US extensive access to Ukraine's rare earth minerals in exchange for American support in Ukraine's conflict with Russia. Zelenskyy stressed that any such agreement must incorporate genuine security guarantees for Ukraine, a point that the Trump administration has thus far neglected. Tensions escalated further when Trump highlighted his amicable relationship with President Vladimir Putin, attributing the stagnation of peace negotiations to Zelenskyy's perceived hostility towards the Russian leader. In response to the Ukrainian President's assertion that the U.S. might experience the repercussions of Putin's actions in the future, Donald Trump reacted strongly, asserting his authority over Zelenskyy:

> Zelenskyy: "First of all, during the war, everybody has problems, even you. But you have nice ocean and don't feel now. But you will feel it in the future. God bless –"
>
> Trump: "You don't know that. You don't know that. Don't tell us what we're going to feel. We're trying to solve a problem. Don't tell us what we're going to feel."
>
> Zelenskyy: "I'm not telling you. I am answering on these questions."
>
> Trump: "Because you're in no position to dictate that."
>
> Vance: "That's exactly what you're doing."
>
> Trump: "You are in no position to dictate what we're going to feel. We're going to feel very good."
>
> Zelenskyy: "You will feel influenced."
>
> Trump: "We are going to feel very good and very strong."
>
> Zelenskyy: "I am telling you. You will feel influenced."

The press conference deteriorated into hostility, with the Vice President J. D. Vance accusing Zelenskyy of being "disrespectful" and questioning whether he had expressed gratitude at any point during the discussions:

> Vance: Have you said thank you once?
>
> Zelenskyy: A lot of times.
>
> Vance: No, in this meeting, this entire meeting? Offer some words of appreciation for the United States of America and the president who's trying to save your country.

> Zelenskyy: Yes, you think that if you will speak very loudly about the war ...
>
> Trump: He's not speaking loud. Your country is in big trouble. No, no, you've done a lot of talking. Your country is in big trouble.[64]

The meeting ended abruptly, with Zelenskyy's team escorted out, leaving the minerals agreement unsigned and its future in doubt. Following the confrontation in the Oval Office, Kaja Kallas, the European Union's high representative for foreign affairs and security policy, made a statement in a social media post:

> Today, it became clear that the free world needs a new leader. It's up to us, Europeans, to take this challenge.[65]

Zelenskyy's reluctance to sign a deal with the U.S. without security guarantees for his country angered Trump. A few days after the verbal spats between the two leaders, J. D. Vance in an interview on Fox News said:

> The president knows that if you want real security guarantees, if you want to actually ensure that Vladimir Putin does not invade Ukraine again, the very best security guarantee is to give Americans economic upside in the future of Ukraine. That is a way better security guarantee then 20,000 troops from some random country that hasn't fought a war in 30 or 40 years. The security guarantee and also the economic guarantee for Ukraine is to rebuild the country and ensure that America has a long-term interest.[66]

The feasibility of U.S. isolationism under the "America First" policy, coupled with its desire to establish agreements for earth minerals with Ukraine, create a certain degree of ambiguity regarding its imperialistic intentions. Nevertheless, the pursuit of resources from a war torn nation underscores a form of non-violent imperialism. According to Monica Duffy Toft, International Politics and Director of the Center for Strategic Studies, The Fletcher School, Tufts University:

AMERICA: THE LAST BASTION OF WESTERN IMPERIALISM 365

> Imperialism does not require military force. Great powers still exert influence over weaker nations, shaping their behavior through economc might and wealth, diplomacy and strategic allainaces.
>
> The U.S. has long engaged in this form of influence. It has often pursued its imperialist agenda in what I would call a more "gentlemanly manner" than historical empires with their bloody physical conquests.[67]

Toff contends that rhetoric is instrumental in influencing perceptions, which subsequently impact behaviour. When a President of the United States suggests the acquisition of foreign territories, such as Greenland, the Panama Canal, or the exploitation of the economic resources of a war-torn nation in return for aid, it signals to both allies and adversaries that the United States is departing from the international framework that has upheld a certain level of global stability for the past 75 years.[68]

The focus of Trumpian politics has shifted away from the preservation of democracy against hostile nations to prioritising economic benefits for the United States. As Collinson reports, "For Trump, all foreign policy is a monetary transaction in which the United States is either winning or being taken advantage of".[69] A week later, on March 5, 2025, following the intense confrontation in the Oval Office, the Trump administration made the decision to suspend military assistance to Ukraine. This action underscored to the Western alliance and democratic nations globally that the United States is a dependable ally. Consequently, this move effectively nullified the Marshall Plan of 1948 and the principles it represented. Given that Article 5 of NATO asserts that an attack on one member is an attack on all, it is evident that Europe can no longer depend on the United States for support in the event of a potential conflict on the continent. According to the French President Emmanuel Macron's warning, Europe is "entering a new era … We have to be united and determined to protect ourselves". Furthermore, he added that, "The future of Europe should not be decided in Washington or Moscow".[70] Concurring with Macron, the French politician Claude Malhuret expressed his strongest disapproval of the shifting United States policy regarding Ukraine by directing his criticism towards President Donald Trump during a general session of the French Senate on 7 March, 2025:

> Europe is at a critical turning point in its history. The American shield is slipping away, Ukraine risks being abandoned, Russia strengthened [...]
>
> Washington became Nero's court, an incendiary emperor, submissive courtiers and a ketamine-fuelled buffoon [Elon Musk] charged with purging the civil service.
>
> It is a tragedy for the free world, but it is first and foremost a tragedy for the United States.
>
> Never in history has a president of the United States capitulated to the enemy. No one has ever supported an aggressor against an ally. Never has anyone trampled on the American Constitution, issued so many illegal decrees, dismissed the judges who could prevent them, suddenly dismissed the military staff, weakened all counter-powers and taken control of social networks.
>
> This is not an illiberal drift, it is the beginning of the confiscation of democracy. Let us remember that it only took one month, three weeks and two days to bring down the Weimar Republic and its Constitution …
>
> The defeat of Ukraine would be the defeat of Europe. The Baltic States, Georgia, Moldova are already on the list. Putin's goal is the return to Yalta where half of the continent was ceded to Stalin …
>
> So we are alone …
>
> Is this the end of the Atlantic Alliance? The risk is great.[71]

In light of its security concerns, Europe seeks to draw lessons from its history. Having triumphed over fascism in World War II and communism at the conclusion of the Cold War, it now faces the challenge of overcoming the totalitarianism represented by Russia, even if it must do so independently.[72]

At this crucial juncture in its history, the acknowledgment of security challenges has instilled a sense of trepidation and unease within Europe. The continent finds itself grappling with a complex web of geopolitical tensions, economic uncertainties, and social upheavals that have collectively shaken its foundational sense of stability. The ongoing conflict in Ukraine, in particular, has not only raised alarms about territorial integrity and national sovereignty but has also forced European nations to confront their own vulnerabilities and the implications of their historical actions on the global stage.

Simultaneously, Malhuret conveyed a viewpoint of civilisational superiority that Europe has held for centuries. He remarked: "The nations of the [Global] South are awaiting the resolution of the conflict [in Ukraine] to determine whether they should maintain their respect for Europe or whether they are now free to trample on it".[73] This statement encapsulates a critical moment of reflection for Europe, as it navigates its role in a rapidly changing world order. Malhuret's assertion suggests that the respect historically afforded to Europe by nations in the Global South is contingent upon how Europe addresses its current crises and engages with the international community.

By alluding to Islam, Malhuret's mention of the Global South in his speech implies that the Muslim 'Other' has historically been depicted as violent terrorists or destitute refugees escaping from dysfunctional and underdeveloped regions, ready to invade civilised Europe at the slightest indication of weakness. This characterisation reflects a longstanding narrative that has often framed non-European societies as threats to European stability and Judeo-Christian values. Such depictions serve to reinforce a binary worldview, where Europe is seen as the bastion of civilisation, progress, and order, while the Global South is relegated to the status of chaos, violence, and backwardness.

With nuanced implications, Malhuret draws a connection between 'civilised' Europe and the 'uncivilised,' 'barbaric' Other. This juxtaposition not only highlights the entrenched prejudices that persist within European discourse but also underscores the fragility of the civilisational narrative that Europe has constructed over centuries. The mindset of a clash of civilisations continues to endure in Europe, perpetuating the dehumanisation of the Other, regardless of whether Europe is in a position of strength or vulnerability. This enduring perspective fosters an environment where dialogue and mutual understanding are often overshadowed by fear and suspicion, ultimately hindering the potential for genuine cooperation and solidarity in addressing global challenges. As Europe and the West find themselves at this crossroads, the significance of Malhuret's comments resonates profoundly, urging European leaders and citizens to reevaluate their perceptions of the Global South, which also encompasses Islamic nations.

Historical Parallelisms: From the decadent Roman Emperors to the Ottomans, 'The Sick Man of Europe'

In examining the perception of the Other from a position where might is right, what insights can we derive from the purportedly 'diplomatic' interactions among Trump-Zelenskyy-Vance? Historical evidence indicates that such verbal exchanges are not a novel phenomenon. The Trump-Zelenskyy-Vance verbal exchange illustrates how, over the centuries, nations wielding economic, military, and technological power have often belittled vulnerable nations, relegating them to submissive roles. Donald Trump's remark to Zelenskyy above, "You are in no position to dictate", succinctly reflects the attitudes of the powerful towards the vulnerable. Throughout history, powerful nations have routinely dictated peace terms to the vanquished. A notable example is the Ottoman Turks, whose conquest of Constantinople in 1453 signified the end of the Eastern Roman Empire. From that point until the unsuccessful Second Siege of Vienna in 1683, the Ottomans imposed their terms on European powers, leveraging their military and technological advantages. However, following their defeat in 1683, the once-formidable Ottoman Empire was compelled to accept the peace conditions established at the Treaty of Karlowitz in 1699, as dictated by the victorious European states, Austria, Poland, Russia, and Venice. During its zenith, after conflicts with Venice and the Habsburgs, foreign diplomats sought to negotiate peace treaties on the Ottomans' terms or to secure military assistance against their own adversaries. Despite retaining political, economic, and military relevance in European affairs after the defeat at Vienna, the empire's gradual retreat from international engagement led to a decline in its status as a military superpower and threat to Europe. This decline was exacerbated by the realisation that its extensive borders were no longer defensible against the more advanced European forces. Ironically, it was the empire's vulnerabilities, rather than its strengths, that kept it pertinent to European imperialist ambitions, which sought to partition it and highlighted European supremacy over the Ottoman territories. As the political, economic, and military dynamics shifted in favour of Europe, the empire's situation deteriorated significantly, leading to its decline over the subsequent two centuries, culminating in its defeat at the conclusion of the First World War in 1918 and its formal dissolution in 1922. This does not suggest that the United States is on the verge of collapse, however, from a historical perspective, a comparable pattern is currently observable with the long decline of the American 'Empire'.

Historians would likely agree that Donald Trump's 'America First' rhetoric and his widely reported misconduct draw a striking parallel to Nero, the notorious Roman emperor recognised for his ambition, controversies, and self-aggrandisement. Similar to Trump, Nero maintained a fiercely devoted following, even as his rule incited significant debate and division among both the elite and the general populace. Nero's confident demeanor, coupled with a series of scandals, attracted both fascination and criticism, reflecting the complexities of Trump's own legacy.

Nero, who ruled from 54 to 68 AD, is often remembered for his extravagant lifestyle and artistic aspirations, which he pursued at the expense of traditional governance. His infamous response to the Great Fire of Rome in 64 AD, where he allegedly played the lyre while the city burned, has become emblematic of his perceived detachment from the suffering of his people. Similarly, Trump's first term presidency was marked by a series of controversies, including his handling of crises such as the COVID-19 pandemic and social unrest, which often drew accusations of self-interest and a lack of empathy. Likewise, his second term commenced amidst foreign policy and economic turmoil, which elicited comments from French minister Claude Malhuret, who referred to Trump as the "incendiary emperor," likening his Washington to the court of Nero.[74] Both Nero and Trump, in their respective eras, faced significant backlash for prioritising personal ambition over the welfare of their constituents, leading to a polarised political landscape.

Moreover, Trump exhibits characteristics akin to the lesser-known Caligula, another Roman emperor notorious for his boldness and unconventional methods. Caligula, who ruled from 37 to 41 AD, is often remembered for his erratic behavior and his willingness to flout established norms. He defied the expectations of the Roman elite, challenging their authority and pursuing his vision without regard for tradition—qualities that resonate with Trump's apparent disregard for the conventions of Washington, the so-called deep state, and established norms. Caligula's infamous acts, such as appointing his horse as a consul, symbolise a radical departure from political decorum, much like Trump's unconventional approach to governance, his frequent disregard for political etiquette, and his womanising past.

Both figures represent an "agitator" archetype that captivated and unsettled their respective societies. Trump's rise to power was characterised by a populist appeal that resonated with many Americans who felt disillusioned by the political establishment. His rhetoric often mirrored Caligula's defiance of the status quo, as he positioned himself as an outsider willing to challenge the entrenched political elite. This disruption, while energising for his supporters, also led to significant unrest and division, echoing the tumultuous reign of Caligula, which ultimately culminated in his assassination due to widespread dissatisfaction with his rule.

Similar historical parallels with the Ottoman Empire can be observed in the recent trajectory of the United States, particularly with the emergence of Trumpian politics. During the 16th century, under the rule of Süleyman the Magnificent (r. 1520-1566), the Ottoman Empire expanded its influence to regions such as Gujarat in India (1538), Aden in Yemen (1538), and Aceh (1565), while also engaging in naval conflicts with the Portuguese (1538-57) to secure dominance over the Indian Ocean. The subsequent ascendance of European powers and the discovery of the Americas led to a significant influx of gold and silver into European treasuries, which in turn contributed to the devaluation of the Ottoman currency. By the 18th century, the Ottomans found themselves unable to effectively counter the challenges posed by European control of the spice trade in the Indian Ocean, particularly from Britain, France, and the Dutch, prompting a retreat to the eastern Mediterranean. Additionally, the aggressive expansion of the Russian Empire under Catherine the Great (r. 1762-1796) posed existential threats, culminating in the loss of Crimea, the first Muslim territory to fall in its history. By 1875, the empire's mounting debt had reached 214.4 million British pounds, leading to its bankruptcy that same year. Despite its weakened economic state, the opulence and decadence of the sultans, Abdulmecid I (r. 1839-1861) and Abdualziz (r. 1861-1876), was evident in the extravagant construction of the Dolmabahce Palace and Beylerbey Palace along the Bosphorus, which sought to emulate European architectural styles as a façade of modernisation. The military defeats suffered against Russia in the Balkans and Caucasus during 1877-78 further underscored the empire's prolonged stagnation and decline, earning it the phrase 'the Sick Man of Europe' as designated by Tsar Nicolas I in 1853. The phrase has since been used by Western historians to describe the long decline and eventual fall of the Ottoman Empire, emphasising its economic collapse, ineptitdue and decadence of the sultans in the 19th century, and failure to protect its territories.

Similarly, just as the Ottomans recognised the untenability of their overextended borders, the United States seems to be confronting the reality that its own stretched resources and military outposts around the world may not be sustainable in the long run. The Ottoman defeat at Vienna in 1683 was a significat blow to morale, resulting in its gradual retreat from global engagement. This is akin to the American decisive and demoralising defeat in Vietnam in 1975, and the chaotic, as well as the tumultuous and chaotic exit from Afghanistan in 2021, which underscores its crumbling global credibility as a symbol of democracy, human rights, and liberty, with little to demonstrate politically and strategically in the regions it sought to influence. The fact that the Ottomans declared bankruptcy in their final decades does not imply that the United States government is on the verge of experiencing a similar economic decline. However, from a historical perspective, it remains uncertain how long the United States can sustain its escalating debt, which currently exceeds $34 trillion. Just as the Ottomans were unable to manage the devaluation of their currency due to the influx of American gold and silver into Europe, the U.S. is facing increasing pressure on the dollar as a result of its strong opposition to the de-dollarisation efforts led by the BRICS nations, with more countries opting to conduct trade in their own national currencies.

The notion of American exceptionalism—the belief that the United States holds a distinctive role in leading the global community—is rapidly diminishing. With the emergence of new global powers, like China and regional powers as noted above, the United States' capacity to shape international relations through diplomacy, cultural influence, and economic strategies is waning. Similar to the fate of the Ottomans, the United States faces the danger of becoming a once-great superpower that desperately clings to its historical prestige—the elusive *Manifest Destiny*, while the world progresses forward. As global power dynamics increasingly shift towards decentralisation, the United States confronts a pivotal decision: either embrace the evolving geopolitical environment or oppose this transformation, potentially leading to greater isolation. The era of unchallenged American dominance is waning, and historical precedents indicate that empires that do not evolve frequently succumb to their own burdens.

Enter Muslims as Peacemakers

As the United States is beginning to retreat from the global and look inward, in this considerable void of global leadership, Islamic nations have stepped forward. In this leadership vacuum, Islamic nations have emerged as peacemakers, highlighting the irony of rising Islamophobia and the West's retreat from traditional diplomacy.

As Western influence wanes, Muslim countries are assuming the role of global diplomatic leaders. Across Europe, the Middle East, and Africa, Muslim diplomats are filling the void created by the West and spearheading international negotiations. The growing diplomatic leadership from the Muslim world contrasts sharply with the rise of Islamophobia in the twenty-first century, particularly in Western countries. While these nations have faced escalating Islamophobia and engaged in violent global conflicts, Muslim diplomats have emerged as key peacemakers. A recent instance is Türkiye's effective negotiations that resulted in the release of five Thai hostages by Hamas in Gaza on 29 January 2o25.[75] This event, notably overlooked by Western media, underscores how an Islamic nation is addressing the void in statesmanship created by the United States and its allies. In December 2024, Turkish President Recep Tayyip Erdogan announced a "historic reconciliation" between Ethiopia and Somalia, following peace talks facilitated by Ankara.[76] Türkiye previously organised the Istanbul Peace talks in 2022, which aimed to end the Ukraine conflict but were hindered by the U.S. and U.K.[77] Türkiye also facilitated discussions between Russia and Ukraine, leading to the Black Sea Grain initiative to protect food and fertilizer shipments for developing nations.[78] Other Islamic countries have joined these efforts; in September 2022, Saudi Arabia and Türkiye helped secure the release of Western prisoners from Russia, and Saudi Arabia hosted a Ukraine Peace summit in Jeddah in 2023. For several years, Qatar served as a venue for negotiations between the United States and the Taliban prior to the chaotic withdrawal of Western forces from Afghanistan in 2021.[79] The UAE has played a key role in negotiating the release of Russian and Ukrainian prisoners of war and the remains of deceased military personnel.[80] In January 2025, Qatar has facilitated the initial phase of the ceasefire in Gaza and is said to have hosted preliminary discussions between Russian and Ukrainian representatives focused on resolving the ongoing three-year conflict.[81] Enhancing Saudi Arabia's status as a prominent international actor, Prince bin Salman and his diplomatic team are anticipated to take on a significant role in facilitating a peace agreement between Russia and Ukraine, as indicated by high official meetings in Riyadh, the Saudi capital, between the United States Secretary and Russian officials on 17 February, 2025. The continuation of high-level meetings involving prominent officials from the United States, Russia, and Ukraine underscores the kingdom's ambitions to establish itself as a significant global player capable of effectively mediating international disputes.⁸²

Furthermore, the nation that has historically faced disparagement and dehumanisation from Europe for centuries, often referred to by derogatory terms such as "the terrible Turk", "uncivilised", "backward", "barbaric", and "the sick man of Europe", is now being reassessed through a different perspective. Although there remains a lack of genuine affection for the Turkish people, the evolving dynamics of global uncertainty—particularly those influenced by the political climate associated with Trumpian politics—have led Europe to recognise Turkey as an essential partner in confronting its security challenges. Following years of distancing itself from Turkey and persistently rejecting its bid for permanent membership in the European Union—often referred to as a "Christian club" by Turkish officials—Europe is now eager to strengthen its ties with Turkey, recognising the importance of its military capabilities for defense and the preservation of peace on the continent.⁸³ Sinan Ulgen, a former Turkish diplomat and the director of the Centre for Economic and Foreign Policy Studies (EDAM), noted that European countries that previously believed they could exclude Turkey are now coming to the realisation that such exclusion is no longer a viable option.⁸⁴ With its troops and military bases in North Cyprus, Iraq, Syria, Qatar, Azerbaijan, Bosnia, Libya, Chad, Somalia, and Sudan, underscores Turkey's increasing status as a regional power. Speaking after talks with the Turkish President Erdogan in Ankara on 12 March 2025, Polish Prime Minister Donald Tusk said he brought a "clear proposal for Turkey to take on the greatest possible co-responsibility" for peace in Ukraine and regional stability.⁸⁵ However, the EU's largest members, France and Germany may be more reluctant to include Turkey in such a partnership.

Turkey, a member of NATO, boasts the second largest military force within the alliance. In recent years, the country has embarked on the development of its own military assets, including aircraft, tanks, and naval vessels, while also becoming a significant exporter of armed drones globally, with notable sales to Ukraine. In 2024, Turkey's defence industry exports reached an impressive total of $7.1 billion.[86] The nation has undergone a remarkable transformation, shedding its historical label as "the sick man" of Europe to emerge as a formidable power, no longer susceptible to the foreign imperial ambitions that once led to the disintegration of the Ottoman Empire. Ironically, those very nations that once dismantled the empire now seek security from its modern descendants. This historical irony is profound, as the interplay of cause and effect reveals a Muslim 'Other' that is actively crafting its own destiny and asserting its influence on the global stage, reminiscent of its Ottoman predecessors who once posed a significant existentialist challenge to Europe and Christendom. For centuries, the fear of the Turk became synonymous with the fear of Muslims, perceived as threats along the civilisational frontier. This historical context has contributed to the Islamophobia that is prevalent in Europe and the West today. The deep-seated fears ingrained in the educational systems of these regions have historically complicated efforts to move beyond this legacy and mindset. Nonetheless, the question of whether Europe is willing to integrate Turkey has become a matter of necessity, as its geopolitical significance in an increasingly dynamic global landscape has established it as a regional player that Europe can no longer afford to overlook, but must instead incorporate into its security framework, potentially paving the way for its inclusion in the European Union for which the Turkish president reinforced at the meeting with his Polish counterpart, "The European Union can only halt and even reverse its decline in influence and stature through Turkey's complete membership".[87] Additionally, it is noteworthy that over three centuries ago, Polish King Sobieski III successfully repelled the Ottomans from central Europe in 1683. In a striking similarity, a contemporary Polish leader is advocating for the inclusion of Turks in Europe, not as invaders, but as allies in the defence against another imminent threat, Russia. Furthermore, Erdogan's aspirations for an Islamic nation to secure a permanent seat on the United Nations Security Council, alongside his ambition for Turkey to achieve membership in the European Union, appear unlikely to be realised in the foreseeable future, if at all, they nonetheless reflect Turkey's revitalised confidence.[88] This confidence is particularly significant as Turkey seeks to establish itself as a more prominent power broker on the global stage and as an essential member of NATO. This positioning comes at a time when the United States is reevaluating its commitments to Europe, further underscoring Turkey's strategic importance in international relations.[89]

America does not aim to strengthen NATO or support its member nations; instead, it centres on shifting the financial obligation of maintaining global security to other countries, while the United States benefits from arms sales. This approach is a continuation of strategies previously utilized with so-called third-world militaries—instigating instability, creating a demand for weaponry, and ensuring that warfare remains a profitable venture indefinitely. Europe is being framed not as a partner but as a new arena for economic exploitation under the guise of security concerns. This path reflects the characteristics of a waning empire; the global influence of the American Empire is receding, not due to a deliberate withdrawal, but because the nations that once thrived under that empire no longer need the facade of national power.[90] The financial corporations, technocrats, and elites have extracted resources from the world and are now draining the United States itself. The nation is being methodically stripped of its assets, which are sold off in pieces, including its citizenship to foreign oligarchs and rich individuals. This indicates that the nation has lost its inviolability and is now treated as a commodity, akin to real estate, available to the highest bidder. Similar to their actions in the Global South for decades, they will leave behind a population encumbered by debt, a government incapable of addressing the needs of its citizens, and a security system designed solely to quell dissent. The same corporate oligarchs, financial institutions, and military contractors that exploited the Global South are now employing these tactics in the West.[91]

Historical hindsight demonstrates that during the 19th century, the imperialist nations of Europe systematically exploited various regions, including Africa, the Indian subcontinent, Latin America, and the Middle East, primarily for their rich mineral resources. This exploitation led to significant environmental degradation, severe resource depletion, and substantial economic indebtedness to global financial institutions in these areas. Consequently, these regions became increasingly dominated by authoritarian and corrupt local elites, which further entrenched their dependence on neo-imperialist powers like the United States and the International Monetary Fund that serves in the interest of the rich elites. In recent decades, the psychological and neo-imperialism exerted by the United States over numerous countries serves as a continuation of the long-standing European devastation inflicted upon subjugated populations. The conflict in Ukraine serves as a contemporary example of this neo-imperialistic agenda, aimed at seizing valuable resources for the benefit of the powerful while perpetuating the subjugation of the Other to achieve its goals. The mindset of Western neo-imperialism remains largely unchanged, firmly rooted in a belief in civilisational superiority that echoes the social Darwinist ideologies prevalent in the 19th century.

History will jude figures like Donald Trump and others of his ilk. They possess a notable trait—*animus dominandi*, a concept introduced by the political scientist Hans Morgenthau (d. 1980), which signifies an insatiable desire for power and dominance. These individuals continually push the boundaries of their influence, pursuing new conquests and triumphs until they confront an opposing force that can restrain their ambitions. In this pursuit, human life often becomes a mere byproduct in the quest for profit and advancement, masquerading as progress and greatness within the framework of civilisation.

The European empires of Britain, France, and Spain regarded their endeavour to "civilise" the world as a divine obligation, believing it to be a hallmark of their greatness. In truth, however, their technological prowess coupled with intolerance towards diverse cultures, they bequeathed a legacy characterised by devastation and cruelty. This self-serving and hubristic ambition ultimately led to their downfall, consigning them to the annals of history alongside ancient empires. In a parallel manner, the American ideology of *Manifest Destiny*, which sought to reshape the world according to its own ideals through a perceived divine mandate, is increasingly revealing itself as a mere illusion like "the golden age of America". This is evidenced by the nation's gradual retreat from global engagement and influence. As the principles of *Manifest Destiny* have proven to be a misleading portrayal of America's greatness, the assessment of America's transformation into what it purports to be "history's greatest civilisation"[92] and "the freest, most advanced, most dynamic and most dominant civilisation ever to exist on the face of this Earth"[93] will be rigorously scrutinised by both contemporary and future historians.

The change in America's foreign policy direction, coupled with a sense of hubris and political arrogance reveals an illusion of American exceptionalism that is visibly eroding. While the United States continues to hold economic, military, and technological advantages for the foreseeable future, the foundations of decline have already begun to take root. However, considering these factors, the critical inquiry is not whether the United States will face a decline, but rather when and in what manner it will address the impending challenges. The complexities of global dynamics, economic shifts, and geopolitical tensions suggest that a decline is not merely a possibility but a likely scenario that will unfold over time. As such, the focus must shift to the strategies and policies that the U.S. will implement in response to these challenges.

Ultimately, the decisions taken in the subsequent years will play a pivotal role in shaping the future of American power. The choices made today will not only impact the immediate landscape but will also set the foundation for the United States' role in the world for generations to come. As such, it is imperative for U.S. leaders to approach these challenges with foresight, strategic planning, and a commitment to adaptability in order to navigate the complexities of an evolving global order.

At these crucial moments in history, individuals leave an indelible mark on the world, often steering the course of history in ways that are both profound and lasting. However, it is essential to recognise that not all influential figures contribute positively to the historical narrative. Conversely, there are also those who arise during such pivotal times, instigating discord, division, corruption, and oppression, often disregarding cultural tolerance, religious freedoms, or alliances. The ultimate assessment of Donald Trump's legacy—whether he will be

AMERICA: THE LAST BASTION OF WESTERN IMPERIALISM 379

remembered as a "peacemaker" or as a figure who undermined democracy, leading to his nation's decline—will only be determined by the passage of time.

Will the United States choose to adapt and rejuvenate, embracing a more collaborative approach to international relations that acknowledges the rise of other powers? Or will it mirror the trajectory of past empires that have entered the pages of history!

CHAPTER 22

FROM EUROPE TO AMERICA
EVANGELICAL WHITE CHRISTIANITY AND ISLAMOPHOBIA

Evangelical Christianity has become a major faith movement in the United States over the past fifty years, rooted in the Christian Fundamentalist movement that began about a century ago. A key moment for this movement was the introduction of Charles Darwin's theory of evolution, which prompted various Christian groups to re-evaluate their beliefs and engage in political and cultural advocacy. Additionally, Amrerican Christian Fundamentalism has perpetuated the intolerant attitudes towards other religious groups that have characterised Christendom in Europe since the Middle Ages.

The animosity directed at Islam has persisted from the medieval Christian societies of Europe to the modern evangelical Christian movements in America. This narrative of othering directed at Islam and Muslims has transitioned from Europe to America since the inception of British settlements in the seventeenth century. Humphrey Prideaux's 1697 publication, *The True Nature of Imposture Fully Displayed in the Life of Mahomet*, was made available in America in 1796 and 1798. In early 18th-century literature, Muhammad was frequently referred to as an "impostor". Notably, Benjamin Franklin, a founding father of the United States, in his annual almanack *Poor Richard* (1732-58), drew a parallel between the malevolent actions of the British towards the colonies and those attributed to Muhammad.[1] This anti-Islam trend has persisted into the current political climate, particularly evident in the first term of Trump administration (2017-20), which has garnered significant support from White Christian evangelicals. Ironically, and in stark contrast to traditional religious doctrines, the populism associated with Trump has resonated deeply with Christian evangelicals, fundamentally rooted in religious nationalism. Massimo Faggioli observes that this form of populism signifies America's departure from its identity as a Christian nation. It reflects the emergence of a post-Christian society, albeit one still influenced by a specific brand of religious nationalism. Consequently, it is not surprising that a significant number of Americans perceive President Donald Trump as a messianic figure—especially following his survival of an assassination attempt in July 2024, alongside the various investigations and trials that did not culminate in the end of his political career.[2]

The intense religious nationalism also fosters the narrative of 'the Muslim threat' to America. This narrative continues to dominate news headlines, often utilised for political gain and to divert blame onto this minority group for societal issues. With a steadfast belief in the End Times and the anticipated Second Coming, coupled with Israel's pivotal role in this eschatological framework, Muslims in the United States are frequently positioned as adversaries of the state, undermining democracy and Western values. Regrettably, history has shown that such dangerous rhetoric and actions have previously manifested under regimes like the Nazis. If historical determinism suggests that similar circumstances yield analogous outcomes, there is a profound lesson to be gleaned from our past. Addressing anti-Muslim sentiments in the United States necessitates confronting the fervent beliefs of Christian evangelical groups.

Christian Zionism and Biblical Prophecy

Christian Zionism stems from evangelical and fundamentalist beliefs that support Israel as a divine obligation tied to apocalyptic prophecies. Evangelicals believe the Second Coming of Christ depends on events like the return of Jews to the "Promised Land" and the establishment of Israel. This view dehumanises Palestinians, portraying them as obstacles to prophecy and justifying oppression and violence against them, while providing theological and political support for their suffering and perpetuating Islamophobia.

The recent Israel-Hamas conflict (2023-25) has once more solidified steadfast backing for Israel, reinforcing its claim to Palestinian territories as legitimate owners, a perspective strongly held by Christian and Jewish Zionists rooted in biblical prophecy. Zeynep Conkar, in her article "Does Israel have biblical right over Palestine? Christian Zionists claim so, Theologians disagree," contends that Christian Zionism is founded on the assertion that Israel possesses a divinely sanctioned entitlement to its land; however, she asserts that this assertion is not supported by a robust theological basis.[3] The idea that Israel has a "biblical" claim to the occupied West Bank has gained support from some political leaders, including Elise Stefanik, who aligns with far-right Israeli officials asserting that the entire West Bank is part of Israel's biblical heritage. Joseph Gedeon from The Guardian newspaper in the article "Trump UN nominee backs Israeli claims of biblical rights to West Bank" (25 January 2025) reported that Donald Trump's nominee for US ambassador to the UN, Elise Stefanik, expressed support for Israeli claims to the entire West Bank during her Senate confirmation hearing, a position that could complicate Middle East diplomacy.[4] The Republican congresswoman from New York aligned herself with the Israeli far right, including figures like Finance Minister Bezalel Smotrich and former National Security Minister Itamar Ben-Gvir. When questioned by Democratic Senator Chris Van Hollen about her stance, Stefanik confirmed, "Yes".[5] This belief goes beyond politics; it is central to Christian Zionism, which has significantly shaped U.S. foreign policy and contributed to human rights abuses against Palestinians.

Is it Israel's 'Biblical Right"?

Christian Zionism holds that Israel has a divinely ordained right to the land, but this claim lacks solid theological support. Proponents cite biblical promises to figures like Abraham to justify modern Israel's territorial claims, particularly referencing the Old Testament passage where Abraham is told, "I will bless those who bless you, and whoever curses you I will curse".[6] However, this interpretation is selective. Stephen Sizer, a former vicar and critic of Christian Zionism, argues that the promise in Genesis was specifically for Abraham and not meant for his descendants indefinitely or for a modern nation-state. He states, "There's nothing in the text to suggest that God intended the promise to apply unconditionally or forever," calling the interpretation a "feeble attempt to justify colonisation from the Bible".[7]

Whose Promised Land?

Sizer argues that the Bible contradicts the notion of unconditional land ownership for Jews, asserting that the land ultimately belongs to God and residency is conditional, as stated in Leviticus 25:23. He notes that even Abraham viewed the "promised land" as temporary, anticipating a heavenly inheritance. Sizer emphasizes that residency is based on faith, not ethnicity, and that the land was never intended as a permanent possession.[8]

On the international front, the claim of a "biblical right" is challenged by UN Resolution 242, which calls for Israel's withdrawal from territories occupied in 1967, including the West Bank. The settlements there violate international law, rendering the "biblical right" argument both flawed and illegal.

Christian Zionism is more than a theological viewpoint; it has significantly shaped U.S. foreign policy, particularly since Israel's founding in 1948. Advocates have promoted pro-Israel policies often at the expense of Palestinians. The movement gained momentum when President Harry Truman recognized Israel as a Jewish state just 11 minutes after its establishment.

Under President Donald Trump, Christian Zionism was prominent again, with his administration recognising Jerusalem as Israel's capital in 2017 and affirming Israeli claims over the Golan Heights in 2019—actions that violated international law.

The influence of Christian Zionism persists beyond Trump's presidency, affecting both major political parties. For instance, former Secretary of State Mike Pompeo argued that:

[Israel] is not an occupying nation. As an evangelical Christian, I am convinced by my reading of the Bible that 3,000 years on now, in spite of the denial of so many, [this land] is the rightful homeland of the Jewish people.[9]

By dismissing Israel's status as an occupying force white evangelical Christians have become some of the strongest supporters of Israel, surpassing other demographic groups in their backing.

Christian Zionism and Islamophobia

Christian Zionism stems from evangelical and fundamentalist beliefs that support Israel as a divine obligation tied to apocalyptic prophecies. Evangelicals believe the Second Coming of Christ depends on events like the return of Jews to the "Promised Land" and the establishment of Israel. This view dehumanises Palestinians, portraying them as obstacles to prophecy and justifying oppression and violence against them, while providing theological and political support for their suffering and perpetuating Islamophobia.

Todd Green from Georgetown University, Berkley Center for Religion, Peace & World Affairs in the 2021 article titled "Confronting Christian Islamophobia: Healing Muslim-Christian Relations in the United States" argues that Islamophobia has a long history among Christians. Its roots are both theological and political. Islamophobia has a historical context that extends back among Christians, with its origins rooted in both theological and political dimensions.[10] During the medieval period, European Christians perceived Muslims as adversaries and, ultimately, as heretics, particularly following the First Crusade. This period saw Christians gaining a basic understanding of Islam, recognising it as a monotheistic faith that shared significant figures and terminology with Christianity.

This theological connection prompted Christian theologians to label Islam as a distortion of the authentic Gospel. Although few of these theologians undertook comprehensive studies of Islamic texts and traditions, they were quick to denounce the Prophet Muhammad (PBUH) as a false prophet, alleging that he intentionally misrepresented the teachings of the Old and New Testaments to propagate misleading doctrines and seize authority. Furthermore, these theologians contributed to the formation of simplistic stereotypes about Islam, which continue to endure today, including the perceptions that Islam is inherently violent and detrimental to women.[11]

The theological challenge that Islam presented to Christianity was rooted in the concept of "supersessionism".[12] This is often referred to as replacement theology, is a Christian doctrine positing that the Christian Church has taken the place of the Jewish people as God's chosen covenant community. This belief asserts that the New Covenant established through Jesus Christ has effectively replaced the Mosaic covenant. Similarly, Muslims asserted that the Prophet Muhammad (PBUH) was the ultimate and final messenger of God, and that the Quran represented the last divine revelation. In contrast, Christians believe that Jesus is the perfect and ultimate revelation of God, serving as the divine means for reconciliation with God and the singular path to salvation. This exclusivist perspective within Christianity struggles to accommodate a faith that acknowledges Christians as People of the Book while simultaneously asserting its superiority in terms of access to ultimate truth.

In addition to these theological disputes, political tensions also emerged, best understood through the lens of imperialism. Islamic empires began to take shape during the Middle Ages, leading to both contact and conflict with European Christian kingdoms and empires. Until approximately the eighteenth century, Islamic empires held a dominant position in this rivalry, exhibiting greater cultural and military advancements. However, by the nineteenth century, the balance shifted as European empires rose to prominence and began to impose various forms of imperial control over numerous Muslim-majority regions.[13]

American Christians not only embraced many negative theological stereotypes that had existed among European Christians for centuries, but they also gradually accepted Europe's imperial inclinations. This legacy was evident in their backing of U.S. imperialism in predominantly Muslim areas after World War II, especially during the Cold War.

Many American Christians perceived irreligious communism as the foremost challenge to U.S. global supremacy during the Cold War. However, by the close of the twentieth century, violent Islamist movements emerged as the primary adversary. Consequently, Muslim communities within the United States became emblematic representations of the supposed Muslim threat overseas. This shift led to a range of exclusionary and discriminatory measures targeting Muslims in the post-9/11 context, including registration systems, government surveillance, profiling, and the implementation of the Muslim ban.[14]

It is essential to recognise the significant role that white Christians, particularly white evangelicals, have played in the political and imperial aspects of Islamophobia. Historically, the church has acted as an instrument of empire, evident during the European civilising missions of the nineteenth and twentieth centuries. In the United States, white evangelicals embraced this supportive role for U.S. imperialism. During the war on terror, they constituted a substantial portion of the political foundation for a government intent on invading and occupying nations under the pretexts of "freedom" and "democracy". As Green states:

> In the initial stages of the war, political leaders relied on both theological and political rhetoric to tap into underlying white evangelical hostility toward Muslims and Islam. President Bush infamously referred to the war as a "crusade". General William Boykin claimed that Muslims attacked America because it was a Christian nation. He labeled Islam's god an idol, an agent of Satan, in contrast to the one true God of Christianity.[15]

The aggressive rhetoric from influential white evangelicals not only continued but escalated over the subsequent two decades. Franklin Graham, the son of the esteemed evangelist Billy Graham, asserted that Islam is intent on the annihilation of Jews and Christians, suggesting that the Christian West is compelled to engage in conflict with Islam. Jerry Falwell, Jr., the former president of Liberty University, implied that if more "good [Christian] people" possessed gun permits, "we could end those Muslims before they walked in".[16] Robert Jeffress, the senior pastor of First Baptist Church in Dallas, maintained that Islam is a repressive and violent faith that endorses paedophilia.[17]

This anti-Muslim sentiment has been echoed by many ordinary white evangelicals. White evangelicals constituted a crucial voting bloc for Donald Trump, with 81% supporting him in the 2016 election, a candidate who declared that "Islam hates us." Their backing for Trump's first presidential campaign subsequently translated into robust support for his anti-Muslim initiatives and policies, including the Muslim ban, with three-quarters of white evangelicals expressing approval for the ban just one month after Trump assumed office. Overall, white evangelicals continue to exhibit negative perceptions of Muslims at rates higher than nearly any other religious group, with 44% holding such views compared to only 13% of Jews, according to a 2019 survey conducted by the Institute for Social and Policy Understanding.[18]

Green argues that for an extended period, Americans have observed the manipulation and endorsement of racial and religious intolerance by numerous white evangelicals, aimed at promoting and safeguarding a white Christian America. The backing of discriminatory policies and actions against Muslims—such as detentions, deportations, extraordinary renditions, torture, surveillance, profiling, and the Muslim ban—should be recognised as both a continuation and a reflection of this white Christian nationalist agenda. According to Green:

> There can be no healing between Muslims and white evangelicals until we confront the racism that drives white Christian Islamophobia, including the effort to preserve a white Christian nation. It's racism that animates Islamophobia among white evangelicals and many other white Christians. It's racism that gives Islamophobia its legs and its life. Of course, Islam is not a race, nor are Muslims. But Muslims are treated as a race, as a monolithic entity collectively presumed guilty of harboring violent impulses. They are viewed as a suspect population

deserving of discrimination. It's a form of racism that is based on both skin color and assumed cultural and religious attributes ... Healing the divide between white evangelicals and Muslims is a noble and necessary endeavor. But there will be no lasting healing or interfaith harmony until we situate the fight against Islamophobia within an antiracist framework, until we end U.S. imperial and militaristic projects that disproportionately target Muslim populations, and until we see more white Christian leaders and communities step up and take greater responsibility for combating Islamophobia.[19]

Entrenched racism and discrimination within evangelical Christian fundamentalism significantly hinder the establishment of understanding, tolerance, and common ground between Christianity and Islam. Furthermore, the United States need to militarily disengage from the Middle East and assume the role of a genuine mediator in the Israeli-Palestinian conflict, as this is essential for achieving "lasting healing" between the two faiths.

Christian Eschatology and Islamophobia

The events of September 2001 undoubtedly brought Islam into the forefront of awareness for many Americans, particularly among Protestant evangelicals. However, it is important to recognise that the relationship between Muslims and Christians has a long and varied history, encompassing both harmonious exchanges and violent conflicts. American Protestants have been engaging with the subjects of Muslims and Islam since before the establishment of the nation. A historical perspective is essential for comprehending the current dynamics between these two groups, even if, as David Johnston suggests, there has been minimal change over the past three hundred years.[20]

Islamic terrorism, which had primarily affected Muslims, now resulted in American deaths on U.S. soil. This shift was likely to heighten anti-Islamic sentiment and rhetoric in America. President George W. Bush, aligning with conservative Protestant values, stressed that the "War on Terror" targeted Muslim extremists, not Islam or Muslims as a whole. This position was supported by mainline Protestants, some evangelicals, and the U.S. Conference of Catholic Bishops, though they opposed his decision to invade Iraq in 2003.

David L. Johnston of St. Joseph's University in Philadelphia and the Fuller Theological Seminary in California, in his article titled "American Evangelical Islamophobia: A History of Continuity with a Hope for Change," contends that the white Christian evangelical movement in the United States has a longstanding history of hostility towards Islam and Muslims. This animosity is fundamentally anchored in their rigid interpretation of biblical eschatology, which encompasses beliefs about the Antichrist, Armageddon, and the Second Coming of Christ, particularly the thousand-year reign of Christ in Revelation 20:1-6. In colonial America, some Protestant groups viewed this period symbolically (amillennial), while most expected it as a future event facilitated by the church (postmillennial). The "premillennial" perspective gained prominence in the late nineteenth century, becoming the dominant view among twentieth-century evangelicals.[21] According to Johnston:

> This view [of the premillennialism] sees all of the prophecies in the book of Revelation as "sealed" and only to be revealed in the Last Days. Though premillennialism comes in several varieties, the dominant view sees the "Rapture" of the church precede a time of tribulation for all of the earth's inhabitants—a period during which the Antichrist gathers his strength and authority. The great battle of Armageddon follows. Then Christ with his heavenly and earthly agents destroys his enemies and rules in Jerusalem for a thousand years. Finally, one last battle breaks out, in which Satan is defeated for good and thrown into the Lake of Fire. Then comes the last judgment.[22]

Until the mid-nineteenth century, English Puritans believed the downfall of the Ottoman Empire would lead to mass Jewish conversions to Christianity and the collapse of the Roman Church. During the 1690 "Glorious Revolution," Cotton Mather saw the rise of English Protestantism as a sign of impending collapse for both powers. By the early eighteenth century, prophetic enthusiasm surged in the U.S., with popular publications and itinerant preachers speculating on visions from Daniel, Ezekiel, and Revelation. Johnston argues that this historicist interpretation suggested that contemporary events reflected eschatological signs, such as the drying up of the Euphrates River in Revelation 16:12[23], seen as a sign of the Ottoman Empire's decline.[24]

The culmination of this historicist interpretation was marked by William Miller (1782-1849), a farmer and Baptist layperson, who is acknowledged for founding the mid-19th-century religious movement in North America known as Millerism. His audacious forecasts regarding the return of Christ in 1843 and 1844 ultimately resulted in his downfall and the waning of this eschatological perspective. Influenced by events like the Greek War of Independence (1821-29) and the Russo-Turkish War (1828-29), Miller identified Muhammad as the "false prophet" from Revelation 16:13, claiming he would inspire infidelity and wage war against the faithful alongside the Papacy and earthly rulers. Ultimately, these forces were expected to be defeated in the final battle of Armageddon.[25]

The Millerites faced embarrassment when their predictions failed, damaging the reputation of historicism and leading to a new conservative Protestant eschatology: premillennial dispensationalism.[26] Initiated by British theologian John Nelson Darby (1800-82), this movement gained popularity in the American conservative Protestant community, especially after C. I. Scofield's Reference Bible was published in 1909. Consequently, the "smoke locusts" in Revelation 9 were reinterpreted from symbols of Islam to representations of "unprecedented activity of demons" linked to the rise of the Antichrist.[27]

In the late twentieth century, especially after Israel's establishment in 1948 and Hal Lindsey's 1970 book, *The Late Great Planet Earth*, the link between political and eschatological themes became clear. Premillennialist futurist eschatology began to focus on current events, suggesting that the countdown to the End Times had started, with Israel as the centre of divine interest. Support for Israel was seen as aligning with God, while opposition was viewed as siding with His enemies. However, not all evangelicals shared the pro-Zionist views of figures like John Hagee. Some, including the organisation Evangelicals for Middle East Understanding, advocate for a peaceful two-state solution, with former President Jimmy Carter as a notable supporter. Despite this, most American evangelicals align with pro-Zionist sentiments, contributing to the Christian Right's collaboration with anti-Islamic figures like Pamela Geller and Glenn Beck. However, the one post-9/11 trend is frightening. According to Thomas Kidd in *American Christians and Islam: Evangelical Culture and Muslims from the Colonial Period to the Age of Terrorism:*

> Perhaps the most distinctive change in Christian eschatology since 2001 has been the rise of speculation in some circles that the Antichrist would come from Islam, and particularly that he would be (mis-)identified by Muslims as the messianic Mahdi.[28]

The actions of American evangelicals within the political and geopolitical landscape are not primarily driven by a wish to instigate an apocalypse; nonetheless, they do not actively seek to avert it either. Evangelicals strive to adhere to what they perceive as God's will, and their shared interpretation of biblical prophecy indicates that Israel should extend its borders to correspond with those of the ancient biblical kingdom promised to the descendants of Abraham, Isaac, and Jacob. Furthermore, they believe that the reconstruction of the temple —currently situated at the site of the Al-Aqsa Mosque complex, which is the third-holiest site in Islam—must occur prior to the arrival of the end times. This conviction significantly influences the persistent support and advocacy among evangelicals for the recognition of Jerusalem as the undivided capital of a Jewish state, a stance that was endorsed by Donald Trump during his first term of presidency on December 6, 2017.

The most harmful consequence of religious Islamophobia may be seen in the area of US foreign policy. Chrissy Stroop, a senior researcher with the Postsecular Conflicts at The University of Innsbruck, argues that key figures like former CIA Director and Secretary of State Mike Pompeo played a crucial role in the Trump administration, which increasingly allowed a fundamentalist interpretation of Christianity— markedly antagonistic towards Muslims—that shaped U.S. foreign policy. White evangelicals not only form a vital part of Trump's support base but also represent the most nativist group in modern America.[29]

During the Cold War, many evangelical Protestants, who adhered to a particular set of eschatological beliefs stemming from a 19th-century interpretation of the Book of Revelation and other prophetic biblical texts, often viewed the Soviet Union as the main enemy of Christ. The unexpected establishment of the modern state of Israel in 1948 was used to bolster their interpretations of biblical prophecy. Furthermore, Hal Lindsey's influential 1970 book, *The Late Great Planet Earth*, became a foundational text for the evangelical perspective on "the end times", popularising the concept known as dispensational premillennialism.[30]

Lindsey identified Russia with the kingdom of Magog, which was foretold to assume a prominent role among the forces of evil during the Battle of Armageddon. Following the conclusion of the Cold War, and particularly in recent years, some evangelicals have shown support for Russian President Vladimir Putin due to his advocacy for "traditional values." This has led to difficulties among evangelicals in reaching a consensus on a suitable alternative candidate for Magog. Concurrently, as anti-Islamic sentiments have grown within evangelical circles, predominantly Muslim nations, such as Iraq during the Iraq War, have occasionally been considered as potential candidates, with evangelical author Joel Richardson proposing that the Antichrist may emerge from Islam.[31] According to Stroop:

> The influence of evangelicals' end-times beliefs on U.S. policy toward Israel is a serious concern. Both these strands of popular evangelical thinking—dispensational premillennialism and Islamophobia—can be found in Pompeo, an Evangelical Presbyterian who has expressed support for the views of Islamophobic conspiracy nut Frank Gaffney, and who has vowed to struggle against evil "until the rapture." To be sure, Pompeo has more recently said, "We're all children of Abraham," but when you understand that evangelicals are taught that Jews are descended from Isaac and Arabs from Ishmael, and that there will never be peace between them, that statement takes on a different, coded meaning.[32]

From this perspective, the second term of the Trump administration is poised to influence the future trajectory of U.S. foreign policy regarding Muslim countries, both on the global stage and within domestic contexts. Before taking office in 2025, Trump's cabinet appointments to key positions within the administration reflect a strong presence of pro-Israel advocates, implying a possible inclination towards Zionist viewpoints. Ultimately, the passage of time and the unfolding of historical events will clarify the implications of this persistent historical vilification of the Muslim 'Other' in the contemporary world.

CHAPTER 23

CHALLENGING WESTERN CULTURAL IMPERIALISM AND SOFT POWER POLITICS

TELEVISION AS A MEDIUM IN REPRESENTING THE MUSLIM OTHER IN THE 21ST CENTURY

Addressing Islamophobia by Muslim nations necessitates their capacity to present themselves effectively on the global stage. For an extended period, Muslims have faced significant challenges in establishing a favourable image in the West. This difficulty in self-representation, which aligns with contemporary global standards while maintaining core faith values, has been a notable limitation. However, in the last twenty years, there has been a noticeable shift, characterised by an increased presence of Muslim culture in Western digital media, as well as in regions such as Latin America, Asia, and Africa. This re-energised culture is dynamic and forward-looking, taking pride in its rich historical and cultural heritage and its contributions to the intellectual and spiritual advancement of humanity. Challenging the dominant Western secular ideologies through a moral framework that emphasises fundamental family values, reverence for the elderly, religious principles, the significance of marriage in society, and the distinct roles of men and women is successfully appealing to non-Muslim audiences. This approach stands in contrast to Hollywood's portrayals of promiscuity, the objectification of women, and the disintegration of the family unit, which is made clear by rising divorce rates in contemporary society.

Western ideology is a complex concept that lacks a definitive definition. It is a collection of beliefs that have evolved over time from various cultures and nations. The dominant ideology is often influenced by the United States, which spreads its influence through popular culture and media outlets such as Hollywood films and news channels like CNN, FOX, and SKY. Many of these media sources will claim to serve as intermediaries, providing the public with unbiased information - a comprehensive update that presents different perspectives on an issue. John Molyneux argues that the idea that media news coverage is politically impartial or simply "reporting the facts" cannot withstand closer examination.[1] Nevertheless, this notion continues to be idealised and demonstrated by journalists who meticulously choose their words to create the impression of spontaneous, unaltered responses. Hollywood films attempt to sell to global audiences the illusion of the American dream and the American hero saving the day.[2] But there is an underlying political and cultural imperialism at play – American soft-power imperialism. To this we can also add the European cultural modes.

According to John Tomlinson's book, *Cultural imperialism: A critical introduction* (2002), he asserts that cultural imperialism is a form of critical discourse that defends the autonomy of cultures by presenting them in terms of the dominant Western culture. This discourse is entangled in ironies that arise from its position of discursive power.[3] Likewise, James Petras, in his article "Cultural imperialism in the late 20th century" (1993), discusses the systematic suppression of cultural imperialism as it attempts to interpret and meddle with the cultural elements of various societies in the Third World.[4]

Stephanie Rohac also contends in her work *Cultural diversity versus US cultural imperialism: The film industry* (2007) that the term US cultural imperialism can be attributed to the US government's tactics of influencing foreign governments and institutions to distribute American films and TV shows that endorse American lifestyle, particularly business practices, political ideologies, and cultural beliefs.[5] Similarly, Bethany Avalos, in her 2019 dissertation titled *A regretted legacy? Literary and cultural responses to U.S. imperialism in Hawaii and Puerto*

Rico, delves into the literature of Hawaii and Puerto Rico that reacts to American cultural imperialism. Avalos argues that the U.S. portrays itself as an imperial power to its citizens, commodifying its island territories as paradises. This creates a social and cultural fascination with otherness, leading to a perception of superiority over, yet desire or envy towards, the Other.[6]

In her work *Justice and the Politics of Difference* (1990), Young discusses the lasting impact of cultural imperialism on the perspectives of minorities. She notes that the experiences and interpretations of social life by oppressed groups are often overlooked by the dominant culture, which in turn imposes its own views on these marginalized communities. This dynamic highlight how cultural imperialism affects both the oppressed and the oppressors.[7]

The dissemination of American culture via Hollywood films presents a dilemma for the international community, as it prompts nations to either embrace or be apprehensive about the prospect of Americanisation. While it may contribute to the emergence of a global culture, it also poses a threat to the national sovereignty and identity of other countries. Moving forward, American culture is poised to maintain its significant influence within the global community. Thomas Friedman argues that the current era is characterised by the dominance of American power, American culture, the American dollar, and the American navy.[8]

The United States is often viewed as the sole superpower globally, and its efforts to spread American culture on the international stage could potentially impact its relationships with other countries. The dissemination of American culture through the medium of Hollywood films can be interpreted as a form of cultural imperialism. Hollywood movies serve as a cultural commodity through which the U.S. seeks to exert influence on a global scale in a more subtle manner. American culture stands as one of the primary exports of the United States, as the nation endeavours to market its cultural values to various states worldwide.[9]

Cultural imperialism involves the dominance of a more established culture over others, serving as a subtle form of colonisation. Tomlinson argues that cultural imperialism entails the dissemination of modernity, rather than cultural expansion, resulting in a loss of cultural identity. This process aims to eradicate the cultures of minority groups or those deemed outdated. Ultimately, cultural imperialism leads to the gradual disappearance of local cultures over time.[10]

U.S cultural imperialism aims to dominate markets and control public consciousness. It exports cultural products for economic gain and influences individuals' desires through advertising. This leads to the alienation and isolation of people from their cultural heritage and collective solidarity.

Cultural Hegemony and Worldwide Exploitation

> Imperialism cannot be understood merely as an economic-military system of control and exploitation. Cultural domination is an integral dimension to any sustained system of global exploitation.[11]

Cultural imperialism in the Developing World involves the West's control over the cultural aspects of the popular classes to reshape their values and identity in line with imperial interests. This has been done through traditional and modern means, with the Church, education system, and public authorities historically playing a role in indoctrination. Today, new modern methods are also used to maintain imperial dominance.

The influence of mass media, advertising, and secular figures is significant in today's society, with Hollywood, CNN, and Disneyland holding more sway than traditional institutions like the Vatican, the Bible, or political leaders' public relations strategies. Cultural influence often aligns with political and economic power, as seen in U.S. military actions in Central America and Evangelical groups spreading messages of submission in Indian villages. Intellectuals convene at international conferences to discuss democracy and the market, while television programs offer an escape from reality. Cultural influence can be viewed as a form of non-military counter-insurgency warfare. According to Petras:

> The mass media as instruments of cultural imperialism today are 'private' only in the formal sense: the absence of formal state ties provides a legitimate cover for the private media projecting imperial state interests as 'news' or 'entertainment'.[12]

One method of cultural imperialism involved normalising mass killings by Western nations, portraying them as routine and acceptable actions. The bombings in Iraq were depicted as video game-like, desensitising the public to the severity of these crimes. This desensitisation leads society to view human suffering as less wrong. The mass media also glorifies Western dominance through highlighting advancements in modern warfare tactics, emphasising technological warfare. Present-day cultural imperialism includes "news" coverage that anthropomorphizes weapons of mass destruction and dehumanizes victims in developing countries as faceless "aggressors-terrorists".[13]

The concept of 'internationalisation' is misleading in the present time. Phrases such as "globalisation" and "internationalisation" are employed to undermine unity, togetherness, and ethical principles. Europe and the U.S. disseminate cultural norms that de-emphasise political engagement and reduce the significance of daily life. The American mass media sector advocates for personal advancement, the notion of the "self-made individual," and a focus on self-interest to influence the developing nations.[14]

Following intense military conflicts, invasions, and incursions by Western powers in Muslim territories over the centuries and in recent past, the powerful American dollar, capitalist market economy and mass exportation of American cultural influence now reign supreme on a global scale. This represents yet another manifestation of a crusade against the economically disadvantaged Muslim nations and countries in the Global South. But, the Muslim 'Other' is beginning to challenge this new wave of Western cultural imperialism.

The Muslim 'Other' is assuming control and directly confronting the long-standing criticisms it has faced from the West for centuries. As mentioned in the previous chapter, the education sector in Muslim countries is now actively challenging the dominance of Euro-American academia. However, there is another realm of soft power politics in the Global South that has recently emerged from its dormant state. It is clear that influential and economically strong nations are exerting their cultural influence and exporting their ideology to other countries in the Global South through media, television, and film. Turkish television industry has recently achieved international recognition, securing the third position in global rankings after Hollywood and Bollywood. Turkey stands out as a country whose storytelling prowess has demonstrated the ability to transcend geographical and linguistic boundaries. Turkish television, according to multiple assessments, ranks as the second most widely distributed television content globally.[15]

Turkey and Soft Power Politics

In contemporary international relations, soft power plays a crucial role in achieving foreign policy goals. Turkey, as a rising economic force, prioritises the development of its soft power, particularly in the Middle East and North Africa (MENA) from 2011 to 2020, during the AK Party's second decade in power. Turkey's influence on Muslim-majority countries in the region despite challenges like the 2016 coup attempt, Gezi Park protests, the Syrian crisis, and currency fluctuations has remained strong in the MENA region during this period.

Soft power, introduced by Joseph Nye in *Bound to Lead: The Changing Nature of American Power* has become a key concept in International Relations. Despite ongoing debates about its definition and implications, it is widely used beyond the U.S., with Turkey receiving significant scholarly attention. Nye distinguishes soft power from hard power, defining it as the ability to influence others through attraction. He identifies three main areas of soft power: "culture," "political values," and "policies." Nations can achieve their goals in global politics when others align with them due to admiration for their values and success. In other words, soft power refers to a nation's ability to influence others through attraction and charm rather than force.[16] It involves inspiring others to support desired outcomes and is derived from a nation's culture, history, political ideals, effective policies, and public diplomacy. Hard power elements, like military strength and economic power, can also enhance soft power, depending on how they are applied.[17]

Turkey's soft power grew significantly in the late 1990s and 2000s, driven by socioeconomic and political advancements compared to its Middle Eastern neighbours. A key factor was Turkey's reform agenda aimed at EU membership, initiated in the mid-1990s under Bülent Ecevit's coalition government and furthered by the Justice and Development Party (AKP) after 2002. In its early years, the AKP enhanced Turkey's soft power by strategically incorporating it into its foreign policy, drawing influence from both its identity and international actions.

The rise of the Justice and Development Party (AKP) enhanced Turkey's appeal, especially in the Islamic world, by showcasing "moderate" Islamism's compatibility with democracy. This model attracted interest from Muslim-majority countries facing "authoritarian resilience." Additionally, the AKP's policies appealed to the U.S., which promoted this model as a solution to the global threat of Islamist radicalism following the September 11 attacks.

The interpretation of the "Turkish model" and its characteristics is still debated. Unlike the narrative of the Justice and Development Party (AKP), Turkey can be viewed as a significant Muslim nation that upholds democratic principles, a secular framework, and global economic integration. It is also a candidate for EU membership and has ties to major Western organisations like NATO and the OECD. This broader context shows Turkey's appeal goes beyond the AKP or moderate Islam, though the "model" was not actively promoted by either the AKP or external entities.

Turkey's foreign policy has significantly boosted its soft power. The Justice and Development Party's opposition to the U.S. invasion of Iraq in 2003 improved Turkey's international standing and showcased its role in mediation and conflict resolution. Additionally, Turkey's development aid and "humanitarian diplomacy," particularly its open-door policy for Syrian refugees, have increased its global appeal. These efforts have enhanced Turkey's influence in the Middle East, Western Balkans, and parts of Africa. In 2010, Turkey established the Office of Public Diplomacy to further strengthen its international branding through collaboration with various actors.

In recent years, Turkey's appeal has significantly declined due to domestic changes since the 2010s, characterized by "competitive authoritarianism" and "populist authoritarianism." This has led to a downgrade in global democracy rankings, with Freedom House labelling it "partly free." The political landscape is polarized, with restrictions on press freedom and expression, further exacerbated by the 2016 coup attempt. Economically, a financial crisis that began in 2018 has resulted in high inflation, a depreciating Lira, and rising unemployment. Turkey's foreign relations have also worsened, with strained ties in the Middle East and increased conflicts with Greece, marking a shift from its 2000s regional policies. While recent medical aid diplomacy and involvement in the Ukraine crisis have slightly improved its standing, Turkey's overall attractiveness remains diminished.

It can be argued that Turkey is achieving its most significant ratings in the realm of scripted television series, which contributes positively to its branding on the international stage. Turkey's investment in television series and soap operas has gained global attention, particularly in the Middle East, enhancing its soft power. By incorporating aesthetic appeal, local dialects, and Arabic names, these productions resonate with audiences' interests in conspiracy narratives. Turkish series have become popular in Arab and Muslim households, making Turkey the second-largest exporter of TV series after the U.S. This surge in popularity reflects Turkey's growing influence in the region.

Turkish TV Series Going Global

Hollywood must move beyond its current limitations by showcasing diverse stories from around the world, rather than solely focusing on actors of colour. Turkish storytelling serves as a prime example of how narratives can transcend borders and language barriers, highlighting the importance of embracing global perspectives in the film industry. Hollywood's tendency to centre its stories around its own experiences, beauty standards, and historical romanticisation hinders its ability to truly resonate on a global scale.

The US culture perpetuates cultural chauvinism by promoting an inward-looking tendency, particularly within the vast film and TV industry. Producers often stick to familiar settings like Los Angeles or New York, neglecting the diverse cultures both within the US and globally. This lack of curiosity leads to a narrow portrayal of cultural experiences, with small-town America either idealised or depicted as a place from which to escape. Numerous narratives from various corners of the globe have the potential to resonate with American viewers, provided they are given the opportunity to immerse themselves in them.

Turkish television series, also referred to as Turkish TV dramas, have made a significant impact on a global scale, captivating audiences worldwide from Vietnam to Mexico. Turkish television series draw from Turkey's rich cultural heritage to effectively convey a wide range of emotions. The unique appeal of Turkish dramas lies in their exceptional production quality, attractive and talented cast members, and emotionally charged family-oriented storylines. A recent feature in The Economist (15 February 2024) has shed light on the global appeal of Turkish TV and OTT series. Citing data from Parrot Analytics, the article highlights how scripted Turkish shows have surpassed entertainment offerings from other nations, such as South Korea, to secure the third spot in global popularity rankings, following only the United States and the United Kingdom. This section of the chapter delves into the realm of scripted Turkish TV series, examining perspectives from a film director, a producer, and viewers from a poll conducted in Egypt,

Pakistan, and Malaysia, where these programs have garnered significant acclaim.[18]

The Ottoman culture and the religion of Islam highly value the expression of various emotions in different ways. Film director Murat Pay, known for his extensive work in feature and documentary films, explains that even if a script for a series does not explicitly incorporate religious or historical elements, the poetic essence of the culture naturally thrives within the scripts.[19] This aspect resonates with international audiences, as they delve into the intricate exploration of the complex human existence, which avoids simplifying emotions for mere excitement. From the diverse forms of love, such as love for the opposite gender, family, nation, and even God, to emotions like jealousy, hatred, and anger, these scripts of Turkish TV and OTT series immerse us in a tumultuous ocean of feelings.[20]

The ability to intricately portray a wide range of emotions on screen is a key factor in the widespread appeal of their narratives across various languages and cultures. A notable distinction between Western and Turkish productions lies in the restrained manner in which emotions are showcased by the former. Turkish scripts not only shed light on lesser-known facets of Turkey and its inhabitants for a global audience but also garner praise from experts for their unique approach. By blending contemporary perspectives with spiritual underpinnings, these series offer a portrayal of Muslims and Islam that diverges from the typical Hollywood depiction. According to The Economist:

> Turkish shows are popular not just in the Middle East but also in Europe and Latin America. Last year the three biggest importers of new Turkish shows were Spain, Saudi Arabia and Egypt. The Istanbul Chamber of Commerce estimates that Turkey's television exports earned $600m in 2022; some analysts predict their sales will soon total billions.[21]

Turkish productions have successfully incorporated the authentic emotions of this region into classical drama, resulting in their widespread popularity abroad. In contrast to British and American productions that focus on thrilling and action-packed narratives, Turkish scripts offer a deeper emotional experience. Recent poll conducted in Egypt, Pakistan and Malaysia of viewers of Turkish series, enjoy romantic storylines and acknowledge the diverse range of emotions portrayed in these stories.[22] Film director Pay emphasises that Islamic culture, with its rich values, plays a significant role in highlighting these emotions, such as love and sacrifice, which resonates with global audiences.[23] The foreign audiences also highlight the cultural parallels in family values and societal norms depicted in Turkish series. Meanwhile, the characters connect with the audience due to the common cosmopolitan values they share. Similarly, the Turkish characters underscore the personal values mirrored in these series that resonate with the heritage and culture of their Muslim viewers.

Combining modernity with "their own roots"

Pay states that Turkish dramas not only showcase modernity but also incorporate the rooted traditions of the country, which resonates with diverse viewers. Emre Avsar, a scriptwriter and producer of these TV dramas, further emphasises that the characters in these narratives effortlessly maintain their rich cultural heritage and values, despite their Western attire and lifestyles. Avsar refers to this as "Anatolian wisdom", encompassing values such as respect for parents, parental and filial rights and responsibilities, manners, and moral boundaries. By seamlessly blending modern and traditional identities, these dramas also generate relatable moral conflicts within their narratives.[24] As The Economist states:

> Arab audiences appreciate that Turkish shows depict Muslims as heroes, not as terrorists or cab drivers, as Hollywood often does. The shows also bow to expectations of modesty. Turkish media watchdogs blur alcohol bottles, forbid sex scenes and issue fines for characters kissing.[25]

Turkey's national sentiment is often reflected through the popularity of specific television programs. Turkish TV's 'breakout role' came with the success of "The Magnificent Century", a series based on the life of

Ottoman Sultan Süleyman the Magnificent, the leader of the Ottoman Empire during its peak in the 16th century. Since its premiere on domestic television in 2011, the show has been exported to various regions reaching 70 countries, including the Balkans, Central Asia, South America, Japan, and eastern European countries, and attracting an audience of more than 250 million viewers. This success story demonstrates the global appeal and reach of Turkish drama, as well as foreign TV in general. Referred to as an "Ottoman-era 'Sex and the City'" by The New York Times in 2012, "The Magnificent Century" indulged in the splendour and political intrigue of the Ottoman court, captivating audiences worldwide.

The appeal of "The Magnificent Century" to countries as distant as Russia and Argentina can be attributed to various factors. While the writing and high production values certainly played a role, there is also a unique cultural essence present in Turkish soap operas. Similar to Arabic soap operas, Turkish dramas often revolve around universal themes such as romance, betrayal, and family dynamics. These themes resonate strongly in societies where faith and family hold significant importance in the public sphere.

"The Magnificent Century" presented an intriguing alternative history of an Islamic empire, offering a refreshing change from the typical American film and TV versions of history. This unique perspective appealed to countries in eastern Europe and audiences seeking alternative narratives. However, in order for Turkish television to compete with Hollywood on a global scale, it must successfully penetrate the markets of western Europe and the US.

The trend known as 'Ottomania', which refers to the fascination with Turkish history, culture, and fashion, has not yet fully reached the Western world in contemporary times. This could be attributed to the emergence of newer Turkish dramas like "Endless Love" (Kara Sevda), which have shifted away from the historical focus of earlier shows. For instance, in 2017, the Turkish drama series "Kara Sevda" made history by winning the International Emmy Award for Best Telenovela at the 45th International Emmy Awards held in New York. This marked the first time a Turkish drama series had received such a prestigious award. Subsequently, Univision, the largest American Spanish-speaking TV network, decided to include "Kara Sevda" in its weeknight programming line-up in 2019, making it the first Turkish drama series to be featured on the network. The show quickly became a ratings success for Univision, attracting over three million viewers for its Finale in 2020.[26] Turkish dramas gained popularity in the United States even before "Kara Sevda", with the release of "Hakan: Muhafız" (The Protector) and "Gönül" on Netflix and Telemundo in 2018. Just like in Latin America, Turkish dramas quickly captivated the Hispanic audience in the United States, leading Univision and Telemundo to plan the release of several more Turkish drama series for their viewers.

Since 2002, close to 150 Turkish television series have been distributed to more than 100 countries across the Middle East, Eastern Europe, South America, and South Asia. It is estimated that annual exports exceeded US$300 million in 2016. These figures grew in 2018, where Turkish dramas were distributed to approximately 150 countries, resulting in a substantial revenue of USD 500 million.[27] Forecasts indicate that this figure is set to double by the year 2023. Consequently, Turkey has emerged as the second-largest television drama exporter globally, surpassing both Brazil and Mexico. It is not uncommon to witness groups of Arab or Iranian tourists in Istanbul, exploring the enchanting locations they have seen on screen.[28]

Turkey's soap operas have achieved unprecedented ratings. The allure of these series extends beyond entertainment, as they have sparked a renewed fascination in contemporary adaptations of Ottoman culture. From the opulence of sumptuous gowns to the intrigue of palace politics, these shows have reignited interest in various aspects of Ottoman life, including calligraphy and cuisine. The popularity of these soap operas has even translated into a surge in visits to Topkapı Palace, the historic residence of the sultans, since shows like "Magnificent Century" first aired in 2011. Tourists visiting Istanbul reached 17.5 million in 2023 making it the most visited city in the world according to "Top 100 City Destinations".[29] Combined with the country's diverse array of cultural components, including its historical and cultural heritage and religious traditions, along with its renowned figures and symbols, Turkey exerts an indirect influence on audiences and captivate the public. Consequently, the growth of Turkey's tourism sector has significantly enhanced its soft power.

The Turkish government has also become involved. In 2012, Turkey's president, Recep Tayyip Erdoğan, criticised "Magnificent Century" for focusing too much on palace intrigues rather than Süleyman's conquests. In response, a Turkish state broadcaster produced its own historical drama, "Diriliş: Ertuğrul" ("Resurrection: Ertuğrul"), centred around a Turkic warrior in the 13th century. Originally aired from 2014 to 2019, the series is centred around Muslim Oghuz Turks in the 13th century. Starring Engin Altan Düzyatan in the leading role, it depicts the life of Ertuğrul, the father of Osman I, the founder of the Ottoman Empire. Despite being banned in Egypt, the show continued to be well-received in Pakistan and several other Muslim-majority nations globally. All five seasons of the show were also accessible for streaming on Netflix until 2023. Widely praised by international viewers, the series is often referred to as the Turkish equivalent of 'Game of Thrones'.[30] The show's popularity in mainly Muslim countries including Azerbaijan, Central Asian Turkic Republics, Pakistan, Bangladesh, Malaysia and those with Muslim minorities including India and Kashmir, suggest a yearning for inspiration and solidarity. By May 2020, during the global lockdown due to covid-19, the series ranked as the fourth most in-demand TV show worldwide, as reported by Parrot Analytics.[31] That same year, Pakistan's former prime minister, Imran Khan, commended the show for its "Islamic values", and a statue of Ertuğrul was erected in Lahore. An Urdu version of the pilot episode has garnered 153 million views on YouTube.[32]

Programs such as "The Magnificent Century" and "Dirilis: Ertuğrul" offer audiences in the Global South, particularly in Muslim countries that have endured centuries and decades of colonial rule by the West, a chance to witness the victories of Muslim heroes from history, rather than the typical Western portrayal of Muslims as "terrorists" in need of rescue by all-American protagonists. These shows have a positive psychological impact, boosting morale and instilling a sense of pride in their rich historical heritage, rather than feelings of despair stemming from subjugation, mockery, and impoverishment. Furthermore, programs like these foster a cultural connection between Turkic and Muslim communities worldwide, while also offering non-Muslim audiences an alternative to the predominantly white-Euro-American narratives in history. It is almost as if the Global South is reclaiming its history and legacy, showcasing it on a global stage to challenge the Euro-American dominance in cultural conflicts and soft power cultural imperialism.

Deep human interactions

Avsar refers to the psychological conflicts present in Turkish drama narratives as the 'East-West synthesis', which subsequently impacts the dynamics of relationships within families. A viewer from Alexandria, Egypt, is particularly interested in series that highlight strong human connections and interactions, finding the intimate encounters between characters captivating. Another from Lahore in Pakistan also believes that robust character development enhances the effectiveness of these narratives. Meanwhile, a viewer from Malaysia favours themes revolving around generational conflicts, societal expectations, and family dynamics that stem from these conflicts, all of which serve to enrich the storytelling.[33]

Ultimately, Turkish series offer a unique exposure compared to Western narratives, allowing viewers to immerse themselves in the distinct emotional world of Turkey. International audiences crave new stories and are intrigued by the lives of individuals from diverse societies. Turkish shows have become very popular in Europe and Latin America, especially in Spain, Chile, Argentina, Colombia, Peru, Uruguay, and Bolivia. According to The Economist:

> In the first half of 2023, the three most popular scripted shows in Spain were Turkish, according to Glance, a tv-data firm. Spaniards and Latin Americans have a history of watching telenovelas, so they are used to the schmaltz and time commitment of Turkish programmes. And some viewers seem to welcome a break from the sex and gore of Western television. Spanish-speaking audiences are drawn to the high production value of Turkish dramas. Latin American telenovelas "look cheap"

in comparison, says one purveyor of shows. People in Turkey and Latin America "express feelings unabashedly", says Carolina Acosta-Alzuru of the University of Georgia: "That's why melodrama works in both cultures."[34]

Turkish dramas may have arrived late to Latin America, but they have managed to establish a strong presence in the region. Chile, Mexico, and Argentina are currently leading the way as some of the biggest markets for Turkish dramas worldwide. Moreover, following Greece, the Turkish TV drama phenomenon continued to expand across the Balkans and the rest of Europe, gaining immense popularity in Serbia, Croatia, Bulgaria, North Macedonia, Montenegro, Albania, Bosnia Herzegovina, Hungary, Slovakia, the Czech Republic, Poland, Sweden, Romania, Italy, France, and Spain. Notably, Spain remains one of the most robust markets for Turkish dramas worldwide to this day.

Binbir Gece (One Thousand and One Nights), the second Turkish drama to be broadcast in Greece after *Yabancı Damat*, achieved unprecedented success in the country, attracting 1.1 million Greek viewers with each episode. Surprisingly, even during the highly anticipated opening game of the 2010 World Cup, *Binbir Gece* managed to captivate 30.5 percent of the audience, surpassing the viewership of the match between France and Uruguay. This marked the first time that a TV drama outperformed a soccer game in terms of ratings in Greece. The triumphs of *Yabancı Damat* and *Binbir Gece* paved the way for the introduction of two new Turkish dramas, *Aşk-ı Memnu* (Forbidden Love) and *Gümüş* (Silver), into the Greek market shortly thereafter. Furthermore, *Binbir Gece* went on to become the first Turkish TV drama to achieve global success, being aired in 80 countries.[35] The program's classic storyline unfolds in Turkey, offering a picturesque backdrop that is considered exotic by numerous viewers in Latin America. It is this very exotic allure that appears to have captivated the Latin American audience. From Colombia to Peru, Uruguay, and Bolivia, viewers are enthralled. Its popularity reached unprecedented levels in Chile and Argentina, to the extent that numerous newborns were named, Onur and Sherezade, after the beloved characters of *Binbir Gece* in the continent.[36]

Turkish soap operas quickly gained immense popularity in Latin America. Mega TV of Chile made history by being the first channel to broadcast Turkish dramas in the region back in March 2014. Among these, *Binbir Gece* stood out as the most-watched program during prime time in the country that same year. The overwhelming success of *Binbir Gece* paved the way for the airing of more Turkish dramas in Chile.

In 2023, Bozdag Film Studios in Istanbul, renowned for its successful series such as 'Dirilis Ertugrul' (Resurrection: Ertugrul), 'Kurulus Osman', and 'Destan', has opened its doors to visitors, drawing Turkish series enthusiasts from around the world. As the third-largest film set globally, after Hollywood and Bollywood, and the largest in Europe, Bozdag Film Studios offers an immersive experience that allows visitors to explore the ancient history of Turkey, with a particular focus on the splendid era of the Ottoman Empire. By strolling through meticulously crafted sets exclusively designed for TV series production, guests are transported back in time to witness the magnificence of Turkish history through authentic historical structures.

Upon entering these meticulously designed sets, specifically crafted for the production of television series, guests are instantly transported back in time to a period where historical structures faithfully replicate the splendour of Turkish history. The studio's impressive filming locations feature a variety of renowned landmarks, such as the Inegol Castle, Urgenc Market, Marmaracik Castle, Yenisehir Market, Kulucahisar Castle, Harzemshah Palace, Sogut, and Kayi Tribe areas. Each setting reveals a unique aspect of the Ottoman Empire's heritage, allowing visitors to fully immerse themselves in the diverse cultural tapestry of Turkey.

Kanal D International, a leading media organisation in Turkey, presented its recent successful productions, such as "Yalan," "İnci Taneleri," and "Annem Ankara," which have garnered attention from audiences worldwide. Murat Yancı, the head of Demirören Medya TV Group, highlighted the significant role of Turkish series in enhancing Türkiye's cultural presence on the international stage. "Our narratives resonate universally, which is our most significant asset," Yancı remarked, noting that these productions play a vital role in promoting the nation's "soft power" by disseminating Turkish culture and values across the globe.[37] At the event, Kanal D International presented a selection of series with extensive global appeal. Throughout 2024, numerous popular programs have been aired on television networks throughout Europe, Asia, and Latin America. Productions such as "Zalim Istanbul," "Poyraz Karayel," and "Fatmagül" have captivated audiences in countries like Vietnam, Portugal, and Bangladesh. Shows like "Siyah Beyaz Aşk" have been transmitted in Thailand and Bosnia, while "Kuzey Güney" has reached viewers in Belgium and Luxembourg. Furthermore, the company revealed new agreements that will introduce "Dilek Taşı" to Mexico and "Zalim Istanbul" to Portugal and Africa.[38] In fact, "Fatmagül" attracted an audience of 70 million viewers across the Middle East.[39] Additionally, this trend is evident in soap operas like "Resurrection: Ertuğrul", which, as of August 2020, has exceeded 1.5 billion views on YouTube alone.[40]

The popularity of Turkish soap operas extends beyond Latin America, with a similar trend emerging in the Arab world that has garnered both fans and critics. This trend can be seen as a response to the perceived dominance of Western media in the developing countries, where societies in the Global South are thought to prefer Western entertainment over other options. These cultural exchanges also raise questions about potential connections between seemingly disparate societies, such as Turkey and Latin America, which share many similarities despite their differences. By facilitating the export and import of soap operas, these exchanges have the potential to democratise what was once a privileged industry, leading to a more equal form of globalisation through the spread of cultural products, even if they are mass-produced, conservative, highly commercial, and come from countries with strict censorship laws.

Turkish television series have played a significant role in promoting Turkish culture worldwide and enhancing Turkey's reputation on the global stage. Furthermore, these series create a demand for Turkish fashion, furniture, and various other products showcased in these productions. As a result, the increased positive perception and visibility of Turkey have led to a rise in the country's soft power, leading to a growing interest in the Turkish language and a surge in international tourism. It is no wonder that the filming locations of Turkish dramas have become popular tourist destinations for fans of Turkish television series.

CONCLUSION

The book has elucidated that as both a religion and a comprehensive way of life, Islam presented a formidable challenge to the established religious ideologies of Christianity, as well as to the political dominance of empires such as the Byzantine Empire, the Sassanian Empire, and the Holy Roman Empire. The intellectual and cultural contributions of Islamic scholars and thinkers during this period were profound, as they sought to reconcile divine revelation with the principles of scientific inquiry. This synthesis not only enriched the Islamic world but also provided the Western world with an intellectual heritage that was unparalleled in its depth and breadth at that time.

The revelations contained in the Qur'an, along with the teachings of the Prophet Muhammad—who was divinely chosen to convey this sacred message—served as a catalyst for a transformative movement that would leave an indelible mark on history. The followers of Islam, inspired by these revelations, established a legacy that encompassed advancements in various fields, including mathematics, medicine, philosophy, and the arts. This legacy not only shaped the cultural and intellectual landscape of the Islamic world but also laid the groundwork for the Renaissance in Europe, demonstrating the interconnectedness of human civilisations.

However, ever since the encounter between Islam and Christendom in the seventh century, European perspectives of the Muslim 'Other' have developed significantly. Over the course of centuries, spanning from the Middle Ages to the European Renaissance, the Age of Enlightenment, nineteenth-century European imperialism, and the challenges posed by orientalism in the twentieth century, the perception of Islam has undergone a transformation. Initially viewed as a military menace, it later became a subject of curiosity, respect, admiration, exoticism, and despotism, ultimately evolving into the sole ideological threat faced by Europe and North America in the present day.

The West is engaged in ongoing discussions regarding Islamic orthodoxy, as opposed to fundamentalism. The effects of Islamic resurgence are causing growing apprehension, especially in the United States. The revival of Islamic orthodoxy in the Muslim world inevitably results in conflicts with the West due to the historical relationship between these two civilisations. The lasting impact of fear, animosity, and suspicion left by the Crusades and the mistreatment of Muslims by Crusaders continues to resonate in the minds of Muslims today. John Esposito observes:

> For Muslims, memory of the Crusades lives as the clearest example of militant Christianity, an earlier harbinger of the aggression and imperialism of the Christian West, a vivid reminder of Christianity's early hostility to Islam. If many regard Islam as a religion of the sword, Muslims down through the ages have spoken of the West's Crusader mentality and ambitions.[1]

In 1453, when the Ottoman Turks conquered Constantinople (now Istanbul), the Byzantine Empire's capital, they proceeded to achieve a series of rapid military triumphs. These victories enabled them to establish Islamic dominance over the present-day Balkan countries, including Albania, Bulgaria, Greece, former Yugoslavia, as well as parts of Hungary, southern Russia, and Romania. Despite their failed attempts to besiege Vienna, the Austrian capital, on two occasions, the Ottoman Turks were renowned as "the Scourge of Christendom" due to their relentless success against Christian European armies. Presently,

Muslims reflect upon the remarkable power of Islam during that era with a sense of pride and yearning.

During the early 19th century, the Islamic rulers of the Ottoman, Safavid, and Mughal empires experienced a series of defeats against the European armies. These defeats were primarily attributed to the advanced technology and weaponry possessed by the Europeans. Sultan Abdul Hamid II of the Ottoman Empire, in particular, gained a reputation as the "Sick Man of Europe", as the survival of his political regime relied heavily on forming alliances with European monarchs. Over time, the Ottoman Turks gradually lost their territories in southeastern Europe, either through successful bids for independence or through peace treaties following unsuccessful wars. Meanwhile, Britain and France established colonial control over Ottoman-Muslim lands in the Middle East. Ultimately, the Ottoman Empire met its demise during World War I, leading to the downfall of its sultan-caliph.

While some argue that Europeanisation in the lands of Islam prepared Muslim peoples for self-governance and the establishment of Islamic nation-states similar to those in modern Europe, a closer examination reveals the failure of representative government institutions in Syria, Iraq, Iran, Saudi Arabia, Libya, and the Gulf states, particularly Kuwait. Among these nations, Turkey stands out as the most western-secular nation in the region today, largely due to the influence of Mustafa Kemal. The puppet governments established by Britain and France in the former Ottoman territories in the Middle East were rooted in a Christian European belief in the separation of church and state. As Bernard Lewis points out:

> The notion of church and state as distinct institutions, each with its own laws, hierarchy, and jurisdiction, is characteristically Christian, with its origins in Christian scripture and history. It is alien to Islam ... From the lifetime of its founder, Islam was the state, and the identity of religion and government is indelibly stamped on the memories of the faithful from their own sacred writings, history and experience.[2]

Hence, in their endeavour to eliminate Islam from governance, European authorities were effectively eradicating the Muslim cultural heritage. Samuel P. Huntington, a renowned political scientist from Harvard University, posits that the post-Cold War era has ushered in a new epoch characterised by the clash of civilisations rather than political or economic competition. According to Huntington, the Islamic civilisation is on a collision course with the Western world. Conversely, dissenting voices argue that Islam is not uniformly anti-Western, but rather a diverse and multifaceted religion.

As the West continues to assert itself as the guardian and champion of the New World Order, developing countries of the Global South, especially Islamic nations, perceive this as a division between Europe, North America, and the rest of the world. This persistent approach only serves to deepen the existing lack of understanding between the Occident and the Orient. Consequently, such policies will only exacerbate the perpetuation of prejudiced stereotypes held by the rest of the world against the Orient.

The Europeans should refrain from adopting the crusader mentality. As Bernard Lewis points out:

> The Ottoman Empire affected Europe in a number of ways. For long it was feared as a dangerous enemy - a fear that long survived the danger. For merchants, manufacturers, and later financiers, it was a rich and increasingly open market, and for many also - and here, too, there is a parallel with the modern confrontation - it exercised a powerful fascination. The disaffected and the ambitious were attracted by Ottoman opportunity, and many whom Europe called 'renegades' and whom Muslims called '*muhtadi*' ('those who have found the true path') made brilliant careers in the Ottoman service. Downtrodden peasants looked hopefully to the enemies of their masters. Martin Luther in his 'Admonition to prayer against the Turk', published in 1541, gave warning that the poor, oppressed by greedy princes, landlords and burghers, might well prefer to live under the Turks rather than under Christians such as these. Even the defenders of the established order

were impressed by political and military efficiency of the Turkish empire at its height.³

A considerable amount of literature produced by Europeans focuses on the Turkish threat, with a significant portion of it emphasising the virtues of the Turkish system and how Europeans could emulate it.

In 1999, Turkey commemorated the seven hundredth anniversary of the founding of the Ottoman Empire by Osman Bey in 1299. This important occasion necessitates a more historically accurate examination of European views regarding the Turks and the Ottoman Empire throughout the last seven centuries. While the legacy of the Crusades, the Inquisition, the pogroms, World War II, and the Holocaust continues to weigh heavily on Europe's collective memory, the impact of the Ottoman Empire remains prominent in the Balkans and the Middle East. This prominence can be attributed to the actions of European imperialist powers following the conclusion of the First World War. Therefore, it is essential for Western historical narratives to present a more equitable portrayal of Ottoman history. As we transition from the last millennium into the next, it is appropriate for Europe to accurately situate the Ottoman Empire within the broader historical context. By consciously engaging in this effort, we can work towards alleviating the hatred, animosity, and mistrust that have historically characterized interactions between different cultures and religions, ultimately promoting a more peaceful coexistence among the world's diverse cultures.

The present difficulties encountered by Europeans concerning the Middle East may not originate from historical religious conflicts established centuries ago. Nevertheless, the Muslim community continues to perceive the tensions, hostilities, misinterpretations, and political inconsistencies of the Western alliance as indicative of a struggle between the Christian and Muslim realms. While secularism has supplanted religious authority in the West, the Muslim world still regards European imperial ambitions, which were evident through colonialism until the 1960s, as a contemporary and ongoing crusade against Islam. This perception is further intensified by the establishment of the State of Israel in 1948, initiated by European Jews with the backing of Europe, which Muslims view as a further extension of Western imperialism within the Muslim world. Israel serves as a persistent reminder and symbol of the remorse and atonement that Christian Europe seeks for the historical atrocities committed against the Jewish people. According to Norman Daniel, "If colonialism is a kind of Crusade, all Western manners and customs are 'Christian', and any 'Christian' writer may justly be called a 'Crusader'".[4] According to Norman Daniel, it is worth noting that the Christian missionary lobby celebrated the humiliation of Islam due to the West's technological advancements. They believed that the triumph of colonialism served as proof of Christianity's righteousness.[5]

The late twentieth century marked a significant period of confidence for the Western world. Unlike the devastating wars that occurred between 1914 and 1945, the West had managed to avoid any major conflicts within itself. This newfound confidence led to a reevaluation of its own progress. However, alongside this self-assurance came the collapse of the Soviet order and the rise of smaller power blocs worldwide. Unfortunately, we are now witnessing a different kind of crusade against the Muslim minority populations in Europe, particularly by the Orthodox Serbian government targeting the Muslim Bosnians and Albanians in Kosovo through ethnic cleansing. If the European Union was established with the aim of preventing Europeans from engaging in destructive wars fuelled by nationalism, it now faces the immense challenge of eradicating racial and religious hatred from the European continent. The year 1995 witnessed the most horrific human atrocities in Europe since World War II, with the Bosnian Serb forces committing heinous acts against their Muslim counterparts in Srebrenica. Once again, the Balkans and southeastern Europe seemed to be a testing ground not only for European diplomacy but also for European unity, just as it was before the outbreak of the First World War in 1914.

The Muslims in Bosnia were well aware that there would be no arms sales to support them during the conflict. It is astonishing that it took NATO three years to intervene and broker a fragile peace agreement among the warring factions. In contrast, when Saddam Hussein invaded the oil-rich kingdom of Kuwait, the world swiftly rallied together to confront him, with 24-hour live telecasts of the Gulf War captivating audiences worldwide within six months. The West was quick to defend the legitimate government of Kuwait, which was controlled by wealthy oil sheikhs and lacked true democracy. The pursuit of oil and oil-related interests seemed to take precedence over saving Bosnian Muslim lives. This disparity was once again evident during the Christmas and Ramadan periods in 1998, when the United States and Britain bombed Iraq for denying access to UN weapons inspectors. Despite global condemnation, these countries were prepared to take action again if necessary. Furthermore, when NATO initiated airstrikes against Serbia during the Kosovo crisis, it not only resulted in a flood of Albanian refugees escaping Serbian forces but also reignited the deep-seated animosities between Christianity (represented by the Orthodox) and Islam in the Balkans. It is ironic that the predominantly Christian West came to the aid of the predominantly Muslim Kosovo Albanians by bombing the mainly Orthodox Serbian Slavs on the eve of the millennium's last Easter.

The former Yugoslav government's ethnic cleansing of Kosovo can be seen as a retaliatory act by Orthodox Christianity against Islam, which had ruled the region since 1389 when the Serbian armies were defeated by the Ottoman Turks. The Bosnian and Kosovo crises of the 1990s became a political concern for Europeans due to their geographical location in the heart of Europe, and finding a solution was crucial to maintain their reputation. These crises also pose a significant challenge for the European Union, as they require breaking down national and political barriers to resolve conflicts on the continent. The ethnic cleansing carried out by the Serbs in southeastern Europe, first in Bosnia and then in Kosovo, raises an important question about the potential threat of Islam to Western and European security. However, it is essential to assert that Islam is not a threat in this context. Instead, one could argue that Christian fundamentalism, along with other radical groups and organisations, poses a destabilising factor for European and Western security.

The topic of Islam in Europe has resurfaced amid rising xenophobia and racism in various European nations, notably France. The National Front Party, previously led by the late Le Pen, gained traction by promoting the repatriation of approximately 2 million Algerian Muslim immigrants to Algeria. Furthermore, anti-Semitic factions, including neo-Nazi groups in Germany, the Netherlands, and Denmark, have directed their hostility towards Muslims, especially those of Turkish descent, as well as Jewish communities.

The future of the European Union is uncertain. Its foreign policy shortcomings over the years, coupled with a dependence on the United States for security, continue to weaken European unity. These circumstances can be perceived as threats to national identity and sovereignty. As a result, the West's and Europe's support for Israel in the Palestinian issue, which has reemerged, is likely to influence European views of Islam throughout the 21st century. The consequences of these changes are yet to be determined.

So, how should the West approach Islam in the contemporary world? According to Norman Daniel ,"It is essential for Christians to see Muhammad as a holy figure, to see him, that is, as Muslims see him".[6] If this can be accomplished, it would pave the way for a Christian-Muslim dialogue that extends beyond religious and theological discussions and encompasses the political realm as well. In essence, one approach to fostering understanding with Islam is to delve into the core principles of the Islamic faith. This does not imply that Christians must believe that God spoke through Muhammad, but rather to empathise with this perspective. Such empathy and understanding are essential. By adopting a sympathetic approach, it becomes feasible to immerse oneself in the mindset of Muslims throughout different eras: from the early Companions of the Prophet Muhammad, to the individuals of the prosperous Abbasid era, to the people of the Ottoman Empire, and finally, to the Muslims of today. However, without this spiritual and intellectual exchange, further progress becomes unattainable.[7]

Yet, contemporary Islam represents a challenge rather than a threat to Western societies. It is essential for the West to engage with the multifaceted nature of the Islamic faith and its adherents. Additionally, Muslim governments should perceive contemporary Islam as a chance to adopt political liberalism, heed the aspirations of their citizens, and encourage greater civic participation rather than stifling peaceful opposition movements. These governments ought to work towards the establishment of strong democratic institutions. For example, during the 1990s, Islamic movements like the Algerian Salvation Front and the Turkish Welfare Party participated in democratic processes to attain power, making it vital for Western nations to uphold the democratic principles they advocate. They must distinguish between populist movements and violent extremists, while recognising the right of the populace to choose their governance and leadership.[8]

The West's support for dictatorial and authoritarian regimes in the Arab states of the Middle East has a direct link to the emergence of anti-Western and anti-American sentiments among Islamic groups. As a result, these groups often view the United States as opposed to Islam and unwaveringly supportive of Israel. The Western narrative, which frequently equates radical Islamic movements, such as the Ayatollahs in Iran, with Islam and fundamentalism, further perpetuates the misconception that these violent factions are intrinsically tied to the religion. In reality, religion is often manipulated for political purposes. Henceforth, certain Western analysts contend that a clash of civilisations exists between Islam and the West. Nevertheless, according to Esposito's perspective, radical movements are often driven by opposition to particular Western policies rather than a deep-seated animosity towards civilisation. To gain a better comprehension of the disparities between Western and Muslim societies, it is more insightful to scrutinise the conflicting political, socioeconomic, and cultural interests rather than ascribing them solely to a clash of civilisations.

The inclusion of religion in discussions is often questioned by Western academics and individuals who are in agreement with Islam's reasoning and logic until the topic of religion arises. This is where the West's understanding reaches its limit. The West's alignment with Islam only goes so far before encountering a barrier. This is not where Islam's rationality, logic, and understanding ends, but rather where the

West's does. The question should not be why Muslim scholars, academics, or individuals bring religion into the discussion and their research, but rather why does the West insist on secularism and atheism? The secular West does not have the right to impose its biases and prejudices on Muslims due to its history with an irrational and illogical religion, ideology, or belief system that does not belong to Muslims. One could make the case that, despite religion, medieval and early modern Islamic civilisation did not impede critical thinking, scientific thought, and rationality. However, the later centuries presented a different picture as the Ottoman Empire experienced a gradual decline from the eighteenth century onwards. The medieval and early modern Islamic civilisation gave rise to numerous scholars known for their intellectual prowess and devotion to their faith. This tradition of rigorous scholarship is experiencing a revival today. The Western world must come to terms with this fact, as it cannot dictate the parameters of Muslim discourse or control the topics of discussion within the Muslim community. Western reluctance to acknowledge the academic contributions of Muslim scholars today, stemming from their adherence to Qur'anic research methodologies that promote epistemological unity, reveals a lack of understanding and a missed opportunity to embrace diversity in knowledge.

The intellectual leaders of the Muslim community surpass their Western counterparts, as their intellects are illuminated by the profound insights of Islamic scholarship. They placed great emphasis on reason and maintained a strong dedication to critical analysis, from the Golden Age of Al-Andalus to the illustrious halls of medieval Baghdad. This tradition continued in the court of Süleyman the Magnificent in the 16th century where his *kanuns* or laws were systematically codified and harmonised with divine Revelation.

Islamic scholars were architects of wisdom, exploring mathematics, astronomy, medicine, and philosophy with profound mastery. Their brilliance stemmed from their religion, not in spite of it. Islamic civilisation's intellectual prowess harmonised with faith, as reason and critical thinking were integral to Islam. The Qur'an served as a guiding beacon for seekers of knowledge, not a constraint on intellect. In

Islamic thought, reason and religion worked in tandem, challenging Western misconceptions. The genius of Islamic civilisation elevated both mind and spirit, a stark contrast to the West's imperfect balance of faith and reason. The resurgence of Islamic intellectualism, characterised by an Islamic Enlightenment that incorporates God rather than relegating Him to the distant heavens as the West has done, along with an Islamic Renaissance, signifies the conclusion of the Western Dark Ages of colonisation and imperialism.

The Muslim philosophers of the medieval period were moving towards comprehending the Almighty Allah, and that was their journey. It is an incredible journey, and people are now starting to recognise it. All that knowledge was wiped out, but the discovery of it for the Muslim will strengthen their belief, structure, gratitude, amazement, and awe at the miracle of the Revelation. When they see Islam for what it truly is in terms of its manifestation, their awe for the Almighty will be overwhelming. The religion remains intact, but our understanding of the manifestation of Islam in history is completely confused and obliterated. Once that is discovered, that is the moment when the Muslims will have the strength to be the witness and the refuge in the storm that is unfolding.[9]

The concepts of East and West should be eliminated from both History and the collective mindset of historical circles. These concepts only serve to perpetuate divisions and foster racism and hatred among people of different cultures. In reality, there are no distinct races in the world, as there is only one human race. The progress of humanity has been achieved not through assimilation, where a minority group becomes like the majority, but through the celebration of cultural diversities. Historians should not interpret history based on ethnicity or nationality. The world has witnessed numerous horrors, especially in the twentieth century, due to nationalism. The primary objective of delving into history is to gain insights from previous blunders and avert their repetition in the current era. Nevertheless, it seems evident that as a collective society, mankind has failed to assimilate the lessons from its past errors. In the new millennium of the twenty-first century, animosities, hatred, and ethnic cleansing continue to prevail in most societies today, even in the heart of Europe. Despite the long-standing dominance of eurocentrism over other cultures, the world once again witnesses the suffering of people based on their ethnic and religious backgrounds.

Instead of engaging with the narrative of civilisational conflict that often dominates global political discussions, it is far more pertinent to advocate for intercultural dialogue as a pathway to achieving the peace that humanity so desperately needs. In light of this historical context, it becomes evident that fostering intercultural dialogue is essential for overcoming the narratives of conflict that have often overshadowed the rich tapestry of human interaction. By recognising the shared heritage and contributions of diverse cultures, we can move towards a more inclusive understanding of our collective history. This approach not only honours the complexities of our past but also paves the way for a future where collaboration and mutual respect can flourish, ultimately leading to the peace that humanity urgently requires.

The three major monotheistic religions of the world have a shared ancestry. The followers of these religions, who all believe in the existence of one Supreme Being, should embrace this common foundation and not let it slip away. Throughout history, we have witnessed the unity, accomplishments, and creativity of these faiths. Whether it was during the era of Muslim Spain in the eighth century or the reign of the Ottomans, Safavids, and the Mughals, all three religions coexisted peacefully and harmoniously for many centuries. Islam should not be perceived as a threat to the world.

Pope Paul VI's open-minded approach during the Second Vatican Council played a crucial role in establishing better relations between the two faiths. He expressed regret over the fact that many Christians had been raised with a mindset of hostility towards Islam, which hindered any meaningful understanding of the religion. As the Catholic Church made preparations for the new millennium, it demonstrated a readiness to extend apologies to Muslims, aiming to overcome the deep-rooted sentiments of mistrust, animosity, and ignorance. Through this act of goodwill from the head of the Catholic community, there arose a sense of optimism that both civilisations could advance and embrace the common values highlighted in the Qur'an, which are shared among the three monotheistic faiths. Islam has long demonstrated the oneness of the Almighty and has called upon all individuals to surrender to His divine will. For over 1400 years, the Qur'an has advocated for interfaith dialogue, encouraging Muslims, Christians, and Jews to pursue a common understanding:

> Say: "O People of the Book!
>
> Come to common terms as between us and you:
>
> That we worship none but God;
>
> That we associate no partners with Him:
>
> That we erect not, from among ourselves,
>
> Lords and patrons other than God."
>
> If they then turn back,
>
> Say: "Bear witness that we (at least)
>
> are Muslims bowing to God's Will." (Sura Al-I-Imran)

Islam calls for unity among all believers rather than hostility and violence. Portraying Islam solely through the lens of radicalism is not only unfair to the faith but also shows a lack of reverence towards the Almighty.

Human nature, as it often reveals, harbours a fear of the unfamiliar and the unknown, leading to the ostracism of those deemed different, particularly in times of crisis. Over the past two centuries, Europe, buoyed by a belief in its economic and military dominance, has viewed itself as a civilising force, characterising non-White, non-European populations as 'barbaric' and 'backward.' This conviction that power equates to righteousness has justified the occupation, invasion, colonisation, extermination, and enslavement of various civilisations and cultures across the Americas, Africa, Asia and the Middle East. A similar ideology of might equating to right is observable today within the US-led global order, which is often framed in terms of freedom and democracy. Europe's apprehension regarding Russia amid the Ukraine conflict overlooks Russian security concerns related to Ukraine's aspirations to join the Western defence alliance, NATO, which brings Western military forces to its borders and poses a threat to its security. When nations fail to recognise or choose to ignore historical parallels in contemporary events, they are prone to repeating past mistakes. This deterministic mindset has resulted in numerous errors by nations. History serves as a teacher, urging us to learn from previous missteps to avoid their recurrence. The ongoing Ukraine-Russia conflict, particularly Russia's apprehensions about Ukraine's potential NATO membership, bears striking similarities to the Cuban Missile Crisis of 1961. The US's vehement opposition to Soviet missiles stationed in Cuba, a mere ninety miles from the Florida coast, triggered significant alarm in Washington, leading President John F. Kennedy to impose a blockade on Cuba and placing the world on the brink of World War III.

In the context of the Israel-Gaza conflict (2023-2025), the unwavering backing provided to Israel by the European Union, alongside the unconditional support from the United States, has once more highlighted the civilisational divide prevalent in the world—us versus them. Although the actions of Hamas on 7 October 2023 are indefensible, the disproportionate response from Israel, which has resulted in the forced displacement of millions, thousands of fatalities, and the devastation of Gaza's infrastructure, suggests a collective complicity among humanity in averting such deliberate actions.

The hesitation of the European Union to welcome Turkey into its ranks serves as yet another illustration of the divide between Christianity and Islam. If the European Union is genuinely dedicated to combating the rising Islamophobic attitudes within its borders, it should extend full membership to Turkey. Turkey's pursuit of strategic autonomy in its foreign policy has led to tensions with the European Union. The nation's relationships with Russia, its views on NATO's expansion, and its response to the ongoing humanitarian crisis in Gaza illustrate a departure from EU interests. Turkey's approach to strategic autonomy is notably in conflict with EU foreign policy, especially regarding the situation in Gaza.

Turkey has established its independent foreign policy in response to the regional dynamics, addressing issues such as the Arab-Israeli conflict by advocating for the Palestinian cause and tackling the Cyprus issue by challenging the European Union's partial stance regarding the rights of Turkish Cypriots on the island. This approach underscores Turkey's role as a stabilising force in both the Middle East and the Eastern Mediterranean. However, the EU has expressed concerns over Turkey's growing ties with Russia, particularly in the energy sector, viewing it as a threat to European unity. In relation to Gaza, Turkey has been outspoken, condemning what it sees as the EU's lack of action in response to Israel's violations of human rights. It is important to acknowledge that the era of the diminished Ottoman Empire, which was exploited and divided by European imperialist powers for their own benefit, has long since passed. In its stead, a more assertive Turkey has emerged, prepared to address the challenges within the geopolitical landscape of the Middle East, prioritising its own national interests above all others.

When Europe and the West conscioulsy confronts its dark past without continuing to demonise and marginilise the Other then it will begin to heal. While for centuries it perceived Islam, the religion, as incompatible with its so-called Western secularist-consumer-materialist values and Judeo-Christian tradition, yet it has been proven again and again that its inherent intolerance of the marginalised manifested its ugliness that lies at the core of its collectvie consciousness. The white dominated Christain Church both in western Europe and Russian orthodox east that sanctioned or simply remianed complicit during the Spanish inquisition against Muslims and Jews that began in 1478 and continued until 1834, pogroms against the Jews by Tsarist Russia, culminating in the 'final solution' of the Jewish problem during World War II by the Germans, as well as the slave trade of Africans by Britain, France, Spain, Portugal, the Netherlands, and Belgium with its social repercussions in the United States, are not easily forgotten.

Europe and the West must consciously address their troubling history without perpetuating the demonisation and marginalisation of others in order to initiate a process of healing. For centuries, Europe and the

West have viewed Islam as fundamentally at odds with their secular, consumer-driven, materialistic values and Judeo-Christian heritage. However, it has repeatedly been demonstrated that this inherent intolerance towards marginalised groups reveals a deep-seated ugliness within the collective consciousness. The largely white Christian Church, encompassing both Western Europe and the Orthodox East, either endorsed or remained complicit to numerous historical injustices and atrocities. These include the Spanish Inquisition targeting Muslims and Jews from 1478 to 1834, the pogroms against Jews in Tsarist Russia (1821-1920), culminating in the horrific 'final solution' executed by the Germans against the Jews and other minorities during World War II, and the genocide committed against Bosnian Muslims by Orthodox Serbs in the latter part of the twentieth century. Moreover, the European Zionist colonialist presence in Palestine, which has persisted since 1948, has failed to acknowledge the historical injustices that were perpetrated against the Jews by their Christian European counterparts. The frequent images broadcasted on our television screens depicting the plight of millions of displaced Palestinians evoke a haunting resemblance to the harrowing suffering experienced by Jews in the concentration camps during World War II. Additionally, the transatlantic slave trade, perpetrated by Britain, France, Spain, Portugal, the Netherlands, and Belgium, has left lasting social repercussions in America that cannot be easily dismissed.

Throughout history, no culture or civilisation characterised by hubristic ambition has managed to endure or avert its eventual downfall. The United States of the 21st century serves as a prime example of such a civilisation. The gradual and protracted decline of America has commenced. Similar to other prominent empires throughout history, such as the Roman and Ottoman empires, the process of decline and eventual disintegration may unfold over centuries. However, the factors contributing to the decline of the American Empire have been set in motion over the past several decades, and Donald Trump may be the president who presides over the erosion of the democratic institutions that have historically represented its most significant strength.

No culture or civilisation has attained greatness in isolation. There has consistently been, and will continue to be, various forms of cross-cultural interactions. The impact of Islam on the development of Western civilisation is significant and should not be overlooked. Unfortunately, the narrative of Islamic influence on Western civilisation is often absent from the curricula of many universities in Western nations. When it is addressed, only a fraction of the extensive fourteen-century legacy is briefly examined, especially in comparison to the broader history of Western civilisation. Such deficiencies in historical education perpetuate cultural prejudices and misconceptions about Muslims that constitutes over one-third of the global population and is frequently misrepresented.

When we come to understand our mortality, the colour of our skin, the hue of our eyes, the language we communicate in, and our ethnic background will become irrelevant as we transition from this life to the next. In that moment of profound realisation, we stand alone, subject to the consequences of our actions, words, and deeds, which ultimately determine our path to salvation or condemnation. Ultimately, truth will prevail over falsehood and malevolence. The irony lies in the fact that the Islam which Europe and the West have vilified for the past fourteen centuries is the same Islam that has consistently reminded humanity of its profound truths:

> Among His Signs is the creation of the heavens and the earth, as well as the diversity of your languages and colours; indeed, in this, there are Signs for those who possess knowledge.[10]

Throughout history, it has been the inherent goodness in humanity that has consistently confronted evil. This inherent goodness will be humanity's eventual triumph.

A concluding remark to encapsulate this book's exploration of viewing others from a standpoint of superiority is to advocate for a transformation of that perspective. Over six decades ago, Yuri Gagarin (d. 1934-1968) became the first human in space, likely experiencing the "overview effect", where viewing Earth from above highlights the insignificance of borders and conflicts related to race, religion, and economics. This phenomenon underscores the planet as a singular, interconnected entity. Astronaut and author Ron Garan argues that fostering a planetary perspective can help tackle many of humanity's and Earth's challenges:

> When I looked out the window of the International Space Station, I saw the paparazzi-like flashes of lightning storms, I saw dancing curtains of auroras that seemed so close it was as if we could reach out and touch them. And I saw the unbelievable thinness of our planet's atmosphere. In that moment, I was hit with the sobering realization that that paper-thin layer keeps every living thing on our planet alive, I saw an iridescent biosphere teeming with life," he continues. "I didn't see the economy. But since our human-made systems treat everything, including the very life-support systems of our planet, as the wholly owned subsidiary of the global economy, it's obvious from the vantage point of space that we're living a lie. We need to move from thinking economy, society, planet to planet, society, economy. That's when we're going to continue our evolutionary process. And when we can evolve beyond a two-dimensional us versus them mindset, and embrace the true multi-dimensional reality of the universe that we live in, that's when we're going to no longer be floating in darkness … and it's a future that we would all want to be a part of. That's our true calling.[11]

At that moment, he realised that humanity needs to reassess its priorities.

EPILOGUE

Throughout history, certain individuals have emerged at critical junctures, significantly influencing the trajectory of events. These pivotal figures often possess a unique vision and the ability to inspire others, allowing them to propel their nations to unprecedented achievements within the annals of civilisation. The question of whether it is individuals who shape history or events that shape leaders remains a topic of considerable debate among historians, prompting a deeper exploration of the interplay between personal agency and historical context.

To illustrate this dynamic, we can examine the profound effects of influential figures such as Karl Marx and Vladimir Lenin on global history. Marx's revolutionary ideas on class struggle and economic theory laid the groundwork for a new political ideology that would inspire countless movements and revolutions around the world. His writings not only critiqued the capitalist system but also provided a framework for envisioning a more equitable society. Lenin, on the other hand, took Marx's theories and applied them to the specific conditions of early 20th-century Russia, leading to the Bolshevik Revolution and the establishment of a communist state. The ripple effects of their ideas reshaped not only Russia but also had far-reaching implications for the global balance of power, influencing the course of the 20th century and beyond.

Similarly, Mustafa Kemal Atatürk's transformative reforms in Turkey during the early 20th century serve as a compelling example of an individual reshaping a nation. As the founder of the Republic of Turkey, Atatürk implemented sweeping changes that modernised the country, promoting secularism, education, women's rights, while allowing his citizens to practice their religion in their native language. His aspiration for a progressive, Western-aligned Turkey that embraced a unique Turkish-Muslim identity not only altered the trajectory of his own nation but also set a precedent for reform in other Muslim-majority countries. The repercussions of his leadership continue to resonate, as nations grapple with the balance between tradition and modernity in the contemporary world.

Atatürk's vision extended beyond Turkey's borders, as he sought to position Turkey as a modern nation-state in a rapidly changing world. His emphasis on nationalism, secularism, and modernisation resonated with various movements across the globe, particularly in post-colonial contexts where nations were grappling with their identities and governance structures. His ideas influenced leaders and reformers in other countries, particularly in the Middle East and North Africa, where similar struggles for modernisation and national identity were underway.

Moreover, the historical significance of Muhammad as both a statesman and a religious leader cannot be overstated. His role in unifying the Arabian Peninsula under the banner of Islam marked a turning point in human history, leading to the establishment of a major world religion that would influence billions of lives. Muhammad's leadership extended beyond spiritual guidance; he implemented social reforms, established legal frameworks, and fostered a sense of community among diverse tribes.

Muhammad's teachings also laid the groundwork for interfaith dialogue and relations. His interactions with Jews and Christians in Medina exemplified a model of coexistence and respect for other faiths.

This aspect of his legacy is particularly relevant in today's globalised world, where understanding and cooperation among different religious and cultural groups are essential for peace and harmony. His legacy continues to shape the political, social, and cultural landscapes of Muslim nations today, illustrating the enduring impact of individual leadership on the course of history. As Michael Hart aptly states:

> My choice of Muhammad to lead the list of the world's most influential persons may surprise some readers and may be questioned by others, but he was the only man in history who was supremely successful on both the religious and secular levels.
>
> [...] Furthermore, Muhammad (unlike Jesus) was a secular as well as a religious leader. In fact, as the driving force behind the Arab conquests, he may well rank as the most influential political leader of all time.
>
> [...] We see, then, that the Arab conquests of the seventh century have continued to play an important role in human history, down to the present day. It is this unparalleled combination of secular and religious influence which I feel entitles Muhammad to be considered the most influential single figure in human history.[1]

In the modern era, Muhammad's life and teachings continue to inspire movements for social justice, human rights, and ethical governance. His emphasis on compassion and community service resonates with contemporary efforts to address issues such as poverty, inequality, and environmental sustainability. Moreover, as the world grapples with challenges related to religious extremism and misunderstanding, revisiting Muhammad's message of peace, tolerance, and respect for diversity is more crucial than ever.

If the complex historical events that have transpired between Christendom and Islam, along with the interactions between Western societies and Islamic cultures since the seventh century, can be traced back to a singular figure, Muhammad, it raises an important question regarding the perception of this individual by the Christian West in the 21st century. An examination of historical attitudes towards Muhammad in Europe reveals a pressing need to reevaluate these past perspectives. For Muslims, Muhammad transcends the role of a mere historical figure; he is regarded as the final prophet in a long line of messengers sent by God to guide humanity. His life and teachings serve as a paradigm for ethical behaviour, spiritual devotion, and social justice. Without a sincere engagement with Muhammad, the central religious figure of Islam, by the various Christian denominations, authentic interfaith dialogue remains unattainable.

In this context, the Christian West is encouraged to approach Muhammad with an understanding of his significance within the Islamic faith. This involves recognising the profound respect Muslims hold for him, as well as the impact of his teachings on the development of Islamic civilisation. Furthermore, it is essential for Christians to engage with the historical and theological nuances that shape Muslim views of Muhammad, which may differ significantly from the narratives often presented in Western discourse.

By fostering a dialogue that emphasises mutual respect and understanding, the Christian world can gain a more nuanced appreciation of Muhammad's role in shaping not only Islamic identity but also the broader historical interactions between Islam and Christianity. This perspective encourages a move away from stereotypes and misconceptions, promoting a more informed and empathetic engagement with the complexities of interfaith relations in the contemporary world.

Keith Ward, an English Anglican priest, philosopher, and theologian, is a member of the British Academy and serves as a priest in the Church of England. He held the position of Regius Professor of Divinity at the University of Oxford from 1991 to 2004. He asserts that Muhammad was a true prophet of God, a view that is shared by nearly all of his fellow Christian theologians. Below are several key points he discussed during an interview on the Blogging Theology podcast on May 2, 2021:

> I believe that Muhammad was a true Prophet of God, divinely appointed, and that the Qur'an represents a form of God's Revelation. As a Christian and a follower of Jesus, I do not identify as a Muslim. However, I strongly oppose the notion that Islam inherently rejects Christianity. This perspective is inaccurate. From my understanding,

Islam, as I perceive it, and Muhammad himself may not have been well-versed in Christianity. It seems he opposed certain views held by the Christians he encountered, which I acknowledge, but I do not share those views, nor do my colleagues. While there are distinct differences between the two faiths, I maintain that Muhammad was a legitimate Prophet of the one true God, who challenged a simplified Christian interpretation that suggests a belief in three gods or distinct entities within God. His stance was justified. I perceive the differences between Islamic and Christian traditions to be comparable to the distinctions I have with conservative Evangelical Christians.

I acknowledge the existence of differing perspectives, and I can respect those who hold views contrary to my own. I do not claim infallibility; rather, I recognise that my understanding may not be absolute. As expressed in the Quran, "God will decide who is right". It is essential to remain true to one's own feelings.

I choose to follow Jesus because I perceive him as a human embodiment of God's wisdom and love. The core message he conveys is that God's love is unconditional and extends to everyone. While some Christians may not share this belief, there are Muslims who do, albeit they may avoid terms such as "Incarnation" or "Trinity", which are considered taboo in their tradition. If we accept that religious language is inherently fluid and that our grasp of God's nature is limited, then Islam and Christianity should not be viewed as entirely separate religions. Instead, they represent different pathways to understanding God, and I often find myself closer to many Muslims than to numerous Christians.

I am aware that you are familiar with the contributions of Wilfred Cantwell Smith, the founder of Harvard University's Center for the Study of World Religions. He was a distinguished scholar in the field of Islam. Smith advocated for a shift away from the term "religion" as if it categorises distinct, monolithic belief systems—suggesting that all Christians belong to one block and all Muslims to another. Instead, he proposed that we should focus on the various pathways of faith and approaches to the divine. I resonate with this perspective, as discussing religion in such a manner can be limiting […]

> Some Christians I know hold beliefs that diverge significantly from my own, despite their use of the name Jesus, which seems to refer to a different figure altogether. This situation highlights a profound divide between the perspectives of academic theologians and many congregants in the United States, Africa, and other regions. These individuals often adopt an exclusivist stance, asserting that only Jesus can lead one to God. I find myself questioning this viewpoint: if Moses did not know Jesus, does that mean he is condemned? What about the other prophets who also lived without knowledge of Jesus? The responses to these questions often reflect a binary, absolutist, and exclusive worldview that starkly contrasts with my own beliefs. "I maintain that Jesus is the saviour of the world, not merely of a select group". Many of my academic colleagues share this perspective—asserting that God is the ultimate saviour of the world, with Jesus serving as a mediator of God's presence. This belief does not exclude others, as we affirm that God's desire is to save all of humanity. I have also found common ground with many of my Muslim friends, particularly through my close association with the Oxford Islamic Centre, as I believe they share a similar understanding.[2]

A significant openness to interact with various religious traditions is evident, which plays a crucial role in overcoming cultural divides. By stepping outside our individual comfort zones, we are able to recognise common themes and similar spiritual dynamics that transcend the confines of specific faiths. This exploration not only enriches our understanding of different belief systems but also fosters a sense of unity among diverse groups. In this context, modern theologians are especially equipped to address these intricate challenges, as they possess the tools and insights necessary to engage thoughtfully with the complexities of our increasingly interconnected global society. Their expertise enables them to facilitate meaningful dialogues that promote mutual respect and understanding among different faith communities.

Finally, one rationale for incorporating an epilogue in this book can be articulated as follows. The existence of this book and similar works is encapsulated in the first image selected for the cover, which features a

14th-century Iranian miniature painting from Tabriz. The division between Christendom and Islam traces back to the moment Muhammad received his initial revelation from God around 610 CE. It is remarkable that a man from seventh-century Arabia was chosen by an omnipotent and omniscient being, recognised by humanity as God, Yahweh, or Allah—the same Divine Being who communicated with Moses and Jesus—thereby creating a significant schism between two civilisations that have profoundly shaped the world as we understand it. The Christian world primarily represented by the West, the Orthodox East, and Latin America, attributes its eventual prominence and Judeo-Christian heritage to the three-year ministry of Jesus and the 'true' Christianity established by St. Paul. Conversely, Muslims contend that the founder of Islam, Muhammad, and his 23-year ministry have left a political, social, cultural, and religious legacy that has endured for over fourteen centuries, rivalling, if not surpassing, that of Christianity. Michael Hart's claim that Muhammad is "the most influential single figure in human history" holds validity not only for the reasons he presents but also because no other historical figure has his name invoked alongside Allah from minarets and places of worship five times daily around the world, calling humanity to pause for contemplation and prayer, thereby encouraging us to prioritise our lives within the broader context of the universe and to honor our Creator. Furthermore, the divine revelation he received served as the inspiration for the second image depicted on the cover of my book: the intellectual revolution that transformed not only the path of Western civilisation but also influenced the broader narrative of human history. As emphasised in the concluding chapter, the call from Islam to Jews and Christians to "come to common terms" continues to hold significance in our present-day troubled world.

NOTES

INTRODUCTION

1. B. Lewis, *Cultures In Conflict - Christian, Muslim, and Jews in the Age of Discovery* (New York: Oxford University Press, 1995), 9-13.
2. The term 'Western' is commonly used to refer to Western Europe and the Americas, in contrast to the Islamic 'East'. It is advisable, therefore, to utilise the term 'occidental' when discussing the civilisation of the white man as a whole. This choice of terminology also serves the purpose of reminding us that Marxism, just like parliamentary democracy, is a product of European culture.
3. H. Djait, *Europe and Islam*, trans., P. Heinegg (Berkeley: University of California Press, 1992), 21.
4. Amy Allen, *The End of Progress: Decolonizing the Normative - Foundations of Critical Theory* (New York: Columbia Unuversity Press, 2016), 1.
5. P. Valery, *An Anthology*, James R. Lawler, ed. (Princeton University Press, 1956), 94.
6. See O. Spengler, *The Decline of the West*, trans., Charles Francis Atkinson (New York: Oxford University Press, 1991), 12.
7. See Spengler, *The Decline of the West*, 15ff
8. Spengler, *The Decline of the West*, 16.
9. See Spengler, *The Decline of the West*.
10. A. Toynbee, *A Study of History* (Oxford: Oxford Uni. Press, 1987), 51.
11. See Toynbee, *A Study of History*.
12. See Toynbee, *A Study of History*.
13. See Toynbee, *A Study of History*.
14. T. Hentsch, *Imagining the Middle East* (Montreal: Black Rose Books, 1991), 170.
15. See Francis Fukuyama, *The End of History and the Last Man* (New York: Free Press, 1992).
16. Samuel P. Huntington, *The Clash Of Civilizations and the Remaking of the World Order* (New York: Simon & Schuster, 1996), 20.
17. Huntington, *The Clash Of Civilizations*, 20.
18. See R. D. Kaplan, "Ground Zero - Macedonia: The Real Battleground", *New Republic*, 2 August (1993): 22-49.
19. See Kaplan, "Ground Zero - Macedonia".
20. Rodinson, *Europe and the Mystique of Islam*, 117.
21. 21 Said, *Orientalism*, 123.

1. THE RISE AND EXPANSION OF ISLAM

1. Qur'an, 112: 104.
2. M. Hodgson, *Rethinking World History* (London: Cambridge University Press, 1994), 166.
3. Lewis, *Cultures in Conflict - Christian, Muslim, and Jews in the Age of Discovery*, 15-16.

442 NOTES

4. For more see Lewis, *Cultures in Conflict Christian, Muslim, and Jews in the Age of Discovery*.

2. ISLAMIC CONTRIBUTION TO WESTERN CIVILISATION

1. Luca Mattei, "Study of the Madrasah of Granada in the light of the Material Culture and Scientific Methods used in the intervention of 2006", University of Granada, Spain, accessed June 7, 2024, https://www.ugr.es/~arqueologyterritorio/PDF5/Mattei.pdf
2. Miguel Rodríguez-Pantoja Márquez, *Patrimonio artístico y monumental de las universidades andaluzas* (Seville: Universidad de Sevilla, 1992), 13-15.
3. Zakaria Virk, "Science and Technology in Islamic Spain", Centre for Islamic Studies, accessed June 7, 2024, https://islamic-study.org/science-and-technology-in-islamic-spain/
4. See Al-Bukhari, Sahih on the Hadiths of the Prophet for more sayings regarding knowledge and wisdom.
5. See P. K. Hitti, *Short History of the Arabs* (Paris: Payot, 1950), Introduction.
6. John Thiem, "The Great Library of Alexandria Burnt: Towards the History of a Symbol", *Journal of the History of Ideas*, Vol. 40, No. 4 (Oct. - Dec., 1979): 507-526, https://doi.org/10.2307/2709356
7. See Gustav Le Bon, *Les Civilisation des Arabes* (Paris: Paris Libraire de Firmin Didot et Cie, 1884).
8. See J. C. Reisler, *Arab Civilisation* (Paris: Payot, Paris, 1955).
9. I. Gardet, *The Mediterranean: A Dialogue of Cultures, Mediterranean Studies*, Summer, No. 1 (1957): 19.
10. See L. A. Sedillot, *Histoire des Arabs* (History of the Arabs) (Paris, 1854).
11. See H. A. R. Gibb, *Modern Tends in Islam* (Chicago, Illinois: The University of Chicago Press, 1974).
12. See Claude C. Fauriel, *Histoire de la Poesie Provencale: Cours Fait à la Faculté des Lettres de Paris* (Paris: Jules Labitte, Libraire-Editeur, 1846).
13. See Fauriel, *Histoire de la Poesie Provencale*.
14. See E. Renan, *Averroes Et L'Averroisme (1861)* (Whitefish, Montana: Kessinger Publishing, 2010).
15. See Renan, *Averroes Et L'Averroisme*.
16. See L. Massignon, "What the Holy Land is for human communities who demand justice", *Journal of Islamic Jerusalem Studies* 11 (2011): 45-58.
17. See M. Vintejoux, *The Arab Miracle* (Paris: Editions Charlot, 1950).
18. See Hitti, *Short History of the Arabs*.
19. See M. Chasles, *Historical overview of the origin and development of methods in geometry*, trans., Charles Graves (Dublin: 1865).
20. Chasles, *Historical overview of the origin and development of methods in geometry*.
21. Chasles, *Historical overview of the origin and development of methods in geometry*.
22. For more details see H. Bammate, *Muslim Contribution to Civilization* Lahore: Kazi Publication, 1981).
23. Haller, cited in Bammate, *Muslim Contribution to Civilization*, 19.
24. See Le Bon, *The Civilisation of the Arabs*.
25. See Reisler, *Arab Civilisation*.

26. See A. M. Goichon, *Avicenna's Philosophy and Its Influence in Mediaeval Europe*, trans., M. S. Khan (Delhi: Motilal Banarsidass, 1969).
27. See Renan, *Averroes Et L'Averrosime*.
28. See Renan, *Averroes Et L'Averrosime*.
29. H. Pirenne, G. Cohen and H. Focillon, *Western Civilisation in the Middle Ages*, Vol. VIII (Paris: Presses Universitaires de France, 1933).
30. R. M. Pidal, *Poesia Arabe y Poesia Europea* (*Arab Poetry and European Poetry*) (Madrid: Espasa Calpe, 1973).
31. See Renan, *Averroes Et L'Averroism*.
32. See Sedillot, *History of the Arabs*.
33. See Sedillot, *History of the Arabs*.
34. See Renan, *Averroes Et L'Averroism*.
35. See Reisler, *Arab Civilization*.
36. The Prolegomena were translated into French by de Slane in 1868.
37. Ibn Khaldun. *The Muqaddimah*, trans., Franz Rosenthal, accessed December 17, 2021, https://delong.typepad.com/files/muquaddimah.pdf

3. IMPACT OF ISLAM ON MEDIEVAL EUROPEAN CONSCIOUSNESS

1. See C. Sanchez-Albornoz, "España y el Islam", *Revista de Occidente*, vol. 24 (1929): 1–30.
2. M. Rodinson, *Europe and the Mystique of Islam* (Seattle: Uni. Washington Press, 1991), 11-15.
3. Rodinson, *Europe and the Mystique of Islam* (Seattle: University of Washington Press, 13.
4. Rodinson, *Europe and the Mystique of Islam*, 15-16.
5. Hentsch, *Imagining the Middle East*, 29.
6. Rodinson, *Europe and the Mystique of Islam*, 24.
7. Hentsch, *Imagining the Middle East*, 31.
8. S. Runciman, *A History of the Crusades* (London: Penguin, 1990), 134.
9. Runciman, *A History of the Crusades*, 116-117.
10. Rodinson, *Europe and the Mystique of Islam*, 10.
11. H. Djait, *Europe and Islam*, trans., Peter Heinegg (Berkeley: University of California Press, 1985), 35-36.
12. B. Lewis, *Islam and the West* (New York: Oxford University Press, 1993), 5.
13. Hentsch, *Imagining the Middle East*, 37.
14. Rodinson, *Europe and the Mystique of Islam*, 17.
15. Rodinson, *Europe and the Mystique of Islam*, 17.
16. M. Hodgson, *Rethinking World History* (London: Cambridge University Press, 1994), 166.
17. Hodgson, *Rethinking World History*, 167.
18. Hentsch, *Imagining the Middle East*, 42.
19. Hodgson, *Rethinking World History*, 169.
20. H. Corbin, *History of Islamic Philosophy*, trans., L.Sherrard (London: Kegan Paul International, 1991), 1192.
21. Hodgson, *Rethinking World History*, 132.
22. Hodgson, *Rethinking World History*, 164.

23. See H. A. R. Gibb, "The Influence of Islamic Culture on Medieval Europe", *Bulletin of the John Rylands Library*, 38 (1955), 82-98.
24. Hodgson, *Rethinking World History*, 166.
25. Hodgson, *Rethinking World History*, 42.
26. Hentsch, *Imagining the Middle East*, 46.
27. Rodinson, *Europe and the Mystique of Islam*, 29.
28. See A. Champdor, *Saladin: le plus pur héros de l'Islam* (Paris: Floch: 1956), 59.
29. For more see Hitti, *History of the Arabs*, 580.
30. See H. Pirenne, *Mediaeval Cities: Their Origins and the Revival of Trade* (New York: Princeton, 1927), 27.
31. See Lewis, *Cultures in Conflict Christian, Muslim, and Jews in the Age of Discovery*, 19-20.
32. For more on the Ottoman Renaissance see Metin Mustafa, *The Ottoman Renaissance: A. Reconsideration of Early Modern Ottoman Art, 1413-1575* (New Jersey: Blue Dome Press, 2019).

4. THE RENAISSANCE MINDSET

1. Ahmed Paul Keeler, *Islam & The West: A New Narrative for the Age of Crises* (Cambridge: Equilibra Press, 2019), 74.
2. For more see Keeler, *Islam & The West: A New Narrative for the Age of Crises*, 68-76.

5. THE OTTOMAN THREAT

1. N. Asrar, *Kanuni Sultan Süleyman ve Islam Alemi*, (Istanbul: Hilal Yayınlar, 1992), 226.
2. Hentsch, *Imagining the Middle East*, 51.
3. Paul Coles, *Ottoman Impact on Europe* (London: Harcourt, Brace & World, 1968), 112.
4. Bernard Lewis, *The Middle East, 2000 Years of History From the Rise of Christianity to the Present Day* (London: Phoenix Giant, 1996), 128.
5. Lewis, *The Middle East, 2000 Years of History From the Rise of Christianity to the Present Day*, 116.
6. Lord Kinross, *The Ottoman Centuries: The Rise and Fall of the Turkish Empire* (New York: Morrow Quill Paperbacks, 1977), 52.
7. F. Babinger, *Mehmed the Conqueror and His Time* (Princeton, New Jersey: Princeton, 1978), 416-17.
8. Coles, *Ottoman Impact on Europe*, 156.
9. J. B. Ross, *The Portable Renaissance* (London: Penguin, 1995), 70.
10. Rodinson, *Europe and the Mystique of Islam*, 32.
11. Babinger, *Mehmed the Conqueror*, 408.
12. Babinger, *Mehmed the Conqueror*, 408-09.
13. Babinger, *Mehmed the Conqueror*, 421.
14. Burckhardt cited in Babinger, *Mehmed the Conqueror*, 421.
15. See Lewis, *Cultures in Conflict*, 2-8.
16. See Lewis, *Cultures in Conflict*, 2-8.
17. R. Lewis, *Everyday Life on Ottoman Turkey* (London: Dorset, 1988), 166.
18. Coles, *Ottoman Impact on Europe*, 150.

19. J. Hale, *The Civilisation of Europe in the Renaissance* (London: Harper Collins Publications 1993), 39.
20. Hale, *The Civilisation of Europe in the Renaissance*, 39.
21. Kinross, *The Ottoman Centuries*, 173.
22. Rodinson, *Europe and the Mystique of Islam*, 32.
23. J. Roberts, *Larousse Encyclopedia of Modern History* (London: Hamlyn, 1981), 31.
24. M. Heath, "Unlikely Alliance: Valois and Ottomans," *Renaissance Studies*, Vol.3, no.3 (1989): 307-8.
25. Kinross, *The Ottoman Centuries*, 272.
26. F. Braudel, *The Mediterranean and the Mediterranean World in the age of Phillip II*, Vols.1 & 2 (London: Fontana Press, 1981), 1185.
27. N. Daniel, *Islam, Europe and Empire*, (Edinburgh: Edinburgh University Press, 1966), 12.
28. Burien, cited in Hale, *The Civilisation of Europe in the Renaissance*, 41.
29. Hale, *The Civilisation of Europe in the Renaissance*, 41.
30. Rodinson, Europe and the Myth of Exoticism, 42.
31. A. Lybyer, *Government of the Ottoman Empire in the time of Suleiman the Magnificent* (Cambridge: Harvard University Press, 1913), 8.

6. OBSERVING THE OTHER AND SHIFTING IDENTITIES IN THE SIXTEENTH CENTURY

1. J. B. Ross and M. M. McLaughlin, *The Portable Renaissance*, (London: Penguin, 1985), 253.
2. Ross and McLaughlin, *The Portable Renaissance*, 253-54.
3. Ross and M. M. McLaughlin, *The Portable Renaissance*, 255.
4. Hale, *The Civilisation of Europe in the Renaissance*, 39.
5. Belon, cited in Hentsch, *Imagining the Middle East*, 62.
6. A. Lybyer, *Government of the Ottoman Empire in the Time of Süleyman the Magnificent* (Cambridge: Harvard University Press, 1913), 60.
7. Belon, cited in Lybyer, *Government of the Ottoman Empire in the Time of Süleyman the Magnificent*, 60-62.
8. Lybyer, *Government of the Ottoman Empire in the Time of Süleyman the Magnificent* , 67.
9. Rodinson, *Europe and the Mystique of Islam*, 38.
10. N. Machiavelli, *The Prince* (London: Everyman, 1995), 20-1.
11. Hentsch, *Imagining the Middle East*, 54.
12. H. İnalcık, *The Ottoman Empire - The Classical Age 1300-1600* (London: Phoenix, 1994), 135.
13. Braudel, *The Mediterranean and the Mediterranean World in the age of Phillip II*, 548-49.
14. Braudel, *The Mediterranean and the Mediterranean World in the age of Phillip II*, 550.
15. İnalcık, *The Ottoman Empire - The Classical Age 1300-1600*, 137.
16. İnalcık, *The Ottoman Empire - The Classical Age 1300-1600*, 137.
17. İnalcık, *The Ottoman Empire - The Classical Age 1300-1600*, 137.
18. İnalcık, *The Ottoman Empire - The Classical Age 1300-1600*, 138-39.
19. B. Lewis, *Islam and the West* (Oxford: Oxford University Press, 1994), 19.
20. Hentsch, *Imagining the Middle East*, 57.
21. Hodgson, *Rethinking World History* , 100.
22. Hodgson, *Rethinking World History*, 99.
23. Hentsch, *Imagining the Middle East*, 58.

24. Hodgson, *Rethinking World History*, 100.
25. Braudel, *The Mediterranean and the Mediterranean World in the age of Phillip II*, 137.
26. Braudel, *The Mediterranean and the Mediterranean World in the age of Phillip II*, 755.
27. Braudel, *The Mediterranean and the Mediterranean World in the age of Phillip II*, 771.
28. Hentsch, *Imagining the Middle East*, 57.
29. Hentsch, *Imagining the Middle East*, 56.
30. Rodinson, *Europe and the Mystique of Islam*, 35-37.
31. Hodgson, *Rethinking World History*, 125.
32. Hale, *The Civilisation of Europe in the Renaissance*, 38.
33. Hale, *The Civilisation of Europe in the Renaissance*, 50.

7. EUROPEAN PERCEPTIONS OF ISLAM AND THE OTTOMAN TURKS IN THE SEVENTEENTH CENTURY

1. See Paul Hazard, *European Mind, 1680-1715*, translated by Lewis May (London: Hollis and Carter, 1953.
2. See M. Foucault, *The Order of Things: An Archaeology of the Human Sciences* (New York: Pantheon Books, 1971).
3. Émeric Crucé, *The New Cyneas of Émeric Crucé; Edited with An Introduction and Translated Into English from the Original French Text of 1623 by Thomas Willing Balch* (Philadelphia: Allen, Lane and Scott, 1909), accessed February 4, 2003), https://archive.org/details/newcyneasofemeri00cruc
4. See Crucé, *The New Cyneas of Émeric Crucé*.
5. See Denis De Rougemont, *Vingt-Huit Siècles d'Europe* (Paris: Payot, 1961), 91.
6. For more see Francesca Russo, "The Utopia of International Peace During the Thirty Years War. 'Le Nouveau Cynée' Written by Eméric Crucé", *Governare La Paura, Journal of Interdisciplinary Studies* 9 (1) (2016), https://doi.org/10.6092/issn.1974-4935/6533.
7. Thevenot, J. cited in Hentsch, *Imagining the Middle East*, 86.
8. Jean de Thevenot, *The travels of Monsieur de Thevenot into the Levant in three parts, viz. into I. Turkey, II. Persia, III. the East-Indies* (London: H. Clark, 1687), 38-56, https://quod.lib.umich.edu/e/eebo2/A64495.0001.001/1:10?rgn=div1
9. Thevenot, *The travels of Monsieur de Thevenot*, 36.
10. Thevenot, *The travels of Monsieur de Thevenot*, 248 (PART I, BOOK II), 98-108 PART II, BOOK II).
11. J. Chardin, *Sir John's Travels in Persia*, Vol.2 (London: Argonaut Press, 1927), 93-4.
12. Chardin, *Sir John's Travels in Persia*, 101.
13. Chardin, *Sir John's Travels in Persia*, Vol.1, 5.
14. J. Racine, *Complete Plays*, translated by S. Solomon (New York: Random House, 1967), 5.
15. Racine, *Complete Plays*, 3.
16. Leibniz cited in Hentsch, *Imagining the Middle East*, 95.
17. Leibniz cited in Hentsch, *Imagining the Middle East*, 96.
18. Hentsch, *Imagining the Middle East*, 96.

8. BIRTH OF MAN'S HUBRIS

1. Keeler, *Islam & The West: A New Narrative for the Age of Crises*, 51.
2. Keeler, *Islam & The West: A New Narrative for the Age of Crises*, 51.
3. Keeler, *Islam & The West: A New Narrative for the Age of Crises*, 51-52.
4. Keeler, *Islam & The West: A New Narrative for the Age of Crises*, 52.
5. Keeler, *Islam & The West: A New Narrative for the Age of Crises*, 52-53.
6. Keeler, *Islam & The West: A New Narrative for the Age of Crises*, 53-54.
7. Keeler, *Islam & The West: A New Narrative for the Age of Crises*, 54.
8. See Richard Rex, *The Making of Martin Luther* (New Jersey: Princeton University Press, 2017).
9. Immanuel Kant, "An Answer to the Question: What is Enlightenment? (1784)", https://donelan.faculty.writing.ucsb.edu/enlight.html
10. Keeler, *Islam & The West: A New Narrative for the Age of Crises*, 55.
11. Friedrich Nietzsche, *The Gay Science: With a Prelude in German Rhymes and an Appendix of Songs*, ed., Bernard Williams, trans, Josefine Nauckhoff (Cambridge: Cambridge University Press, 2001), 120.
12. Keeler, *Islam & The West: A New Narrative for the Age of Crises*, 56.

9. THE AGE OF ENLIGHTENMENT AND THE ORIENT IN THE EIGHTEENTH CENTURY

1. Hentsch, *Imagining the Middle East*, 98.
2. Rodinson, *Europe and the Mystique of Islam*, 43.
3. Hentsch, *Imagining the Middle East*, 100.
4. See Richard Simon, *Histoire Critique du Vieux Testament* (Rotterdam: Reinier Leers, 1685).; also see Rodinson, *Europe and the Mystique of Islam*, 46.
5. Rodinson, *Europe and the Mystique of Islam*, 47.
6. Cassirer cited in Hentsch, *Imagining the Middle East*, 101.
7. Bayle cited in Hentsch, *Imagining the Middle East*, 101.
8. Rodinson, *Europe and the Mystique of Islam*, 46.
9. Rodinson, *Europe and the Mystique of Islam*, 47.
10. A. Hourani, *Islam in European thought* (New York: Cambridge University Press, 1995), 10.
11. Rodinson, *Europe and the Mystique of Islam*, 48.
12. P. Hazard cited in Rodinson, *Europe and the Mystique of Islam*, 48.
13. Simon Ockley, *History of the Saracen Empires* (London: Frederick Warne & Company, 1870), 54.
14. Hentsch, *Imagining the Middle East*, 102.
15. Henri de Boulainvilliers, *Life of Mahomet* (London: Darf, 1983), 3.
16. For more see P. Hazard, *European Mind, 1680-1715*, translated by Lewis May (London: Hollis and Carter. 1953), 14.
17. See Hazard, *European Mind, 1680-1715*, 14.
18. Voltaire, cited in Hazard, *European Mind, 1680-1715*, 14.
19. Voltaire cited in Hentsch, *Imagining the Middle East*, 106.
20. Hentsch, *Imagining the Middle East*, 107-08.
21. Montesquieu, *The Persian Letters*, translated by J. R. Loy (New York: Meridian Books, World Publishing, 1961), Letter XIX, 72.

22. Montesquieu cited in Hentsch, *Imagining the Middle East*, 113.
23. For more see Hourani, *Islam in European thought*.
24. Sermons preached before the University of Oxford , in the year 1784, at the Lecture founded by Rev. John Bampton, 2nd edition (London, 1785), 165f.
25. E. Gibbon, *The Decline and Fall of the Roman Empire* (London: Penguin, 1985), 652.
26. Gibbon, *The Decline and Fall of the Roman Empire*, 653.
27. Gibbon, *The Decline and Fall of the Roman Empire*, 660.
28. Hentsch, *Imagining the Middle East*, 113.
29. Rodinson, *Europe and the Mystique of Islam*, 48.
30. A. Galland cited in Hentsch, *Imagining the Middle East*, 99.
31. Robert Irwin, interview from documentary, *East to West: The Untold Story of the Modern World, Episode 7: The Ottomans and the West*. Produced by Lion Television and Bahçeşehir University, Turkey, 2011.
32. B. Lewis, *Islam in History - Ideas, People and Events in the Middle East* (Chicago: Open Court), 29.
33. A. L. Croutier, *Harem - The World Behind the Veil* (London: Bloomsbury, 1989), 178.
34. D. Murphy, *Embassy to Constantinople - The Travels of Lady Mary Wortley Montagu* (London: Century, 1988), 179.
35. A. Palmer, *The Decline and Fall of the Ottoman Empire* (London: John Murray, 1993), 35.
36. Murphy, *Embassy to Constantinople*, 130.
37. See Murphy, *Embassy to Constantinople*.
38. Croutier, *Harem*, 179.
39. Croutier, *Harem*, 176.
40. P. Kappert, "From Romantisation to Colonial Dominance: Historical Changes in the European Perception of the Middle East," Hippler & Lueg, *The Next Threat - Western Perceptions of Islam* (Amsterdam: Pluto Press, 1995), 39.
41. Croutier, *Harem*, 177.
42. See Croutier, *Harem*, 177.
43. Croutier, *Harem*, 177.
44. Croutier, *Harem*, 177.
45. Nikolaus Harnoncourt, *Die Entführung aus dem Serail Wolfgang Amadeus Mozart* (Hamburg: Teldec, 1988), 22.
46. Harnoncourt, *Die Entführung aus dem Serail Wolfgang Amadeus Mozart*, 22.
47. Harnoncourt, *Die Entführung aus dem Serail Wolfgang Amadeus Mozart*, 22.
48. Harnoncourt, *Die Entführung aus dem Serail Wolfgang Amadeus Mozart*, 8.
49. Harnoncourt, *Die Entführung aus dem Serail Wolfgang Amadeus Mozart*, 8.
50. Rodinson, *Europe and the Mystique of Islam*, 48.
51. Bettany Hughes interview from documentary, *East to West: The Untold Story of the Modern World, Episode 7: The Ottomans and the West*. Produced by Lion Television and Bahçeşehir University, Turkey, 2011.

10. A CRITIQUE OF ORIENTALISM

1. Huntington, *The Clash Of Civilizations and the Making of the New World Order*, 50.
2. For more see Huntington, *The Clash Of Civilizations*.
3. Huntington, *The Clash Of Civilizations*, 51.
4. E. Said, *Orientalism* (London: Penguin, 1995), 40
5. Hentsch, *Imagining the Middle East*, 121.

6. Said, *Orientalism*, 331.
7. Said, *Orientalism*, 352.
8. Said, *Orientalism*, 352.
9. Said, *Orientalism*, 17-19.
10. Lewis, *Islam and the West*, 108.
11. Said, *Orientalism*, 317.
12. Said, *Orientalism*, 317.
13. Said, *Orientalism*, 354.
14. Rodinson, *Europe and the Mystique of Islam*, 117.
15. Said, *Orientalism*, 3.
16. Said, *Orientalism*, 204.
17. F. Halliday, 'Orientalism and its Critics', *British Journal of Middle Eastern Studies*, Volume 20, No.2 (1993): 149.
18. Halliday, 'Orientalism and its Critics', 158.
19. Halliday, 'Orientalism and its Critics', 158.
20. Halliday, 'Orientalism and its Critics', 158.
21. Halliday, 'Orientalism and its Critics', 158.
22. Halliday, 'Orientalism and its Critics', 158.
23. Halliday, 'Orientalism and its Critics', 160.
24. Halliday, 'Orientalism and its Critics', 162.
25. C. Dodd, 'The Critique of Orientalism: A Review', *British Society For Middle Eastern Studies Bulletin*, Volume 6, No.2 (1979): 88.
26. Dodd, 'The Critique of Orientalism: A Review', 88.
27. Dodd, 'The Critique of Orientalism: A Review', 88.
28. Dodd, 'The Critique of Orientalism: A Review', 88.
29. T. Asad, ed., *Anthropology and the Colonial Encounter* (London: Ithaca Press, 1973), 15.
30. For more see Dodd, 'The Critique of Orientalism: A Review'.
31. B. A. Roberson, 'Islam and Europe: An Enigma or a Myth?', *Middle East Journal*, Volume 48, No. 2 (1994): 288.
32. Roberson, 'Islam and Europe: An Enigma or a Myth?', 289.
33. Roberson, 'Islam and Europe: An Enigma or a Myth?', 290.
34. Roberson, 'Islam and Europe: An Enigma or a Myth?', 290.
35. Roberson, 'Islam and Europe: An Enigma or a Myth?', 291.
36. Roberson, 'Islam and Europe: An Enigma or a Myth?', 297.
37. Roberson, 'Islam and Europe: An Enigma or a Myth?', 299.
38. For more see Roberson, 'Islam and Europe: An Enigma or a Myth?'.
39. Roberson, 'Islam and Europe: An Enigma or a Myth?', 307.
40. Rodinson, *Europe and the Mystique of Islam*, 117.
41. M. Hodgson, *Rethinking World History* (Cambridge: Cambridge University Press, 1994), 292-93.

11. THE ERA OF IMPERIALISM AND THE SUBSERVIENCE OF THE OTHER

1. Lewis, *Islam and the West*, 19.
2. Lewis, *Islam and the West*, 20.
3. Lewis, *Islam and the West*, 19.
4. Lewis, *Islam and the West*, 20.
5. See Lewis, *Islam and the West*, 21.

6. Lewis, *Islam and the West*, 21.
7. Palmer, *The Decline and Fall of the Ottoman Empire*, 45.
8. Palmer, *The Decline and Fall of the Ottoman Empire*, 45.
9. Lewis, *Islam and the West*, 21.
10. Rodinson, *Europe and the Mystique of Islam*, 52.
11. Hentsch, *Imagining the Middle East*, 119.
12. Kappert, "From Romantisation to Colonial Dominance", 37.
13. Volney, cited in Hentsch, *Imagining the Middle East*, 122.
14. Hentsch, *Imagining the Middle East*, 122; also see Rodinson, *Europe and the Mystique of Islam*, 51.
15. A. Wheatcroft, *The Ottomans* (London: Viking, 1993), 223.
16. Wheatcroft, *The Ottomans* (London: Viking, 1993), 223.
17. Wheatcroft, *The Ottomans*, 223.
18. R. Curzon, *Armenia: A Year at Erzurum, and on the Frontiers of Russia, Turkey, and Persia* (London: John Murray, 1854), 93.
19. Wheatcroft, *The Ottomans*, 164.
20. Halit, cited in Wheatcroft, *The Ottomans*, 165.
21. Kappert, "From Romantisation to Colonial Dominance", 39.
22. Charles A. Frazee, *The Orthodox Chruch and independent Greece. 1821-51* (Cambridge. 1869), 13
23. Wheatcroft, *The Ottomans*, 165.
24. Charles A. Frazee, *The Orthodox Chruch and independent Greece. 1821-51* (London: Cambridge University Press. 1869), 13.
25. S. Runciman, *The Great Church in Captivity: A Study of the Patriarchate of Constantinople from the Eve of the Turkish Conquest to the Greek War of Independence* (Cambridge: Cambridge University Press, 1986), 411.
26. Stanford Shaw and Ezel Kural Shaw, *History of the Ottoman Empire and Modern Turkey*, Vol.2 (London: Cambridge University Press, 1985), 18.
27. Shaw and Shaw, *History of the Ottoman Empire and Modern Turkey*, 162.
28. Shaw and Ezel Kural Shaw, *History of the Ottoman Empire and Modern Turkey Vol. 2*, 162.
29. Shaw and Shaw, *History of the Ottoman Empire and Modern Turkey Vol. 2*, 162.
30. Wheatcroft, *The Ottomans*, 165.
31. Shaw and Shaw, *History of the Ottoman Empire and Modern Turkey Vol. 2*, 203-204, 314-320.
32. D. Feldman, *Englishmen and Jews : social relations and political culture 1840-1914* (New Haven: Yale University Press, 1994), 13.
33. Wheatcroft, *The Ottomans*, 204-05.
34. Wheatcroft, *The Ottomans*, 205.
35. Lewis, *Islam in History*, 69.
36. Adolphus Slade, *Records of Travels in Turkey, Greece, &c, and of a Cruise in the Black Sea with the Capitan Pasha, in the years 1829, 1830 and 1831, Vol. 1* (London: Saunders and Otley, 1833), 96.
37. See Slade, *Records of Travels in Turkey, Greece, &c, and of a Cruise in the Black Sea with the Capitan Pasha, in the years 1829, 1830 and 1831*, 97.
38. See Slade, *Records of Travels in Turkey, Greece, &c, and of a Cruise in the Black Sea with the Capitan Pasha, in the years 1829, 1830 and 1831*.
39. Said, *Orientalism*, 219.
40. Said, *Orientalism*, 219.
41. Said, *Orientalism*, 219.

42. Renan, cited in Hentsch, *Imagining the Middle East*, 132-33.
43. Lamartine, cited in Hentsch, *Imagining the Orient*, 134.
44. Lewis, *Islam and the West*, 19.
45. Lewis, *Islam and the West*, 19.
46. See Hegel, *Lectures on the Philosophy of World History* (London: Cambridge University Press, 1975); also see Hegel, *Philosophy of History*, trans., J. Sibree (New York: Dover, 1956).
47. Hegel, *Lectures on the Philosophy of World History*, 197.
48. Hegel, *Lectures on the Philosophy of World History*, 202-03.
49. Hegel, *Philosophy of History*, translation by J. Sibree (New York: Dover, 1956), 358.
50. Johann Wolfgang (von) Goethe, *Noten und Anhandlungen zum West-östlichen Divan*, translated by Martin Binder and Peter Anton von Arnim (Notes and Essays to the Divan) (Global Academic Publishing, 2010), WA 1, 6, 128.
51. Goethe, *Noten und Anhandlungen zum West-östlichen Divan*, WA 1, 7, 32 and 1, 6, 23.).
52. Johann Wolfgang (von) Goethe, *Noten und Anhandlungen zum West-östlichen Divan*, WA 1, 7, 32).
53. Letter to A. O. Blumenthal, 28.5.1819, WA IV, 31, 160.
54. Goethe's letter to Carlyle on 20.7.1827, WA IV, 42, 270.
55. Kappert, "From Romantisation to Colonial Dominance", 41.

12. FROM THE IMAGINED ORIENT TO THE ORIENT EXPRESS

1. For more on the history of the Orient Express see E. H. Cookridge, *Orient Express: The Life and Times of the World's Most Famous Train* (New York: Random House, 1978); also see Kenneth Branagh, *Orient Express: The Story of a Legend* (London: Acc Art Books, 2018).
2. For more see Metin Mustafa, *Oriental Imaginings, Occidental Refashioning: Turquerie, the Tulip Age and Ottoman Modernity, 1683-1867* (Sydney: Centre for Ottoman Renaissance and Civilisation, 2023).
3. Pramod K. Nayar, *The Transnational in English Literature: Shakespeare to the modern* (London: Routledge, 2015), 76.
4. Agatha Christie, *Appointment with Death*, Internet Archive, accessed September 4, 2023, https://archive.org/stream/agathachristie/Agatha%20Christie/English/Agatha%20Christie%20-%20Appointment%20With%20Death_djvu.txt
5. Christie, *Appointment with Death*, Internet Archive.
6. Agatha Christie, *Murder in Mesopotamia* (New York: Berkley Book, 1984), 3.
7. Agatha Christie, *They Came to Baghdad* (Leicester: Thorpe, 2012), 109.
8. Christie, *They came to Baghdad*, 111.
9. Agatha Christie, *Murder on the Orient Express*, Internet Archive, accessed September 4, 2023, https://archive.org/details/murder-on-the-orient-express-agatha-christie_202103/mode/2up?q=mosques
10. Christie, *Murder on the Orient Express*, Internet Archive.
11. Christie, *Appointment with Death*, Internet Archive.
12. Christie, *Appointment with Death*, Internet Archive.
13. Christie, *They Came to Baghdad*, 229.
14. Agatha Christie, *Destination Unknown* (London: Harper Collins, 2011), 58, 66-67.
15. Christie, *Destination Unknown*, 73.
16. Christie, *Destination Unknown*,120.

17. Christie, *Destination Unknown*,120.
18. Agatha Christie, *Death on the Nile*, Internet Archive, accessed September 8, 2023, https://archive.org/details/death-on-the-nile-1937-copy/mode/2up?q=flies

13. WHERE DID THE MUSLIMS GO WRONG?

1. Sinan Meydan, *Atatürk ile Allah arasında* (Istanbul: Inkilap Kitapevi, 2009), 372.
2. Meydan, *Atatürk ile Allah arasında*, 372.
3. Erol Güngör, "Mederese, Ilim ve Modern Düşünce", *Tore Dergisi*, Kasım (1980): 114, 11-12.
4. Turhan Olcaytu, "Dinimiz Neyi Emrediyor, Atatürk Ne Yaptı", in N. Mirkelamoğlu, *Din ve Laiklik: Atatürkcü düşünce ve uygulamada* (Istanbul: Çev, 2000), 29-95, 397.
5. Abdullah Manaz, *Atatürk Reformları ve Islam* (Izmir, 1995), 142.
6. M. A. Ubucuni, "Türkiye 1850", in N. Mirkelamoğlu, *Atatürkcü Düşünce ve Uygulamada Din ve Laiklik*, ff. 140.
7. N. Mirkelamoğlu, *Din ve Laiklik: Atatürkcü Düşünce ve Uygulamada Din ve Laiklik* (Istanbul: Çev, 2000), 128.
8. Abdulhak Adnan Adivar, *Osmanlı Türklerinde Bilim* (Istanbul: Maarif Matbaası, 1943), 195.
9. Manaz, *Atatürk Reformları ve Islam*, 84.
10. Fahir Iz, *Eski Türk Edebiyatında Nesir* (Istanbul: Osman Yalçın Matbaası, 1964), 61.
11. Manaz, *Atatürk Reformları ve Islam*, 143.
12. Manaz, *Atatürk Reformları ve Islam*, 143.
13. Iz, *Eski Türk Edebiyatında Nesir*, 88, 161.
14. Manaz, *Atatürk Reformları* ve Islam, 198-99.
15. Meydan, *Atatürk ile Allah arasında*, 639.
16. Şakir Kocabaş, "Islam and Science," in *Islam and Scientific Debate: Searching for Legitimacy*, Rais Ahmad, ed. (New Delhi: Global Vision Publishing House, 2017), 24.
17. Ekmeleddin Ihsanoğlu, "An Overview of Ottoman Scientific Activities," *Foundation for Science and Civilisation* (December 2006): 9-10, accessed May 27, 2024, https://muslimheritage.com/uploads/An_Overview_of_Ottoman_Scientific_activities2.pdf
18. Ihsanoğlu, "An Overview of Ottoman Scientific Activities," 10-11.
19. See Meydan, *Atatürk ile Allah arasında*, 634-639.
20. See Meydan, *Atatürk ile Allah arasında*.
21. For more on this see Y. N. Öztürk, *Arapçılığa Karşı Akılcılığın Öncüsü İmamı Azam Ebu Hanife* (Istanbul: Yeni Boyat, 2014).
22. B. Bayraklı, "Atatürk ve Din," Yolu Tube, October 29, 2021, https://www.youtube.com/watch?v=fzN-LG47s0I
23. See Meydan, *Atatürk ile Allah arasında*, 661.
24. Öz, *Quotations from Mustafa Kemal Atatürk*, 51-51.
25. See Qur'an, 12:2, 14:4, 26:193-95, 41:44.
26. Qur'an, 14:4.
27. See Qur'an, 30:22.
28. See Y. Nuri Öztürk, Cuma Sohbetleri. "Atatürk'ü Okuyabilmek", Hürriyet, 1998.
29. See Meydan, *Atatürk ile Allah arasında*, 690-95.
30. See Meydan, *Atatürk ile Allah arasında*, 690-95
31. Ducane Cundioğlu, *Türkçe Kur'an ve Cumhuriyet İdeolojisi* (Istanbul: Kitabevi Yayınları, 1998), 188-191.

32. O. Keskioğlu,' "Yeni Islam Düşüncesi" Üzerine Bazı Görüşler,' https://dspace.ankara.edu.tr/xmlui/bitstream/handle/20.500.12575/49561/9395.pdf?sequence=1&isAllowed=y
33. Keeler, *Islam & The West: A New Narrative for the Age of Crises*, 77, 79-80.
34. See Abdul Hameed Siddiqi, *Main Springs of Western Civilisation* (Lahore: Kazi Publication, 1979), 83-85.
35. Muhammad Iqbal, *The Reconstruction of Religious Thought in Islam* (Lahore: Muhammad Ashraf, 1962), 155.
36. Muhammad Iqbal, *The Reconstruction of Religious Thought in Islam* (Lahore: Muhammad Ashraf, 1962), 8-9, 181.
37. See Siddiqi, *Main Springs of Western Civilisation*, 86.
38. Yaşar Nuri Öztürk, *Islam Nasıl Yozlaştırıldı* (Istanbul: Yeni Boyut, 2020), 422-24.
39. Bayraktar Bayraklı, "Sermons," You Tube, https://www.youtube.com/@bbayrakli/videos
40. Qur'an, 42:38.
41. Bayraktar Bayraklı, Kur'an'dan Gonule, You Tube 05-03-2020, https://www.youtube.com/watch?v=nfUMCpSfWL4&list=PL7z5mUYzRqisz1vJsmbrOWKDPqOV-zQBn&index=6

14. CHALLENGING IMPERIALISM, EUROCENTRISM & MUSLIM RADICALISM

1. Said, *Orientalism*, 109.
2. Henri Pirenne, *Mohammed and Charlemagne* (New York: Dover Publications, 2001), 152.
3. Said, *Orientalism*, 223.
4. Said, *Orientalism*, 220.
5. Said, *Orientalism*, 123.
6. Shaw and Shaw, *History of the Ottoman Empire and Modern Turkey*, Vol. 2, 329.
7. Calthorpe, cited in Shaw and Shaw, *History of the Ottoman Empire and Modern Turkey*, Vol. 2, 329.
8. For more see Mustafa, *Oriental Imaginings, Occidental Refashioning: Turquerie, the Tulip Age and Ottoman Modernity, 1683-1867*.
9. Patrick Kinross, *Atatürk - The Rebirth Of A Nation* (Virginia: K. Rustem, Weidenfeld and Nicholson, 1981), 297.
10. Lewis, *Islam and the West*, 30.
11. Eleftheira Daleziou, "Britain and the Greek-Turkish war and settlement of 1919-1923: the pursuit of security by "proxy" in Western Asia Minor", University of Glasgow, PhD Thesis (2002), 257, accessed March 17, 2025, https://theses.gla.ac.uk/1578/1/2002dalezioughd.pdf
12. Atatürk's speech to the Parliament of Turkey, *Nutuk* (Istanbul: Can Yayınları, 2023), 846-848.
13. H. Howard, *The Partition of Turkey* (New York: H. Fertig, 1966), 313.
14. Y. Öz, *Quotations from Mustafa Kemal Atatürk* (Ankara: Ministry of Foreign Affairs, Republic of Turkey, 1982), 36.
15. Öz, *Quotations from Mustafa Kemal Atatürk*, 44.
16. For more see Mustafa, *Oriental Imaginings, Occidental Refashioning*.
17. Z. Gökalp, *Türkçülüğün Esasaları* (Istanbul: Varlık, 1963), 118-119.

18. For a detailed analysis of Mustafa Kemal's reforms see Shaw and Shaw, *History of the Ottoman Empire and Modern Turkey, Vol. II: Reform, Revolution, and Republic – The Rise of Modern Turkey 1808-1975*, 373-396.
19. See The Qur'an, 2:256.
20. M. E. Bozkurt, *Atatürk Ihtilali* (Istanbul: Burhaneddin Matbaasi, 1940), 188.
21. See U. Azak, *Islam and Secularism in Turkey, Kemalism, Religion and the Nation State* (London: IB Tauris, 2010), 148; also see Z. Gökalp, *Türkçülüğün Esaslari* (Istanbul: Varlik, 1963), 118-119.
22. Huntington, *Clash of Civilisations*, 74.
23. Lewis, *Islam and the West*, 30-31.
24. See The Qur'an, 2:104.
25. See The Qur'an, 10:49.
26. Muhammad Iqbal, *The Reconstruction of Religious Thought in Islam* (Lahore: Dodo Press, 1930), 182.
27. Iqbal, *The Reconstruction of Religious Thought in Islam*, 181.
28. For analysis of the reforms by Mustafa Kemal in Turkey see Iqbal, *The Reconstruction of Religious Thought in Islam*, 183-188.
29. See Iqbal, *The Reconstruction of Religious Thought in Islam*, 184.
30. Qur'an, 4:59.
31. Iqbal, *The Reconstruction of Religious Thought in Islam*, 184.
32. See Iqbal, *The Reconstruction of Religious Thought in Islam*, 184.
33. See Ibn Khaldun, *The Muqadimmah*, trans., Franz Rosenthal 256-296, accessed March 13, 2024. https://asadullahali.files.wordpress.com/2012/10/ibn_khaldun-al_muqaddimah.pdf; also see Iqbal, *The Reconstruction of Religious Thought in Islam*, 184.
34. Iqbal, *The Reconstruction of Religious Thought in Islam*, 184.
35. Iqbal, *The Reconstruction of Religious Thought in Islam*, 185.
36. Iqbal, *The Reconstruction of Religious Thought in Islam*, 186.
37. Qur'an, 49:13.
38. See Murat Bardakçı, "Even Einstein once asked for a job in Turkey, which today discusses men shaking hands with women," *Hürriyet*, October 29, 2006, https://www.hurriyet.com.tr/bugun-erkegin-kadinla-tokalasmasini-tartisan-turkiye-den-bir-zamanlar-einstein-bile-is-ricasinda-bulunuyordu-5335137; also see Arnold Reisman, *Turkey's Modernization: Refugees from Nazism and Atatürk's Vision* (New Academia Publishing, 2006); Video (in Turkish) "Einstein'in Atatürk'e Mektubu" (Einstein's Letter to Atatürk): http://www.cankaya.edu.tr/duyuru/einstein.php; see Eurasia Digital News, https://eurasiadigital.medium.com/einsteins-letter-to-ataturk-s-turkey-7449ada946a5; also see Arnold Reisman, "Jewish Refugees from Nazism, Albert Einstein, and the Modernization of Higher Education in Turkey (1933-1945)." Aleph: Historical Studies in Science & Judaism, The Hebrew University of Jerusalem, and University of Indiana Press, No. 7, Pages 253-281, http://inscribe.iupress.org/doi/abs/10.2979/ALE.2007.-.7.
39. See Reisman, *Turkey's Modernization*.
40. Arnold Reisman, "Turkey's Invitations to Nazi Persecuted Intellectuals Circa 1933: A Bibiliographic Essay on History's Blind Spot," (June 12, 2007), accessed May 28, 2024, https://ssrn.com/abstract=993310 or http://dx.doi.org/10.2139/ssrn.993310, 14-15. (1-25)
41. Reisman, "Turkey's Invitations to Nazi Persecuted Intellectuals Circa 1933," 15.
42. See Reisman, "Turkey's Invitations to Nazi Persecuted Intellectuals Circa 1933."

43. Albert Einstein, Letter to the Prime Minister of the Republic of Turkey (İsmet İnönü), September 17, 1933. Republic of Turkey State Archives (T.C. Devlet Arşivleri Başkanlığı, 030.10/115.805.10), Ankara.
44. "Teklifin mevzuat? kanuniyeyle telifi mümkün degildir."
45. "Bunlar? bugünkü şeriat eriata göre kabule imkan yoktur."
46. See Reisman, *Turkey's Modernization*, 474-478.
47. See Reisman, "Turkey's Invitations to Nazi Persecuted Intellectuals Circa 1933".
48. See Reisman, "Turkey's Invitations to Nazi Persecuted Intellectuals Circa 1933."
49. See Reisman, *Turkey's Modernization*, 215, 290, 312-317, 331, and 332.
50. *Le Journal d'Orient* October 20, 1933, Courtesy Rockefeller [Foundation], Archives Center. Collection RF; Record Group 1.1; Series 717; Box 1; Folder 1.
51. See Reisman, *Turkey's Modernization*, 215, 290, 312-317, 331, and 332.
52. These figures are based on 2006 statistics. See Reisman, *Turkey's Modernization*, 443.
53. See Bardakçı, "Even Einstein once asked for a job in Turkey, which today discusses men shaking hands with women," *Hürriyet*, October 29, 2006.
54. See Max Plank, *Scientific Autobiography and Other Papers* (New York: Philosophical library, 1950), 33, 97.
55. See http://rescomp.stanford.edu/~cheshire/EinsteinQuotes.html, accessed May 28, 2024.
56. Mark. A. Epstein, "A Lucky Few: Refugees in Turkey," in M. A. Berenbaum and A.J. Peck (Eds), *The Holocaust and History: The Known, The Unknown, The Disputed, and The Re-examined* (Washington, DC: United States Holocaust Museum and Bloomington, IN, Indiana University Press, 1998), 536, 537.
57. Grand National Assembly of Turkey, on the occasion of the Bill Specifying the Duties and Powers of the Council of Ministers, 1 December 1921, ASD, Vol. 1, 215.
58. Paul Taylor, 'Between two stools: the EU's Foreign Policy', 20 October, 2023, https://www.friendsofeurope.org/insights/critical-thinking-between-two-stools-the-eus-foreign-policy/
59. See Taylor, 'Between two stools: the EU's Foreign Policy'.
60. Taylor, 'Between two stools: the EU's Foreign Policy'.
61. See Maria Chiara Cantelmo, "The Fall of Kemalism and the New Face of Political Islam: 20 Crucial Years in Turkey's History (1980-2002)", Athens Journal of History (2018): 37-53.
62. See Cantelmo, "The Fall of Kemalism and the New Face of Political Islam: 20 Crucial Years in Turkey's History (1980-2002)", 37-53.
63. See Cantelmo, "The Fall of Kemalism and the New Face of Political Islam: 20 Crucial Years in Turkey's History (1980-2002)", 37-53.
64. See Yılmaz Öz, *Quotations from Mustafa Kemal Atatürk* (Ankara: Ministry of Foreign Affairs, Republic of Turkey, 1982), 51-54.
65. See Cantelmo, "The Fall of Kemalism and the New Face of Political Islam: 20 Crucial Years in Turkey's History (1980-2002)", 37-53.
66. See Öz, *Quotations from Mustafa Kemal Atatürk*, 51.
67. Speech delivered by the President of Indonesia to the Turkish Parliament on 10 April, 2025, Sozcu, 10 April 2025, https://www.sozcu.com.tr/endonezya-cumhur baskani-prabowo-subianto-dan-ataturk-sozleri-benim-ikonum-evimde-heykeli-var-p161629
68. Huntington, *Clash of Civilisations*, 20.
69. Ahmed El Amraoui and Faisla Edroos, "Why Ataturk's legacy is debated 80 years after his death", Al Jazeera, 11 June, 2018, https://www.aljazeera.com/features/2018/6/11/why-ataturks-legacy-is-debated-80-years-after-his-death

70. Lally Waymouth, 'A Turning Point for Turkey," Washington Post, December 23, 1997, https://www.washingtonpost.com/archive/opinions/1997/12/23/a-turning-point-for-turkey/26929323-efcc-427f-afa4-abb00fe681b4/
71. Z. Onis, "Turkey in The Post-Cold War Era: In Search Of Identity", *Middle East Journal*, Volume 49, No. 1, Winter (1995):54.
72. Onis, "Turkey in The Post-Cold War Era: In Search Of Identity", 55.
73. Onis, "Turkey in The Post-Cold War Era: In Search Of Identity", 53-54.
74. Onis, "Turkey in The Post-Cold War Era: In Search Of Identity", 54.
75. Ottoman Muslim Caliphate (1517-1924).

15. RE-AWAKENING OF ISLAM

1. Berger, cited in Said, *Orientalism*, 285-86.
2. Morroe Berger, cited in Said, *Orientalism*, 288.
3. Said, *Orientalism*, 299.
4. E. Said, *Covering Islam: How the Media And The Experts Determine How We See The Rest of The World* (London: Vintage, 1997), 26.
5. Said, *Covering Islam*, 25.
6. D. Hiro, *Between Marx and Muhammad* (London: Harper Collins Publishers, 1994), 63.
7. Said, *Covering Islam*, 29.
8. Said, *Covering Islam*, 71.
9. Hippler & Lueg, *The Next Threat*, 1.
10. Der Spiegel, No. 5 (1993): 108.
11. See Paul Williams, "Europe'a Forgotten Genocide", Blogging Theology Podcast, You Tube, August 14, 2024, https://www.youtube.com/watch?v=kgK02HMwL1c&t=935s
12. See Williams, "Europe'a Forgotten Genocide".
13. *Prosecutor v. Radislav Krstic (Trial Judgement)*, International Criminal Tribunal for the former Yugoslavia (ICTY), 2 August 2001, accessed March, 19, 2025, https://www.refworld.org/jurisprudence/caselaw/icty/2001/en/40159
14. See Williams, "Europe'a Forgotten Genocide".
15. See See Abdal Hakim Murad, *Travelling Home: Essays on Islam in Europe* (Cambridge: Quilliam Press, 2020).
16. Michael Sells, *The Bridge Betrayed: Religion and genocide in Bosnia* (Berkeley: University of California Press, 1996), 144.
17. Hippler & Lueg, *The Next Threat*, 12-13.
18. Hippler & Lueg, *The Next Threat*, 10.
19. See T. Meyer, *Fundamentalism* (Reinbek: Rowholt Publ., 1991).
20. J. Esposito, *The Islamic Threat - Myth or Reality?* (New York: Oxford Uni. Press, 1992), 9.

16. THE CLASH OF CIVILISATIONS OR DIALOGUE OF CULTURES?

1. On the 20th of March in 1923, he spoke to the youth of Konya and made a statement during the tea reception held at the Turkish House, cited in Meydan, *Atatürk ile Allah arasında*, 828-29.

2. Seyyed Hossein Nasr, *Islam and the Plight of Modern Man* (London: Longman, 1975), 135.
3. Davutoğlu, "From Fukuyama to Huntington," in *Medeniyetler Çatışması*, M. Yılmaz, ed (Istanbul: Vadi Yayınlar, 1995), 242-248.
4. Davutoğlu, "From Fukuyama to Huntington," in *Medeniyetler Çatışması*, M. Yılmaz, ed (Istanbul: Vadi Yayınlar, 1995), 242-248.
5. Davutoğlu, "From Fukuyama to Huntington," in *Medeniyetler Çatışması*, M. Yılmaz, ed (Istanbul: Vadi Yayınlar, 1995), 242-248.
6. See K. Kahraman, "Is it a Clash of Civilisations", in *Medeniyetler Çatışması*, 249-254.
7. Kahraman, "Is it a Clash of Civilisations", 249-254.
8. B. Toprak, "Huntington and Western Supremacy," in *Medeniyetler Çatışması*, 264.
9. D. Perinçek, "Christian-Muslim Clash," in *Medeniyetler Çatışması*, 265-268.
10. Perinçek, "Christian-Muslim Clash," in *Medeniyetler Çatışması*, 265-268.
11. Perinçek, "Christian-Muslim Clash," in *Medeniyetler Çatışması*, 265-268.
12. I. Kiras, "Islam delays the 'End of History,'" in *Medeniyetler Çatışması*, 275.
13. Huseyin Hatemi, "Islam Yegâne Mümkün Çözümdür," in *Medeniyetler Çatışması*, 274.
14. Hatemi, "Islam Yegâne Mümkün Çözümdür," in *Medeniyetler Çatışması*, 274.
15. Ozdağ, "Medeniyetler Çatışması Üzerine (Mülakat)," in *Medeniyetler Çatışması*, 284-286.
16. Pope John Paul II apology, accessed March 13, 2000, https://www.theguardian.com/world/2000/mar/13/catholicism.religion
17. Ozdağ, "Medeniyetler Çatışması Üzerine (Mülakat)," in *Medeniyetler Çatışması*, 284-286.
18. Ozdağ, "Medeniyetler Çatışması Üzerine (Mülakat)," in *Medeniyetler Çatışması*, 284-286.
19. Ozdağ, "Medeniyetler Çatışması Üzerine (Mülakat)," in *Medeniyetler Çatışması*, 284-286.
20. Sami Şener, "Medeniyetler Arası Çatışma Teorileri ve Tarihin Sonu Üzerine," in *Medeniyetler Çatışması*, 289-305.
21. Şener, "Medeniyetler Arası Çatışma Teorileri ve Tarihin Sonu Üzerine," in *Medeniyetler Çatışması*, 289-305.
22. Şener, "Medeniyetler Arası Çatışma Teorileri ve Tarihin Sonu Üzerine," in *Medeniyetler Çatışması*, 289-305.
23. Şener, "Medeniyetler Arası Çatışma Teorileri ve Tarihin Sonu Üzerine," in *Medeniyetler Çatışması*, 289-305.
24. Şener, "Medeniyetler Arası Çatışma Teorileri ve Tarihin Sonu Üzerine," in *Medeniyetler Çatışması*, 289-305.
25. Mustafa Özcan, "Meş'um Teori, Barbar ve Medeni," in *Medeniyetler Çatışması*, 306-310.
26. R. Zakaria, *Muhammad and the Qur'an* (London: Penguin, 1991), 59.
27. TIMES Newspaper cited in Mustafa Özcan, "Meş'um Teori", in *Medeniyetler Çatışması*, 307.
28. TIMES Newspaper cited in Özcan, "Meş'um Teori, Barbar ve Medeni," in *Medeniyetler Çatışması*, 307.
29. Özcan, "Meş'um Teori, Barbar ve Medeni," in *Medeniyetler Çatışması*, 306-310.
30. Özcan, "Meş'um Teori, Barbar ve Medeni," in *Medeniyetler Çatışması*, 306-310.
31. Z. Sayın, "Western Modernism, Islamic Fundamentalism!" in *Medeniyetler Çatışması*, 311-318.
32. Sayın, "Western Modernism, Islamic Fundamentalism!", 311-318.

33. Ömer Laçiner, "New World Order and Cultures", in *Medeniyetler Çatışması*, 319-339.
34. Laçiner, "New World Order and Cultures", 319-339.
35. Laçiner, "New World Order and Cultures", 319-339.
36. Y. Aktay, "From the End of Eschatology to the Continuation of Conflict", in *Medeniyetler Çatışması*, 340-349.
37. Yılmaz, "Medeniyetler Çatışmasından Medeniyetin Tahribine", 350-362.
38. Yılmaz, "Medeniyetler Çatışmasından Medeniyetin Tahribine", 350-362.
39. Andrea Lueg, "The Perceptions of Islam in Western Debate", in *The Next Threat: Western Perceptions of Islam*, edited by Jochen Hippler and Andrea Lueg (London: Pluto Press, 1995), 7-29.
40. Esposito, *The Islamic Threat - Myth or Reality?*, 243.

17. THE NEW MILLENNIUM AND THE MUSLIM OTHER

1. Speech made by Pope Urban II in 1095 heralding the call for a Crusade against the Muslims. In 1094 or 1095, Emperor Alexios I Komnenos of the Byzantine Empire reached out to Pope Urban II, seeking assistance from the western powers against the Seljuq Turks, who had seized control of most of Asia Minor from him. During the council of Clermont, Pope Urban II delivered a powerful speech to a large audience, urging them to support the Greeks and reclaim Palestine from Muslim rule. While the official records of the council's proceedings have not survived, we do have four written accounts of Urban's speech, all penned by individuals who were present and heard his words. One such account was written by the chronicler Fulcher of Chartres. It is worth noting how the principles of the peace and truce of God, which aimed to establish peace within Christendom, are directly linked to the call for a Crusade. However, one may question whether this amounts to the promotion of violence and the clash of civilisations debate today? Medieval Sourcebook: Urban II: Speech at Council of Clermont, 1095, according to Fulcher of Chartres, https://web.mit.edu/aorlando/www/SaintJohnCHI/Church%20History%20Readings/Urban%20II%20on%20First%20Crusade.pdf
2. Jonathan Phillips, *The Fourth Crusade and the Sack of Constantinople* (London: Pimlico, 2011), ix.
3. Jeffrey Haynes, "Twenty Years of Huntington's 'Clash of Civilizations'", in *The Clash of Civilizations: Twenty Years On*, J. Paul Baker, ed. (Bristol: E-International Relations, Edited Collections, 2013), 11.
4. Haynes, "Twenty Years of Huntington's 'Clash of Civilizations'", 12; also see Huntington, *The Clash of Civilizations?*, 35.
5. See David A. Welch, "Enemy Wanted: Apply Without", in *The Clash of Civilizations: Twenty Years On*, 15.
6. Welch, "Enemy Wanted: Apply Without", 15.
7. Welch, "Enemy Wanted: Apply Without", 18.
8. See Syed Mansoob Mursheed, "The Crescent and the Cross", in *The Clash of Civilizations: Twenty Years On*, 22.
9. See Mursheed, "The Crescent and the Cross", 22-23.
10. Johan Eriksson, "The 'Clash of Civilizations' and Its Unexpected Liberalism", in *The Clash of Civilizations: Twenty Years On*, 29.
11. Eriksson, "The 'Clash of Civilizations' and Its Unexpected Liberalism", in *The Clash of Civilizations: Twenty Years On*, 30.

12. Dieter Senghass, "How to Promote a Perspicacious Intercultural Dialogue?", in *The Clash of Civilizations: Twenty Years On*, 40.
13. Amir Taheri, *Holy Terror* (London: Hutchinson, 1987), 20.
14. A. Bonnett, "Occidentalism: The Uses of the West", presented at the NORFACE seminar Towards a Post-Western West? The Changing Heritage of 'Europe' and the 'West', Tampere Peace Research Institute, Finland, 2-3 February 2006, 5.
15. S. J. Al-Azm, "Orientalism and Orientalism in Reverse", *Khamsin*, 8 (1981): 5-26.
16. See Al-Azm, "Orientalism and Orientalism in Reverse".
17. See Said, *Orientalism*.
18. B. Lawrence, *Messages to the World: The Statements of Osama bin Laden* (London and New York: Verso, 2005), 113-114.
19. Lawrence, *Messages to the World*, 114.
20. B. Harlow, *Resistance Literature* (London and New York: Methuen, 1987), 7.
21. F. Fanon, *The Wretched of the Earth* (London: Penguin, 2001), 169.
22. P. Childs and P. Williams, *An Introduction to Post-Colonial Theory* (London: Prentice Hall / Harvester Wheatsheaf, 1997), 209.
23. See N. Lahoud, *The Jihadis' Path to Self-Destruction* (New York: Columbia University Press. 2010),119; also see Z. Lockman, *Contending Visions of the Middle East: The History and Politics of Orientalism* (Cambridge: Cambridge University Press, 2004), 230.
24. K. Marx, *The Eighteenth Brumaire of Louis Bonaparte* (Maryland: Wildside Press, 2008), 15.
25. B. Lawrence, ed., *Messages to the World: The Statements of Osama bin Laden* (New York and London: Verso, 2005), 121.
26. Lawrence, *Messages to the World*, 108.
27. Lawrence, *Messages to the World*, 124-25.
28. Cited in, B. Lia, *Architect of Global Jihad: The Life of Al-Qaida Strategist Abu Mus'ab al-Suri*, (London: Hurst and Company, 2007), 238.
29. F. Halliday, "'Orientalism' and Its Critics", *British Journal of Middle Eastern Studies*, 20(2) (1993): 155.
30. Fanon, *The Wretched of the Earth* (London: Penguin, 2001), 171.
31. See Lawrence, *Messages to the World*, 218; also see A. B. Naji, A. B., and W. McCants (trans.), 'The Management of Savagery: The Most Critical Stage Through Which the Umma Will Pass', John M. Olin Institute for Strategic Studies, Harvard University, 23 May 2006, accessed, August 26, 2023, <http://www.wcfia.harvard.edu/olin/images/Management%20of%20Savagery%20- %2005-23-2006.pdf> (21 March 2012), 29, 214.
32. See S. Schmitt, *Concept of the Political* (New Brunswick: Rutgers University Press, 1976).
33. J. Esposito, *The Islamic Threat: Myth or Reality?* (New York: Oxford University Press, 1999) xix.
34. See David G. Kibble, "The Attacks of 9/11: Evidence of a Clash of Religions?" *The US Army War College Quarterly: Parameters 32*, No. 3(2002): 35.
35. Lewis, "License to Kill", 15.
36. Bin Laden, *Declaration of War (I)*, http://msanews.mynet.net/MSANEWS/199610/19961012.3.html.
37. Lawrence, *Messages to the World*, 166.
38. Lawrence, *Messages to the World*, 166-68.
39. Naji, 'The Management of Savagery', 256.
40. Lia, *Architect of Global Jihad*, 311, 329.

41. George W. Bush, "Full transcript of George Bush's statement", The Guardian, September 11, 2001, https://www.theguardian.com/world/2001/sep/11/september11.usa19
42. Naji, 'The Management of Savagery', 208-09.
43. Naji, 'The Management of Savagery', 208-09.
44. A. Al-Awlaki A., 44 Ways to Support Jihad, NEFA Foundation, 5 February 2009, accessed March 5, 2023, <http://www.nefafoundation.org/file/FeaturedDocs/nefaawlaki44wayssupportjihad.p df> (15 March 2012), 6.
45. Naji, 'The Management of Savagery', 43.
46. Schmitt, *Concept of the Political*, 54.
47. Lawrence, *Messages to the World*, 112.
48. Christopher Sims, "Occidentalism at War: Al-Qaida's Resistance Rhetoric", *Altre Modernita*, Milan (2012): 218.
49. Matthew 28:19.
50. Bassam Tibi, *Islam Between Culture and Politics* (Basingstoke, England: Palgrave, 2001), 216.
51. Powell's speech can be found on the Union of American Hebrew Congregations website: http://www.seekpeace.org/articles/powell.shtml. In April 2002, President George Bush Snr. and British Prime Minister Tony Blair both advocated for a separate Palestinian state. President Bush's speech is also available on the same website at: http://www.seekpeace.org/articles/bushspeech.shtml.
52. Powell's speech can be found on the Union of American Hebrew Congregations website: http://www.seekpeace.org/articles/powell.shtml. In April 2002, President George Bush Snr. and British Prime Minister Tony Blair both advocated for a separate Palestinian state.

18. DECOLONISING ORIENTALISM

1. Neil de Grasse Tyson, "Nobel laureates in Science: Contributions from Jews and Muslims," You Tube, https://www.youtube.com/watch?v=VQl7k7lQTns
2. The figure 609 refers to the total recipients of Nobel Prize for science from 1901 to 2011.
3. The figure 609 refers to the total recipients of Nobel Prize for science from 1901 to 2011.
4. "Turkish-American Nobel winner says prize would be out of reach if he worked in Turkey", Turkish Minute, 8 November 2024, accessed November 12, 2024, https://www.turkishminute.com/2024/11/08/turk-american-nobel-winner-says-prize-would-be-out-of-reach-if-he-worked-in-turkey/
5. Steven Weinberg cited in Hillel Ofek, "Why the Arabic World Turned Away from Science", *The New Atlantis*, No. 30 (2011): 3-23, accessed June 20, 2024, https://www.thenewatlantis.com/publications/why-the-arabic-world-turned-away-from-science
6. See Pervez Amirali Hoodbhoy, "Science and the Islamic world—The quest for rapprochement", *Physics Today* 60, (2007): 49-55, accessed June 19, 2024, https://doi.org/10.1063/1.2774098
7. For more see Duncan Madden, "New Research Ranks The 10 Smartest Countries In The World", Forbes, January 28, 2025, accessed January 30, 2025, https://www.forbes.com/sites/duncanmadden/2025/01/28/new-survey-ranks-the-ten-smartest-countries-in-the-world/
8. See Madden, "New Research Ranks The 10 Smartest Countries In The World".

9. See Madden, "New Research Ranks The 10 Smartest Countries In The World".
10. Cited in Madden, "New Research Ranks The 10 Smartest Countries In The World".
11. See Ofek, "Why the Arabic World Turned Away from Science", *The New Atlantis*, No. 30 (2011): 3-23.
12. See Mert Müstecaplıoğlu, "Turkey has extended R&D and design centers incentive program", Norton Rose Fulbright, March 29, 2021, https://www.nortonrosefulbright.com/de-de/inside-turkiye/blog/2021/03/turkey-has-extended-rd-and-design-centers-incentive-program
13. Royal Society. *The Atlas of Islamic World Science and Innovation* (Royal Society, 2014); also see, N., Osama, A. Guessoum, "Institutions: Revive universities of the Muslim world," *Nature* 526 (2015): 634–636 (2015), https://doi.org/10.1038/526634a
14. See Ministry of Industry and Technology of Turkey, https://www.sanayi.gov.tr/anasayfa
15. Expenditure on research and development pertains to the total spending in this field relative to the GDP of each country (expressed as a percentage). It encompasses both capital and current expenses in the four primary sectors: Business enterprise, Government, Higher education, and Private non-profit. R&D encompasses fundamental research, applied research, and experimental development.
16. See UNESCO Institute for Statistics (UIS). UIS.Stat. Bulk Date Download Service, accessed May 8, 2024, apiportal.uis.unesco.org.bdds
17. See Guessoum, "Institutions: Revive universities of the Muslim world," 634-636.
18. See *Nature* 514 (2014): 550–553.
19. See Scopus Database, https://www.scopus.com/; and Scimago, https://www.scimagojr.com/
20. See Times Higher Education, World Universtiy Rankings 2025, https://www.timeshighereducation.com/world-university-rankings/latest/world-ranking
21. 'Turkish universities achieve significant success in 2025 global rankings'. Daily Sabah, 29 January, 2025. https://www.dailysabah.com/turkiye/turkish-universities-achieve-significant-success-in-2025-global-rankings/news
22. E. Hazelkorn, "Striving for World Class Excellence: Rankings and Emerging Societies," in D. Araya and P. Marber (Higher Education in the Global Age: Universities, Interconnections and Emerging Societies. Routledge Studies in Emerging Societies Series, 2012), 1.
23. See Joseph E. B. Lumbard, "Decolonizing Qur'anic Studies," *Religions* 13, No. 2(2022): 1, accessed May 5, 2024, https://doi.org/10.3390/rel13020176
24. Times Higher Education University Rankings 2024, https://www.timeshighereducation.com/world-university-rankings/2024/world-ranking#!/length/25/locations/TUR/sort_by/rank/sort_order/asc/cols/scores
25. See https://www.timeshighereducation.com/world-university-rankings/2024/world-ranking
26. See Guessoum, "Institutions: Revive universities of the Muslim world," 634-636.
27. John Henrik Clarke, "Origin and Impact of Racism" Great Lectures of Dr. John Henrik Clarke (podcast), November 30, 2021, accessed April 28, 2024, https://www.spreaker.com/podcast/great-lectures-of-dr-john-henrik-clarke--5282513
28. See Boaventura de Sousa Santos, *Epistemologies of the South: Justice Against Epistemicide* (New York: Taylor & Francis, 2015).
29. See Ahmed Paul Keeler, *Islam & The West: A New Narrative for the Age of Crises* (Cambridge: Equilibra Press, 2019), 76.
30. Joseph E. B. Lumbard, "Islam and the Challenge of Epistemic Sovereignty," *Religions* 15: 406 (2024): 3, accessed May 5, 2024, https://doi.org/10.3390/rel15040406

31. See Joseph E. B. Lumbard, "Decolonizing Qur'anic Studies *Religions,*" 13, no. 2, 176 (2022): 1, accessed, April 28, 2024, https://doi.org/10.3390/rel13020176
32. Lumbard, "Decolonizing Qur'anic Studies *Religions,*" 13, no. 2, 176 (2022): 1.
33. Lumbard, "Decolonizing Qur'anic Studies *Religions,*" 1.
34. Muzaffar Iqbal, "The Qur'an, Orientalism and the Encyclopaedia of the Qur'an", *Journal of Qur'anic Research and Studies* 3 (2008): 5–45.
35. Coloniality denotes the persistence of colonialism even after the abandonment of different forms of "settler colonialism". See Lumbard, "Decolonizing Qur'anic Studies *Religions,*" 12; also see Ramón Grosfoguel, "Colonial Difference, Geopolitics of Knowledge, and Global Coloniality in the Modern/Colonial Capitalist World-System," *Review (Fernand Braudel Center)* 25 (2002): 203–24.
36. See Grosfoguel, "Colonial Difference, Geopolitics of Knowledge, and Global Coloniality in the Modern/Colonial Capitalist World-System," 203–24.
37. See Nicolai Sinai, *The Qur'an: A Historical-Critical Introduction* (Edinburgh: Edinburgh University Press 2017).
38. Amy Allen, *The End of Progress: Decolonizing the Normative Foundations of Critical Theory* (New York: Columbia University Press, 2016), 3.
39. See Allen, *The End of Progress: Decolonizing the Normative Foundations of Critical Theory*, 3.
40. See Babatunde Lawal, *The Gẹlẹdé Spectacle: Art, Gender, and Social Harmony in an African Culture* (Seattle: University of Washington Press, 1996), xvi; also see Joseph E. B. Lumbard, "Islam and the Challenge of Epistemic Sovereignty," *Religions* 15, no. 4: 406 (2024): 7, accessed April 28, 2024, https://doi.org/10.3390/rel15040406
41. See Seyyed Hossein Nasr, *Islam and the Plight of Modern Man* (Chicago: Kazi Publications, 2001), 42-43.
42. Jay Garfield, *Empty Words: Buddhist Philosophy and Cross-Cultural Interpretation* (New York: Oxford University Press, 2002), 260.
43. See Lumbard, "Islam and the Challenge of Epistemic Sovereignty," 8.
44. See Lumbard, "Islam and the Challenge of Epistemic Sovereignty," 8.
45. Max Planck, *Where is Science Going?* (New York: AMS Press, 1932), 107, 168.
46. See See Lumbard, "Islam and the Challenge of Epistemic Sovereignty," 8; also see Ngugi wa Thiong'o, *Politics: A Re-Engagement with Issues of Literature and Society* (Oxford: James Currey, 1997), 10.
47. See *Die Zeit*, February 20, 2003.
48. See E. Seligmann, ed., *Desperately Seeking Europe* London: Archetype Publications, 2003), 198–210; also see the German version in Valery Giscard d'Estaing, Ralf Dahrendorf, eds., *Europa Leidenschaftlich Gesucht,* (München-Zürich: Piper Verlag, 2003), 210–224.
49. See the Russian political journal, *Chelovecheskiy Faktor: Obschestvo i Vlast,* (2004): 4.
50. See PhD thesis by Yusuf Çelik, "Critical Hermeneutics Contemporary Philosophical Perspectives in Turkey on the Understanding and Interpretation of The Qur'an", The University of Edinburgh, 2020, https://era.ed.ac.uk/bitstream/handle/1842/37651/Celik2020.pdf?sequence=1&isAllowed=y; also see the thesis by G. Bacik, "Contemporary Rationalist Islam in Turkey: The Religious Opposition to Sunni Revival," Columbus State University, https://library.columbusstate.edu/eds/detail?db=edsebk&an=2941956&isbn=9780755636761
51. See https://time.com/search/?q=Yasar+Nuri+Ozturk; also see http://hyeforum.com/index.php?showtopic=4997
52. See Susan Leigh Star, *Ecologies of Knowledge: Work and Politics in Science and Technology* (New York: State University of New York Press, 1995).

53. Santos, *Epistemologies of the South: Justice against Epistemicide*, 237.
54. Santos, *Epistemologies of the South: Justice against Epistemicide*, 237.

19. RELIGION, POLITICS AND THE EMERGING WORLD ORDER

1. Stan Grant, "Vladimir Putin's invasion of Ukraine is not just a war of politics – it's a holy war" (20 March 2023), https://www.abc.net.au/news/2022-03-20/vladimir-putin-invasion-ukraine-politics-holy-war/100921102
2. See Jocelyne Cesari, *We God's People: Christianity, Islam and Hinduism in the World of Nations* (Cambridge: Cambridge University Press, 2021).
3. See Cesari, *We God's People*.
4. See Grant, "Vladimir Putin's invasion of Ukraine is not just a war of politics – it's a holy war".
5. See Grant, "Vladimir Putin's invasion of Ukraine is not just a war of politics – it's a holy war".
6. See Grant, "Vladimir Putin's invasion of Ukraine is not just a war of politics – it's a holy war".
7. See Grant, "Vladimir Putin's invasion of Ukraine is not just a war of politics – it's a holy war".
8. See Cesari, *We God's People*.
9. See Cesari, *We God's People*.
10. See Grant, "Vladimir Putin's invasion of Ukraine is not just a war of politics – it's a holy war".
11. See Grant, "Vladimir Putin's invasion of Ukraine is not just a war of politics – it's a holy war".
12. For more see Joram Van Klaveren, "Can Western liberalism tolerate anything at all but itself?" (September 2023), https://www.trtworld.com/opinion/can-western-liberalism-tolerate-anything-at-all-but-itself-14582950
13. For Van Klaveren, "Can Western liberalism tolerate anything at all but itself?"
14. See Anton Fedyashin, "End of Wilsonianism: Ukraine, Gaza wars will shape new global order" (February 2024), https://www.trtworld.com/opinion/end-of-wilsonianism-ukraine-gaza-wars-will-shape-new-global-order-16594254
15. See Fedyashin, "End of Wilsonianism: Ukraine, Gaza wars will shape new global order."
16. See Fedyashin, "End of Wilsonianism: Ukraine, Gaza wars will shape new global order."
17. See Fedyashin, "End of Wilsonianism: Ukraine, Gaza wars will shape new global order."
18. See Fedyashin, "End of Wilsonianism: Ukraine, Gaza wars will shape new global order."
19. See Fedyashin, "End of Wilsonianism: Ukraine, Gaza wars will shape new global order."
20. See Fedyashin, "End of Wilsonianism: Ukraine, Gaza wars will shape new global order."
21. See Fedyashin, "End of Wilsonianism: Ukraine, Gaza wars will shape new global order."
22. See Fedyashin, "End of Wilsonianism: Ukraine, Gaza wars will shape new global order."

20. THE GLOBAL SOUTH IN THE 21ST CENTURY

1. See Daniel Drezner, "Never mind hypocrisy, the West faces another challenge", 21 March 2024, Chatham House, accessed August 15, 2024, https://www.chathamhouse.org/publications/the-world-today/2024-02/never-mind-hypocrisy-west-faces-another-challenge
2. See Daniel Drezner, "Never mind hypocrisy, the West faces another challenge".
3. See Donald Markwell, *John Maynard Keynes and International Relations: Economic Paths to War and Peace* (Oxford: Oxford University Press, 2006).
4. Steil Benn, *The battle of Bretton Woods John Maynard Keynes, Harry Dexter, and the making of a new world order* (Princeton: Princeton University Press, 2014); also see Lawrence E. Blume; Steven N. Durlauf, eds., *The new Palgrave dictionary of economics* (2nd ed.) (Basingstoke, Hampshire: Palgrave Macmillan, 2008), 544–546.
5. For more see Jordan Bleischer and Josh Lipsky, "The Geopolitical Imperative to Upgrade the Dollar", Project Syndicate: The World's Opinion Page (June 24, 2024), accessed June 26, 2024, https://www.project-syndicate.org/commentary/swift-alternatives-could-undermine-american-national-security-interests-by-jordan-bleicher-and-josh-lipsky-2024-06
6. Joschka Fischer, "Will Europe be the world's biggest loser?", Project Syndicate: The World's Opinion Page (23 May, 2023), accessed June 25, 2024, https://www.project-syndicate.org/commentary/europe-biggest-loser-in-multipolar-world-by-joschka-fischer-2023-05
7. See Fischer, "Will Europe be the world's biggest loser?", Project Syndicate?"
8. See Fischer, "Will Europe be the world's biggest loser?", Project Syndicate?"
9. William R. Rhodes and Stuart P. M. Mackintosh, "How the Sino-American Rivalry Is Reshaping the World Order", Project Syndicate: The World's Opinion Page (June 7, 2024), accessed June 25, 2024, https://www.project-syndicate.org/commentary/us-china-conflict-will-increase-importance-of-regional-alliances-by-william-r-rhodes-and-stuart-p-m-mackintosh-2024-06
10. See Rhodes and Mackintosh, "How the Sino-American Rivalry Is Reshaping the World Order".
11. See Rhodes and Mackintosh, "How the Sino-American Rivalry Is Reshaping the World Order".
12. See Mike Maharrey, "Dollar reserves have dropped by 14 percent since 2002", Money Metals Exchange, 19-08-2024, https://www.fxstreet.com/analysis/dollar-reserves-have-dropped-by-14-percent-since-2002-202408191736
13. See Rhodes and Mackintosh, "How the Sino-American Rivalry Is Reshaping the World Order".
14. See Rhodes and Mackintosh, "How the Sino-American Rivalry Is Reshaping the World Order".
15. See Rhodes and Mackintosh, "How the Sino-American Rivalry Is Reshaping the World Order".
16. See Maharrey, "Dollar reserves have dropped by 14 percent since 2002", Money Metals Exchange."
17. DAILY SABAH, "Fidan holds talks in Russia as Türkiye inches closer to BRICS" (June 11, 2024), accessed June 25, 2024, https://www.dailysabah.com/politics/fidan-holds-talks-in-russia-as-turkiye-inches-closer-to-brics/news
18. TRT AFRIKA, "Relations between Ankara, Moscow going really well: Turkish FM Fidan" (June 11, 2024), https://trtafrika.com/turkey/relations-between-ankara-

moscow-going-really-well-turkish-fm-fidan-18172251
19. Aslı Aydıntaşbaş cited in "Russia's BRICS summit: What's on the agenda and why it matters to Putin" Al Jazeera, 22 October 2024, accessed October 23, 2024, https://www.aljazeera.com/news/2024/10/22/russias-brics-summit-whats-on-the-agenda-and-why-does-it-matter
20. Haluk Direskeneli, "India Blocks Turkey's BRICS Membership Bid Due To Relations With Pakistan – OpEd", Eurasia Review: News & Analysis, 24 October, 2024, accessed October 27, 2024, https://www.eurasiareview.com/25102024-india-blocks-turkeys-brics-membership-bid-due-to-relations-with-pakistan-oped/
21. Ben Norton, "BRICS grows, adding 13 new 'partner countries' at historic summit in Kazan, Russia", 24 October 2024, Eurasia, accessed October 27, 2024, https://geopoliticaleconomy.com/2024/10/26/brics-13-partner-countries-summit-kazan-russia/
22. See Norton, "BRICS grows, adding 13 new 'partner countries' at historic summit in Kazan, Russia".
23. See Norton, "BRICS grows, adding 13 new 'partner countries' at historic summit in Kazan, Russia".
24. R. T. Erdogan, "Peace has no losers', Erdogan says, vowing to step up efforts to end war in Ukraine", United Nations News, accessed September 24, 2o24, https://news.un.org/en/story/2023/09/1141047
25. Erdogan, "Peace has no losers', Erdogan says, vowing to step up efforts to end war in Ukraine".
26. For more see the opinion piece by Mehmet Celik, "OPINION - President Erdogan's UNGA speech: From Gaza to the "world is bigger than five", 25-09-2024, Anadolu Agency, accessed September 25, 2024, https://www.aa.com.tr/en/opinion/opinion-president-erdogan-s-unga-speech-from-gaza-to-the-world-is-bigger-than-five/3340985
27. For more see "UN veto power a must now for one Islamic nation — Erdogan", TRT Global, 3 March, 2025, https://trt-global.com/world/article/5510f6f25b40
28. See "UN veto power a must now for one Islamic nation — Erdogan".
29. Recep T. Erdogan, "Muslims deserve fair representation in global decision-making bodies", Daily Sabah, 3 MArch 2025, https://www.dailysabah.com/politics/diplomacy/muslims-deserve-fair-representation-in-global-decision-making-bodies
30. George W. Bush, "Address to a Joint Session of Congress and the American People", The White House, September, 20, 2001, https://georgewbush-whitehouse.archives.gov/news/releases/2001/09/20010920-8.html
31. Richard Falk, "Twilight of the Nation-State at a Time of Resurgent Nationalism", Global Justice in the 21st Century, https://richardfalk.org/category/global-governance/
32. Falk cited in Edibe Beyza Caglar, "Trump's Gaza takeover plan condemned as 'betrayal' by former UN official", TRT World, 20 February, 2025**,** https://www.trtworld.com/magazine/trumps-gaza-takeover-plan-condemned-as-betrayal-by-former-un-official-18267285
33. See Falk, Falk, "Twilight of the Nation-State at a Time of Resurgent Nationalism".
34. See Falk, Falk, "Twilight of the Nation-State at a Time of Resurgent Nationalism".
35. Shahid Bolsen, "Revoke America's License to Kill", Middle Nation, You Tube, February 12, 2025, https://www.youtube.com/watch?v=ch3O4n9QRdI
36. Charter of the United Nations, Article 6, Codification Division Publication, Repertory Practice of United Nations Organs, https://legal.un.org/repertory/art6.shtml
37. Bolsen, "Revoke America's License to Kill".

38. See Hope O'Dell, "How the US has used its power in the UN to support Israel for decades", Bluemarble, 18 December, 2023, https://globalaffairs.org/bluemarble/how-us-has-used-its-power-un-support-israel-decades
39. See O'Dell, "How the US has used its power in the UN to support Israel for decades".
40. James Landale and Patrick Jackson, "US sides with Russia in UN resolutions on Ukraine", BBC, February 25, 2025, https://www.bbc.com/news/articles/c7435pnle0go
41. Bolsen, "Revoke America's License to Kill".
42. Bolsen, "Revoke America's License to Kill".
43. Bolsen, "Revoke America's License to Kill".
44. Bolsen, "Revoke America's License to Kill".
45. Bolsen, "Revoke America's License to Kill".

21. AMERICA: THE LAST BASTION OF WESTERN IMPERIALISM

1. See Mike Hawkins, *Social Darwinism in European and American Thought 1860–1945: Nature and Model and Nature as Threat* (London: Cambridge University Press, 1997).
2. See "The Inaugural Address", White House, 20 January, 2025, https://www.whitehouse.gov/remarks/2025/01/the-inaugural-address/
3. For more on Manifest Destiny see Trevor B. McCrisken, "Exceptionalism: Manifest Destiny", in *Encyclopedia of American Foreign Policy* (2002), Vol. 2, Alexander DeConte, ed. (New York: Charles Scribner's & Sons, 2001), 68; also see John O'Sullivan, *Manifest Destiny*, Digital History ID 362, https://www.digitalhistory.uh.edu/disp_textbook.cfm?smtID=3&psid=362
4. See "The Inaugural Address".
5. Dan Steinbock, "What's driving Trump's quest for expansion, domination and influence?" TRT World, 12 February, 2025, https://www.trtworld.com/opinion/whats-driving-trumps-quest-for-expansion-domination-and-influence-18264192
6. Nadim Siraj, "Trump's Gaza gambit is just a continuation of America's dark legacy", TRT World, 13 February, 2025, https://www.trtworld.com/opinion/trumps-gaza-gambit-is-just-a-continuation-of-americas-dark-legacy-18264654
7. See Siraj, "Trump's Gaza gambit is just a continuation of America's dark legacy".
8. See "The Inaugural Address".
9. Artyom Lukin, "Will Trump 2.0 usher in a new age of imperialism?", Think China, 28 January, 2025, https://www.thinkchina.sg/politics/will-trump-2-0-usher-new-age-imperialism
10. Franco Ordonez and Deepa Shivaram, "Trump says he wants the U.S. to take ownership of the Gaza Strip", NPR Network, 4 February, 2025, https://www.npr.org/2025/02/04/nx-s1-5287012/trump-netanyahu-ceasefire-gaza
11. See Ordonez and Shivaram, "Trump says he wants the U.S. to take ownership of the Gaza Strip".
12. "Full text of Trump and Netanyahu's explosive news conference", Middle East Eye, 5 February, 2025, https://www.middleeasteye.net/news/full-text-trump-and-netanyahus-explosive-news-conference
13. See Ordonez and Deepa Shivaram, "Trump says he wants the U.S. to take ownership of the Gaza Strip".

14. See Ordonez and Deepa Shivaram, "Trump says he wants the U.S. to take ownership of the Gaza Strip".
15. See Ordonez and Deepa Shivaram, "Trump says he wants the U.S. to take ownership of the Gaza Strip".
16. See "Full text of Trump and Netanyahu's explosive news conference", Middle East Eye, 5 February, 2025, https://www.middleeasteye.net/news/full-text-trump-and-netanyahus-explosive-news-conference
17. See "Full text of Trump and Netanyahu's explosive news conference", Middle East Eye, 5 February, 2025, https://www.middleeasteye.net/news/full-text-trump-and-netanyahus-explosive-news-conference
18. James Mackenzie and Doina Chiacu, "Trump says Israel would hand over Gaza after fighting is over, no US troops needed", Reuters, 7 February, 2025, https://www.reuters.com/world/middle-east/israels-defense-minister-orders-army-prepare-gaza-residents-departure-media-2025-02-06/
19. See Ordonez and Deepa Shivaram, "Trump says he wants the U.S. to take ownership of the Gaza Strip".
20. Michael R. Allen, "Trump's Ethnic Cleansing of Gaza Is a Brutal Form of Colonial Capitalism", Common Dreams, 5 February, 2025, https://www.commondreams.org/opinion/trump-ethnic-cleansing-gaza-2671102101
21. Rania Abu Shamala, 'Take Israelis to Alaska, Greenland,' Saudi official mocks Trump's Gaza plan", Anadolu Ajansı, 9 February, 2025, https://www.aa.com.tr/en/americas/-take-israelis-to-alaska-greenland-saudi-official-mocks-trump-s-gaza-plan/3476754#
22. "Arab states reject Trump plan for Gaza, Egypt foreign minister tells Rubio", Reuters, 11 February, 2025, https://www.reuters.com/world/middle-east/arab-states-reject-trump-plan-gaza-egypt-foreign-minister-tells-rubio-2025-02-10/
23. Kevin Liptak and Donald Judd, Trump says 'all hell is going to break out' if Hamas doesn't release hostages by Saturday at noon", CNN, 10 February, 2025, https://edition.cnn.com/2025/02/10/politics/trump-palestinians-no-right-return-gaza/index.html
24. Kevin Liptak, "Trump stands by his Gaza plan in meeting with Jordan's Kng Abdullah", CNN, 11 February, 2025, https://edition.cnn.com/2025/02/11/politics/trump-jordan-king-abdullah-gaza-plan/index.html
25. Liptak, "Trump stands by his Gaza plan in meeting with Jordan's Kng Abdullah".
26. "Francesca Albanese calls for US isolation over Gaza takeover proposal", SBS News You Tube Channel, February 6, 2025, https://www.youtube.com/watch?v=ZAAHHH_BFVo
27. See Arik Ascherman, "The Demagoguery of Pharaoh and the Demagoguery of Donald Trump", The Times of Israel, January 11, 2021, https://blogs.timesofisrael.com/the-demagoguery-of-pharaoh-and-the-demagoguery-of-donald-trump/
28. Shahid Bolsen, "Shahid Bolsen gives a scathing commentary on Trump's America Warning of Inevitable Collapse Of USA", You Tube, 4 March, 2025, https://www.youtube.com/watch?v=kSfdmdrxcsA
29. Cited in "'Pure evil' — Trump, Musk, Netanyahu feature in grotesque AI Gaza clip", TRT World, February 26, 2025, https://www.trtworld.com/middle-east/pure-evil-trump-musk-netanyahu-feature-in-grotesque-ai-gaza-clip-18269114
30. See "'Pure evil' — Trump, Musk, Netanyahu feature in grotesque AI Gaza clip", TRT World, February 26, 2025.
31. Olivia Holmes and Paul Owen, "Trump faces Truth Social backlash over AI video of Gaza with topless Netanyahu and bearded bellydancers", The Guardian, February

26, 2025, https://www.theguardian.com/us-news/2025/feb/26/backlash-trump-shares-ai-created-video-reimagined-gaza
32. Ben Goggin, "'Trump Gaza' video shared by president originated from pro-Israel accounts that have embraced AI", NBC, February 27, 2025, https://www.nbcnews.com/tech/internet/trump-gaza-video-shared-president-originated-israel-accounts-embraced-rcna193891
33. Cited in "'Pure evil' — Trump, Musk, Netanyahu feature in grotesque AI Gaza clip", TRT World, February 26, 2025.
34. Tom O'Connor and Amira El-Fekki, "Hamas Responds to Trump's AI Gaza Video", Newsweek, February 26, 2025, https://www.newsweek.com/hamas-israel-ai-video-donald-trump-gaza-palestinians-war-2036693
35. See "The Inaugural Address".
36. Phyllis Bennis, "Trump's Big, Bad, Destructive, and Unpeaceful Imperialism", Common Dreams, 31 January, 2025, https://www.commondreams.org/opinion/trump-imperialism-2671040104
37. Shahid Bolsen, "Trump: Overseeing the Downfall", Middle Nation, You Tube, January 29, 2025, https://www.youtube.com/watch?v=kE7UwSc_Z6s
38. See Bolsen, "Trump: Overseeing the Downfall".
39. See Lukin, "Will Trump 2.0 usher in a new age of imperialism?"
40. See Bolsen, "Shahid Bolsen gives a scathing commentary on Trump's America Warning of Inevitable Collapse Of USA".
41. See Bolsen, "Trump: Overseeing the Downfall".
42. See Bolsen, "Trump: Overseeing the Downfall".
43. Shahid Bolsen, "America Will Own Gaza", Middle Nation, February 7, 2025, https://www.youtube.com/watch?v=7UTpJYZ6Eec
44. See Bolsen, "America Will Own Gaza".
45. Trita Parsi, "What Rubio said about multipolarity should get more attention", Responsible Statecraft, 3 February, 2025, https://responsiblestatecraft.org/marco-rubio/
46. Bolsen, "America Will Own Gaza".
47. Bolsen, "America Will Own Gaza".
48. Bolsen, "America Will Own Gaza".
49. Bolsen, "America Will Own Gaza".
50. Julius Sello Malema, "South Africa Sends SHOCKWAVES to America | Explosive Warning to Elon Musk & Trump!" You Tube, 12 February, 2025, https://www.youtube.com/watch?v=gzL-rQMnRWY
51. These nine Global Nations include: South Africa, Malaysia, Namibia, Colombia, Bolivia, Chile, Senegal, Honduras, and Belize.
52. Zeynep Conkar, "How the Hague Group is set to challenge US-backed Israeli impunity", TRT World, 15 February, 2025, https://www.trtworld.com/magazine/how-the-hague-group-is-set-to-challenge-us-backed-israeli-impunity-18265079
53. Cited in Conkar, "How the Hague Group is set to challenge US-backed Israeli impunity".
54. Amelia Gentleman, "African and Caribbean nations agree move to seek reparations for slavery", The Guardian, 18 November, 2023, https://www.theguardian.com/world/2023/nov/17/african-and-caribbean-nations-agree-move-to-seek-reparations-for-slavery
55. Martin Lynn, "How many Africans were transported to the Americas as a result of the European slave trade? Has anyone tried to quantify how many died as a result?"

The Guardian, 2011, https://www.theguardian.com/notesandqueries/query/0,,-1255,00.html
56. United Nations, The Question of Palestine, 21 November, 2024, https://www.un.org/unispal/document/icc-arrest-warrant-netanyahu-21nov24/
57. Bolsen, "America Will Own Gaza".
58. Stephen Collinson, "How the world changed in a month", CNN, February 22, 2025, https://edition.cnn.com/2025/02/22/world/trump-vance-zelensky-europe-intl-latam/index.html
59. Collinson, "How the world changed in a month".
60. Collinson, "How the world changed in a month".
61. Collinson, "How the world changed in a month".
62. Collinson, "How the world changed in a month".
63. "UK PM Starmer says he does not accept that US is an unreliable ally", Reuters, March 3, 2025, https://www.reuters.com/world/uk/uk-pm-starmer-says-he-does-not-accept-that-us-is-an-unreliable-ally-2025-03-02/
64. See "Trump's explosive clash with Zelenskyy: read the full transcript", The Guardian, March 1, 2025, https://www.theguardian.com/us-news/2025/feb/28/trump-zelenskyy-meeting-transcript
65. Mazoe Ford, "After Trump and Zelenskyy's heated clash in the Oval Office, what now for Ukraine?", ABC News, 28 February, 2025, https://www.abc.net.au/news/2025-03-02/analysis-trump-zelenskyy-oval-office-what-now-for-ukraine/104999758
66. J. D. Vance, "Vice President JD Vance reveals the moment the Trump-Zelenskyy meeting 'went off the rails'", Fox News, You Tube, 4 March, 2025, https://www.youtube.com/watch?v=HOJS3qQlVjE
67. Monica Duffy Toft, "Trump's threats on Greenland, Gaza, Ukraine and Panama revive old-school US imperialism of dominating other nations by force, after decades of nuclear deterrence", The Conversation, 21 February, 2025, https://theconversation.com/trumps-threats-on-greenland-gaza-ukraine-and-panama-revive-old-school-us-imperialism-of-dominating-other-nations-by-force-after-decades-of-nuclear-deterrence-249327
68. See Toft, "Trump's threats on Greenland, Gaza, Ukraine and Panama".
69. Stephen Collinson, "Trump makes fateful wager by testing his lifelong faith in the power of tariffs", CNN, 4 March, 2025, https://edition.cnn.com/2025/03/04/politics/trump-tariffs-economy-gamble/index.html
70. Laura Gozzi, "Europe 'at turning point in history', French president warns", BBC News, 6 March, 2025, https://www.bbc.com/news/articles/c3w14gw3wwlo
71. "Speech by French Senator Claude Malhuret on Ukraine and European security", Diplomatizzando, 7 March, 2025, https://diplomatizzando.blogspot.com/2025/03/speech-by-french-senator-claude.html
72. See "Speech by French Senator Claude Malhuret on Ukraine and European security".
73. See "Speech by French Senator Claude Malhuret on Ukraine and European security".
74. See "Speech by French Senator Claude Malhuret on Ukraine and European security".
75. Utku Simsek and Seda Sevencan, "Turkish intel helps release of 5 Thai hostages in Gaza via negotiations with Hamas," Anadolu Ajansı, 30 January, 2025, https://www.aa.com.tr/en/turkiye/turkish-intel-helps-release-of-5-thai-hostages-in-gaza-via-negotiations-with-hamas/3466970

76. Kalkidan Yibeltal and Basillioh Rukanga, "Ethiopia and Somalia agree to end bitter Somaliland port feud", BBC, 12 December, 2024, https://www.bbc.com/news/articles/cvgr7v1evvgo
77. "Russia, Ukraine 'close to agreement' in negotiations, says Turkey", Al Jazeera, 20 March, 2022, https://www.aljazeera.com/news/2022/3/20/turkey-says-russia-ukraine-close-to-agreement
78. Peter Wintour, "What was the Black Sea grain deal and why did it collapse?" The Guardian, 20 July, 2023, https://www.theguardian.com/world/2023/jul/20/what-was-the-black-sea-grain-deal-and-why-did-it-collapse
79. "Security Council Thanks Qatar for Facilitating Afghan Peace Negotiations", Qatar Ministry of Foreign Affairs, 18 September, 2020, https://mofa.gov.qa/en/qatar/latest-articles/latest-news/details/1442/02/01/security-council-thanks-qatar-for-facilitating-afghan-peace-negotiations
80. "Russia and Ukraine swap 25 POWs each in UAE-mediated exchange", Reuters, 16 January, 2025, https://www.reuters.com/world/europe/russia-ukraine-swap-25-pows-each-uae-mediated-exchange-moscow-says-2025-01-15/
81. "Qatar reiterates its support for international efforts to resolve Russian-Ukrainian crisis peacefully", Qatar Ministry of Foreign Affairs, 25 January, 2025, https://www.wam.ae/en/article/bhv929e-qatar-reiterates-its-support-for-international
82. Kevin Liptak and Jeff Zeleny, "Trump leans on close ties to Saudi prince as he looks for a deal on Ukraine", CNN, 17 February, 2025, https://edition.cnn.com/2025/02/17/politics/trump-saudi-arabia-ukraine/index.html; also see, Mostafa Salem, "Why is Saudi Arabia hosting talks to end the Ukraine war?", CNN, 11 March, 2025, https://edition.cnn.com/2025/02/17/middleeast/saudi-riyadh-us-russia-talks-analysis-intl-latam
83. In 2003, during a session of question time in the European Parliament, a significant discussion unfolded among ministers concerning the portrayal of the European Union as a "Christian Club." This conversation was ignited by remarks made by Recep Tayyip Erdogan, who was then the Turkish Minister of State. Erdogan proposed the idea of partitioning the Mediterranean into separate entities for Christians and Muslims. At the same event, he, in his capacity as Prime Minister of Turkey, reinforced his stance by asserting, "We would not like the EU to become a Christian club." See European Parliamentary question - H-0652/2003, 'The EU as a Christian club', 24 October 2003, https://www.europarl.europa.eu/doceo/document/H-5-2003-0652_EN.html
84. Tuvan Gümrükçü, "Turkey could be a vital partner as Europe, Ukraine seek new security framework", Reuters, 13 March, 2025, https://www.reuters.com/world/europe/turkey-could-be-vital-partner-europe-ukraine-seek-new-security-framework-2025-03-13/
85. See Gümrükçü, "Turkey could be a vital partner as Europe, Ukraine seek new security framework".
86. See Gümrükçü, "Turkey could be a vital partner as Europe, Ukraine seek new security framework".
87. "Polish prime minister urges Turkey to play key role in Ukrainian peace process", Euronews, 12 March, 2025, https://www.euronews.com/my-europe/2025/03/12/polish-prime-minister-urges-turkey-to-play-key-role-in-ukrainian-peace-process
88. Selcan Hacaoglu, "Erdogan Tries to Leverage Turkey's NATO Muscle as US Retreats", Bloomberg, 13 March, 2025, https://www.bloomberg.com/news/articles/2025-03-13/turkey-s-erdogan-seeks-closer-ties-with-europe-as-us-retreats
89. See Hacaoglu, "Erdogan Tries to Leverage Turkey's NATO Muscle as US Retreats".

90. For more see Bolsen, "Shahid Bolsen gives a scathing commentary on Trump's America Warning of Inevitable Collapse Of USA".
91. For more see Bolsen, "Shahid Bolsen gives a scathing commentary on Trump's America Warning of Inevitable Collapse Of USA".
92. See Donald Trump's inaugural speech, January 20, 2025.
93. Donald Trump, "Transcript of President Donald Trump's speech to a joint session of Congress", Associated Press News, March 4, 2025, https://apnews.com/article/trump-speech-congress-transcript-751b5891a3265ff1e5c1409c391fef7c

22. FROM EUROPE TO AMERICA

1. See David L. Johnston, "American Evangelical Islamophobia: A History of Continuity with a Hope for Change", Fuller Studio (Fuller Theological Seminary), accessed November 12 2024, https://fullerstudio.fuller.edu/american-evangelical-islamophobia-a-history-of-continuity-with-a-hope-for-change/
2. Massimo Faggioli, "Donald Trump captured American Catholicism — and the ramifications are being felt around the world", ABC News, 19 February, 2025, https://www.abc.net.au/religion/massimo-faggioli-trump-captured-american-catholicism/104955542
3. Zeynep Conkar, "Does Israel have biblical right over Palestine? Christian Zionists claim so, Theologians disagree", TRT WORLD, 29 January, 2025, accessed January 29, 2025, https://www.trtworld.com/magazine/does-israel-have-biblical-right-over-palestine-christian-zionists-claim-so-18259150
4. Joseph Gedeon, "Trump UN nominee backs Israeli claims of biblical rights to West Bank", The Guardian, 25 January, 2025, accessed January 30, 2025, https://www.theguardian.com/us-news/2025/jan/21/trump-un-elise-stefanik-israel
5. See Gedeon, "Trump UN nominee backs Israeli claims of biblical rights to West Bank".
6. See Genesis in the Bible, 12:3.
7. See Stephen Sizer, "A Biblical Refutation of Christian Zionism", You Tube, April 28, 2024, accessed January 30, 2025, https://www.youtube.com/watch?v=LohMNT_Xtas&t=1s
8. See Sizer, "A Biblical Refutation of Christian Zionism".
9. See Conkar, "Does Israel have biblical right over Palestine? Christian Zionists claim so, Theologians disagree."
10. See Todd Green, "Confronting Christian Islamophobia: Healing Muslim-Christian Relations in the United States", May 24, 2021, Berkley Center for Religion, Peace & World Affairs, Georgetown University, accessed November 13, 2024, https://berkleycenter.georgetown.edu/responses/confronting-christian-islamophobia
11. See Green, "Confronting Christian Islamophobia: Healing Muslim-Christian Relations in the United States".
12. See Green, "Confronting Christian Islamophobia".
13. See Green, "Confronting Christian Islamophobia".
14. See Green, "Confronting Christian Islamophobia".
15. See Green, "Confronting Christian Islamophobia".
16. See Green, "Confronting Christian Islamophobia".
17. See Green, "Confronting Christian Islamophobia".
18. See Green, "Confronting Christian Islamophobia".
19. See Green, "Confronting Christian Islamophobia".

472 NOTES

20. See Johnston, "American Evangelical Islamophobia: A History of Continuity with a Hope for Change".
21. See Johnston, "American Evangelical Islamophobia: A History of Continuity with a Hope for Change".
22. See Johnston, "American Evangelical Islamophobia".
23. Revelation 16:12, "The sixth angel poured out his bowl on the great river Euphrates, and its water was dried up to prepare the way for the kings from the East."
24. See Johnston, "American Evangelical Islamophobia".
25. See Tim LaHaye and Jerry B. Jenkins, a series of sixteen books (Carol Springs, IL: Tyndale, 1995-2007).
26. See Johnston, "American Evangelical Islamophobia".
27. See Johnston, "American Evangelical Islamophobia".
28. Thomas S. Kidd, *American Christians and Islam: Evangelical Culture and Muslims from the Colonial Period to the Age of Terrorism* (Princeton, NJ, and Oxford: Princeton University Press, 2009), 159.
29. See Chrissy Stroop, "America's Islamophobia Is Forged at the Pulpit: White evangelicals' apocalyptic fantasies are driving U.S. policy", Foreign Policy, accessed November 12, 2024, https://foreignpolicy.com/2019/03/26/americas-islamophobia-is-forged-in-the-pulpit/
30. See Stroop, "America's Islamophobia Is Forged at the Pulpit".
31. See Stroop, "America's Islamophobia Is Forged at the Pulpit".
32. See Stroop, "America's Islamophobia Is Forged at the Pulpit".

23. CHALLENGING WESTERN CULTURAL IMPERIALISM AND SOFT POWER POLITICS

1. J. Molyneux, *Will The Revolution Be Televised? A Marxist analysis of the media* (London: Bookmarks Publications, 2011), 55.
2. See Willow H. Wood, "Essays, Politics: Hollywood and Western Ideology," (August 14, 2013), https://willowhwood.com/2013/08/14/hollywood-and-western-ideology/
3. J. Tomlinson, *Cultural imperialism: A critical intro- duction* (London, England: Continuum, 2002), 13.
4. J. Petras, "Cultural imperialism in the late 20th century", *Journal of Contemporary Asia*, 23(2), (1993): 140, 139-148, accessed May 21, 2024, http://dx.doi.org/10.1080/00472339380000091
5. S. Rohac, (2007). *Cultural diversity versus us cultural imperialism: The film industry* (München, Germany: GRIN Verlag, 2007), 4; also see Stephanie Rohac, *Cultural diversity versus US cultural imperialism: The film industry* (2007), 4.
6. Bethany Avalos, *A regretted legacy? Literary and cultural responses to U.S. imperialism in Hawaii and Puerto Rico*, 2019 (Doctoral dissertation). Retrieved from Pro-Quest LLC (22584785), 6.
7. I. M. Young, *Justice and the politics of difference* (New Jersey, NJ: Princeton University Press, 1990), 60.
8. T. Friedman, "The Trajectory of American politics, power and prestige: A conversation with Tom Friedman," United States Studies Centre, Podcast, Episode 56, August 19, 2024, https://www.ussc.edu.au/the-trajectory-of-american-politics-power-and-prestige-a-conversation-with-tom-friedman

9. See Wanwarang Maisuwong, "The Promotion of American Culture through Hollywood Movies to the World," *International Journal of Engineering Research & Technology*, Vol. 1 Issue 4, June – 2012: 1, accessed May 21, 2024. 1-7
10. Tomlinson, in *Cultural imperialism: A critical introduction* (2002), 13.
11. See Petras, "Cultural imperialism in the late 20th century".
12. See Petras, "Cultural imperialism in the late 20th century".
13. See Petras, "Cultural imperialism in the late 20th century".
14. See Petras, "Cultural imperialism in the late 20th century".
15. Turkey's Minister of Culture and Tourism announced on November 16, 2017, that Turkey holds the second position in television series exports globally, following the United States. During a session with the Planning and Budget Committee of the Parliament, Numan Kurtulmuş emphasized the significance of exporting Turkish television series. Kurtulmuş stated that Turkey is the second-largest exporter of television series after the U.S., highlighting that 48 percent of the Turkish population watches domestic productions, with Turkish films leading in Europe. The widespread popularity of Turkish TV series has led to exports to more than 200 countries, fuelling growth in the domestic television industry.
16. Joseph Nye, *Soft Power: The Means to Success in World Politics*, (New York: Public Affairs, 2004), 5.
17. Nye, *Soft Power: The Means to Success in World Politics*, 85.
18. See "The third-largest exporter of television is not who you might expect: After America and Britain, Turkey is the biggest seller of scripted shows", The Economist (15 February, 2024), accessed August 15, 2024, https://www.economist.com/culture/2024/02/15/the-third-largest-exporter-of-television-is-not-who-you-might-expect
19. Ayşe Isin Kirenci, "Climbing to top 3 in global market, what makes Turkish series different?" (March 2024), https://www.trtworld.com/turkiye/climbing-to-top-3-in-global-market-what-makes-turkish-series-different-17260108
20. Kirenci, "Climbing to top 3 in global market, what makes Turkish series different?"
21. See The Economist (15 February 2024), "The third-largest exporter of television is not who you might expect," https://www.economist.com/culture/2024/02/15/the-third-largest-exporter-of-television-is-not-who-you-might-expect
22. For more detail Kirenci, "Climbing to top 3 in global market, what makes Turkish series different?"
23. For more detail Kirenci, "Climbing to top 3 in global market, what makes Turkish series different?"
24. For more detail Kirenci, "Climbing to top 3 in global market, what makes Turkish series different?"
25. See "The Economist" (15 February 2024), "The third-largest exporter of television is not who you might expect."
26. See New York City Turkish Club, "Turkish Drama Craze", https://www.nycturkishclub.com/turkish-dramas/
27. See New York City Turkish Club, "Turkish Drama Craze", https://www.nycturkishclub.com/turkish-dramas/
28. See William Armstrong, "What a TV Series Tells Us About Erdogan's Turkey," The New York Times (May 14, 2017), accessed May 16, 2024, https://www.nytimes.com/2017/05/14/opinion/erdogan-tv-show-turkey.html
29. Euromonitor International's report reveals world's Top 100 City Destinations for 2023, accessed November 16, 2024, https://www.euromonitor.com/press/press-

releases/dec-2023/euromonitor-internationals-report-reveals-worlds-top-100-city-destinations-for-2023
30. See Pradeep Menon, *Resurrection: Ertugrul*, currently on Netflix, far exceeds its reputation as a 'Turkish Game of Thrones'", (9 July, 2020), accessed May 26, 2024, https://www.firstpost.com/entertainment/resurrection-ertugrul-currently-on-netflix-far-exceeds-its-reputation-as-a-turkish-game-of-thrones-8576051.html ; also see *"Greater Kashmir*, (24 April 2020), accessed May 26, 2024, https://www.greaterkashmir.com/todays-paper/op-ed/ertugrul-turkish-game-of-thrones/
31. See The Economist (15 February 2024), "The third-largest exporter of television is not who you might expect."
32. See The Economist (15 February 2024), "The third-largest exporter of television is not who you might expect."
33. For more detail Kirenci, "Climbing to top 3 in global market, what makes Turkish series different?"
34. See "The Economist" (15 February 2024), "The third-largest exporter of television is not who you might expect."
35. See New York City Turkish Club, "Turkish Drama Craze", https://www.nycturkishclub.com/turkish-dramas/
36. See Global Voices Online, "Why some Latin Americans are naming their children 'Onur' and 'Sherezade'", May 21, 2015, httpsa://the world.org/programs/global-voices-online
37. For more see "Türkiye continues to emerge as leading force in TV exports", Hürriyet Daily News, 28 October, 2024, accessed October 30, 2024, https://www.hurriyetdailynews.com/turkiye-continues-to-emerge-as-leading-force-in-tv-exports-201986
38. See "Türkiye continues to emerge as leading force in TV exports", Hürriyet Daily News, 28 October, 2024.
39. "Arab World Remains Biggest Market for Turkish TV Series," *Arab News*, (2017), accessed November 15, 2024, https://www.arabnews.com/node/1197036/media.
40. "Ertuğrul: How an Epic TV Series Became the 'Muslim Game of Thrones',," *The Guardian*, (August 12, 2020), accessed November 15, 2024, https://www.theguardian.com/tv-and-radio/2020/aug/12/ertugrul-how-an-epic-tv-series-became-the-muslim-game-of-thrones.

CONCLUSION

1. Esposito, J., *The Islamic Threat: Myth or Reality?*, 40.
2. Lewis, *Islam and the West*, 135.
3. Lewis, *The Middle East, 2000 Years of History from the Rise of Christianity to the Present Day*, 128.
4. N. Daniel, *Islam And The West - The Making of an Image* (London: Oneworld Oxford Publications, 1997), 333
5. Daniel, *Islam And The West*, 326.
6. Daniel, *Islam And The West*, 326.
7. Daniel, *Islam And The West*, 326.
8. Esposito, *The Islamic Threat*, 242.
9. For more see Ahmed Paul Keeler, *Rethinking Islam & the West: A New Narrative for the Age of Crises* (CITY: Equilibra Press, 2019).
10. Qur'an, 30:22.

11. Tod Perry, "Astronaut shares the profound 'big lie' he realized after seeing the Earth from space: This change in perspective could change humanity", Upworthy, accessed November 22, 2024, https://www.upworthy.com/astronaut-shares-big-lie-space-ex1

EPILOGUE

1. Michael H. Hart, *The 100: A Ranking of the Most Influential Persons in History* (New York: Hart Publishing Company, 1992), 33-39.
2. Paul Williams, "Reverend Professor Keith Ward on Muhammad as a Prophet of God", Blogging Theology Podcast, You Tube, May 2, 2021, https://www.youtube.com/watch?v=FkeoGRT_ATE

BIBLIOGRAPHY

Adivar, A. A. *Osmanlı Türklerinde Bilim*. Istanbul: Maarif Matbaası, 1943.

Al-Awlaki A. 44 Ways to Support Jihad. NEFA Foundation, 5 February 2009. Accessed March 5, 2023. <http://www.nefafoundation.org/file/FeaturedDocs/nefaawlaki44wayssupportjihad.p df> (15 March 2012).

Al-Azm, S. J. "Orientalism and Orientalism in Reverse". *Khamsin*, 8 (1981): 5-26.

Allen, A. *The End of Progress: Decolonizing the Normative - Foundations of Critical Theory*. New York: Columbia Unuversity Press, 2016.

Allen, Michael R. "Trump's Ethnic Cleansing of Gaza Is a Brutal Form of Colonial Capitalism". Common Dreams, 5 February, 2025. https://www.commondreams.org/opinion/trump-ethnic-cleansing-gaza-2671102101

Asad, T. (ed.). *Anthropology and the Colonial Encounter*. London: Ithaca Press, 1973.

Ascherman, A. "The Demagoguery of Pharaoh and the Demagoguery of Donald Trump". The Times of Israel, January 11, 2021. https://blogs.timesofisrael.com/the-demagoguery-of-pharaoh-and-the-demagoguery-of-donald-trump/

Asrar, N., *Kanuni Sultan Süleyman ve Islam Alemi*. Istanbul: Hilal Yayınlar, 1992.

Aydıntaşbaş, A. "Russia's BRICS summit: What's on the agenda and why it matters to Putin". Al Jazeera, 22 October 2024. Accessed October 23, 2024. https://www.aljazeera.com/news/2024/10/22/russias-brics-summit-whats-on-the-agenda-and-why-does-it-matter

Azak, U. *Islam and Secularism in Turkey, Kemalism, Religion and the Nation State*. London: IB Tauris, 2010.

Babinger, F. *Mehmed the Conqueror and His Time*. 2nd ed.Edited by W. C. Hickman. Translated by R. Manheim. Princeton: Princeton University Press, 1992.

Bardakçı, M. "Even Einstein once asked for a job in Turkey, which today discusses men shaking hands with women." *Hürriyet* (October 29, 2006). Accessed May 29, 2024. https://www.hurriyet.com.tr/bugun-erkegin-kadinla-tokalasmasini-tartisan turkiye-den-bir-zamanlar-einstein-bile-is-ricasinda-bulunuyordu-5335137

Bayraklı, B. "Atatürk ve Din." Yolu Tube. October 29, 2021. https://www.youtube.com/watch?v=fzN-LG47s0I

Bayraklı, B. "Sermons." You Tube. https://www.youtube.com/@bbayrakli

Benn, S. *The battle of Bretton Woods John Maynard Keynes, Harry Dexter, and the making of a new world order*. Princeton: Princeton University Press, 2014.

Bennis, P. "Trump's Big, Bad, Destructive, and Unpeaceful Imperialism". Common Dreams, 31 January, 2025. https://www.commondreams.org/opinion/trump-imperialism-2671040104

Bleischer, J., and Josh Lipsky. "The Geopolitical Imperative to Upgrade the Dollar". Project Syndicate: The World's Opinion Page (June 24, 2024). Accessed June 26, 2024. https://www.project-syndicate.org/commentary/swift-alternatives-could-undermine-american-national-security-interests-by-jordan-bleicher-and-josh-lipsky-2024-06

Blume, Lawrence E. and Steven N. Durlauf (eds.). *The new Palgrave dictionary of economics* (2nd ed.). Basingstoke, Hampshire: Palgrave Macmillan, 2008.
Bin Laden. *Declaration of War (I)*. http://msanews.mynet.net/MSANEWS/199610/19961012.3.html.
Bolsen, S. "America Will Own Gaza". Middle Nation. February 7, 2025. https://www.youtube.com/watch?v=7UTpJYZ6Eec
Bolsen, S. "Revoke America's License to Kill". Middle Nation. You Tube, February 12, 2025. https://www.youtube.com/watch?v=ch3O4n9QRdI
Bolsen, S. "Trump: Overseeing the Downfall". Middle Nation. You Tube, January 29, 2025. https://www.youtube.com/watch?v=kE7UwSc_Z6s
Bolsen, S. "Shahid Bolsen gives a scathing commentary on Trump's America Warning of Inevitable Collapse Of USA". You Tube, March, 4, 2025. https://www.youtube.com/watch?v=kSfdmdrxcsA
Bonnett, A. "Occidentalism: The Uses of the West". Presented at the NORFACE seminar Towards a Post-Western West? The Changing Heritage of 'Europe' and the 'West', Tampere Peace Research Institute, Finland, 2-3 February 2006.
Boulainvilliers, H. *Life of Mahomet*. London: Darf, 1983.
Braudel, F. *A History of Civilisation*. New York: Penguin, 1993.
Braudel, F. *The Mediterranean and the Mediterranean World in the age of Phillip II*, Vol. II. Translated by Sian Reynolds. London: Fontana Press, 1987.
Caglar, E. B. "Trump's Gaza takeover plan condemned as 'betrayal' by former UN official". TRT World, 20 February, 2025. https://www.trtworld.com/magazine/trumps-gaza-takeover-plan-condemned-as-betrayal-by-former-un-official-18267285
Cantelmo, Maria Chiara. "The Fall of Kemalism and the New Face of Political Islam: 20 Crucial Years in Turkey's History (1980-2002)". *Athens Journal of History* (2018): 37-53.
Chardin. *Sir John's Travels in Persia*, Vol.2. London: Argonaut Press, 1927.
Childs, P., and P. Williams. *An Introduction to Post-Colonial Theory*. London: Prentice Hall / Harvester Wheatsheaf, 1997.
Clarke, John Henrik. "Origin and Impact of Racism" Great Lectures of Dr. John Henrik Clarke (podcast), November 30, 2021. Accessed April 28, 2024. https://www.spreaker.com/podcast/great-lectures-of-dr-john-henrik-clarke--5282513
Coles, P. *Ottoman Impact on Europe*. London: Harcourt, Brace & World, 1968.
Conkar, Z. "Does Israel have biblical right over Palestine? Christian Zionists claim so, Theologians disagree". TRT WORLD, 29 January, 2025. Accessed January 29, 2025. https://www.trtworld.com/magazine/does-israel-have-biblical-right-over-palestine-christian-zionists-claim-so-18259150
Corbin, H. *History of Islamic Philosophy*. Translated by L. Sherrard. London: Kegan Paul International, 1991.
Croutier, A. L. *Harem: The World Behind the Veil*. London: Bloomsbury, 1989.
Crucé, E. *The New Cyneas of Émeric Crucé; Edited with An Introduction and Translated Into English from the Original French Text of 1623 by Thomas Willing Balch*. Philadelphia: Allen, Lane and Scott, 1909. Accessed February 4, 2003). https://archive.org/details/newcyneasofemeri00cruc
Cundioğlu, D. *Türkçe Kur'an ve Cumhuriyet İdeolojisi*. Istanbul: Kitabevi Yayınları, 1998.

DAILY SABAH. "Fidan holds talks in Russia as Türkiye inches closer to BRICS" (June 11, 2024). Accessed June 25, 2024. https://www.dailysabah.com/politics/fidan-holds-talks-in-russia-as-turkiye-inches-closer-to-brics/news

Daleziou, E. "Britain and the Greek-Turkish war and settlement of 1919-1923: the pursuit of security by 'proxy' in Western Asia Minor". University of Glasgow, PhD Thesis (2002), 257. Accessed March 17, 2025. https://theses.gla.ac.uk/1578/1/2002dalezhiouphd.pdf

Daniel, N., *Islam, Europe and Empire*, Edinburgh, 1966.

Daniel. N. *Islam And The West - The Making Of An Image*. London: Oxford Publications, 1997.

De Rougemont, D. *Vingt-Huit Siècles d'Europe*. Paris: Payot, 1961.

Direskeneli, H. "India Blocks Turkey's BRICS Membership Bid Due To Relations With Pakistan – OpEd". Eurasia Review: News & Analysis, 24 October, 2024. Accessed October 27, 2024. https://www.eurasiareview.com/25102024-india-blocks-turkeys-brics-membership-bid-due-to-relations-with-pakistan-oped/

Djait, H. *Europe and Islam*. Translated by P. Heinegg. Berkeley: University of California Press, 1985.

Drezner, D. "Never mind hypocrisy, the West faces another challenge", 21 March 2024, Chatham House. Accessed August 15, 2024. https://www.chathamhouse.org/publications/the-world-today/2024-02/never-mind-hypocrisy-west-faces-another-challenge

East to West: The Untold Story of the Modern World. Produced by Lion Television and Bahçeşehir University, Turkey, 2011.

"Einstein'in Atatürk'e Mektubu" (Einstein's Letter to Atatürk). Video (in Turkish). http://www.cankaya.edu.tr/duyuru/einstein.php

El Amraoui, Ahmed and Faisla Edroos. "Why Ataturk's legacy is debated 80 years after his death". Al Jazeera, 11 June, 2018. https://www.aljazeera.com/features/2018/6/11/why-ataturks-legacy-is-debated-80-years-after-his-death

Eriksson, J. "The 'Clash of Civilizations' and Its Unexpected Liberalism". In *The Clash of Civilizations: Twenty Years On*. Edited by J. Paul Baker, 28-30. Bristol: E-International Relations, Edited Collections, 2013.

Esposito, J. *The Islamic Threat: Myth or Reality*. New York: Oxford University Press, 1992.

Eurasia Digital News. https://eurasiadigital.medium.com/einsteins-letter-to-ataturk-s-turkey-7449ada946a5

Faggioli, M. "Donald Trump captured American Catholicism — and the ramifications are being felt around the world". ABC News, 19 February, 2025. https://www.abc.net.au/religion/massimo-faggioli-trump-captured-american-catholicism/104955542

Fischer, J. "Will Europe be the world's biggest loser?" Project Syndicate: The World's Opinion Page (23 May, 2023). Accessed June 25, 2024. https://www.project-syndicate.org/commentary/europe-biggest-loser-in-multipolar-world-by-joschka-fischer-2023-05

Falk, R. "Twilight of the Nation-State at a Time of Resurgent Nationalism". Global Justice in the 21st Century. https://richardfalk.org/category/global-governance/

Fanon, F. *The Wretched of the Earth*. London: Penguin, 2001.

Foucault, M. *The Order of Things: An Archaeology of the Human Sciences*. New York: Pantheon Books, 1971.

Gibb, H .A. R. "The Influence of Islamic Culture on Medieval Europe". *Bulletin of the John Rylands Library*, 38 (1955): 82-98.

Gibbon, E. *The Decline and Fall of the Roman Empire*. London: Penguin, 1985.

Gökalp, Z. *Türkçülüğün Esasaları*. Istanbul: Varlik, 1963.

Güngör, E. "Mederese, Ilim ve Modern Düşünce". *Tore Dergisi*, Kasım (1980).

Hacaoglu, S. "Erdogan Tries to Leverage Turkey's NATO Muscle as US Retreats". Bloomberg, 13 March, 2025. https://www.bloomberg.com/news/articles/2025-03-13/turkey-s-erdogan-seeks-closer-ties-with-europe-as-us-retreats

Hale, J. *The Civilisation of Europe in the Renaissance*. London: Harper Collins Publications, 1993.

Halliday, F. "'Orientalism' and Its Critics". *British Journal of Middle Eastern Studies*, 20(2) (1993): 145-163.

Harlow, B. *Resistance Literature*. London and New York: Methuen, 1987.

Harnoncourt, N. *Die Entführung aus dem Serail Wolfgang Amadeus Mozart*. Hamburg: Teldec, 1988.

Hawkins, M. *Social Darwinism in European and American Thought 1860–1945: Nature and Model and Nature as Threat*. London: Cambridge University Press, 1997.

Haynes, J. "Twenty Years of Huntington's 'Clash of Civilizations'". In *The Clash of Civilizations: Twenty Years On*. Edited by J. Paul Baker, 10-13. Bristol: E-International Relations, Edited Collections, 2013.

Hazard, P. *European Mind, 1680-1715*. Translated by Lewis May. London: Hollis and Carter, 1953.

Hegel. *Lectures on the Philosophy of World History*. London: Cambridge University Press, 1975.

Hegel, *Philosophy of History*, translation by J. Sibree. Dover: New York, 1956.

Hentsch, T. *Imagining the Middle East*. Montreal: Black Rose Books, 1991.

Hippler, J. and Lueg, A. *The Next Threat - Western Perceptions of Islam*. Amsterdam: Pluto Press, 1995.

Hiro, D. *Between Marx and Muhammad*. London: Harper Collins Publishers, 1994.

Hodgson, M. *Rethinking World History*. London: Cambridge University Press, 1994.

Hoodbhoy, Pervez Amirali. "Science and the Islamic world—The quest for rapprochement." *Physics Today* 60, (2007): 49-55. Accessed June 19, 2024. https://doi.org/10.1063/1.2774098

Hourani, A. *Islam in European thought*. Cambridge: Cambridge University Press, 1995.

Howard, H. *The Partition of Turkey*. New York: H. Fertig, 1966.

Huntington, S. "The Clash Of Civilizations and the Remaking of World Order". Foreign Affairs (1993):

Huntington, Samuel P. *The Clash of Civilizations?* Foreign Affairs, Vol. 72, no. 3, Summer (1993): 22–49. Accessed March 27, 2019. https://www.foreignaffairs.com/articles/united-states/1993-06-01/clash-civilizations

Huntington, S. *The Clash Of Civilizations and the Remaking of World Order*. New York: Simon & Schuster, 1996.

Ibn Khaldun, *The Muqadimmah*. Translated by Franz Rosenthal. Accessed March 13, 2024. https://asadullahali.files.wordpress.com/2012/10/ibn_khaldun-al_muqaddimah.pdf

Ihsanoğlu, Ekmeleddin. "An Overview of Ottoman Scientific Activities". *Foundation for Science and Civilisation* (December 2006): 1-12. Accessed May 27, 2024. https://muslimheritage.com/uploads/An_Overview_of_Ottoman_Scientific_activities2.pdf

İnalcık, H. *The Ottoman Empire - The Classical Age 1300-1600*. London: Phoenix, 1994.

Iqbal, M. *The Reconstruction of Religious Thought in Islam*. Lahore: Muhammad Ashraf, 1962.

Iz, F. *Eski Türk Edebiyatında Nesir*. Istanbul: Osman Yalçın Matbaası, 1964.

Kant, I. "An Answer to the Question: What is Enlightenment? (1784)". Accessed August 4, 2024, https://donelan.faculty.writing.ucsb.edu/enlight.html

Kappert, P. "From Romantisation to Colonial Dominance: Historical Changes in the European Perception of the Middle East". In *The Next Threat – Western Perceptions of Islam*. Edited by Hippler & Lueg. Amsterdam: Pluto Press, 1995.

Keeler, Ahmed Paul. *Islam & The West: A New Narrative for the Age of Crises*. Cambridge: Equilibra Press, 2019.

Kibble, David G. "The Attacks of 9/11: Evidence of a Clash of Religions?" *The US Army War College Quarterly: Parameters* 32, No. 3(2002): 34-45.

Kinross, L. *The Ottoman Centuries - The Rise and Fall of the Turkish Empire*. New York: Morrow Quill Paperbacks, 1977.

Kocabaş, Ş. "Islam and Science". In *Islam and Scientific Debate: Searching for Legitimacy*, Rais Ahmad, ed., 13-35. New Delhi: Global Vision Publishing House, 2017.

Lahoud, N. *The Jihadis' Path to Self-Destruction*. New York: Columbia University Press, 2010.

Lawrence, B. *Messages to the World: The Statements of Osama bin Laden*. London and New York: Verso, 2005.

Le Journal d'Orient (October 20, 1933), Courtesy Rockefeller [Foundation]. Archives Center. Collection RF; Record Group 1.1; Series 717; Box 1; Folder 1.

Lewis, B. *Cultures In Conflict - Christian, Muslim, and Jews in the Age of Discovery*. New York: Oxford University Press, 1995.

Lewis, B. *Islam and the West*. New York: Oxford University Press, 1993.

Lewis, B. *The Middle East, 2000 Years of History from the Rise of Christianity to the Present Day*. London: Phoenix Giant, 1996.

Lewis, R. *Everyday Life in Ottoman Turkey*. New York: Dorset, 1988.

Lia, B. *Architect of Global Jihad: The Life of Al-Qaida Strategist Abu Mus'ab al-Suri*. London: Hurst and Company, 2007.

Lockman, Z. *Contending Visions of the Middle East: The History and Politics of Orientalism*. Cambridge: Cambridge University Press, 2004.

Lukin, A. "Will Trump 2.0 usher in a new age of imperialism?" Think China, 28 January, 2025. https://www.thinkchina.sg/politics/will-trump-2-0-usher-new-age-imperialism

Lumbard, Joesph E. B. "Islam and the Challenge of Epistemic Sovereignty." *Religions* 15, no. 4: 406 (2024): 1-14. Accessed, May 5, 2024. https://doi.org/10.3390/rel15040406

Lumbard, Joseph E. B. "Decolonizing Qur'anic Studies." *Religions* 13, No. 2(2022): 1-14. Accessed, May 5, 2024. https://doi.org/10.3390/rel13020176

Lybyer, A. *Government of the Ottoman Empire in the Time of Süleyman the Magnificent*. Cambridge: Harvard University Press, 1913.

Machiavelli, N. *The Prince*. London: Everyman, 1995.

Mackenzie, James and Doina Chiacu, "Trump says Israel would hand over Gaza after fighting is over, no US troops needed". Reuters, 7 February, 2025. https://www.reuters.com/world/middle-east/israels-defense-minister-orders-army-prepare-gaza-residents-departure-media-2025-02-06/

Malema, Julis Sello. "South Africa Sends SHOCKWAVES to America | Explosive Warning to Elon Musk & Trump!" You Tube, 12 February, 2025. https://www.youtube.com/watch?v=gzL-rQMnRWY

Manaz, A. *Atatürk Reformları ve Islam.* Izmir, 1995.

Markwell, D. *John Maynard Keynes and International Relations: Economic Paths to War and Peace.* Oxford: Oxford University Press, 2006.

Márquez, Miguel Rodríguez-Pantoja. *Patrimonio artístico y monumental de las universidades andaluzas.* Seville: Universidad de Sevilla, 1992.

Marx, K. *The Eighteenth Brumaire of Louis Bonaparte.* Maryland: Wildside Press, 2008.

Mattei, L. "Study of the Madrasah of Granada in the light of the Material Culture and Scientific Methods used in the intervention of 2006." University of Granada, Spain. Accessed June 7, 2024. https://www.ugr.es/~arqueologyterritorio/PDF5/Mattei.pdf

McCants, W. (trans.) 'The Management of Savagery: The Most Critical Stage Through Which the Umma Will Pass', John M. Olin Institute for Strategic Studies, Harvard University, 23 May 2006. Accessed, August 26, 2023. <http://www.wcfia.harvard.edu/olin/images/Management%20of%20Savagery%20- %2005-23-2006.pdf> (21 March 2012).

McCrisken, Trevor B. "Exceptionalism: Manifest Destiny". In *Encyclopedia of American Foreign Policy* (2002), Vol. 2. Edited by Alexander DeConte, 68. New York: Charles Scribner's & Sons, 2001.

Medieval Sourcebook: Urban II: Speech at Council of Clermont, 1095, according to Fulcher of Chartres. https://web.mit.edu/aorlando/www/SaintJohnCHI/Church%20History%20Readings/Urban%20II%20on%20First%20Crusade.pdf

Müstecaplıoğlu, M. "Turkey has extended R&D and design centers incentive program", Norton Rose Fulbright, March 29, 2021, https://www.nortonrosefulbright.com/de-de/inside-turkiye/blog/2021/03/turkey-has-extended-rd-and-design-centers-incentive-program

Meydan, S. *Atatürk ile Allah arasında.* Istanbul: Inkilap Kitapevi, 2009.

Ministry of Industry and Technology of Turkey, https://www.sanayi.gov.tr/anasayfa

Montesquieu. *The Persian Letters.* Translated by J. R. Loy. New York: Meridian Books, World Publishing, 1961.

Montesquieu, C. *The Persian Letters.* Translated by J.R. Loy. New York: Meridian Books, World Publishing, 1961.

Murad, Abdal Hakim. *Travelling Home: Essays on Islam in Europe.* Cambridge: Quilliam Press, 2020.

Murphy, D. *Embassy to Constantinople - The Travels of Lady Mary Wortley Montagu.* London: Century, 1988.

Mursheed, Syed M. "The Crescent and the Cross". In *The Clash of Civilizations: Twenty Years On.* Edited by J. Paul Baker, 20-27. Bristol: E-International Relations, Edited Collections, 2013.

Mustafa, M. *Oriental Imaginings, Occidental Refashioning: Turquerie, the Tulip Age and Ottoman Modernity, 1683-1867.* Sydney: Centre for Ottoman Renaissance and Civilisation, 2023.

Mustafa, M. *The Ottoman Renaissance: A Reconsideration of Early Modern Ottoman Art, 1413-1578.* New Jersey: Blue Dome Press, 2019.

Nietzsche, F. *The Gay Science: With a Prelude in German Rhymes and an Appendix of Songs.* Edited by Bernard Williams. Translated by Josefine Nauckhoff. Cambridge: Cambridge University Press, 2001.

Norton, B. "BRICS grows, adding 13 new 'partner countries' at historic summit in Kazan, Russia", 24 October 2024, Eurasia. Accessed October 27, 2024. https://geopoliticaleconomy.com/2024/10/26/brics-13-partner-countries-summit-kazan-russia/

Nye, J. *Soft Power: The Means to Success in World Politics.* New York: Public Affairs, 2004.

O'Dell, H. "How the US has used its power in the UN to support Israel for decades". Bluemarble, 18 December, 2023. https://globalaffairs.org/bluemarble/how-us-has-used-its-power-un-support-israel-decades

Ofek, H. "Why the Arabic World Turned Away from Science." *The New Atlantis,* No. 30 (2011): 3-23. Accessed June 20, 2024. https://www.thenewatlantis.com/publications/why-the-arabic-world-turned-away-from-science

Olcaytu, T. "Dinimiz Neyi Emrediyor, Atatürk Ne Yaptı". In N. Mirkelamoğlu, ed., *Din ve Laiklik: Atatürkcü düşünce ve uygulamada.* Istanbul: Çev, 2000.

Ordonez, Franco and Deepa Shivaram. "Trump says he wants the U.S. to take ownership of the Gaza Strip". NPR Network, 4 February, 2025. https://www.npr.org/2025/02/04/nx-s1-5287012/trump-netanyahu-ceasefire-gaza

O'Sullivan, J. *Manifest Destiny.* Digital History ID 362. https://www.digitalhistory.uh.edu/disp_textbook.cfm?smtID=3&psid=362

Öz, Y. *Quotations from Mustafa Kemal Atatürk.* Ankara: Ministry of Foreign Affairs, Republic of Turkey, 1982.

Öztürk, Y. N. *Arapçılığa Karşı Akılcılığın Öncüsü İmamı Azam Ebu Hanife.* Istanbul: Yeni Boyat, 2014.

Öztürk, Y. N. Cuma Sohbetleri. "Atatürk'ü Okuyabilmek". Hürriyet, 1998.

Palmer, A. *The Decline and Fall of the Ottoman Empire.* London: John Murray, 1993.

Perry, T. "Astronaut shares the profound 'big lie' he realized after seeing the Earth from space: This change in perspective could change humanity". Upworthy. Accessed November 22, 2024. https://www.upworthy.com/astronaut-shares-big-lie-space-ex1

Phillips, J. *The Fourth Crusade and the Sack of Constantinople.* London: Pimlico, 2011.

Pirenne, H. *Mediaeval Cities: Their Origins and the Revival of Trade.* New York: Princeton, 1927.

Pirenne, H. *Mohammed and Charlemagne.* New York: Dover Publications, 2001.

Pirenne, Henri, G. Cohen and H. Focillon. *Western Civilisation in the Middle Ages,* Vol. VIII. Paris: Presses Universitaires de France, 1933.

Plank, M. *Scientific Autobiography and Other Papers.* New York: Philosophical Library, 1950.

Planck, M. *Where is Science Going?* New York: AMS Press, 1932.

Prosecutor v. Radislav Krstic (Trial Judgement), International Criminal Tribunal for the former Yugoslavia (ICTY), 2 August 2001, accessed March, 19, 2025, https://www.refworld.org/jurisprudence/caselaw/icty/2001/en/40159

Qur'an.

Racine, J. *Complete Plays*. Translated by S. Solomon. New York: Random House, 1967.

Reisman, A. "Jewish Refugees from Nazism, Albert Einstein, and the Modernization of Higher Education in Turkey (1933-1945)." Aleph: Historical Studies in Science & Judaism, The Hebrew University of Jerusalem, and University of Indiana Press, No. 7, Pages 253-281. Accessed May 30, 2024. http://inscribe.iupress.org/doi/abs/10.2979/ALE.2007.-.7

Reisman, A. "Turkey's Invitations to Nazi Persecuted Intellectuals Circa 1933: A Bibliographic Essay on History's Blind Spot," (June 12, 2007), 1-25. Accessed May 28, 2024. https://ssrn.com/abstract=993310 or http://dx.doi.org/10.2139/ssrn.993310

Reisman, A. *Turkey's Modernization: Refugees from Nazism and Atatürk's Vision*. New Academia Publishing, 2006.

Rex, R. *The Making of Martin Luther* (New Jersey: Princeton University Press, 2017).

Rhodes, William R., and Stuart P. M. Mackintosh. "How the Sino-American Rivalry Is Reshaping the World Order". Project Syndicate: The World's Opinion Page (June 7, 2024). Accessed June 25, 2024. https://www.project-syndicate.org/commentary/us-china-conflict-will-increase-importance-of-regional-alliances-by-william-r-rhodes-and-stuart-p-m-mackintosh-2024-06

Roberts, J., and Wasserstein, B. *Larousse Encyclopedia of Modern History From 1500 to the present day*. London: Hamlyn, 1981.

Rodinson, M. *Europe and the Mystique of Islam*. Seattle: Uni. Washington Press, 1991.

Ross, J. B., and McLaughlin M. M. *The Portable Renaissance*. London: Penguin, 1985.

Runciman, S. *The Great Church in Captivity: A Study of the Patriarchate of Constantinople from the Eve of the Turkish Conquest to the Greek War of Independence*. Cambridge: Cambridge University Press, 1986.

Runciman, S. *A History of the Crusades*. London: Penguin, 1990.

Russo, F. "The Utopia of International Peace During the Thirty Years War. «Le Nouveau Cynée» Written by Eméric Crucé". *Governare La Paura, Journal of Interdisciplinary Studies* 9 (1) (2016). Accessed February 4, 2003. https://doi.org/10.6092/issn.1974-4935/6533.

Said, E. *Orientalism*. London: Penguin, 1995.

Said, E. *Covering Islam: How The Media And The Experts Determine How We See The Rest of The World*. London: Vintage, 1997.

Salem, M. "Why is Saudi Arabia hosting talks to end the Ukraine war?" CNN, 11 March, 2025. https://edition.cnn.com/2025/02/17/middleeast/saudi-riyadh-us-russia-talks-analysis-intl-latam

Santos, Boaventura de Sousa. *Epistemologies of the South: Justice Against Epistemicide*. New York: Taylor & Francis, 2015.

Schmitt, S. *Concept of the Political*. New Brunswick: Rutgers University Press, 1976.

Sells, M. *The Bridge Betrayed: Religion and genocide in Bosnia*. Berkeley: University of California Press, 1996.

Senghass, D. "How to Promote a Perspicacious Intercultural Dialogue?". In *The Clash of Civilizations: Twenty Years On*. Edited by J. Paul Baker, 39-41. Bristol: E-International Relations, Edited Collections, 2013.

Shaw, S., and Shaw, E. K. *History of the Ottoman Empire and Modern Turkey*, Vol.2. London: Cambridge University Press, 1985.

Siddiqi, Abdul Hameed. *Main Springs of Western Civilisation*. Lahore: Kazi Publication, 1979.

Sims, C. "Occidentalism at War: Al-Qaida's Resistance Rhetoric". *Altre Modernita*, Milan (2012): 206-220.

Sizer, S. "A Biblical Refutation of Christian Zionism". You Tube, April 28, 2024. Accessed January 30, 2025. https://www.youtube.com/watch?v=LohMNT_Xtas&t=1s

Slade, A. *Records of Travels in Turkey, Greece, &c, and of a Cruise in the Black Sea with the Capitan Pasha, in the years 1829, 1830 and 1831, Vol. 1*. London: Saunders and Otley, 1833. Second Edition.

Speech delivered by the President of Indonesia to the Turkish Parliament on 10 April, 2025. Sozcu, 10 April 2025. https://www.sozcu.com.tr/endonezya-cumhurbaskani-prabowo-subianto-dan-ataturk-sozleri-benim-ikonum-evimde-heykeli-var-p161629

"Speech by French Senator Claude Malhuret on Ukraine and European security". Diplomatizzando, 7 March, 2025. https://diplomatizzando.blogspot.com/2025/03/speech-by-french-senator-claude.html

Spengler, O. *The Decline of the West*. London: George & Allen Unwin Ltd., 1926.

Steinbock, D. "What's driving Trump's quest for expansion, domination and influence?" TRT World, 12 February, 2025, https://www.trtworld.com/opinion/whats-driving-trumps-quest-for-expansion-domination-and-influence-18264192

Taheri, A. *Holy Terror*. London: Hutchinson, 1987.

"The Inaugural Address". White House, 20 January, 2025. https://www.whitehouse.gov/remarks/2025/01/the-inaugural-address/

Thiem, J. "The Great Library of Alexandria Burnt: Towards the History of a Symbol". *Journal of the History of Ideas*, Vol. 40, No. 4 (Oct. - Dec., 1979): 507-526. Accessed February 20, 2025. https://doi.org/10.2307/2709356

Tibi, B. *Islam Between Culture and Politics*. Basingstoke, England: Palgrave, 2001.

Toynbee, A. *A Study of History*. Oxford: Oxford University Press, 1987.

TRT AFRIKA. "Relations between Ankara, Moscow going really well: Turkish FM Fidan" (June 11, 2024). https://trtafrika.com/turkey/relations-between-ankara-moscow-going-really-well-turkish-fm-fidan-18172251

Tuğal, C. *The fall of the Turkish model. How the Arab uprisings brought down Islamic liberalism*. London: Verso Books, 2016.

"Turkish-American Nobel winner says prize would be out of reach if he worked in Turkey". Turkish Minute, 8 November 2024. Accessed November 12, 2024. https://www.turkishminute.com/2024/11/08/turk-american-nobel-winner-says-prize-would-be-out-of-reach-if-he-worked-in-turkey/

"Türkiye continues to emerge as leading force in TV exports". Hürriyet Daily News, 28 October, 2024. Accessed October 30, 2024. https://www.hurriyetdailynews.com/turkiye-continues-to-emerge-as-leading-force-in-tv-exports-201986

Tyson, Neil de Grasse. "Nobel laureates in Science: Contributions from Jews and Muslims". You Tube. https://www.youtube.com/watch?v=VQl7k7lQTns

Ubucuni, M. A. "Turkiye 1850". In N. Mirkelamoğlu, *Din ve Laiklik: Atatürkcü düşünce ve uygulamada*. Istanbul: Çev, 2000.

Union of American Hebrew Congregations. http://www.seekpeace.org/articles/powell.shtml

Vance, J. D. "Vice President JD Vance reveals the moment the Trump-Zelenskyy meeting 'went off the rails'". Fox News. You Tube. 4 March, 2025. https://www.youtube.com/watch?v=HOJS3qQlVjE

Virk, Z. "Science and Technology in Islamic Spain.", Centre for Islamic Studies, California. Accessed June 7, 2024. https://islamic-study.org/science-and-technology-in-islamic-spain/

Welch. D. A. "Enemy Wanted: Apply Without". In *The Clash of Civilizations: Twenty Years On*. Edited by J. Paul Baker, 14-19. Bristol: E-International Relations, Edited Collections, 2013.

Wheatcroft, A. *The Ottomans*. London: Viking, 1993.

Williams, P. "Europe's Forgotten Genocide". Blogging Theology Podcast, You Tube, August 14, 2024. https://www.youtube.com/watch?v=kgK02HMwL1c&t=935s

Williams, P. "Reverend Professor Keith Ward on Muhammad as a Prophet of God". Blogging Theology Podcast, You Tube, May 2, 2021. https://www.youtube.com/watch?v=FkeoGRT_ATE

www.ingramcontent.com/pod-product-compliance
Lightning Source LLC
Chambersburg PA
CBHW050608230426
43670CB00009B/1319